Bloody Skies

Much has been written about the U.S. Army Air Corps in World War II, but the contributions of each aircrew member to that effort have been largely neglected. Also, the importance of the unity of the crew has not been sufficiently emphasized.

BLOODY SKIES is the story of a Fifteenth Air Force, Second Bomb Group (H), Twentieth Squadron, B-17 crew that often flew the notorious '*Old Flak Holes*,' and how they learned to respect and trust each other. Training made them cohesive; crisis and tragedy bonded them.

They arrived at Amendola, Italy, on the day their entire squadron, the Twentieth, and some of the Second Bomb Group, had been wiped out by the Luftwaffe. That legacy was their introduction to war.

Through McGuire and Hadley the reader will watch these enthusiastic, bright-eyed, cocky boys lose that brightness and confidence. When fatigue and weariness become so overpowering and seem to go deep into the bones, it is only their pride in themselves, their crew, and their country that keeps them returning to the skies to face another day of that dreaded flak and German fighters. There appeared to be no way to survive.

In the midst of the horrors of aerial combat, they can still find humor living in the 'Amendola Ritz,' compassion for those innocent victims of every war—the children, marvel in the early morning song of a bird, and enjoy the historical sights of Rome.

These ten men, from the economic, cultural, and geographic spectrum of 1940s America, were representative of the best their country had to offer. They vehemently deny any claim to hero status. The Soldier's Prayer was their credo:

> Let me fight well today, O Lord,
> Let me do nothing to bring shame or disgrace on my family,
>   my comrades, my unit, my country.
> Let me conduct myself in such a manner that
>   there is no dishonor.
> Let me not be wasted, but if I die, let me die
>   like a soldier should.

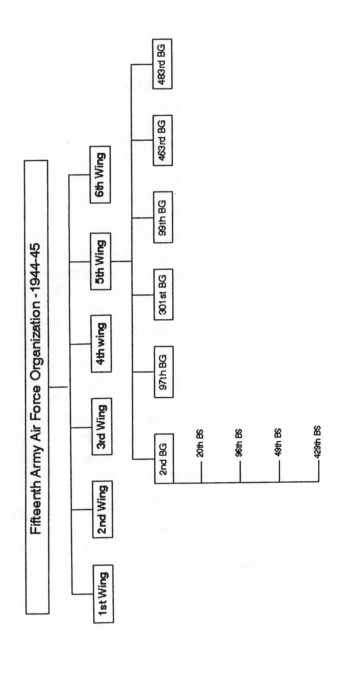

Fifteenth Army Air Force Organization - 1944-45

1st Wing   2nd Wing   3rd Wing   4th wing   5th Wing   6th Wing

2nd BG   97th BG   301st BG   99th BG   463rd BG   483rd BG

20th BS

96th BS

49th BS

429th BS

Bloody Skies

A 15th AAF B-17 Combat Crew:
How They Lived and Died

by

Melvin W. McGuire
and
Robert Hadley

Yucca Tree Press

First Printing   December 1993

First Paper Edition Printing   October 1998
Second Paper Edition Printing   June 2000

McGuire, Melvin W., and Robert Hadley

   BLOODY SKIES: A 15th AAF B-17 Combat Crew: How They
          Lived and Died
       1. World War, 1939-1945 - Aerial Operations, American
       2. World War, 1939-1945 - Personal narratives, American
       3. United States Army Air Corps - Fifteenth Air Force
       I. Melvin W. McGuire.   II. Robert Hadley.
       III. Title.

Library of Congress Catalog Card Number: 92-061289

ISBN: 1-881325-07-5

Cover photos: Case Kowall/Amador Studio
Cover design: John Cole/Cole Graphics

 PRINTED IN CANADA

Acknowledgments

Fifteenth Air Force Association and Colonel Ben Franklin, Executive Director.

Second Bombardment Association Archivist John Stephen

Second Bombardment Association Newsletter Editor Rudolph Koller, Jr.

Eighth Air Force Museum and Second Wing Museum Curator Buck Rigg of the Barksdale Air Force Base.

Twentieth Bombardment Squadron and all its personnel

Second Wing, Barksdale Air Force Base

West Texas Wing *Log Book*, Confederate Air Force

Duane L. Neifert, Dallas/Fort Worth Wing Leader Confederate Air Force

Col. Tom Hall

Col. Edward 'Jerry' Bishop

Case Kowall, Amador Studios

Wallace and Martha Dillard - This talented and diligent couple has taught me, again, the meaning of friendship.

Ralph Bischoff - His knowledge, assistance, and records helped make this book possible.

War Eagle Air Museum, Santa Teresa, New Mexico

Ralph and Rachel Chambers

Wayne Lesher

Louis M. Scofield

J. Warren Karsten

John Fenstermaker

Donald Stern

Arthur L. Valdez, Sr.

Oscar and Charlotte Gorbitz

Ozzie Hans Gorbitz

William McCormick

Darrell Lassiter

Juraj Rajnenic

Vicente J. Martinez - a former POW, shot down on Mission 263

Gene Gephart, Arizona Wing Leader, Confederate Air Force

Janie Matson, a good friend, without whose willingness to do the dirty work, this book would never have been published.

Dedication

March 1939, the citizens of Czechoslovakia awakened early one morning to the sound of Hitler's Nazi legions marching through their country. Within a few hours, the Republic of Czechoslovakia was no more; it had been incorporated into Hitler's new Third Reich. Their sons were conscripted into the German military machine, and other citizens into the numerous labor battalions that serviced Hitler's Nazi Empire.

They were a people with a will to fight, they wanted to fight, but had nothing with which to fight and no allies. France, with its huge army, was defeated in a very few weeks. The British had retreated to their islands and were embattled there. The Czechs had no hope, no champion. As the months passed, the Germans became more demanding and the Czechoslovakians had less and less.

Then word filtered to them that the Americans were bombing Germany in broad daylight. Can you imagine their joy when they learned that Berlin had been bombed! Perhaps there was hope. In late 1943 and early 1944, American bombers— B-17s and B-24s—appeared regularly over Czechoslovakia, hitting strategic targets. They admired the 'Amis' (Americans) because they never turned back. It was soon apparent that the Americans were winning the air battle over Czechoslovakia. With their own eyes they had seen German fighters burning and crashing to the ground. They observed those battles where, occasionally, the Americans lost and their B-17s and B-24s crashed to the ground.

The Americans were the Czechs only hope and they cheered wildly, much to the displeasure of their Nazi captors, when American bomber formations passed overhead. They adopted the Americans as their sons. Many times, at great personal risk, they retrieved the bodies of those American airmen that the Germans had buried in shallow, unmarked graves. They built coffins for these adopted sons, often draped with home-made American flags, and buried them in honored positions in their family cemeteries, with appropriate religious ceremonies and erected monuments to them. As late as 1983 most of these monuments they had built to these fallen airmen still stood all over Czechoslovakia, well maintained and occasionally decorated with flowers.

The day of 29 August 1944, when my squadron, the Twentieth Bomb Squadron of the Second Bomb Group, lost their fight to stay alive, the Czechoslovakians retrieved all but a few of the seventy men shot down that day, and buried them lovingly and tenderly, as if they had been their own sons. It was the Czechs' way of saying, "We thank you."

So, on behalf of my squadron, the Twentieth Bomb Squadron of the Second Bomb Group, Fifteenth Air Force, be you Czech, or be you Slovak, I say, "Thank you," and dedicate this book to you for burying our dead so compassionately.

Melvin W. McGuire

This book is respectfully dedicated to

Sergeant Jim D. Brown, my father,

56th Armored Infantry Battalion, 12th Armored Division,

3rd and 7th United States Armies, 1944-1946.

Robert Hadley

Table of Contents

List of Photographs

List of Maps, Illustrations and Documents

Introduction

In April 1993, laborers clearing land for the building of a trade market in the southern province of Hunan, China, were interrupted by a singular discovery. They crowded around a rusty piece of metal embedded in the ground. Much dirt had to be removed before the object could be recognized: It was an unexploded bomb dropped during World War II. The laborer who first struck it with his shovel completed the task of unearthing it. A passing villager saw the bomb, and, perceiving potential value in the explosives still inside the rusty metal, purchased the bomb from the laborer for a small sum. The villager hired two other men to help him open the bomb and extract the explosives. The three men squatted and began hammering on the bomb. . . .

So very much more than a forgotten bomb in China reminds us of that war: The fabric of our existence today was woven in the mindless, ruthless chaos that descended over the world from 1939 until 1945. World War II was the largest single event in history, a war fought by most of the populations of fifty nations, over all the oceans and above or upon six of seven of the planet's continents. There had been nothing like it before. Figures vary because there can never be a thorough tally sheet, but it is generally accepted that this war cost the lives of at least fifty to fifty-five million humans, and also displaced and wounded, in body or soul, hundreds of millions of others. A generation of men and women, summoned by their respective governments across the globe, attended the harsh curriculum of total war. One of those soldiers was Melvin W. McGuire of Las Cruces, New Mexico.

McGuire was a new breed of soldier to Twentieth Century warfare; he was an airman, a gunner in a B-17. He served with the Fifteenth Air Force, flying strategic bombing missions out of Italy with the Twentieth Squadron, Second Bomb Group, from late August until late December 1944, completing fifty missions against a witches' cauldron of targets in Germany, Poland,

Greece, Italy, Yugoslavia, Czechoslovakia, Hungary, and Rumania. He was nineteen years old. He rotated home at the end of his tour and was training B-29 gunnery crews when atomic bombs effectively and unexpectedly shortened and ended the war. As with millions of others, he returned home. During those months when he flew over the heartland of an enemy who fought hard and smart, carried aloft in a thin aluminum tube in the company of nine other frightened but determined men, astride thousands of gallons of flammable gasoline and thousands of pounds of explosives and bullets, McGuire early on gave up believing that one day he would indeed have something precious at the end of it all, a life to live.

In that life he has subsequently successfully lived, the sights and smells, laughter and agony, fear and triumph of the crucible of those hard months of air combat literally remained with him. His hands remain sensitive, still reddened, from the burns he sustained when he picked up a large, white-hot, burning Pathfinder flare and stuffed it out of his aircraft, saving himself, the plane and his friends—his fellow crewmen—from certain death.

As with thousands of surviving airmen, he still carries German steel in his body. Most of the subcutaneous shards of anti-aircraft shrapnel had worked their way out of his body by the late 1950s, but there still remain deeply embedded pieces that trouble him during some seasons, pieces which have become part of his flesh, blood and sinew.

More importantly, the war has permanently become part of his psyche, as the nightmares still intrude, although not nearly so frequently as once before. While in Italy, they called the nightmares, 'pulling missions.' Nights at the Amendola Ritz, the patched and worn old canvas tent, home for McGuire and his crew, were frequently interrupted by screams, yells, and the urgent conversations of him and his crew as they pulled missions in their sleep. The nightmares have continued. McGuire is especially bothered by two recurring nightmares: In one, an airman falls eternally through a bomber formation, arms and legs flailing wildly; in another, McGuire is hopelessly trapped inside a fire-swept B-17.

That crucible of combat in torn and bloody skies has remained with him, especially in memory: The evil stench of

German anti-aircraft fire, smelling like rotten eggs as it tore through metal and flesh; A B-17, straggling far behind formation, engines afire, the focus of every German battery on the ground, heading straight and level towards target, finally successfully dropping its bombs before plunging to earth; the cracked, reddened hands of the dedicated ground crews, feverishly working in the harsh elements to patch up more planes for the next day's mission; a navigator who became so physically ill during flights that he kept metal tins at his navigator's table and was constantly regurgitating in them during missions, calmly sitting through mission after mission, doing his job, holding up his responsibility until his tour was completed, the bravest man McGuire ever knew where bravery was commonplace; the beautiful, unexpected sound of a song-bird serenading McGuire on the morning he calmly awaited his death, for a mysterious voice in his dreams had announced that he would die that day.

Perhaps the most compelling memories, however, were those of the members of his crew, from the soft-spoken pilot Ralph Chambers to James Thompson the tail gunner, the "baby" of the crew, nine friends with whom he trained and fought. It is memories about these friends that are especially poignant to McGuire because a month later, after he had rotated to Naples and just two days prior to his departure for home, he was told they had been killed when their beat-up, loyal and tough old veteran airplane *Flak Holes*, which had always brought them home despite its cantankerousness, finally took a direct hit in the bomb bay and blew to pieces in a flash. McGuire lived for forty-eight years with the guilt, sorrow, and certainty that they were dead.

What is essential to know is that McGuire started taping his memoirs of the war not as a monument to his particular experiences, but instead to honor these men with whom he fought, to bring them back to life, perhaps for the last time. In these pages you will read of the unfailing purpose and resolve that held together his crew, his generation, his nation, in unity of form and spirit. It is that which needed expression, that which held him to his purpose and resulted in the publication of this book.

Today, during the fiftieth anniversary of that conflict, one generation looks back over its shoulder at the war its parents fought, when a world turned upside down, when a mindless god devoured its children. In looking back at that conflict, the mind numbs at its breadth, its scope, the depth of its horror; yet despite its size, we seek some way to understand it all, what it must have been like for that generation. We get our truest emotional insight of that conflict—far from the flying bullets and dropping bombs, far from the academic, dry pages of history—when we know how the personal lives of the combatants were swallowed by that great mouth of war.

McGuire is able to perceive value and worth inside the horror and sadness of that experience, much the same as the Chinese observed potential value inside the bomb on which they hammered. They hammered too long and too hard; the bomb blew up, and World War II claimed three more victims almost fifty years after it officially ended. McGuire also hammered away at the crusty, often-times unyielding metal of memory to produce this book. What he brings us is a faithful picture of a time which is becoming increasingly nostalgic, a snapshot of a war so large it is almost incomprehensible to see. McGuire's narrative, however, reminds us that history is never woven of whole cloth, that it is a fabric spun one thread at a time. Whether warp or woof, German or American, airman or infantryman, present or past, it is in the individual narrative that a war of this magnitude can be surely grasped, for there is a common feeling many sense in the mystery of life and conflict, a sense of commonality of experience, that what is most personal is also most universal.

Robert Hadley
La Mesa, New Mexico
September 1993

Prologue

Several years ago some former Second Bomb Group members from World War II and their wives returned to Amendola, Italy to see the site of the Second Bomb Group encampment and the old air field. They knew those rows of pyramid, olive-drab tents set in the old olive grove would be gone, but they did not expect the cave to be closed and the old Italian buildings and courtyards which had housed the Second Bomb Group Headquarters, infirmary, and orderly rooms to be gone. They did not expect the little tuffa huts, or the old, bent, gnarled, ugly olive trees to be gone. And they did not expect the ancient rock wall that formed the back boundary of the Second Bomb Group encampment to be gone. Even the scars behind the wall where that British bomber hit were gone. Its crew had been fighting for their lives as they came out of the midnight skies, furrowed the earth, and burned. All was gone.

The old straw stack on the far side of the vacant field that had harbored so many cooties, lice, fleas and multitudes of other vermin was gone. Even the out buildings and the old two-storied house that had belonged to villainous old Umberto, the bootlegger, counterfeiter, black marketeer, con artist, and former Fascisti, were also gone. Nothing was left to indicate that the Second Bomb Group had ever lived there for a year and a half. Even the crudely drawn direction signs were gone. Everything that could possibly indicate the existence of the Second Bomb Group was gone.

Instead, the area where the old olive grove and wall had stood was now planted in neat rows of new trees, grape arbors, and vegetable crops. Everything that indicated that the Second Bomb Group had ever been there was gone. When they talked to some of the younger workers in the vineyards, those workers remembered their parents and grandparents had told them that once upon a time the *Americani*, the *aviatori* had lived there. Occasionally they found a relic or two. They, personally, didn't remember anything about the Second Bomb Group of the Fifteenth Air Force. It wasn't until the party talked to the older workers, those in their late fifties and sixties, who remembered and smiled. They remembered the GI Joes, the *aviatori*, the Yanks, the *molte bombe* men who gave them the *ciocolate*, the *sigarette*, the *mangiare*, the K-rations, clothing, shoes, medicine, and friendship, when they were the dirty, shivering, hollowed-eyed, ill-clothed, barefooted, sickly, scared, hungry children of the war. Yes, they smiled and remembered. They also remembered the thunder of the Wright Cyclone engines leaving every morning after sun-up to do battle with *Te Deschi*. They remembered the roar of those engines that went on all night, every night, while the ground crews repaired the previous day's damage so the Fortresses would be ready at sun-up. They remembered.

Leaving the Second Bomb Group site, they drove past the former encampment of the Ninety-seventh Bomb Group, the Second's sister bomb group. There, too, there were no signs, no buildings, no evidence that the Ninety-seventh had ever been there. It was all gone. What had once been a key American bomber base in the war against Germany was completely gone. The Marston matting runways and the hard stands were gone. 'Darn Thing' tower, the parachute rooms, the equipment shacks, the little trailers and tuffa huts, and the telephone lines were gone. The scorched spot in the middle of the east-west runway where one damaged Fortress rode upon top of another crippled Fort whose landing gear had collapsed, burning both aircraft and most of the crews, was gone. The furrows, the ditches, the craters, the blackened spots beside the runways where so many B-17s had bellied in coming back from missions, were covered and gone. Even that big mound of dirt on the approach end to the east-west runway and the mutilated shrubbery that had been the graveyard for a B-17 were gone. That battle-damaged B-17, riddled by flak and fighters, had fought its way from deep inside of enemy territory, only to run out of luck and fuel fifteen hundred yards from the runway. All of that was gone.

Now sheep grazed peacefully, and neatly planted rows of grape arbors and tomatoes grew over this once chaotic air field. It was as if the Second and Ninety-seventh Bomb Groups had never existed. It was all gone.

It wasn't until they arrived in Bari, Italy at the United States Air Force cemetery, did they find anyone else who remembered. The custodians remembered the Second Bomb Group well because all they had to do was look out the window at those beautiful acres with the row after row of neat, white crosses, to remind them.

And I remember. I remember Row 1500. That's where my tail gunner, James Thompson, was buried. Thinking of him, I am reminded of the possibility that someplace in Central or Eastern Germany there are one or two unmarked graves, final resting places of one or two of my fellow crew members. They are gone.

I begin with an apology to the reader. This book has been extremely difficult to write. I am particularly ill-suited to writing anything other than a letter, and my mind is no longer that keen. To compound my research difficulties, the bag that was shipped from Italy to my home in Hatch, New Mexico, in January 1945, arrived two years later via Guam. When packed in Italy it contained my personal records, souvenirs, memorabilia, and address books. Upon its arrival in Hatch, it was full of fungus, rot and goo. All means of contact with my crew and their families were lost to me. In addition, most of my official records were burned in that giant fire where so many thousands and thousands of American Army, Navy and Air Corps records were stored in the U.S. Military Records Depot in St. Louis, Missouri. They were irretrievably lost.

When I left Italy, I believed I was the only survivor of my crew. I was bitter, with a survivor's complex, "Why me, Lord?" I was tired and emotionally drained. After the war I buried the memories in a closet in the deepest recesses of my mind and nailed the door shut. I simply willed myself to forget that it had ever happened. There are several combat days I still cannot recall. Those were the bad days that I willed away. Now and then I see tantalizing glimpses and little flashes of what happened, but not enough to write about them. Only three months ago did I learn what I did on Christmas Day of 1944. So, forgive the inadequacies, the inaccuracies and the mistakes that will crop up. It is an honest book in that I have tried my best to tell it like it was, as accurately as possible.

This is not an autobiography. This is the story of a very good combat B-17 crew and how we lived, how we laughed, and how we died. It is the story of our accomplishments and our failures, of the good times and the bad, of how we fought the enemy and how we fought that numbing cold in airplanes with open windows flying at twenty-eight to thirty thousand feet. It is the story of our fears, of our pride, of our cohesiveness, and of our bonding. It is the story of our crew's part in that little corner of the world during World War II.

I want the reader to understand how we believed in the two Latin words on our Second Bomb Group patch we wore on our jackets: "*Libertatem defendimus,*" which means "In the defense of liberty." I want to tell what it was like and how it felt to attack some of the worst, the toughest targets during that tragic period of history called World War II. I want to tell about how we never turned back because of enemy action, and of the many times each of us straggled home alone in a battle-damaged aircraft, sometimes with dead and wounded aboard, fighting for our lives.

I am writing this for those who will come later. I am writing this for my grandchildren because, in a few short years, they will say about us, "They're all gone. . . , but we remember."

Melvin W. McGuire
Las Cruces, New Mexico
September 1993

Bloody Skies

– 1 –

Home

I was born in Fort Bayard, New Mexico in September 1924. My maternal grandfather was the civil housing and maintenance officer for that federal installation. My father, a baseball player, had come to the nearby Silver City area seeking employment in the mines. In those days baseball was truly the great American pastime. The West and Southwest areas of the United States were dotted with giant copper and other mineral mining conglomerations. In those days, the giant copper mines all sponsored baseball teams. For a baseball player, it not only meant steady employment, but a little extra in each month's pay envelope for playing on the company team. Also, it was the quickest way to attract the attention of the major league professional baseball teams. This was the forerunner of the present-day farm club system. Major league team scouts attended most of the Copper League games. A big, agile, talented, athletic man, Dad's major aspiration, of course, was to be a major league baseball player.

Silver City had been a hotbed of baseball for some time and interest increased even more when William Wrigley of the chewing gum fortune began using the health spa at Faywood, a few miles southeast of Silver City, as a place to treat athletes' nagging injuries and for sore-armed pitchers. Faywood, grew rapidly because of Wrigley's interest. For centuries Indians had visited the hot mineral waters for their therapeutic and healing properties. Recuperating players could keep in condition by continuing to play high-caliber baseball. Some of the major league teams using the Faywood facilities were the Washington Senators, the White Soxs, and Wrigley's own team, the Chicago Cubs.

After their marriage, my parents lived in the Silver City area for almost five years while Dad was a journeyman electrician as well as a baseball player.

Situated at the foot of the Gila National Forest, Silver City was a pleasant place to live. It was a shipping point for the many very large ranches in the area and the nearby mines. Big game hunting was very good and hunters had their choice of deer, bear, elk, antelope, lion and turkey. The air was beautiful and crystal clear.

It was a good life until the Depression hit. The mines closed and workers were laid off. Cattlemen couldn't sell their beef and couldn't afford to feed them. When the banks failed, my parents, like millions of other Americans, lost their savings. They were left with a few dollars and a new gas-guzzler car they couldn't afford to operate.

Dad's second driving ambition was to be a farmer and experiment with his many novel ideas about farming. Therefore, we moved to the beautiful Hatch Valley. For eons the Valley had been the bed of the Rio Grande. About a mile wide at its medium point, the land would grow anything in abundance within its growing season, but was subject to seasonal flooding. Now, with the installation of two large dams several

2

miles to the north, built to check the flood waters, the land was put up for sale. It was relatively cheap because the majority had to be cleared of heavy cottonwood trees and very heavy undergrowth. Dad was willing to tackle this task because of the model irrigation system which was a part of the dam installations. We believed our fortunes were to be made here. Dad occasionally worked during the daylight hours for somebody else for cash. During those periods he and Mother often cleared and farmed our place by lantern light. After much, much work, by 1934, the McGuires had a model farm.

We never went hungry but there were times when we didn't have more than we needed. Dad spent much time at the Agricultural Department of New Mexico A & M College, forty miles to the south in Las Cruces, working with them and experimenting on new seeds, different farming methods, new crops, and innovative marketing methods. They encouraged him because he was willing to experiment and put his ideas to work. He also learned a valuable lesson during that time; he never planted a crop that wasn't sold before its planting. Due to his hard work and willingness to take chances, by 1936, the McGuires were prospering. We raised our own livestock for our beef and pork. Life was now very good and we enjoyed it in a new house which Dad wired for electricity, in anticipation of rural electrification. By the mid-Thirties when electricity arrived, all we had to do was flip the switch.

My father believed in the Golden Rule. Many of our neighbors were illiterate and they depended upon him for help with their income tax forms and to see if they had been paid the proper amount for their crops. He was also involved in school board activities. Without realizing it, he became very potent politically. Seldom did a week go by that a congressman, governor, or legislator didn't visit our home.

Hunting and fishing were a way of life in the whole Valley. Fishing was great in New Mexico in those days. Big game was available in the Gila Forest or the Sacramento Mountains, both less than a two-hour drive away. Little did I realize how those trips and camp outs would help me in times to come.

3

Bloody Skies

I received my first small .22 rifle when I was six. Under the watchful eye of my father and uncles, I soon became a very good shot. Later they gave me a better rifle, and by seven I was hunting on my own. Our house was set back from U.S. Highway 85, the main north-south artery in New Mexico. We were separated from the nearby foothills and the canyons by U.S. 85 and one field. The area was abundant with small game—rabbits, quail, bobcat, coyotes and even deer. They were a nuisance to neighboring truck farmers. By then my brother Danny, who was five years younger, and I had a saddle horse we named Peg. This little quarter horse became a part of the family. She loved children and it was not uncommon to see her carrying three or four, and all enjoying the experience. From the time he was three, Danny was a very proficient rider. Peg would lower her head for him to climb between her ears, and then she would toss her head until he managed to get into the proper position. We had saddles, but preferred to ride Indian-style. Feeding the livestock was an after-school chore, and all I had to do was hold up an ear of corn and she would trot over. Before long I could raise my little rifle and she would come trotting over to me. She thoroughly enjoyed our hunting trips into the canyons.

After several of these trips I noticed a young man following me. When I arrived at the canyons, in the base of the foothills, he would be sitting on a little point with a sack and old battered .22 rifle. On a badly deformed leg, he followed me from a distance. His behavior worried me until I realized he was feeding his family with rabbits I rejected. His leg made him unemployable and this was his means of taking care of his family. Thereafter, I made it a point to kill several extra rabbits and leave them on the trail.

At ten I received my first big game rifle and could actively participate in Dad's hunting trips. For a young boy, life couldn't have been better.

When we moved to the Hatch Valley, I was due to start second grade. The Salem Elementary School was a four or five-room schoolhouse. Shortly before the beginning of the fall term

4

I became sick and was very ill for about three weeks, with an additional two weeks spent in recuperation. That put me five weeks behind the other second graders. My mother, not knowing the dress code for that area, was anxious that I make a good impression on the teachers. That first morning she dressed me in my new Buster Brown outfit with the frilly shirt and short pants with patch pockets on the back, knee-length argyle socks, and polished brogan shoes. Dad walked the mile to school with me and handed me the papers I was to present to the second grade teacher.

I knocked tentatively on the second grade door and will never forget the look of dismay on Mrs. Shipe's countenance when she looked down into my eager, shining little face. Dressed in all my sartorial elegance, I carried a Big Chief tablet, a little pencil box, my Crayolas, and a little lunch bucket with fairies and flowers painted on the side. She stood for a moment before taking my papers. I offered the explanation that I had been sick and that was why I hadn't been there earlier. Could I come in? She said, "Yes Melvin, you can come in."

She looked around the room for a vacancy among the two-person desks. The only empty space was in a desk set all by itself and away from the windows, and finally said, "You'll have to share this desk."

That's when I met Pablo. It didn't take but a few seconds to realize that not only did Pablo not floss, Pablo had probably never heard of a toothbrush and he was not a regular bather. The best that could be said about Pablo was that he didn't smell, he reeked from every pore in his body.

As I looked around the room after the teacher's introduction, there was much giggling from the class. Only a few were wearing shoes, and most of those were girls. A majority of the boys weren't even wearing shirts. The shirts I saw were worn and patched. One of the boys shook his fist at me. I knew then how the Christians felt when they were led into the arena to face the lions.

Mrs. Shipe kept me in for the first recess, but when the lunch bell rang she said to another teacher, "I guess I better let him go outside. He's got to eat, so we might as well get this over. Let's all make a point of dropping by and checking on him during the lunch hour."

I took my little lunch bucket and sat down near some students. A fourth grader ate my lunch and trashed my lunch bucket with the fairies and flowers. Two sixth graders held me while a third yanked down the patch pockets on my little short pants. The events of the next ten days could be used as a curriculum guide for Green Beret training. I had seven fights—six boys and one girl. I batted about sixty percent with the boys, but was soundly whipped by the girl. After ten days I had found my place in the pecking order and the appeal of beating me had palled. Meanwhile, each night my mother tried repairing my clothing and re-sewing my patch pockets. Then she bought me two pair of corduroy pants. Each pair weighed about as much as a flak vest and they made weird noises when you walked. I hated them!

Mercifully, the weather started cooling and the new desks arrived. Mrs. Shipe, aware of my plight, separated me from Pablo and put me in one of the new desks in the front of the class, and near a window. After that, Salem Elementary School was an enjoyable experience.

Times were harsh during the Depression and many Salem students suffered dietary and nutritional deficiencies, particularly during the winter months when fresh fruits and vegetables were unavailable. They were surviving on molasses, coarse biscuits, and water gravy. Water gravy was made with flour and water, the same concoction used for pasting wallpaper. Their evening meal generally consisted of cornbread made from rough corn and watered milk. In the summertime wild asparagus and other fruits and vegetables supplemented their diet. Students on this diet often fainted after strenuous exercise.

Sixth through eighth grades were taught in the same room under the greatest teacher I've ever known. Katherine Griffith was also the principal. Mrs. Griffith was energetic and dedicated. She realized that most of the students who graduated from her eighth grade would never continue their education. They would need to drop out and work on the family farm to help feed the family. She also recognized that many of her students, and their parents, couldn't speak English. If she could teach these students correct English, a love of reading, and a desire to keep abreast of current events, then they might have a chance to survive in life.

Learning English was difficult for those students, but under Mrs. Griffith's encouragement, they learned quickly. As they read to their families, this accomplishment was soon reflected in their parents' lives. Katherine Griffith's secret was to teach you to enjoy reading. She believed if a child could read, he could educate himself. Two hours of every school day were set aside for reading from *The National Geographic*, *The Reader's Digest*, *Life Magazine*, and other current periodicals. Each day she selected an article and a student to read it aloud to the class. While the child read, she pointed to the location on the big roll-up map, thereby incorporating geography into the reading lesson. Sometimes she interrupted the reader for a class discussion on the subject of the article. Not only were we learning to read, we were learning public speaking. Her method was very successful.

Every Saturday this wonderful woman drove the forty miles to Las Cruces and loaded her car with library books. Each book was individually selected for a particular student. I loved to read and did not need to be encouraged. Later, at college, I was surprised to learn that, because of this woman, I had read most of the classics. My theory then was, 'the smaller the book, the harder it was to understand.' She definitely instilled the desire to read in all of us, but the other 'Rs,'—'riting and 'rithmetic didn't suffer either. She graduated many exceptional students who later enjoyed national honors in the educational field. I am sorry to say that Pablo and I weren't among them.

About 1933, my father read an ad in the local newspaper that a governmental entity, possibly the WPA, was selling surplus, new National Park Service outhouses. The ad heralded them as being of the latest design. Dad left early one Friday morning, took one of our large trailers and several helpers to Las Cruces where he purchased one of these new, three-hole outhouses. The outhouse had a concrete base and was quite heavy. By Friday night it was operational. As usual with the government, they take the lowest bidder. In this case, the lowest bidder sold green paint. Not a soft pastoral green, but a vivid, ugly, bilious green that could be seen for miles.

Danny, and I were extremely proud of it. To us it was a magnificent edifice. Much to my mother's horror and embarrassment, she looked out the window the next morning and saw us giving our neighbors guided tours through our new outhouse. People were pouring out of cars parked along the roadway. They had heard about these outhouses and wanted to examine the first one in Salem. Danny and I were enthusiastically exhibiting the latest technology in outhouses. After we pointed out the lime bin and all the other marvelous details, they would knock on the door and ask Mother what Dad had paid for it and where he bought it.

Mother detested that green thing. No matter how nice the yard and house looked, this green monstrosity stood out like a sore thumb. We tried to disguise it by stacking mesquite firewood on three sides. Even stacks of corded wood couldn't hide that green. Years later, when we purchased another farm near Deming, Mother said the first thing Father had to do was move that ugly thing to the new farm.

The fall after graduation from Salem Elementary School, I entered Hatch High School. Hatch was then a busy little community. Its trade area was the large ranches which surrounded it, the valley farmers, and the small satellite villages. Hatch was right out of a Norman Rockwell painting. Only the geography, architecture, and lack of Yankee dialects made it different. It was a place where the pharmacist would leave his bed at 2:00 a.m. to fill a critical prescription. The local grocer was chief of the volunteer fire department and the blacksmith and mechanics would work late into the night to complete repairs on a much-needed piece of equipment. It was a pleasant, wonderful place to live. Even though the inhabitants were prospering, there was not much available money. People were busy paying off indebtedness incurred during the Depression, purchasing equipment, and buying that extra bit of acreage. Barter was still a way of life. Saturday afternoon was the general shopping day for farmers and everyone came into town. I can still remember the lobby of the local theater, which was so popular with all the children and townspeople. After the Saturday afternoon's shopping the lobby was piled with sacks of green chile, roasting ears, and poultry products. Mr. McMahon, the owner, spent much of his time arguing about how many tickets equaled a sack of fine cornmeal. He didn't make much money either, but he was the best-fed man in the whole Valley.

The community was very supportive of the high school as it was also the center of much of the town's entertainment. Hatch Union High School was a relatively modern facility with a fine gymnasium, pleasant campus, a good stadium, and the teachers were superior. Salaries were very poor, but the cost of living in Hatch was quite low, so most teachers were reluctant to leave for higher paying jobs. Twice I was blessed, in elementary and high school, with superior teachers.

One of the things, besides the teachers, which made high school so special was the students themselves. No one in the student body had any money so we did everything together. When one acquired temporary use of the family car it was immediately loaded with classmates. If other transportation was needed, teachers and parents pitched in to help. There were no social distinctions between haves and have-nots. My children don't understand it, and I wish they could have had the same opportunities. Class members still maintain close contact and we try to have at least one gathering every year or two. It's like a gigantic family reunion. Any former teachers still living are considered a part of the group.

We had an excellent football team, super track teams, and a good music department. I chose football. It was tough the first year as the high school was plentifully supplied with big, tough, strong, farm- and ranch-bred athletes. At 140 pounds I took quite a beating. My sophomore year, in the 150-160 pound class, wasn't quite so bad. The next year, at 177 pounds, it was better. By graduation, I was crowding 190 pounds, a little over six feet tall, and considered a very good football player.

Those four high school years were the happiest of my life. December 6, 1941, we all attended a normal Saturday evening high school social function.

December 7th, was a beautiful Sunday in southern New Mexico. We were completely unaware that what had happened earlier, half-way around the world, would have a lasting impact upon all of our lives. About mid-morning I rode horseback to Tom Case's house. We talked for awhile and decided to visit Paul Norviel who had been sick. As we walked to Paul's house, people were returning from church, walking or driving.

Everybody waved at one another in those days. We visited along the short distance to Paul's house. When we arrived Mr. and Mrs. Roy Norviel were still involved with their customary Sunday Bible study. They sent us upstairs where Paul was in bed, anxious to get out. As usual with teenage boys, we were trying to figure out what to do that afternoon. Should we go hunting or to the movie in Hatch? Another option was riding our horses to the remains of an old cavalry remount and Butterfield Stage station that we had discovered west of the Rio Grande.

About noon Mr. Norviel came upstairs, visibly shaken, and announced that the Japanese had attacked Pearl Harbor. Many had been killed and much American property had been damaged. Even though the attack had been beaten off, many ships were either sunk or burning. This was sobering news. Uncle Ross, my father's brother, was stationed in Pearl Harbor as a regular Navy man. Only five years older than I, Uncle Ross had been my childhood hero. I thought of him. Tom mentioned Frank Simpson, who had graduated a few years ahead of us; he was there on the *USS California*. Stunned, we sat thinking of the local boys who were in the service and might be in Pearl Harbor. We looked at one another and it became very quiet.

Then Paul said, "I'm gonna go, as soon as I can, and try to join the Marines or the Navy." Tom said the Navy would also be his choice. My choice was already made. For the past few years my goal had been to be an Army Air Corps pilot and I was making plans toward that end. Everything had been worked out in my head, but reality never coincided with my plans. We examined our options. Tom and I were a year younger than Paul. I would have to wait, unless they changed the entrance age. Finally, I left to give my parents the news, if they had not already heard it. They would be very concerned about Ross.

On my way home I stopped at a little store run by a World War I veteran, Seaton Higgenbotham. He owned a large, high-powered radio, and residents had drifted in to listen to the news. There were quiet discussions about what they should do. One was concerned about the danger of the Japanese invading the U.S. Most thought it was too far, but we had better get ready. Everyone was very pensive. I rode home and, after turning the horse loose, went inside to see the folks.

They were there. Dad was white-faced and Mother had tears in her eyes. Danny, had appreciated the situation and was sitting very quietly and listening. Mother immediately asked, "Have you heard the news about Pearl Harbor?"

I said, "Yes."

She continued, "You know Ross is there." After a while, Dad left to find another brother and the McGuire clan gathered.

Several days passed before we learned that Ross had survived the attack on Ford Island Naval Aviation Station. Frank Simpson's parents were not so fortunate. The *California* had been sunk and Frank was missing.

A letter from Ross arrived about two weeks later. The night before that attack, December 6, Ross had purchased a new car and had parked it in the Ford Island parking area. After the battle, all he could find in his parking space was some debris. All that was left of that new car was a fender and all the payments.[1]

On December 8th, my family drove into Hatch. Townspeople were gathered in clusters talking soberly. We knew war was inevitable. Many New Mexico sons were in the 200th Coast Artillery (AA) (formerly the New Mexico National Guard), and they were already in the Philippines facing the Japanese onslaught. These New Mexicans were captured at Bataan and later Corregidor, and many participated in the Bataan Death March. Other neighbors' sons were in the military with quite a few at Pearl Harbor, including Ross. It was a sober group that met to talk and ponder about the future. Everyone sympathized with those who had family at Pearl Harbor.

At school we attended a general assembly the teachers had spent most of the night preparing. The principal and coach agreed that war was inevitable, but stressed the need for a diploma. Much high-technology would be employed in this war and we would be more valuable to our country with an education. They encouraged us to stay in school and not let our hearts rule our heads and enlist prematurely. There was time to get our diploma and then be a vital asset to our country. Later that day the entire student body gathered to hear President Roosevelt address Congress and ask for a declaration of war against Japan.

After the assembly, the Superintendent called me into his office. "Melvin, I understand you are anxious to be an Army Air Corps pilot. Here is some material that I want to give you. You have several strikes against you if that is what you really want. One, you're not old enough now. Two, you're going to have to have two years of college. Therefore, you're going to have to start studying harder. I understand there is an equivalency exam, but you have the time, and if you want it badly enough, I'll give you everything I can to help you get into the Army Air Corps."

A few months later, my father gave the commencement address. When he called me forward to receive my diploma, it was only the third time in my life that I'd ever seen my father with tears in his eyes.

Chapter 1

[1] As a footnote to our family's experience with Uncle Ross at Pearl Harbor, June, my wife of forty-three years, had a very different situation at their home in Cheyenne, Wyoming. Their brother, Walter, had been in the Navy for about two years and was an Able Seaman on the *USS Oklahoma*. They had received no word and feared the worst. On that Sunday they had been to church. When they heard the news, their family gathered. As the reports came, their chances of finding Walter alive diminished. Then the rumors began circulating, in spite of the censorship, that the *Oklahoma* had been sunk and capsized. A few days later, while their mother Marie sat sewing and her youngest brother Johnny, and sister Betty, were talking, the doorbell rang. A Navy officer stood at the door. All knew what this meant. Very quietly, he told them that Walter Stein, Able Seaman on the *USS Oklahoma* was missing and presumed dead.

About a year later the Navy notified the family that Walter Stein's body was being returned to Cheyenne for burial at the local cemetery. He was buried with appropriate military honors. Approximately a year after that, one of Walter's life-long friends, a Navy diver, came to see them. He said Walter was still interred in the *Oklahoma*. The diver friend had been inside the *Oklahoma* on several dives and had found Walter, with five others, in a water-tight compartment, perhaps the library. He was plainly identifiable and he was still there. After several rounds of letters inquiring into this possibility, the family dropped the matter, but they still firmly believe their brother, Walter, is still aboard the *Oklahoma*.

– 2 –

In The Army

Following graduation, several universities and colleges offered me athletic scholarships. I had considered accepting one at a Southern military academy, but it was a cavalry school and I didn't want to get stuck in tanks or cavalry. New Mexico A & M's scholarship was attractive for two reasons: It was close to home and it had a very fine ROTC (Reserve Officer Training Corps) program. Being a Land Grant College, ROTC was compulsory for two years and, I thought, that would be good preparation for what I intended to do. That fall, after registering and being placed in the McFie Hall dorm, I enjoyed playing intramural football until the coach realized that too many of his brute athletes were being hurt playing with the pee-wees. Then we were moved to Kent Hall, across from the gymnasium and football stadium in the heart of the campus.

The ROTC program kept abreast of military happenings and regulations. My counselor, Jack Baird, knew I was aspiring to be an Army Air Corps pilot and my second choice was infantry. He told me that representatives from the Army would be on campus shortly to give the Army General Classification Test (AGCT). I eagerly looked forward to this test as it was necessary, regardless of what I would be doing in the service. The following week I was notified to report for the AGCT. It was a difficult test and lasted about four hours, but I felt confident about my effort. Two days later a notice appeared on the bulletin board telling us where to go to learn our test scores. Mine was a very good score and qualified me for several choices of service, and it was also above the minimum required for aviation flight training. I was pleased.

The next step was an interview with the Army Air Corps representatives who would conduct interviews and do counseling at the ROTC building. They would furnish information and materials to those interested in joining the Army Air Corps Aviation Training Program. I was there thirty minutes early. Two officers interviewed me and were particularly interested in why I wanted to fly. After the interview they said I would receive a letter telling me where and when to take the cadet entrance exams for flight school training.

About two weeks later a notice arrived, stating that the exam would be given on the campus. As usual, I was there early. This was a very difficult test and even longer than the AGCT. When they said, "Time's up," I left the building feeling that I'd failed. The only question I felt confident about was the one on how a carburetor worked. The previous weekend I had been home and Dad asked me to take a tractor with carburetor problems to a mechanic in town. Until then, I couldn't spell the word, much less describe how it worked. That mechanic loved to talk and explained every step he took. When the test asked for a labeled drawing of a carburetor, I blessed that old mechanic. About a week later a letter arrived advising me that I had made a satisfactory score, but would need my parent's permission to go any further since I was under age. After obtaining their signatures, I was to mail the papers back.

I had grave doubts that my parents would sign the papers. That weekend I went home and all four of us gathered. I explained about the tests I had taken and passed, but I couldn't go any further without their signatures giving their permission for me to go into flight training if I was selected.

My father mumbled something about, "If God had wanted us to fly he would have given us feathers." Mother, with quivering lips, said she would rather I had chosen another branch of the service. Then she surprised me and said, "I know your heart is set on this, so if your Dad signs, I'll sign."

Dad looked at me for a long time. Finally, I said, "Dad, this is very important to me. This is what I want to do. I want to make my life's work out of it if I can. I have worked hard taking a bunch of tests, so please sign." He signed with shaking hands and the papers left in that day's mail for the War Department. After the usual two-week wait another letter informed me that within the next ninety days I would receive information on when and where to appear for a medical examination and submit to psychological testing. Details would be furnished in the next letter, but the location would probably be Fort Bliss (El Paso, Texas).

Meanwhile, I enjoyed the new-found freedom of college life. I liked football and was doing well on the team, although we wondered if there would even be a regular season. Rumors said that conference games had been suspended. The coach told us we would have a few scrimmage games that wouldn't count, but would be good experience.

In about a month another letter arrived from the War Department ordering me to report to Fort Bliss, Texas for my medical examination and to receive psychological testing. My appearance before the qualification and interview board was to be just a few blocks away at Biggs Field, and would be the afternoon following the tests. Transportation would be furnished from Fort Bliss to Biggs Field. That letter would be my pass to get onto both installations. I couldn't wait.

The night before my exams we scrimmaged against the Texas Western College Miners. It was a rough game, with two bench-clearing brawls, and I left the game with a skinned forehead, elbows and knees, a fat lip, and shin bones full of lumps. In general, I looked a mess. Since the game was in El Paso, I splurged and spent the night at the Cortez Hotel.

The next morning a medical technician took a lengthy medical history from me and then told me to disrobe and wait. The doctor probed and pushed, looked in my ears, throat and nose, and examined everything, including my hands and fingers. After a very thorough and business-like exam he asked, "Mr. McGuire, are you a football player?"

"Yes, sir."

"Did you get all of those bruises and contusions last night in the game against the Miners?"

"Yes, sir."

"I had a boy playing with the Miners in that game. It was a good game."

I thought, "Oh Lordy, as if I haven't got enough problems. Now I've got a doctor that's a Miner sympathizer."

He laughed and continued with the examination. After submitting to all the usual indignities associated with physical exams, he stopped when the rumbling from my stomach became loud enough to disrupt conversation and asked, "McGuire, did you have any breakfast?"

"No, sir."

"Why not?"

I blurted, "Doctor, I'm afraid of the weight limit. I have been trying to diet and thought last night's game might help me lose some more, but I still weigh more than two hundred pounds."

"What do you ordinarily weigh?"

"I vary between 208 and 216 pounds."

He replied, "Well, we have to take some lab tests."

"Sir, if I eat I'm sure I can't make that weight limit and this is very important to me."

He laughed and told me to get on the scales. "Let's see what you weigh."

I prayed as I climbed on the scales. "You're two hundred-two pounds and this old scale always weighs heavy anyway. Let me tell you this. You have to come back at 1300 for some lab tests, so you have a good lunch at the place where they'll take you in a few minutes. You can eat plenty and still rest easy because your skeletal development is what determines your weight limit. The two-hundred-pound limit would be waived in your instance anyway, because of your height."

I felt a million years younger. After lunch I returned to the doctor's office. I liked him and hoped to see him again, but that didn't happen. After more tests, they handed me a number and the number of another building where I was to report. It was the psychiatric section of the hospital and within walking distance. A sergeant was ahead of me in the waiting room. This Regular Army man, who also wanted to be an aviation cadet, seemed to know all the answers, so I asked many questions. According to him, the psychological exam requirements were very high and the psychologists washed out a large proportion of the applicants. That scared me.

Shortly after that they called his number and he left me. In a very short time I heard loud voices and shouting coming from that room. Several orderlies entered the room and brought the sergeant out. He was livid. Then my number was called.

I entered, scared to death. The psychiatrist apologized for the disturbance and told me not to let it bother me, and then asked me to sit. The first questions were very logical. Then, suddenly, he became extremely personal. Had I ever had an incestuous relationship? Only by reminding myself that this was an exam was I able to keep from losing my temper. I bit my lip and answered his questions.

From there it was back to the doctor's office. My tests completed, I was instructed to catch the transportation in front of the building at 1430 for the short ride to Biggs Field for my appearance before the interview board.

While waiting for the transportation I continually reviewed my perceived errors during the psychiatric exam. I had tried not to show emotion or feelings, but wasn't convinced that I had been too successful. The interview board was running behind schedule and we would need to make our appearance at 0900 the next morning. With that, they returned us to the main gate and we caught a bus into town.

A boy from Big Springs, Texas, who was behind me in the interview line, asked where I was staying. "I stayed at a hotel downtown last night," I replied, "but can't afford another night there." He was broke and couldn't afford to stay by himself in a hotel, but he could share a room. We left the bus in front of a sleazy looking hotel not far from Fort Bliss. A room with a double bed, water pitcher, washbasin, cracked mirror, and a dresser was $3.50. Once we were settled in, it only took a few minutes to discover we were lodging in a cat house. We barricaded the door with the dresser and spent the remainder of the night refusing the girls offered by those who knocked.

The next morning we barely made it in time to go through the main gate at Biggs Field and join the interview board line. It took thirty minutes before my name was called. Dressed in my best suit, I entered and they asked to me sit. The interviewers were older, very pleasant, Army Air Corps men and all wore wings. Two were from World War I. The chairman congratulated me on passing the different tests and examinations, and told me theirs would be the final procedure. They urged me to relax. They wanted to know more about me and asked about my childhood, why I was so interested in Army Aviation, and my choice of aircraft to fly. They were a bit surprised when I said the A-20, until I explained that if I couldn't stay in the service after the war, I wanted to be a commercial pilot. For years I had been reading everything available about all types of aircraft, so I could knowledgeably answer their technical questions. In a little while they said, "Mr. McGuire, you take a chair outside and we'll soon let you know our decision."

During the next candidate's interview I died a thousand deaths. When his interview was concluded, they called me back. This time I wasn't asked to sit down and took that for a bad omen. Instead, they congratulated me for successfully passing the exams for entrance into the Army Air Corps Aviation Flight

Training. There would be other tests later, but there would be a long wait because the classes were backlogged. Until more airplanes were available and new bases came on-line, they could not train more pilots.

Fort Bliss

In early March 1943, my parents delivered me to a building topped by a large sign: 'Logan Heights Induction Center.' Logan Heights, an annex to Fort Bliss, was where all inductees and draftees reported. I took my little blue AWOL bag[1] and shaving kit from the car. After shaking hands with my father and brother and kissing my mother goodbye, I headed for the door that proclaimed, 'Inductees Enter Here.' It might as well as have said, 'Abandon all hope, all who enter here.'

Naturally excited, as this would be my first day in the Army, we arrived at the Induction Center around 0745. The sign announced the center would open at 0800. Twenty-five or thirty other men were already there bidding goodbye to sweethearts, wives, and families. At eight o'clock sharp the doors opened. I was one of the first to the counter. They asked for my name, which I gave them. After an extensive perusal of the list, they finally said, "You're not on it."

Shook to the core, I produced my orders that stated I was to report at eight o'clock that morning. Finally, a nearby soldier overheard our exchange and said, "Just a minute, what's his name?"

They said, "McGuire."

"I have his folder here." He brought out a very official looking folder and said, "He's one of those Air Corps things. I just got it." My murderous look didn't appear to bother him as he continued, "Take a seat and you'll be called when we get around to it." To the clerks he continued, "There's another different one here, too. The Captain will have to examine his paperwork also. His name is Jesús Hinojosa (pronounced Hay-soos He-no-ho-sah), a damn car thief. It's one of those deals where the Captain has to sign the court papers, so he'll have to handle these."

Jesús came forward upon hearing his name. He was a nice-looking Hispanic male about my age. They told him to take a seat, which he did beside me. He was quite embarrassed, as I was by association, because everybody in the building had heard the car thief reference. He appeared to be a nice guy and was neat and clean. The longer I knew him, the better I liked him. Much later I learned that he had borrowed a car without permission, and driven it across the state line, but for what he considered an emergency. The judge told him he could serve time or go into the service. Since he had been trying to get into the service, this suited him fine. Jesús and I shared many adventures those first thirty days. Through a mixture of my border Spanglish and Jesús' marginal English, we got along fine.

The line continued to move and no one called our names. Finally, a medical technician approached and held out two little jars. He needed a urine specimen. When I explained this to Jesús, he was horrified. "The Army wants my pee?"

"Yes."

"¿Por que? (Why?)"

"They can tell whether you have some diseases, I guess, but you've got to fill that little bottle for them."

We followed the technician into the clinic restroom where Jesús finally filled his bottle. At that point Jesús adopted me as his spokesman, translator, and advisor. Later we were told to disrobe. Then we sat for what seemed like hours. Since we were stark naked we stuck to the chairs. To increase our discomfort, those chairs had small holes in the seat which transferred their pattern to our posteriors. Finally, a line of men came back into our area. As their names were called they were to dress and go to another building for the swearing-in. Those rejected could talk to one of the examiners. It was a production-line process. Throughout it all Jesús and I remained stuck to our chairs.

Finally, after everyone had marched out, a smock-garbed Captain entered and called, "McGuire, Hinojosa."

We stood, chairs sticking to our backsides, and responded, "Here, sir."

"McGuire, you just had a physical. Why are you here? Are you going to OCS or what?"

"I'm going to the Army Air Corps, sir."

"Yes, I can see there are some War Department circulars and you have a thick file already."

"I'm going to flight training if I can."

"Very well." To Jesus he said, "I have to sign your papers and mail them to a judge. Apparently, you were charged with inter-state car theft."

Jesus shamefacedly said, "Yes, sir."

The preliminaries completed, he told us to get on the scales and we went through that physical in record-breaking time. It was the usual turn your head and cough, and bend over with the usual indignities, but within an hour the doctor said, "Both of you are fit. You will be sworn in today, but we're going to have to hurry to get you in on the regular swearing-in."

We hastily dressed and one of the men working at the center took us to another building. Everybody was leaving and he announced, "We have two more to be sworn in. They have been processed. One of them is a car thief and I don't know what this other is."

That introduction started me off on the wrong foot with the Army. Finally, they corralled a second lieutenant and a sergeant and Jesús and I were duly sworn into the United States Army. Next, we had to draw our clothing, so we headed for the warehouse with a sergeant who kept looking at his wristwatch. Most of the clerks had already gone and they were ready to lock up. They did not view our late arrival with favor. Before he entered his little glass-enclosed cubicle, the sergeant said, "Issue these knuckle-heads some clothing and send them back to me."

One clerk looked at Jesús' file and said, "Jailbirds," including me in his condemnation.

"Here comes some more trouble," I thought, and sure enough it came.

He said, "Take this," and threw a helmet liner at me, which I grabbed, followed with an overcoat and a raincoat. He literally threw them at me. When he threw the pants and shirt, I looked at them and said, "These are too big," and gave him my size.

The clerk, a Japanese Nisei,[2] said, "You'll take what I give you."

I threw them back and said, "They're too big. I wear a 16 1/2-34 shirt and this is about a 20 or something." He threw it back, this time hitting me in the face. All of the day's indignities boiled to the surface and I started to climb over the counter after him. The sergeant emerged from his office, grabbed me and said, "Calm down. What's this all about?"

The clerk answered, "He doesn't like the clothes he's been issued."

The sergeant told me, "You'll wear them anyway." Then he issued the rest of my socks, clothes, and belt. I could rope a steer with the belt, it was so long. At least my G.I. shoes fit. I had stood there with the customary pail of sand in each hand to simulate the weight of a backpack, as your feet flatten when you are carrying heavy weights. As I put the clothing in my barracks bag, I promised myself that someday I was going back and get the proper size clothing.

Seething, I left the clothing warehouse. Outside the sergeant told us to fall in single file, shoulder our barracks bags and then march forward. Giving it my best ROTC marching display, I immediately discovered that Jesús was not a natural born marcher as he continually stepped on my heels and bumped into my barracks bag. Finally, I said, "There must be twenty thousand damn acres on this reservation. Would you move back a little and quit stepping on my heels?" Then the sergeant chewed me out for talking in ranks.

We arrived at A Company Orderly Room. An NCO meeting was in process and the participants looked rather perturbed when the sergeant handed them our files and said something about a couple of criminals. I believed it was my duty to protest and said, "I'm not a criminal, I'm here to join the Army Air Corps and I didn't steal a car." I might as well have been a criminal because they didn't like the Army Air Corps, as I soon discovered. The first sergeant turned to a corporal and said, "They're yours. Get them assigned to quarters. And see they get haircuts first thing in the morning."

I started to say, "Sir, I've already had a haircut," and then shut my mouth. The day before our hometown barber had given me a very close haircut and I thought there wasn't much left to cut.

The corporal got up mumbling and marched the two of us to a vacant half-lumber, half-canvas tent. After he had assigned our cots, he ordered us to clean up the place. It looked pretty tidy to me, but I quickly discovered that was not the Army way of doing things. Another corporal came by and I told him we hadn't had anything to eat all day, so he took us over to one of the mess halls and they fed us. He was one of the few nice guys. Otherwise we would have gone to bed hungry.

We tried to make the beds the best we could and struggled into our fatigues. I had enough room in mine for two more guys. Soon it was lights out. Thus ended my first, most unsatisfactory day, in the United States Army.

If anything, the second day was worse. With bugles blaring and whistles blowing, guys hollering, I started my second day in the Army. They required us to shave, although I didn't have much need to shave then. I hastily went through the process and dressed in my fatigues. I looked like a walking tent. Then the whistle blew again and somebody hollered, "A Company, fall in." We fell in. Actually, we looked more like a big mob. The corporal called roll for the morning report. When he got to the 'H's' he hesitated, started, hesitated again, and then began laughing hysterically. "One thing about my job, I meet all the dignitaries. Last week I had Napoleon. This week I've got Jesus." Jesús looked uncomfortable and a few others snickered. When the corporal tried to get us into some semblance of formation, I was very careful not to be placed in front of Jesús. "Now," he said, "we're going to go to the barber shop and start to get you looking like soldiers. Be sure you have your money."

With that we proceeded in a disorganized march to the barber shop. One company was already there. I was about one-hundredth in line and not paying too much attention. Before I realized it, I was in the barber shop and only about ten back from the barber chairs. Two men were frantically sweeping up what looked like bales of hair from the floor. I was curious to see what kind of haircut we would get when it appeared to be taking only about a minute-and-a-half to two minutes per man. A soldier in one of the chairs squalled and hit his head. The barber remedied the nick by applying a little septic pencil to the bloody spot. After your haircut, you went to a sink where they poured disinfectant shampoo on your head. Two minutes later you resembled a survivor from brain surgery.

I commented to the guy behind me, "It ought to be a felony to give a haircut like that and charge for it." The room suddenly became very quiet. Although I was still about ten people back, the corporal said, "You're next."

"But there are still some guys ahead of me."

"YOU'RE NEXT," he snarled.

"Me?"

"Yeh, you loudmouth."

The barber grinned as I climbed into his chair. Those clippers were red-hot and in about two minutes I sported his version of a haircut and had my septic pencil treatment and disinfectant shampoo. A look in the mirror made me sick. Little tufts and lines of hair stuck up wherever he'd missed with the clippers. The tufts alternated with the bloody patches from the nicks. I looked terrible! Angry, I knew better than to say any more. I'd already said too much. Jesús looked like a plucked chicken. With that previous mass of black, wavy hair, I hadn't realized his nose was so big.

Now my oversized fatigue hat came down over my eyes. The only way I could see was to turn the brim up all the way around. It looked like I was wearing a giant hand-operated orange juicer. The rest of that frustrating day we spent in learning to march in close order drill. ROTC had not prepared me for anything as bad as that day's collective effort.

That evening we watched Army VD films, after which I almost took a vow of celibacy. Thus ended my second day in the United States Army, a most unpleasant portent of things to come while I was at Logan Heights. That second day was no accident, it was going to get worse. After that, it was endless days of marching, filling fire buckets and fire barrels, cleaning latrines, picking up pebbles, odd-ball menial details, and KP, KP, KP. Finally, I was sent back to the induction center for what I hoped would be a soft job. Unfortunately, it was in the urinalysis section. Fortunately, I didn't spend much time there. Nearly every day we ran up the side of Mount Franklin and back. It was boring.

New groups moved in about every five or six days and other groups shipped out on the same schedule. As each new group arrived, I was ordered to join them for shots. My arms were swollen from so many shots. Mercifully, one of the medics recognized me. "How many times are you going to go through here?"

"Well, they keep sending me back."

He understood. "O.K. Come over here, have a seat and enjoy yourself. They're trying to find something for you to do." Thereafter, a favorite pastime was sitting outside the shot clinic and making bets with innocent bystanders on whether the big guy was going to faint or not. My discovery, that the bigger they were the more apt they were to faint, earned me quite a few quarters from betting that the big men would faint before the little ones. Nobody bothered you when you were outside the clinic.

The first sergeant came by one day when I was working. "Turn the brim down on that damn hat," he commanded. I demonstrated how it fell down over my face. He barked, "Give me that damn thing and I'll be back in about an hour." Sure enough, about an hour later he handed me one that fit properly. At least now I had a fatigue hat that fit.

Rumors had been floating around that each company was going to have a baseball team. To me, that meant practice and I wasn't that wild about baseball, but it would beat what I had been doing. One morning the corporal asked, "Are there any baseball players or college athletes here?" Here's my chance, I thought, to get off some of these details. Knowing better than to volunteer, I still raised my hand. He picked about ten and then said, "Alright, how many are college athletes?" Again my hand went up. "Alright, all the college athletes and baseball players come up here. Now I want all the rest of you to follow these guys who, in turn, are going to follow me." Then he turned to the select group and said, "You're going to show all these other knuckle-heads how to load and unload boxcars." We'd been had! Unloading a boxcar and loading the contents on trucks was backbreaking work. It was a shipment of uniforms for the induction center. These uniforms we unloaded and stacked in the clothing warehouse.

In spite of the arduous work, it was a lucky break for me. During that detail, I discovered the location of some nice, pre-war uniforms. Between unloading and stacking, I copied the lot numbers for those uniforms. Pre-war uniforms were made of very fine material and were of much better cut and quality than the ones issued to recruits coming through the reception center. The Fifth and Seventh Cavalry had left behind some of these pre-war uniforms. Cadre (leadership group) at Logan Heights had set aside these pre-war uniforms for their personal use, and I was determined to get into that lot.

While on that detail, I observed an interesting phenomenon. Anyone who looked like he was on official business, wore a uniform that fit, and carried a clipboard with official-looking papers, could literally terrify the clerks and the permanent party soldiers (those permanently stationed at Logan Heights). Permanent party had regular hours, no drill, and lots of time off. All had wives or girlfriends, and El Paso was a good leave town. Logan Heights was considered a very good assignment and none of them wanted to lose it. Consequently, when an official-looking unknown from headquarters appeared with a clipboard and roster, they were afraid they had been trans-ferred or reassigned to a unit elsewhere. They avoided you like poison. Mentally, I began formulating my plans to make life more tolerable. And acquire uniforms that fit.

Meanwhile, Jesús was still waiting for more documentation from the judge to expunge the classification 'criminal' from his record. He volunteered for KP duty. I said, "Jesús, you're crazy. You'll spend all day down there cleaning out grease traps, washing dishes and emptying garbage cans. That's hard work. You sweat all the time. You're out of your cotton pickin' head."

"No, Mack, I've always wanted to own a restaurant like my uncle. I want to be a cook and this is all part of it. If I can learn to cook in the Army, I'm going to open a restaurant when I get out. There's lots of money to be made in the restaurant business."

One day, while on KP at Jesús' mess hall, I commented to one of the cooks, "That guy wants to be a cook real bad as he wants to open a restaurant after the war. Is there anything you can do for him?"

The cook, a nice guy, replied, "We don't have too many volunteers because it's hard work. If he's interested, I'll talk to him." A few days later Jesús bid me a tearful farewell. He was being permanently assigned to a mess hall until he could attend Cook's and Baker's School. He was thrilled. His record was now clean and he was no longer a car thief. I wished him well. That was the last time I saw Jesús.

One day, while on latrine duty, a runner came in and said the first sergeant wanted to see me right away. What kind of trouble was I in now? At his office I sat down and waited. In a few minutes the sergeant came out. "McGuire, come in. Have you had a pass since you've been here?"

"No, sir, I sure as hell haven't."

"Your parents are waiting for you in front of the recreation hall at the induction center. They're parked out in front. I'm going to give you a two-day pass. It will be ready by the time you go down to your tent and change into your Class A's. I want to look at you before you go and pick up your pass. Have a good time."

I quickly returned to the tent and hastily put on my clean set of those awful clothes. The shirt was so big the cuffs hung down to the end of my fingers. Rubber bands around my arms held them up. The shirt was folded over several times around my hips and I could put my hand between my throat and the collar button. The pants were also folded back and forth. By then I'd cut the belt to the proper length and it was the only item I was wearing that fit, besides my shoes. The collar was so big that when I tied my tie, the knot was almost belt level. I was the saddest looking sight that ever wore an Army uniform.

The first sergeant inspected me and shook his head, "Well, it's too late to do anything about it now, but here's your pass." I high-tailed it to the parking lot in front of the recreation hall where my mother, father, and little brother were sitting in the car. Danny recognized me first and began laughing hysterically. Mother and Dad were out of the car by then.

Mother looked at me and said, "Oh my God, Melvin, don't you have any clothes that fit? You look terrible. Terrible."

When I removed my overseas cap, that went down almost to my nose, to kiss her, Danny saw my hair and erupted in even louder laughter. "You look like a shaved cat." By then my hair had grown back considerably but it was still a horrible sight. I'd had it with Danny's sense of humor and growled at him, "You're not too big to get a fat lip if you don't shut up." Mother was actually in tears when she saw my head.

Dad was very indignant. "It's a damned disgrace that somebody trying to serve his country is fitted in a uniform that looks like that. Nothing fits him. By God, I'm going to tell somebody about that. That uniform is disgraceful looking." Dad declared he was going to call somebody about this disgrace.

Horrified, I said, "No, no, no, no, no, please no."

Mother said, "Mac, let's take him to a uniform store and get him some clothes that fit."

Dad asked, "Melvin, do you know where one is?"

"Yes, sir. There are several downtown and I understand they do alterations while you wait."

"Why don't you have clothes that fit?" he asked.

"This is what they issued me." I decided not to go into the details. We immediately drove to the largest of several fine military shops in downtown El Paso. To my great embarrassment, Dad told one of the clerks, "I want this boy fitted in some decent uniforms. It's a damned disgrace the things they issue. I want some nice uniforms for him."

The store was full of Fifth Cavalry, old-time Regular Army men, and they were all holding their sides trying to keep from laughing, but not succeeding. My face was scarlet. Even the clerk tried to suppress his giggles, and I was frantically trying to quiet my parents.

"Where shall we start?" asked the clerk.

Mother said, "He has to have shirt and trousers, and look at that awful cap. It comes almost to his shoulders. We want a cap, too."

The clerk lead us over to their most expensive suntan uniforms. I was trying to get out of there as soon as possible, without further embarrassment to myself, so I provided him with my sizes. As more men came into the store, the others enlightened them about my predicament and they, too, would look and start laughing. My parents bought two complete uniforms.

During the fitting, Mother came back with a cap in my size trimmed with blue pipping. She said, "This is a real nice one."

"Mother, I can't wear that. That blue pipping indicates it is infantry."

"Where do they keep the Air Corps ones?"

"I can't wear that one either. I'm not yet assigned to the Air Corps. I'll take care of the hat if all of you will go over there and sit down until I'm fitted out."

Dad promised the tailor an extra five bucks if he could get one uniform in an hour. He could. The fitting finished, we crossed the street for lunch and then returned to the clothing store. An hour later I looked in the mirror. In my new uniform I looked one hundred percent better. In fact, I could have been part of the cadre. I was most pleased, and even Danny approved.

Two days later I volunteered for duty at the induction center as way to implement my plan to get my hands on those cavalry uniforms. They began work very early in the morning and quit at noon, then they were free the rest of the day. I was surprised to receive the assignment and requested the illiterate section for the pre-induction physical classifications. That group processed the fewest number and, therefore, those working there had less to do. As a part of my job I had acquired a clipboard to hold lists of names, etc. When they closed for lunch I quickly returned to our headquarters to collect rosters and official-looking orders out of the A Company wastebaskets. Then I headed for the clothing warehouse to put my theory to the test. The Army was going to issue me some proper clothing, even if I had to do it myself. My operational time frame was between 1215 and 1300 when the non-coms and a majority of the clerks would be at lunch. I was in luck, only one clerk, engrossed in reading a magazine, was on duty. Carrying all those ill-fitting clothes in a bundle under my arm, I marched in with my clipboard. After slamming the bundle onto the counter, I asked the guy his name and looked at the roster. That got his attention. "I want to talk to the sergeant," I demanded.

"The sergeant is not here."

"Well, where the hell is he?"

"He's gone to lunch."

"All he does is eat and he probably won't get back until 1315 or 1330."

"He has to eat."

"But he doesn't have to eat all day long. I have to exchange these clothes for this man. They are waiting on him and these were issued by mistake. Let me exchange them." On a sheet of paper I had written my clothing sizes and the lot numbers of those pre-war clothing boxes with 'cadre' written across the front.

He said, "But I don't know anything about the paperwork entailed in exchanges."

"There is no paperwork in an exchange. You put these back in their proper size bins and you exchange one for one. I have two pairs of pants and two shirts, khaki shirts and khaki pants. You put these back according to their size in the bins and you go over to that lot number and you get me this size out of that bunch there."

"But I don't know anything about lot numbers."

I marched him over to the pre-war clothing I had located earlier and said, "That's the lot number. See right here. Now I need two 16 1/2-34 shirts out of that lot number. Just get into that box and let me have two shirts."

He looked as though he was being led to his execution, but complied. We went through the same routine with the pants, underwear, and everything else that didn't fit. I left about forty-five minutes later, practically on a run as I didn't want some sergeant to catch me. I had finally evened the score with the Army.

Suddenly, all my dirty details—cleaning latrines, KP, fire guard duty—mysteriously stopped and I was drawing rather reasonable duty. I couldn't explain it, but made the most of this pleasant change. Dressed in my new-issue uniforms and carrying my clipboard, I would go to the PX for a malt and then sightsee around the base. My theory was correct, nobody bothered you as long as you looked official and carried a clipboard. That clipboard allowed me to take many liberties.

One day, sometime later, while involved with some menial task, I was told to report to the first sergeant, on the double. He came out and said, "McGuire, come in." I went in. "Well, flyboy, this ought to make you very happy. As of 2400 you belong to the Uuuunited States Army Air Corps. I know this is going to make you very happy. I have your orders here and you're to report to Sheppard Field in Wichita Falls, Texas. There'll be a truck here at the orderly room at 0430. Have everything ready and your barracks bag packed. They'll take you and some others to the El Paso depot to catch the train to Wichita Falls. Be here at 0430. There'll be an early mess for your breakfast.

"McGuire, I know you got the short end of the stick for a while here. The troops were upset because they thought they had some criminals dumped on them. That was finally straightened out. We knew you had been getting an awfully lot of dirty details, so I put a stop to it. Several weeks ago I told them to back off because they might even have to salute you one of these days. I hope life was a little more livable for you.

"I'm sorry about your clothes. Until I saw you when your parents were visiting I didn't know what kind of clothing you had been issued. That's not ordinarily the way it's done. I was always going to do something about it, but I kept forgetting. But, McGuire, I see that you have done all right for yourself. Right now you're sitting here wearing a uniform that was made in 1939. I don't know how you got it, but I have a feeling that you will go far in the service. Congratulations on going to the Air Corps. I know this is going to make you very happy."

I liked that old sergeant. In a peacetime army he would have been reaching retirement age. Before I left he said, "By the way, we could never figure out what you've been doing around here for the last two or three weeks, but seeing that uniform, I have an idea that I know some of it. Now get out of here."

Sheppard Air Force Base

My plan to get basic training out of the way by joining the Army backfired. The Air Corps didn't accept Army basic training, so I had it to do over again. Air Corps basic was as hard as infantry basic training.[3]

Immediately after our arrival, a guy ran into my barracks, and asked us if anybody had any ink. My folks had given me a brand-new gold Parker pen and ink to go with it before I left, so I said, "Yea, I've got some ink," and handed him the bottle. He took it, and drank it. I was horrified. He ran into another room from where we heard a crash. Somebody said, "He's eating a light bulb!" The guy was a Corporal Klinger-type, trying to get out of the service on a Section 8. Soon a first sergeant came over to the barracks with his clipboard, and I told him the guy had drunk my ink and eaten a light bulb. He said, "That son of a bitch!" Apparently the ink drinker was a repeat case. Whether or not he was eventually successful, I don't know.

Basic training was physically tough. Wichita Falls in the summer is humid and dusty and we were always filthy from

33

falling into the oil sumps. The ropes we used to swing across those sumps were deliberately not long enough. We spent hours at night trying to clean that oil and dirt out of our clothes. I was tired all the time. It got to where I could sleep any place big enough for me to lie down. By the time it was over, I was delighted to get out of there, and we hadn't even seen an airplane.

I did, however, pass, and in early 1943 I was immediately assigned to the Aviation Student Program at the University of Xavier and Lunken Field in Cincinnati. This was it. I was about to start learning how to fly. I was going to be a pilot. This had been my dream ever since I was old enough to walk. My fellow students had previously had little contact with New Mexicans and they razed me about my accent. When they wanted to get a rise out of me they would say, "Say something in New Mexican, Mack." It was an intense time. They crammed the normal two-year course into a frantic crash course in the academic portion. In addition to long hours of classwork, we had military drill and guard duty. We flew twenty hours over a period of four months. Finally, we were sent to Randolph Field for classification, i.e. pilot, navigator, bombardier, or civilian.

And then they washed me out.

Because of allergies, I have always had sinus problems. This condition worsened when I was sent to Ohio. My looks were not helped by my allergy to ragweed, which kept my eyes red and teary. During the flight physical, one of the flight surgeons noticed my bloodshot eyes, runny nose and the streaks down my face from sinus infections. Shortly thereafter I was called into a review board. They took a look at my records, asked questions about my sinus problems and said they would take my case "under advisement," and excused me. In a little while a doctor called me into his office and told me I was medically not fit for flight training, and washed me out of flight school. He cautioned me about ever flying.

Even today I'm bitter about that. After the war I returned home and quickly and easily became a pilot, a good one. I would have been a good pilot then, too, but they didn't want me. It was a bitter, bitter blow.

While still at the review board, they said since I was of above-average intelligence and had scored highly on all my exams, I was eligible for Army Officer Candidate School. I told them I would take that. My heart had been set on flying, not being an infantryman. That was next to the worst day of my life. I was so upset I didn't even want to call home.

While sitting outside the building, a fellow soldier walked up to me. He had been immediately behind me at the review board and I recognized him as another flight school candidate. The board had grounded him as well. After he sat down beside me, we introduced ourselves. He said the board didn't know what it was doing; he had between four and five thousand hours of flying in civilian life as a test pilot, and he wasn't going to quit trying to get into flight training. He asked if I wanted to keep trying too. When I told him that I did, he said, "Come with me, I've got some connections."

While we marched to the nearest telephone booth, he told me he had been offered a commission as a service pilot, but he wanted to be a fighter pilot and that was the reason he had ended up in cadet school. A close friend was a commander at an Air Force base, and he was going to see if this friend could pull some strings.

After borrowing some coins from me, he entered the booth and placed his call. After a few minutes his face broke into a wide grin, and he leaned out of the booth. "Quick," he yelled, "give me your name, rank, and serial number. We're going to get in some kind of flight training through the back door!"

The next day we were en route to Air Force Armament School at Buckley Field, Denver, Colorado. I was now officially training with the Army Air Corps. It wasn't exactly what I had anticipated or wanted, but at least I would be closer to flying.

Buckley Field

I subsequently trained in both pursuit and bombardment armament schools for at least thirty-two weeks where I learned everything there was to learn about machine guns, both .30

caliber and .50 caliber,[4] in pursuit planes. There we learned how to break the guns apart and put them back together again, how to bore sight them, feed ammunition, and synchronize their firing through propellers. I also learned electrical wiring and firing systems.

Upon completion of my pursuit armament training phase, I was immediately sent to bombardment armament school, which was an entirely different system. There we learned all about turrets, and the electrical firing systems and compensating sights, and flexible systems unique to bombers. We studied explosives, repairs, and bombs—how to load them, fire them off the racks, and wire them for safety.

In the early fall of 1943, they came around to one of our classes and asked if anybody was interested in becoming a gunner. They were taking applications for gunnery school. My form had been filled out and waiting in my 201 file[5] for this day. Acceptance meant I could fly.

Las Vegas Army Air Base

In the back of my mind I wanted to complete gunnery school and then reapply to flight school. If I could get through gunnery school without physical problems—to prove my sinus wouldn't cause difficulties—maybe I could get accepted to flight school. But things didn't work out that way.

My gunnery school was taught at Las Vegas Army Air Base (Nellis AFB) in Las Vegas and Indian Springs, Nevada. Gunnery school was a snap since the expert training in armament school. Besides, I had been handling firearms and shooting since I was a child. They first ran us through classroom training on ballistics and explosives. Primary instruction was on the .50 caliber, the main gun for all contemporary bombers. We also received a little instruction on the 20-mm cannon, because some bombers carried a few of these. Also, throughout gunnery school they had us breaking apart and putting back together .50 caliber machine guns—again, this was no problem because of my previous armory school training. In armament school we had been required to detail strip them blindfolded.

Then we started shooting. They first put us on a skeet range to give us some idea of how to lead a target effectively. This was called deflection shooting. We shot 12-gauge shotguns so much our shoulders were always sore.

Next they put us in AT-6 training planes. We stood in the back of the plane and fired a .30 caliber machine gun at ground targets or at tow targets as the plane dived.

Finally, we graduated to firing out of turrets, but in a strange way. They drove us around in pickups over a banking figure-eight roller-coaster style raceway and fired skeet clay targets at us. We had to bust the clay birds while shooting from the turrets. Instead of twin .50 caliber machine guns mounted in the turrets, they mounted twin shotguns. The turrets were open. The birds were fired at different angles and directions from the course. One of the positions fired the clay birds right at the turret, and if you didn't bust it, it smacked you in the head. A clay bird is extremely painful when it hits, and I stopped some with my face.

They also put us in a crude electric simulator. It was a big cavernous building. As we sat in the turrets, they projected fighters on the sides of the building in a three-dimensional effect, swooping toward you in the classic fighter pursuit curve. A fighter pursuit curve always reminded me of a *banderillero* at a bull fight swooping down on a bull, only to curve away at the last second.

Once they believed we had mastered deflection shooting, they flew us over Death Valley area for strafing runs. Huge canvases, painted with bulls-eyes, were set up on the desert floor. The canvases were raised above the ground so the dust kicked up would register any hits. Obviously, they didn't want anybody killed, so this was a closed and restricted area. One day while we were strafing I cut loose on a target ahead of us, and just as I was starting to tear up the canvas, suddenly, out from under it in absolute panic ran an old man and his jackass. The man ran out one side and the jackass ran out the other, and I couldn't tell which was running faster. That day's strafing was halted while crews raced out and located him and his animal.

The crews discovered several other desert dwellers who had been seeking shade under the canvases. Fortunately, no one was injured, but they were arrested and forced to leave the area.

Next we graduated to firing at towed targets. They took us up in bombers and we shot at targets towed by B-26 bombers. The targets were large canvas strips twenty feet long and about three or four feet wide attached to the bomber by three- or four-hundred foot cables. Often, the tips of each gunner's ammunition were painted with different colors. When you hit either the ground canvas or the towed targets, the paint colored the holes, so the instructors could tell who was shooting. Each gunner had to qualify at all gun positions, turrets as well as tail and waist positions.

About a week before graduation they circulated a form for us to list our three preferences for types of bombers. I'd been waiting for it. I wanted to go to Europe very badly and knew the Eighth Air Force[6] had been suffering heavy casualties. Also, I wanted to be a tail gunner, in spite of the numerous newspaper articles about a tail gunner's life expectancy in Europe. In spite of the short average life expectancy of a bomber tail gunner, as well as being too big for that position, that was still my preference. I liked being on my own, somewhat isolated from the crew, as well as having a better view of what was going on in the air. Base scuttlebutt also said that B-25s, B-26s, and A-20s were going to the South Pacific in large numbers. While I preferred the B-25, I believed I would be better off in the B-17. During training I had become very fond of the B-17 and developed a great deal of respect for it. Therefore, when I filled out the form they would put in my file after graduation, my preferences were B-17, B-25, and B-26, in that order.

My sinuses did hurt all the time we had been in the air, but it wasn't too bad. I lived in fear that someone would find that damning statement, "medically unfit to fly," in my records. At the end of the course they added up our scores and I passed and received my wings. Now I had wings to go with the patch from bombardment school. This patch, worn on your left sleeve just above the cuff, was triangular with a Horizontal gold bomb on a blue background.

Before we left Las Vegas, we were told to have a new ID photo made and given forms for the photograph. After returning to Las Vegas from Indian Springs I completed the ID form and went to the PX photo studio and made arrangements to have a picture made upon graduation and a copy mailed to my parents.

On graduation afternoon I pinned on my new wings, went to the photo studio and had my picture taken. The next morning I returned to pick the ones I wanted developed. While there two WAC sergeants and a WAC private kept talking and pointing at me. I could tell it was serious and wondered what was the problem. I left and forgot about them. The next day, when I went to get my photographs, one of the WAC sergeants from the previous day, two WAC privates, and two MPs entered the studio. One of the MPs approached and said, "I need your ID and I'd like to look at your dog tags."

That was highly unusual, so I said, "What's this all about?"

Their reply left me speechless. "We've had a problem with a peeping tom and these women think you're it. Did you just graduate?" His voice resonated throughout the PX and everyone within range stopped and looked at us.

"Yes."

"Were you in Indian Springs last week?"

"Sure as hell was," I responded. "And what's this all about?"

One of the WACs chimed in, "Why don't you sit on somebody else's foot locker?"

Totally confused, I said, "I don't know what you're talking about."

One of the MPs intervened, "You just wait here a minute and we'll have some people brought over that can positively identify the suspect. If you're him you're going to get locked up. Somebody has been over at their dorms and when they woke up he was sitting on the footlocker and peeking in the shower or something."

Melvin McGuire after gun-
nery school graduation day
in Las Vegas, Nevada. Note
the new wings, the sparkle
in the eyes and the jaunty air.
(Courtesy M. McGuire)

Just hours after returning
to the States, McGuire's
face shows the fourteen
pounds he gained on the
voyage home. Gone is the
sparkle, and the air is of
one who wants to forget.
(Courtesy M. McGuire)

I was very indignant. By then, another MP and two women had entered. One of the women said, "This isn't him. He's bigger than that guy."

About that time another MP and another two WACs came in and announced to the group, "We got him. Peggy identified him and they're taking him to the stockade now."

They looked at me and said, "We're real sorry. It's all a mistake."

I said, "You ought to be. I haven't done any peeking toming for a long time."

One of the MPs assured me, "You couldn't have been him if you had been at Indian Springs 'cause I was there too and your class was there."

Rather coyly, the WAC sergeant said, "You can set on my footlocker if you'll just notify me ahead of time. We're sorry if we embarrassed you."

Still a little indignant, I took my photos and ordered prints sent to the folks. On my way out of the studio I started thinking and asked the MP, "How about taking me down to the stockade and letting me look at the SOB that's been peeking at women. I want to see if he looks like me."

He agreed, "But you've got to get a ride back." We rode down and they took me in. I didn't think he looked like me. That mistaken identity could have been serious. Everyone else thought it was funny. I was indignant.

Chapter 2

[1] A small canvas bag that held personal necessities and a change of underwear and shower clogs. It acquired its name because soldiers being Absent WithOut Leave took a minimum of luggage with them, usually in a bag of this type.

[2] American-born, second generation Japanese.

[3] McGuire was one of many enlistees to the U.S. Army Air Force that would swell this organization from a pre-war total of 25,000 personnel and 4,000 aircraft to a war's end total of 2,411,294 men and 75,000 aircraft. Elizabeth Ann Wheal, et al., *A Dictionary of the Second World War*. (New York: Peter Bedrick Books, 1990), 494, 496.

[4] The .50 caliber machine gun, or "big fifty," was one of the most versatile and effective guns of the war. It was initially designed as a .30 caliber weapon in 1917 by John Browning, but in the 1920s it was upgraded to a .50 caliber for use on tanks and aircraft, as well as ground support. It is a hardy, extremely accurate, absolutely reliable weapon still being used by the U.S. Army. S.L. Mayer, *The Rand McNally Encyclopedia of World War II.* (Chicago: Rand McNally & Company, 1977), 40.

[5] An individual's personnel record file.

[6] The Eighth Air Force, based in southern England, was formed and dedicated to the strategic bombing of Germany and German-held territory in Europe. Its first mission was flown against Rouen, France in August 1942. Wheal, et al., 495.

Overseas Training Unit

After leaving Las Vegas Army Air Base I spent a few days in Hatch with my family. It was a pleasant interlude before I took the train to Lincoln, Nebraska. I'd arrived a day early because of train schedules out of my home area. A note left for me at the transient barracks told me to report to a sergeant in the personnel assignment area. After showering and changing clothes, I went to see him. I walked into his office and could see by his sleeve patch that he was an aerial gunner and armorer.

On the walk over I had noticed some B-24s[1] flying patterns and this disturbed me. *I did not want to be assigned to a B-24.* After our introduction, I asked, "Is this a B-24 base? I asked for B-17s[2] if I could get them. Am I going to be on a B-24?"

He assured me, "No, no, we have both kinds. Don't worry, McGuire, you're going on 17s alright." After his first glance, he exclaimed, "McGuire, you're bigger than a horse. How big are you?"

"I'm a little over six foot and weigh around two-ten."

"Yeh, you're pretty big. Let's sit down and talk a minute about your application. On your aircraft request you asked for flexible guns—tail or waist."

I agreed that I had asked for the tail.

"That's one of the things I want to talk to you about. You're a little big for the tail. Since you're going to be the AG (armorer/gunner) and you wouldn't do the crew a lot of good back in the tail as you're responsible for the armament on that airplane. It's better that you stay in the waist as it's a more central area and you can get around easier. That position has some disadvantages, but you're pretty big to be crawling in and out of the tail and, given your size, you'd be uncomfortable back there. Anyway, we believe the armorer should be in the waist.

"McGuire," he said, "my recommendation is that you report as waist gunner. You're so big you're going to have a hell of a time, not only crawling back into that tight position, but also you'll have trouble sitting on your knees during missions. It will be awfully uncomfortable. Besides there's another guy on the crew who has asked for tail, so if you'll voluntarily take the waist, we'd certainly appreciate it.

"I don't have to tell you what the disadvantages are in the waist. One, you're going to be in an open window—its going to get awfully cold with the wind blowing through there from the slip stream. The engine noise is pretty bad, too, but at least it's where you can walk around."

Sitting on my knees, with my football injured knee, would be a problem and I didn't want anyone to know about it, so I agreed.

"The crew will be formed tomorrow. It looks like you're going to have a good group. It's almost complete now. I believe you'll like the two pilots. The aircraft commander (A/C) and co-pilot are both southern boys and they'll be able to understand your drawl. You'll meet them about eleven o'clock tomorrow at this building. It's near where you're quartered. If we can do anything for you, we will. You'll probably be here for a few days while they draft your orders. You will be getting some more shots before you leave for an OTU (Overseas Training Unit). It's up to the pilot to tell you about that, but you have what I think is a very good crew. All of you have done well in your classes."

"Can you tell me the pilot's name?" I asked.

"He'll tell you all that tomorrow."

My attempts at pumping him for news resulted in little new information. "Can you tell me what's new in trends? Are the 17s still going to Europe pretty fast?"

"We supply crews for the South Pacific, Pacific, and China, as well as Europe, so you'll be told when the time comes. Right now," he continued, "it looks like they're issuing suntans like mad. The Pacific, I think is where you are being assigned, but I don't have a sure fix on that."

I certainly didn't want to go to the Pacific, for several reasons, including fungus, snakes, spiders, heat, and lack of girls. Life in the Pacific was primitive, and my goal was an assignment with the Eighth Air Force in England.

Irrespective of whatever theater I was assigned, I was very relieved to have not been assigned to a B-24. I had much contact with them all during gunnery and armament schools, and it seemed the B-24s were always cracking up; they were always having problems. I didn't want anything to do with them. It was faster than the B-17, and could carry a bigger bomb load and even fly higher, but it didn't have as many guns, and for a long time it didn't even have a nose turret. Also, the B-24 had a bad reputation. We'd been hearing rumors of a higher ratio of B-24s to B-17s going down. Pilots liked the B-17. It could take much more punishment. Anyway, wherever I was going, I was going there in a B-17, and that was a considerable relief.

We loved the B-17. It was beautiful to look at and it was beautiful to fly. We knew the Germans could shoot it to pieces, and, even when in unbelievable condition, the damned thing would still come home. But we also knew it was obsolete, even at that stage in the war.

The B-24 wasn't the answer either, and we talked about that. It could fly faster, and carry bigger bomb loads, but we still would not have swapped with them. It seemed to be a more fragile airplane and couldn't survive the punishment the B-17 could take. Of course, the guys flying them also swore by them the way we swore by the B-17. They considered the B-24 the greatest thing since Wheaties. Later in my career, I had many near fist-fights from needling B-24 crews.

I liked that sergeant and later discovered that changing positions was very good advice, although at first I wasn't too happy in the waist. Besides being noisy and too cold, you had to stand up. It was hard on your legs as it was like walking the deck of a ship in rough waters. You were constantly moving up, down and sideways as the aircraft moved in flight. Once I became used to the movement, I liked it very well, particularly the unobstructed view without structural braces blocking my vision. In training, I had liked flexible gunnery better than turrets. I prepared to meet my crew the following morning at eleven o'clock.

The next morning I left my quarters about thirty minutes early. Anxiety was mixed with curiosity as I waited to meet my crew and assess them. When I reached the building where we were to meet the A/C and the rest of the crew, some others joined me. We shook hands and chatted. We weren't sure we were on the same crew. Some of them had been at the transient quarters the evening before or that morning. We lined the stairs and made idle chit-chat until two pilots approached. We stood at attention and saluted. One said, "Let's get inside fellows and we'll start the meeting."

Inside we gathered around a big table. It was rather informal with some sitting and others standing. Each pilot carried a stack of files and I could see parts of my own file in one stack. One pilot read a list of names and we answered, "Here," when we heard our name. When he finished there were only eight members for what should have been a ten-man crew.

In a very soft southern voice, he introduced himself. "My name is Ralph Chambers and I'm going to be your aircraft commander. This is John Warren Karsten, the co-pilot. We're here this morning to meet one another and to tell you that we're going to leave very shortly for a B-17 Overseas Crew Training Unit in Ardmore, Oklahoma. It will be a very intense school. I don't know how long it will take , but they're going to mold us into a good fighting crew. I don't know about the rest of you, but I like what I see here. How about each of you telling us where you're from?"

We represented North Carolina, two from Missouri, Michigan, Wyoming, Pennsylvania, Maryland, New Mexico, Indiana, and one from there in Lincoln, Nebraska. He had spent the night at his parent's house before joining us. We pretty well covered the geographic spectrum.

They spoke briefly about our orders and issued a copy to each of us. We were to leave in the early morning hours and they told us where to catch transportation for Ardmore. I was impressed with the pilots. I particularly liked the pleasant twinkle in the pilot's eyes when he laughed. He didn't appear to be a martinet. Trying to categorize the co-pilot, I finally decided he was an individual who made very few mistakes and didn't tolerate them from anyone else. We all liked what we saw, and the atmosphere became more relaxed. During this time a tall, slender man came in, took a seat in the back and listened.

Just before we broke for lunch he walked up and said to Chambers, "Lieutenant, my name is John Fenstermaker. I'm a flight engineer, a damn good one. I've crew chiefed on UC-78s and worked on B-18s," and he named several others. "I've got lots of experience on engines and maintenance and I graduated from the full treatment in gunnery school. Also, I'm a good gunner. Do you have an engineer yet?"

Chambers looked at him quizzically and said, "No, Fenstermaker. We're supposed to have one by this afternoon. I understand he is coming from some distance and won't arrive until this afternoon."

John said, "If you don't have an engineer yet, you have one now. I'd like to be a member of this crew."

After looking at him for a long time, Chambers finally said, "Alright, Fenstermaker, we need to make the arrangements so we had best go before it gets too close to lunch time."

The man grinned from ear-to-ear, and Karsten, Chambers and Fenstermaker left. John was Regular Army and knew all the paperwork ins and outs. He was assigned to our crew that afternoon and his orders cut. Our crew was complete except for the navigator who was to join us a little later. The pilots, keys to a good crew, looked very good to me. I sensed that both were competent and would be good officers.

In those few minutes, we each assessed the others, these men who would play such important roles in our lives for the next few months. Chambers, from Winston-Salem, North Carolina, immediately struck me as a gentleman; a nice, pleasant, soft-spoken guy, but he was as tough as a boot, as we later discovered. Never officious, he always spoke very quietly. He had been attending a junior college when the war began. His father was employed by R.J. Reynolds Tobacco Company.

The copilot, Karsten, was also a good pilot. A Missourian, 'Jack' came from a family of cotton farmers who also owned cotton gins.

The navigator was from East Lansing, Michigan. Wayne Lesher was a year older than I, about twenty, and with myself and the tail gunner, one of the three babies of the crew. He had been attending Michigan State when the war started. Medium-sized and muscular, he was also tough, as we later discovered. He was the only unmarried officer on our crew.

Engineers on B-17s also served as top-turret gunners. Our engineer was John Fenstermaker, and what a jewel of a man he was. A tall, skinny man, Fenstermaker was hot-headed and had been in the Army since the start of the war. He had served as flight engineer on two or three different aircraft before his arrival in Lincoln. John was born and raised in a large, Pennsylvania coal-miner's family. Later I discovered he was actually the first one of us to arrive in Lincoln. Fenstermaker became our engineer, and without him, none of us would have survived the war. I believe Fenstermaker *was* the best engineer in the Army Air Corps. He was constantly reading technical manuals about the B-17, studying things such as engines and fuel transfer. He was all business. He was the best.

Our bombardier was John McDonnell, from Wyoming. We called him 'Grandpa' or 'Pop,' but obviously not to his face, because he was a ripe twenty-six years old. McDonnell had been a teacher before the war started and his wife was a nurse. He was very, very quiet, the kind of guy you could have a long conversation with and then walk away feeling that you never had a conversation at all.

James Sutton, from St. Louis, was our radio operator. He was about twenty or twenty-one years old, a golfer, and a practical jokester. He had become engaged just before being shipped to Lincoln, and he really missed Lorraine. He was a very likable guy.

The right waist gunner was Charles Graham, from Baltimore, where his family was in the grocery business. He, too, was a very quiet guy, but had a good sense of humor and laughed a lot. Initially trained as an engineer, he decided he didn't want to fly as an engineer, although he was a good engineer. He and Fenstermaker made a good team in emergencies. Graham had enlisted as a career gunner. We called him 'Snaf,' short for 'Snafu,' because he reminded us of a popular cartoon character. He was a small, very handsome man. Everybody liked him.

Louis Scofield was our ball-turret gunner. In being assigned to Lincoln to get on a crew, he had returned home. None of us were slouches as gunners, but Louis was absolutely the best shot among us. It was unbelievable how good a shot he was.

Our tail gunner was James Thompson, from Columbus, Indiana. He was a big, rangy kid, and the baby of the group, although he was only a few months younger than I. Jim was the nicest guy that ever lived. He was the All-American Boy that any parent would have been proud to acknowledge. Everybody's favorite on our crew, Jim always did his work, smiled a lot, and had a great attitude. A quiet lad, he never asked for help because he was always there to help you. Everyone was very protective of Thompson.

49

That was my crew, my airborne family. Two pilots, a navigator, a bombardier, an engineer/top turret gunner, radio operator/gunner, ball turret gunner, right waist gunner, myself at left waist, and tail gunner.

We didn't know it at the time, but we had been put together as a top-flight crew. During the training period, school officials often picked the top scorers in each of the positions to form crews that might develop into squadron lead crews.

After lunch we packed our gear and started preparations for departure.

Ardmore, Oklahoma

Early in the morning, two days later, we were in the base theater in Ardmore, Oklahoma, waiting to be addressed by the base commander. About fifteen or twenty crews were there, ready to begin this phase of their training. The base commander told us to sit and welcomed us to Ardmore and to OTU. Our training, he said, would be very intense. There was a great need for B-17 crews overseas and we should train with the expectation that we would be leaving for overseas shortly after graduation.

Other officers from the OTU unit spoke. One of the last, the Provost Marshal, mentioned a problem at that particular OTU base. Beer drinkers used to drinking 3.2 beer, would not be able to get it there. Oklahoma was dry and they served only near beer. He cautioned us about the easy availability of moonshine in the area. Some of the moonshine had been disastrous for earlier crew members. They had had several cases of jake leg.[3] It caused blindness, paralysis, loss of motor functions and even death. He didn't know if they were actually making it in a radiator, but officials were in the process of closing down known moonshiners. One of the biggest sources was a local gas station that operated a still in a chicken house behind the station. If we expected to buy something that was pure, he told us to forget it. His advice, which we took, was to stay away from the homegrown variety. We wanted no part of jake leg. Liquor wouldn't be allowed on the base and we couldn't bring any in.

Ardmore was a small, friendly town and we would enjoy the people, but if we liked to drink that wasn't going to be the place to do it.

The next morning we met in another building where our crew received its number, #5676. From that point on, every assignment was prefixed by our crew number. #5676 waist gunners report to. . . . We were admonished to memorize that number as it would control our lives throughout OTU.

Our days were filled with classroom activities and much flying—both day and night. The navigators worked on long-range, day and night navigation in bad weather. Both pilots practiced formation flying, learning the airplane and sharpening their skills. Gunners fired at tow targets and practiced strafing. In the classroom we studied turrets, flexible guns and ballistics. Flight engineers received special courses in the Wright Cyclone engine. Radio operators worked on navigation problems using radio and code. They learned the Morse Code to the point they would never forget it. Bombardiers studied the Norden bombsight, wind speeds and all the technical aspects associated with that position. On our practice flights from Ardmore to locations throughout the United States, the navigator had to find the site and then the bombardier dropped his 'bombs' on the target. These bombs were a mixture of sand and flour. The flour marked the point of impact so the bombardier could be graded for accuracy. Everyone went through all phases of flying. The navigator had joined us there in Ardmore and quickly became an integral part of our system.

We flew old, tired B-17s. It seemed like a B-17 took off and landed every minute of the day. When we returned from a flight, the airplane was refueled and ground crews loaded ammunition, checked barrels in .50 caliber guns, and loaded the practice bombs. Then another crew took the airplane back into the air. The planes were constantly in the air. After lunch we were back in the classrooms. The pace was very intense as they tried to ready us for overseas assignments. All the instructors were tops in their line. We spent days and long nights on long-distance navigation assignments to points in Nevada or other remote bomb sites.

B-17 Statistics

Crew: 10-man crew. Pilot, Co-Pilot, bombardier, Navigator, Flight Engineer, Radio Operator, Ball Gunner, 2 Waist Gunners, Tail Gunner.

Powerplant: Four 1,200 HP Turbocharged Wright R-1820-97 Cyclone radial piston engines.

Performance: Maximum speed 287 mph at 25,000 feet.
Cruising speed 182 mph.
Service ceiling 35,800 feet.
Range with 6,000 pound bomb load, 2,000 miles.

Weights: Empty - 36,135 pounds (16 tons); Maximum take-off 65,500 pounds (29 tons).

Dimensions: Span 103 ft; Length 74 ft; Height 19 ft 1 in; Wing area 1,420 sq. ft.

Internal Fuel Capacity: Maximum 2,810 gallons, giving about 2,000 range at 180 mph, with a gross take of weight of 65,000 pounds.

The maximum effective range was in the region of 1,700 miles, giving a radius of action of 850 miles. It took 37 minutes to reach 20,000 feet, with a take-off weight of 65,500 pounds under ideal conditions.

Armament: Thirteen .50 caliber machine guns, plus up to 17,600 pounds of bombs. The bomb bay could accommodate 8 x 1,600 pound bombs as a maximum load. More usual loads were:

12 x 500 pounds
6 x 1,000 pounds
4 x 1,600 pounds
2 x 2,000 pounds.

M2 .50 Browning Machine Gun:

Effective range: 1,200 yards   Length: 57 inches
Weight of round: 1.71 ounces   Extreme range: 7,200 yards
Rate of fire: 800 rounds per min.   Weight of 100 rounds - 301 lb
(13.5 rounds per second)   4 ozs
Muzzle velocity: 2,810ft/sec   Length of round: 5.47 in.

In the spring of 1944, the aircraft factories were completing 300 new aircraft per day. The cost of a B-17 was $220,000. Approximately 4,750 B-17s were lost on combat missions.

(Courtesy: Arizona Wing of the Confederate Air Force.)

The B-17, illustrating the location of the various gun positions.

(Courtesy: Arizona Wing of the Confederate Air Force)

#4

#3

Starboard Wing

#2

#1

Port Wing

Top Turret/Flight Engineer

Radio Operator's Gun

Cockpit

Navigator's Eyebrow Gun
(one each side)

Chin Turret

Ball Turret - 2 guns

Waist gun
(one each side)

Tail Guns - 2 hand-operated

During this time we learned to recognize one another's voice. This ability would be extremely important later on in combat. Our signals and language were standardized so there would be no confusion. Everybody worked hard. Classroom activities were divided into career gunners and technical gunners. The former—tail, ball, and right waist—had different classes than the technical gunners—the flight engineer, radio operator and armorer/gunner-left waist. As AG for that particular crew, I had additional training on the bomb rack electrical systems, maintenance of the bomb rack, compensating sights, and how to drop the bombs under different circumstances. A day or two later the others received similar training, so we were all cross-trained. Much of my time was spent with the bombardier.

As the weeks passed we became molded into a very cohesive crew. If anything, our respect for one another grew. Our trust of one another grew, as did our fondness for one another. We all believed ours was a very special crew, and subsequent circumstances proved the truth of this statement. The pilots were excellent. We flew from just above tree-top level, to the twenty thousand-foot altitude level where we worked on oxygen problems. We were convinced we were ready.

It was during Overseas Training that we had an opportunity to see what a .50 caliber machine gun could do. One day a sergeant took all the gunners out to a special range. This particular sergeant was an excellent gunner and instructor. We called him Falstaff because a great, big belly was evidence that he had let his figure get away from him. His nose was bright red, as well.

One day Falstaff took us out on the firing range. In front of us was an old frontier-type log cabin, about half fallen in. He ordered me and another gunner to step behind two machine guns which had been placed on tripods about two-hundred-fifty yards in front of the cabin. Falstaff handed each of us an ammunition belt, and turned to the group. "We want to show you," he said, "what a .50 caliber will do to that log cabin. This is for anybody who believes that a .50 caliber is an insufficient gun to take overseas and shoot at a Focke-Wulf 190." We were already hearing stories about the heavily armored FW-190.[4]

Falstaff turned to me and the other guy and said, "When I tell you to fire, I want you, McGuire, to take it from left to right, and you," indicating the other gunner, "to take it from right to left." He gave us the word, and we started firing away. Logs and pieces of logs flew through the air. It looked like somebody was taking boxes of stove matches and throwing them in the air. We each fired the entire belt of ammunition given to us. We easily shot the old cabin to pieces. After that demonstration, I was impressed with the gun's capabilities, and I believe all the other gunners were as impressed. That experience gave us all the confidence in the world in our guns. It provided us with a strong foundation of trust in that weapon.

Some of the gunnery instructors were veterans recently returned from the Eighth Air Force in England. They had been wounded and sent home to recuperate, and were in the Overseas Training Unit teaching gunnery. They were experienced not only in the mechanics and fundamentals of gunnery, but gave us invaluable insights into combat itself. They were eager to share everything they knew with us.

That was when we first heard about the 'Yellow Noses.' The term slipped in easily during gunnery sessions. When one of us did something incorrectly, such as not properly leading a target, an instructor would cryptically comment, "Now, if that had been a Yellow Nose, you would have been wiped out," or "Wait until you get one of the Yellow Noses parked out there, you've got to fire short bursts. You need to conserve ammunition, because if its a Yellow Nose, he'll be back."

Everybody seemed to know about the Yellow Noses. We heard about them not only from our instructors, but also from the newspapers. The 'Yellow Noses' were German fighters of the JG. 26 Fighter Wing. The name came from their distinctively painted yellow cowlings. Everybody knew they were a crack outfit, the best fighter pilots in the Luftwaffe.

We had one narrow escape. The airplanes from the dawn patrol group had landed and been re-loaded by the ground crews. The Oklahoma summer temperatures were extremely high that afternoon. That day we were using the shortest runway, the one with a row of tall trees at the end. The trouble began at take off. Perhaps the airplane was getting tired, but with the density altitude[5] the aircraft wasn't performing very well. We ran and ran along the runway and could sense the concern in the cockpit. The airplane simply didn't want to climb. When we finally lifted off we staggered off the ground and through the tops of those trees. We returned from that flight with leaves in the wheel well and the waist of the plane, and branches stuck in the landing gear. Fortunately, they were small. After that experience, we shuddered every time we thought of trees at the end of a runway. I can still see that row of trees in my sleep.

It wasn't all work. On our days off we tried to get to Oklahoma City. The people were great. We weren't supposed to hitchhike, but you could walk out the main gate—you didn't even have to hold your thumb out—and in just a minute or two somebody came along and gave you a ride. Transportation off the base was never a problem.

Our flight clothing was always saturated with salt stains. Because of the heat, we were issued enormous amounts of salt tablets. OTU was a tremendous learning process which turned us into a cohesive, well-trained crew. On graduation day we changed into clean clothes for a crew picture. With sunburnt and peeling noses, we were plainly identifiable as flight crews. We were a fit crew. Then we were issued a new set of orders. These orders sent us back to Lincoln, Nebraska. This time to a different area of the base for combat crew assignments. After a ten-day delay en route (furlough) we would be going overseas. The word coming down to us was that we were to be assigned to the Eighth Air Force in England. Only B-17s were flown at Ardmore, and it seemed as though every crew training there was being sent to England. We, too, hoped for an assignment in England.

The Ralph Chambers crew at Ardmore, Oklahoma in July 1944, after completing the Overseas Training Unit and awaiting orders to depart for Lincoln, Nebraska. *(back, l. to r.)* Melvin Mc.Guire, Charles Graham, James Sutton, Louis Scofield, John Fenstermaker, and James Thompson. *(front, l. to r.)* John McDonnell, John Warren Karsten, Ralph Chambers, and Wayne Lesher. *(Courtesy M. McGuire)*

A Few Days at Home

We left Ardmore the following morning, each heading to his own home. Hatch, New Mexico, was my destination. My leave was pleasant and satisfying. With no wake-up bugles and reveille at 0545, I could sleep as late as I liked. The neighbors came to call and wish me well when they heard I was on my way to an overseas assignment. It was a pleasant time spent with my family.

The last Sunday at home, I had dinner with a favorite aunt and uncle, John and Ora, at my cousin Betty's in the little town of Rincon. Here, too, the neighbors came over to say goodbye. We had a beautiful dinner. The only problem was their Chihuahua dog. Rosita shook all the time and made me nervous. I didn't care for that dog and the feeling was mutual. Rosita looked like a rat that had been on weak steroids. During dinner Rosita bit my ankle with her needle-like teeth. That was the only unfriendly gesture I encountered during my leave.

Just before we left the dinner table Uncle John said, "Mick, I've bought a bottle of real good Scotch, and when you get back we'll drink it. If you don't get back, when I know you're not coming, I'll drink it. So good luck." That bottle of Scotch became a symbol to me and to some of the neighbors.

Lincoln, Nebraska

Ever since gunnery school I had sensed an increased level of urgency. The newspapers announced we were short of combat air crews. American day-light bombing during that period had been costly. This sense of urgency had reached the training bases in the States. It was evident at OTU that they wanted us to finish school successfully and depart for overseas. At Lincoln the urgency was almost frantic.

After our furlough, it was a good feeling to be reunited with the crew in Lincoln. Our schedule began without delays. First, we went to the records section to bring our files up to date, make our wills, and purchase additional war bonds if we wished. Some changed their dependents' allotment and made necessary corrections in their records. After record processing we went to the medical facility and received a cursory physical and a very careful dental check. They were very particular about teeth as cavities and poor filings would be extremely painful when flying at high altitudes, and few dentists were available on front-line air bases. I needed a filling replaced. This was accomplished quickly and without fanfare in a thirty-minute period. I had been worried about the physical, but they didn't spend much time on it. Their major concern was whether we had something contagious and gave us more booster shots. In the frantic race from one building to another, you felt the urgency.

Our schedule at Lincoln was extremely busy. In the equipment room our parachute bags, neatly stenciled with our names and serial numbers, were awaiting us. We were fitted with a parachute harness, issued a Mae West, side arms, a knife, and our oxygen mask, which had been carefully fitted to our own face. Much time was spent on that fitting and in explaining how it should be treated. Our helmets were fitted. Our old flight clothes were well-worn by then, so we turned them in for new ones and several types of jackets.

I was the first of our group in line to receive the new flight suits. The sergeant in charge took my name and size. We could try them on if we wanted. As they issued me two flight suits, I noticed at the bottom of that particular bin there were two of a darker color. When I asked for those, the clerk handing them out said, "No, you've been issued these."

Being somewhat paranoid about quartermaster clerks after my first day in the Army, I resisted. He and I stood eyeball-to-eyeball and chin-to-chin, while I gave him my best 'where do you want the remains sent, buster?' look. He flinched and appealed silently to the sergeant who said, "They're here to be issued, so if he wants those, let him have them."

Sutton and Graham were standing behind me and giggling. To add to the fellow's woes, Sutton asked if he could have one of each color. Soon we were outfitted with new flight clothes which we tucked neatly into our parachute bags. The last item issued was the parachute itself. They had fresh inspection slips on them. I had my own English-made glass goggles and passed up the issue rubber-framed Polaroid goggles. Now, we were equipped for high-altitude flying.

From there we attended another orientation. More bond talk. I decided not to increase my bond purchases until we were overseas as I didn't know what expense I might incur along the way. We were delighted to discover that we would be paid seven dollars per day per diem until we reached our final destination. That was very good pay in those days.

Chambers announced that at three o'clock we were all going to the flight line to see our airplane. We had been issued #428, and we would fly it the following day. We could hardly wait. At the appointed time, we were all anxiously awaiting the truck which would drive us to the transient aircraft flight line. There they were—a whole row of parked B-17s. Next was a row of B-24s. As we drove down the flight line it didn't take long to spot '428' near the end of the line. '428' was a G Model B-17 with a chin turret. As we drove up and saw it, each man had a lump in his throat. There stood a gleaming Boeing B-17, glistening in the sun. That was going to be our permanent aircraft—we thought.

We piled out of the truck and proceeded to go over it microscopically. We investigated every crevice and recess. When I had finished my inspection, I backed up and admired the airplane. Without a doubt, this was the prettiest B-17 I had ever seen. I don't know why I thought it would be an OD (olive drab) color, but this was a bright, shiny natural aluminum color. It was a true beauty.

That night another briefing brought us up-to-date on current events and on our flight the next morning. At sun-up we stood by the airplane, ready to take it on our maiden flight. We flew #428 all morning, making notes on changes we wanted made, improvements or minor adjustments. Fenstermaker was not happy with several of the instruments. A sharp corner that could pose a problem down the line if someone became hung on in it needed smoothing. We marked that down to be trimmed and filed. Each man had his own list. I looked for the manufacturer of the gun barrels and the guns, having developed my own ideas about the best barrel for a flexible gun. The airplane performed well in spite of changes that needed to be made to the trim. The compasses badly needed swinging. After landing, we calculated it to the compass rose. When we left, all of the compass instruments were perfectly aligned with the compass rose.

Throughout the next few days we worked on the airplane, constantly hitting the parts depot for items we needed. During this tinkering stage a captain and major came out to the airplane. I spotted them and called the crew standing outside to attention. He asked, "Which one of you is McGuire?"

After I had identified myself, he handed me two little boxes and said, "I don't know what the hell these things are for but you asked for them, so they found some."

"Thank you sir, they are boxes for the spare light bulbs for the gun sights," I replied. Those bulbs were very expensive and we had acquired several. The boxes were similar in size to

The beautiful, new #428 in Lincoln, Nebraska awaiting overseas orders. *(Courtesy L. Scofield)*

penny match boxes and, taped on the side of the sight, or elsewhere in the turret, would offer protection and easy access to the bulbs.

"You've got spare light bulbs?" he belligerently questioned.

"Yes sir."

He shook his head. "You know, I think it would be cheaper to take this airplane back to the factory. It would cost the government less, but it looks good from the outside."

The major nodded approvingly as they circled the aircraft. They went through the inside and it was sparkling clean. We had cleaned and polished and cleaned and polished until the entire airplane glittered. Fenstermaker was installing instruments, the navigator was doing something, the bombardier was busy. He asked, "Where is the aircraft commander?"

We said he had been called to administration and he and the co-pilot are over there right now. He said, "Well, it looks ready to go. Before you leave we want our tools back, and what the hell are you going to do with Kelvinator gun barrels?"

"We've changed them," I said.

"Why?" he wanted to know.

"Because they are better machined than the other barrels."

He nodded. I could see amusement in the major's eyes. Before he left he said, "You fellows have got it looking real nice. Just don't forget to return my tools."

I wanted two pads of insulation to help reduce noise and provide padding in the waist, but decided that might not have been the best time to ask.

The next few days were equally as busy. Finally, Chambers called us together and announced we would be leaving early the next morning. We were to pack our bags and leave them in the airplane. They would be secure. Only our shaving kits and flight gear were to be kept out. Our orders would arrive soon and we were all anxious to see if our destination was the Pacific, Europe, or elsewhere. Headquarters was being very close-mouthed. In fact, Chambers wasn't sure they even knew themselves, but we would know shortly.

On our last day we said goodbye to Mrs. Chambers and Mrs. Karsten. They had been with us through OTU and had also joined us in Lincoln. The two women had rented a small home outside the Ardmore air base to stay with their husbands as long as possible.

Mr. and Mrs. Scofield, Louis's parents, invited us to dinner in their home in Lincoln the night before our departure. As usual, we were famished. It was a beautiful and enjoyable meal and evening.[5]

At sunup the following morning we were ready to go. Then the delays began. Chambers and Karsten, along with the navigator Lesher, had gone to pick up our orders. The rest of us sat under the wing and waited anxiously. Upon their return, we gathered around and excitedly asked, "Lieutenant, is it Europe?"

He said, "Well, I don't know. It looks like it. There is a way to go to the Pacific through Africa and India to China. But all I know for sure is we've got to be in Manchester, New Hampshire tonight. At Manchester we'll receive our final overseas orders and then know our destination. Until then I don't know anything. It's a long haul from here to Manchester, so fellows, let's get aboard and get on our way."

In late August 1944, we departed Lincoln for Grinier Field in New Hampshire. Our flight was a mixture of fifteen to twenty B-24s and B-17s, all headed for Grinier. It was a long haul to Manchester and we didn't arrive until just before dark. Ground crews swarmed over the airplanes loading boxes and equipment aboard. All our B-4 bags and luggage had been stowed in the bomb bay. They removed our personal gear and loaded supplies in their place. At the time we didn't know what we were carrying, just, that from the weight, it was heavy. Then they carefully re-packed our luggage.

Upon our arrival at Grinier Field in Manchester, we were transferred from a training command to a transportation command responsible for the control of overseas troop movements. They had complete authority over us from that point on. About ten o'clock the next morning we received our overseas orders which were not to be opened until we left Gander, Newfoundland. We were curious as to where in the world Gander was. The next morning we took off and left the Continental limits of the United States.

Chapter 3

[1] The Consolidated B-24 heavy bomber, known as the "Liberator," was designed in 1939. A radical wing design, in combination with a newly developed airfoil, gave the plane a remarkable range and load-carrying capability at high altitudes, making it a very effective weapon. It weighed 65,000 pounds and flew a maximum bomb load of 12,000 pounds. It had a range of 2,100 miles carrying a bomb load of 4,000 pounds, a ten-man crew, and defended itself with ten .50 caliber machine guns. It could reach speeds of 300 mph at 30,000 feet, which made it roughly twice as fast as B-17s. From 1941 until the end of the war, 18,400 B-24s were built. Although it had superior range and bomb-carrying capacity, the bomber was difficult to handle above 20,000 feet, making defensive formations hard to maintain. It was especially valuable in the Pacific where long distances affected bombing capabilities. Ronald H. Bailey, *The Air War in Europe*. (Chicago: Time-Life Books, Inc., 1981), 196; Thomas Parrish, ed., *The Simon and Schuster Encyclopedia of World War II*. (New York: Cord Communications, 1978), 42; Wheal, et al., 43-44.

[2] The Boeing B-17 "Flying Fortress" weighed 65,000 pounds and had a maximum bomb load of 12,800 pounds, although the preferred combat bomb load was approximately 6,000 pounds. When introduced into the U.S. Army Air Corps in 1937 it was considered the most advanced bomber in the world. Carrying a 4,000-pound bomb load, it had a maximum range of 1,850 miles. It carried a crew of ten men who had thirteen .50 caliber machine guns on defense. The B-17 was one of the greatly admired planes of the war. It handled well and could take great damage yet remain in the air. Between 1935 and 1945, 12,731 B-17s were built. 4,750 of them were shot down on combat missions. Bailey, 193; Edward Jablonski, *Flying Fortress* (Garden City, NY: Doubleday & Co., Inc., 1965), 309; Wheal, et al., 43.

[3] Peripheral neuropathy.

[4] This very powerful and versatile German aircraft, powered by a 1,700-hp BMW radial engine, was considered Germany's best all-around fighter. It operated within a 942-mile radius and could carry extra fuel tanks. It had a maximum speed of 408 mph at 20,670 feet, and was armed with two 13mm machine guns and up to four 20mm cannon. It could also carry rockets and aerial bombs. It was swift, agile, highly maneuverable, tough, and deadly. The Allies called it the "Butcher Bird." Bailey, 194-5; Martin Caiden, *Black Thursday*. (New York: Ballantine Books, 1960), 54.

[5] Density altitude refers to a condition where the combination of high altitude and high temperatures adversely affect an airplane's performance, particularly on take-offs and landings.

[6] Mrs. Scofield, now in her 90s, still remembers the big guy from New Mexico who ate all that food. She had never seen anyone eat that much before.

— 4 —

Through A Storm,
To A Storm

Gander, Newfoundland

Approaching Gander, we threaded our way through storms as the weather had changed drastically since leaving Grinier. Gander was a transient base for United States aircraft, as well as an RAF and RCAF (Royal Air Force and Royal Canadian Air Force) base. Because its principal duty was to protect maritime shipping, they were submarine hunters. Throughout our stay in Gander, even in bad weather, we would hear their seaplanes and ships going out at all hours. The war was beginning to take on an international look as we saw the blue RAF uniforms and British soldiers in battle dress.

After landing we were taken to the transient barracks—very sparse and very cold as far as we were concerned—where we received a quick briefing. Pilots and navigators, again, were called into special meetings.

While in Gander we met some military air transport command crews that regularly flew the route we were to take. They answered our questions and gave us valuable pointers. One bit of advice was to stock up on cigarettes, chewing gum, nylons, peroxide, lipstick and similar items while in Gander. Cigarettes and the other items were cheap in Gander, but rationed overseas, and they were good barter. I beat it to the PX. Apparently everybody else had received the same advice. There were only two or three packages of recognizable brand cigarettes left on the shelves, except for Kool mentholated cigarettes and English-brand cigarettes. Having no other choice, I bought thirteen cartons of Kool cigarettes and thirteen cartons of Juicy Fruit gum, all I could afford. At that time I didn't smoke, but I grimly hung on to those Kool cigarettes. Not having enough money to purchase all of the suggested items, I concentrated on cigarettes and gum. Later, I was grateful for that advice.

Meanwhile the rest of us learned about the big, tasty Dolly Varden fish available in the nearby water. That night we enjoyed that fish for supper. It looked like the weather was worsening in the Atlantic and snow squalls were being reported in the area. If our crew had a layover, we could go fishing.

They were correct. The next morning we awoke to several inches of snow. The weather canceled our flight, but it didn't keep dedicated fishermen, like Lesher, from going fishing. He borrowed some gear, took the rest out of an old survival kit, rented a boat, rowed out, and started fishing. Until it was time to go home, he didn't realize he had floated several miles, so he spent until late in the evening rowing back to the base wharf.

The evening we landed, our bombardier heard that some British troops in a nearby anti-aircraft battery were selling top-quality Scotch whiskey. The rumor was that this particular gun crew sold Scotch for ten dollars a bottle. That was a fantastic price to pay for whiskey at that time. Being the only crew member unoccupied at that moment, McDonnell asked me to go over and buy some. That's how I learned, the hard way, about *savate*, or foot fighting.

I meandered over to the gun crew, full of Lend-Lease[1] good feelings and asked if the rumors were true that they had whiskey for sale. One of them said, "Yes, sir, how many bottles do you want?" I asked how much it was, and he said about fifteen dollars a bottle. We haggled over the price and I told him I'd pay ten dollars. He agreed. I gave him a twenty, and he handed me a bottle of Scotch, but no change.

Upset, I said, "Hey, you guys owe me ten bucks." One of the Brits laughed and told me how dumb I was. His accent was difficult to understand, but I was plenty offended. I invited him to come out of the battery and I would give him a lesson in English. Out he came with his fists up, like he was going to fight according to the Marquess of Queensberry rules, and I thought to myself, "This is going to be real easy." He twirled and the next thing I knew I was getting up off the ground, wondering where I was.

He had kicked me hard and quickly in the head with his hobnail boots. I got up in a daze. Even the Scotch was gone. Returning to the plane, I grabbed a pistol. With it as my authority, I returned to their battery. They returned my twenty dollars, but I never did get the Scotch. That was my first, but not last, encounter with our Allies the British. I never did have any luck with them.

Each day it snowed more. Then it would rain and get everything muddy before it snowed again. Would we ever leave Newfoundland? It was certainly not the August weather we'd had in Oklahoma. One day it started to clear and we were scheduled to leave Gander early the next morning, not to England as we had thought, but to Africa instead. We were part of a mixed group of B-17s and B-24s. Our plane was loaded with extra food rations for the long flight. We were all ordered to our planes, and warm-up procedures began. By then about two dozen B-17s and B-24s had arrived and were stranded there. When it came our turn to fall in line, snow flurries crossed the field and they called us back.

The following morning we were to try again. Wake-up was at three o'clock. After cleaning frost, ice and snow from the airplane we ran it out to top the tanks, getting it as ready as we could in the poor light. Everything was loaded, engines warmed, and tanks topped to the absolute maximum as it was a long haul. By then we knew our immediate destination was the Azores Islands,[2] little specks in the Atlantic off the coast of Portugal and Africa. That was all we did know. If we missed the Azores, and were lucky enough, and had enough fuel, we could put down on the beaches in Africa. This was not an attractive alternative. In reality, if we missed the Azores, we would most likely wind up in the ocean and no one would know what had happened to us.

Finally, it was our turn. Fenstermaker followed his usual routine. He liked to stand outside with the fire guards in order to listen to the airplane start. After looking at the color of flame coming from the exhaust and assuring himself that each engine was performing well, he would then run under the wings, yank away the wheel blocks, enter the plane through the waist, and take his position between the pilots. Satisfied with his inspection, he started to run. Unfortunately, the brakes started thawing, the ground was soft from the rain and snow, and the airplane began creeping. When he ducked, he didn't duck far enough. A very sharp drain valve protruding from the wing gave him a severe cut in the forehead and almost scalped one part of his head.

Chambers immediately shut down the engines and radioed that we had a bad injury. The flight continued without us and we took Fenstermaker to the base clinic. They stitched his head wounds and, because of his concussion they kept him for observation.

Weather reports indicated we would be able to break out the next morning. If so, they told us we would have to leave without him. This we weren't willing to do. Five of us, including one of the officers, went to the clinic and demanded to see him. They said he was resting. We entered his room, and other than looking shaky, he didn't appear all that bad to us. When we left we had one more in our group than we had coming in. We simply bootlegged him out of the clinic and onto the airplane.

He wasn't much help on the crossing because he really wasn't aware of what was happening to him until we reached the Azores. I have often wondered what the clinic personnel thought when they discovered he was missing and had left without permission. We didn't know it at the time, of course, but Fenstermaker's injury saved our lives.

We took off in bad weather. Visibility was poor and a hundred or so miles into the Atlantic, we ran into one of the worst storms I've ever encountered in an airplane.[3] We flew all day in heavy, heavy rain, black as night. It rained so hard that water began seeping into the plane, wetting our bags and soaking those of us in the waist. During that flight, we had our first encounter with St. Elmo's Fire.[4] Static electricity danced around the prop tips and ran up and down the wings. It even came into the cockpit and ran across the control panel. It looked like Casper the Ghost and his friends were having a party. The display was spooky, but not dangerous.

The storm was so severe that Lesher could not take star sightings, sun readings, or even get drift readings. He used all of his skills to keep us on course. About the time we were due at the Azores, we were beginning to think we might have to swim to Africa.

Chambers told him, "We hope you are right. If not, we're all going to take a bath." They had held faithfully to the headings he had given them during the day.

When the British had captured the Azores from Germany, it had been a submarine base and supply point for the German wolf packs in the Atlantic. German submarines homed in on that signal to reach the Azores. The Germans had left an ADF (Automatic Direction Finder) homer radio in place and the British continued to use it. Gander had provided us with the ADF frequency before we had departed and cautioned that its maximum range was sixty miles. That was the only navigational aid available to us on that crossing.

About when our ETA was up, we popped out into scattered, broken weather conditions. The rain had finally quit. Ditching drills went through our heads, but looking at the white caps and the height of the waves, we believed there wasn't much chance of ditching and surviving. A big raft was stowed aboard and we were wearing our Mae Wests, but we didn't have much confidence in the adequacy of those measures. I mentally reviewed the ditching drill and worried about moving that big raft from its compartment in the top of the airplane out into that rough water and then operating the Gibson Girl.[5] Suddenly Fenstermaker said, "The needle is moving a little bit on the ADF!"

Chambers agreed and said, "I can't get the identifier, but it looks like our ADF needle is starting to move a little bit. It's fluctuating, and I think we're trying to get a signal on something." A few minutes later he continued, "It's starting to hold a little bit. It's showing about eight degrees to the port side."

Holding our breath and uttering prayers, we heard Karsten reply, "I can get the identifier now, it sounds like Azores. Tell me what you get."

Sutton added, "I'm getting an identifier but having problems reading it. It could be our homer. There's a lot of static in it, but the signal strength is getting a little bit better."

In the rear we looked at one another and started to grin. With this welcome news we relaxed and simultaneously exhaled. Our chances had just improved immeasurably. Soon Sutton called, "We're starting to come within range and I'm only showing a few degrees to the starboard side of it. It's definitely the Azores homer."

Karsten dashed our hopes a bit when he reminded us that the Germans occasionally used a substitute homer to mislead incoming aircraft. The Germans were wily. Once they discovered our bombers were homing in on this beacon, they occasionally put a submarine on the surface far away from the Azores and broadcast a higher-powered, false beacon on the same frequency. Many bombers, misled by this false signal, were lost in the Atlantic. Our luck held and within a minute or two Lesher called and asked, "Are you getting a good signal out of the ADF, Jim? I'm showing that we're about sixty-eight miles from the Azores."

The radio operator soon responded. "I'm getting a good strong signal, a firm needle. It looks like we're not more than a few degrees from dead on." With that news, we all became several years younger.

It wasn't long before Lesher announced, "According to my calculations you should be seeing the Azores anytime now. If it's not there, fellas, I can't help it. I've given it my best shot."

Karsten responded, "Fellows, unless I'm wrong, I'm looking at an island with a mountain on it that's sticking out of a cloud, up there about 11:30."

Chambers told Lesher, "Old buddy, we all owe you a beer for this one. I don't know how you did it, but we're grateful. Thanks a lot."

That was my first experience in an extremely stressful situation. None of us had looked forward to going down in that wild stretch of the Atlantic. It was almost a miracle. As we approached the island and contacted the tower, Karsten commented, "It looks like we have an airplane splattered on the side of the hill up here. You fellows get set up back there. We're going to be down wind pretty quick and turning on base leg."

Just before flare out, before landing, Karsten exclaimed, "Ralph, he's going to cross right in front of us!" We held our breath. A peasant with oxen and a cart had meandered very casually, and slowly across the runway dead ahead of us. He didn't even look disturbed when the wing of that big bomber passed within a few feet of his head. Chambers almost ground-looped the bomber trying to avoid them. There we were in a modern aircraft, almost destroyed by a vehicle that looked at least four hundred years old! After we had taxied up and stopped, we all climbed out and offered silent prayers of thanks, and congratulated Lesher.

It was a grateful crew that put down on that runway. The runway was down hill and short, but it was land. The pilots were soaked with perspiration. That flight had been extremely demanding on them. Lesher was equally as wet, with perspiration running down his forehead and his flight clothes sticking to his back. He looked very tired.

We spent that night in our airplane. We'd gone to eat, but passed up the quarters offered to us. They weren't all that great, and we were concerned about the equipment and personal gear we had aboard.

The next day was cloudy. When the navigator and pilots returned from the briefing at the meteorology shack, we gathered around. Ralph said, "Now, fellows, I can tell you our next stop will be French Morocco at Marrakech. It's not going to be that long a flight and I hope it will not be like yesterday's. It's a much shorter flight to Africa. Our final destination in Africa will be Tunis in Tunisia. We'll see a lot of Africa on the way up, so that ought to be a better flight since we'll not be flying over as much water on this trip."

We eagerly looked forward to French Morocco. By then we were sure our destination was either the Eighth or the Fifteenth Air Force.[6] The orders we had received in Gander had mentioned South Hampton, England, so we believed we were destined for the Eighth Air Force. This suited me and the rest of the crew. At that time we knew very little about the Fifteenth. By eleven o'clock we were airborne. The weather was broken, with scattered clouds. During this flight we experienced our first flak.[7] It was thrilling. Looking back on that encounter, the flak wasn't even close. Graham reported anti-aircraft fire at about one o'clock, level with us. It was a few hundred yards off our starboard wing. We couldn't figure out what had happened. It was heavy-type flak but not much of it. Looking down through a hole in the clouds, we could see several naval vessels, warships. Only one was firing; the rest were quiet. Apparently they had just signaled us to move away from them. There didn't appear to be any hostile intent.

Later we heard it was the Free French Fleet,[8] but we never knew for sure whose naval vessels they were. Nevertheless, we quickly understood their message. It was far enough away that it couldn't have bothered us, but we got the feeling that if we didn't move away, the next ones would be up there with us. We detoured around them.

McDonnell sighted land when we weren't too far off shore. The temperature rose quickly as we dropped to lower altitudes.

The pilots contacted the base at Marrakech and were quickly answered and told to make a long, wide pattern. The ground temperature was 112° or above at that time. They advised us to be careful of mirages and density altitude. Those of us in the back were enjoying our sightseeing. It was exactly my image of Africa—sand, with little oases here and there. Finally, as we turned around we saw Marrakech. It didn't look like any of our cities, but you could tell it was a very large place.

As we started to land the sink rate on the airplane became excessive. It was extremely hot and the mirage was very disorienting. Chambers and Karsten called for a go-round. Chambers finally resorted to a "drag-in," landing under power and dragging the tail. Our pilots really earned their pay on that landing. Our airplane suffered no damage. Later that day a B-24 and another B-17 followed us in. They didn't crash, but did damage their aircraft. The air was so thin in that heat that it didn't have much lift. The pilots learned about flying when the air density was very light.

We disembarked after shutting down the plane and were taken to the barracks—a half-barracks, half-tent facility. At the transient area overnight accommodations we were told the local dos and don'ts and where we would be fed. That evening before bed, we mooched a ride from Marrakech to an old French Foreign Legion outpost we had seen from the air. It was almost unbelievable, like something out of a picture book. The scene fit my youthful idea of the Foreign Legion. We had previously been told to stay out of Marrakech as it was a religious holiday. Since we were considered infidels, they did not want us around. Several of us decided this Foreign Legion outpost would be more interesting, anyway.

Chills went over my body after my first glimpse of the outpost. I had definitely seen this fort before. Climbing out of the truck, I knew the location of all the facilities. Everything— headquarters, the barracks, the kitchen facilities, the gate, the well, even the palm trees—looked familiar. As we walked around the old post, everything was exactly where I knew it would be. It was an eerie feeling. I was beginning to believe in reincarnation by the time we returned to our quarters. The next morning we were told this post was where *Beau Geste* had been filmed. I must have seen that movie five or six times, so no wonder everything looked familiar.

We were quite tired from the long flight, and upon arriving at our quarters, were ready for sleep. The first thing we noticed were mosquito nets over the cots. I asked, "Why the hell do you need mosquito netting in a place like this? There hasn't been a mosquito here in a million years, has there?"

Our guide replied, "They ain't for mosquitoes my friend. They're for snakes like cobras, and scorpions. You'd better read the signs in here. Don't leave your bags open. When you get out what you need, zip your bags shut. They love to ride in B-4 bags." I thought this was the 'green crew' treatment. It was a hot, miserable night.

The next morning I awoke, lifted my net, and swung my feet to the ground. My boots were placed near my cot and I put on one boot. Reaching for the other boot, I glanced at a big sign hanging on the wall that read: "Shake your boots and shoes for scorpions before putting them on." With one shoe already on, I shrugged my shoulders and half-heartedly lifted the boot. When I turned it upside down, the grand champion of scorpions fell out. It may not have been all that big, but it looked like a bull elephant to me. Graham and Scofield had seen them running back and forth on the rafters. At that point, Africa lost much of its glamour.

Marrakech was off-limits. With nothing else to do, we spent the day going over the airplane with a fine-tooth comb, readying it for the next leg of our journey to Tunis.

It was on this day I heard a very disquieting story. Somebody at the base told me the Germans had been known to hunt small game with their 88s.[9] He said an American infantryman had actually observed an 88 crew taking shots at a jackal while it was chasing an antelope. They fired at it and killed it. With its extremely flat trajectory, they didn't have to allow for big ballistic drops. The 88 was one of the finest anti-aircraft guns ever made, and it was this gun, in the thousands, that was soon to be aimed at me and my airplane. True or not, it was not a comforting story. After flying through the flak we encountered over Europe, I believe the Germans could have successfully shot rabbits with the 88.

"Army 428, this is Tunis tower. You're cleared to land on Runway 27. Land long, go completely to the end of the runway and follow the jeep with the yellow sign on the back. Stay in the middle of the taxi way. Land long. There's another Baker 17 turning on base now, over."

"Roger Wilco, Tunis tower, this is Army 428. Thank you." With that cryptic message the Ralph Chambers crew, whose journey had begun several days ago in Lincoln, Nebraska, prepared to land before making the last leg to their combat unit. We had left Marrakech early that morning and had been all day en route to Tunisia, via Casablanca, and now to the shores of the Mediterranean. Crossing many battle sites, wrecked vehicles, burned out tanks, and overturned guns, we saw the debris of war everywhere. From the air you could see miles and miles of tracks going off into the desert. Truly, the fighting in North Africa had been savage.[10] As we circled the harbor prior to landing, we could see sunken ships—German, Italian, French, British, and American—both inside and outside the harbor. Piers had been demolished and wharves extensively damaged. The area was covered with overturned cranes, bomb craters, shell pock marks, and miles of abandoned and burnt vehicles. The wages of war were rapidly coming home to us. We had never seen such destruction and it gave us a new appreciation for the carnage two great armies could inflict upon themselves and each other.

As Army 428 followed the jeep to the transient dispersal area, the highly polished B-17 we had flown from Lincoln was beginning to show the wear and tear of the trip. Heavy snows in Newfoundland, near hurricane conditions in the Atlantic, the Moroccan heat, and oil streaks had dimmed the shine. Before their departure from Tunis, the Germans had mined sections of the runway. Therefore, we carefully followed that jeep to avoid falling victim to a, as yet undiscovered, mine.

The carnage of war. A wrecked hanger and carcass of a
German airplane at Tunis. *(Courtesy R. Chambers)*

Burned out hangers with dangling girders, wrecked airplane
graveyards, wrecked vehicles, and abandoned gun emplace-
ments lined our route to the transient dispersal area. There
they signed us to shut down the engines. As we opened the
hatches, the heat hit us like a blast furnace, in spite of the fact
that it was late afternoon. Off came our leather A-2 jackets.

A truck arrived and we received our instructions: Chambers
was to report to the assignment room for modification of the
orders we were carrying; the rest of us were to leave everything
on the plane except our personal gear and shaving kits, and wait
for transportation to our overnight quarters. The plane would
be guarded during the night.

While awaiting our transportation, we stood drinking in the
sights. Shortly, a 'follow-me' jeep lead a B-24 to a spot near
where we were standing. Their engineer hopped out and stood
next to the ground crewman who was giving the pilot directions
for parking. At first we were concerned about how close they
were getting to our airplane. The wingtips of the two aircraft

were only about four feet apart. We couldn't understand why they had to park so close to us. There was plenty of space.

Looking over this B-24, I was very impressed. Through the wear and tear of the trip, you could see it was shined and polished. It appeared to have a crew like ours. They had spent much time on their new pet and were very proud of it. They finally parked and the engineer helped put the chocks under it, waved, and the engines were cut off.

Doing what any self-respecting B-17 crewman would do, I approached their engineer and commented. "How about moving that ugly monstrosity. It detracts from the beauty of our B-17. Besides it's likely to blow up, catch on fire or collapse and damage our airplane. You cannon-fodder types are always doing this." One of our favorite names for the B-24 was 'milk stools,' because of their three wheels.

He glared at me. The pilot yelled at him and he said something about a wise ass. We all stood around admiring their plane. The glares we received from the disembarking crew indicated I had struck a nerve. Sutton, laughing hysterically, acknowledged that I had managed a real zinger. The pilot was a big, red-headed, freckle-faced man. After a short conversation with the engineer, I was identified to the pilot. This left me wondering what kind of trouble I was about to get into. Fortunately, the truck arrived and we climbed into it. I forgot about the incident.

The transient crew quarters, we discovered, weren't the regular quarters assigned to transient crews. This was an old, old, French hotel that had been in the middle of a battle. There wasn't a door in the hotel that we could see. The windows were all broken and the walls pock marked by bullets, where there weren't huge, gaping shell holes. Inside we found cots with fresh blankets. It was definitely an experience to lie in the middle of the room and see in all four directions through the shell holes.

The faucets and fixtures were rusty and could not be turned either on or off, so water continually dripped in the sink and shower. For your personal needs, you had to make do with drips. Life in combat was going to be pretty grim if this was what they had to offer in a non-combat zone.

We also discovered there was a tremendous difference in the time zones between Lincoln and Tunisia. We had arrived late in the day and the mess hall had closed. Our last meal had been in Marrakech.

After dropping my gear in my airy room, I decided to wander about, see the sights and scrounge up something to eat. In my naivete I thought there would be cafes available. About a quarter of a mile from our quarters I could see tents set up in a bombed-out lot. As a last resort, I could go by there and mooch some K-rations.

About that time the most delicious smell floated by me. It smelled like bar-b-que! I hot-footed it around the corner of a bombed-out warehouse and, sitting on some debris were about half a dozen men. From their dress I knew they weren't Arabs. They hummed and chanted while a goat was roasting over a homemade spit. What I interrupted I don't know, my only thought was to buy part of that goat.

My sudden appearance in the middle of their group, and wearing a sidearm, scared them to death. They jumped up and looked shaken. I asked to buy a part of their bar-b-que. They looked at each other and one held out his hand, palm up to indicate they didn't know what I said. After trying to panto-mime eating and pointing to the roasting meat, I finally showed them the twenty dollar bill that I had been kicked in the head for in Newfoundland. They all understood an American dollar. I had not changed my dollars to francs. Walking over to the spit, I again tried to show that I would like to buy one of the hind quarters. After discussing it among themselves, they agreed and hastily cut off a part. It smelled so delicious. Even though it was so hot I could hardly hold it, I tried to take a couple of bites and did manage to eat a few mouthfuls. The rest I planned to take back to the hotel for the others.

Being raised in ranching country, eating mutton was a no-no, and I was curious as to whether this was sheep or goat. Several goats were grazing nearby. Again, through pantomime, I tried to ask them what it was, mutton or goat. They looked even more confused when I went, "Baa, baa." Finally one grinned, nodded his head and walked over to an old blanket or piece of cloth. From within its folds he reached down and held this thing up by the tail. It still had the head and pelt on it. It was a dog! I almost up-chucked. They ended up with both my twenty dollars and the hind quarter. Ashamed to tell the crew about this, I didn't mention it to them.

The area with the G.I. tents was now my last resort for food. There I managed to mooch some K-rations from a soldier at one of the tents. Years later I met that same man in Santa Fe, New Mexico where he was a major with the National Guard. He remembered me coming around that night trying to get rations for my crew. Ironically, we later learned that a large portion of the load we were carrying to Italy was K-rations.

After a bitter cold, hungry, sleepless night in that hotel full of artillery holes, we awoke early on 29 August for our final leg to Italy and the Fifteenth Air Force. Breakfast was something French. Leaving the transient mess hall, Scofield solemnly announced, "One more meal like that and I'm switching sides. The Luftwaffe couldn't eat worse than that."

Arriving at the flight line, we noticed all kinds of activity and several vehicles parked by the B-24. The tail was unusually high in the air. The mechanics had just buttoned up the cowling to our engines, after making some minor adjustments requested by the pilots. While loading our bags into the airplane, I noticed we were carrying a full complement of ammunition for all the guns, as well as several boxes of equipment destined for the Fifteenth. The ground crews had been busy during the night. Out came our Mae Wests, which we carefully examined for the flight across the Mediterranean. The dinghies were checked and the newly stowed boxes secured. Our pre-departure chores completed, we were told to wait near the plane.

Having these few extra minutes, I walked over to the B-24, grinning from ear to ear. During the night the nose wheel's strut seals had turned loose. The strut was flat and oil was all over the tire and the ground. That red-haired pilot was there in his shirt sleeves working with the mechanics trying to get jacks under the plane. Unable to resist the temptation to throw another zinger, I walked up to enjoy the scene and at the same time commiserate with them.

One of the men noticed me and said, "Hey, lieutenant, that guy's back." The pilot stopped what he was doing and walked up to me. He was not only big, he was uglier than sin.

Standing eyeball-to-eyeball he said, "Unless you want your teeth scattered aaaall over this ramp, you better get the hell out of here and keep your mouth shut!"

I didn't even waste time saying, "Yes, sir," but got the hell out of there. When I was back under our airplane, there was Sutton, sitting and laughing. Unfortuntely, the lieutenant's appearance prevented me from delivering the ultimate sting, "The problem there is you've got the tail wheel on the wrong end."

Sutton commented, "You'll learn one of these days, if you don't get killed first."

As we taxied out I couldn't resist waving at them through the waist window. They responded with several obscene gestures. I left feeling very smug. The B-17s had easily won that round. The Ralph Chambers crew of B-17 #428 was headed for the Italian Theater of War.

Amendola, Italy

At Tunis we had received new orders and were given instructions for the flight to Bari, Italy. It didn't take long to fly over the Mediterranean. Arriving at a field near Bari, our navigator received coordinates to our base in Amendola, near Foggia.[11] We also received a radio frequency to call for landing instructions and where to taxi when we landed. Within minutes we were on the way to our new field.

Approaching Amendola, the pilots began circling in and calling for 'Darn Thing' tower. 'Darn Thing' tower, as we later learned, was the call sign for the Amendola field. Our first look at that tower was very unimpressive. It was not much more than a large box on stilts. One of the crew commended that he had built a tree house bigger and better than that. On taxiing in, we were shocked at what we saw. There were no hangers, just an odd assortment of buildings and empty hard stands.[12] A few airplanes with some major-looking repairs, a few buildings, many tents, a trailer or two and several parked vehicles were all we could see. Off in the distance loomed a boneyard of wrecked airplanes—German, Italian, British, and American—but mostly German, ME-109s,[13] ME-210s,[14] and JU-88s.[15] Amendola is on the Adriatic side of Italy, the opposite side of Italy from our take off point in Tunis. The only landmark we could identify was the little fishing village of Manfredonia, four miles from the base. It was about as bleak a location as you could imagine.

Once on the ground, we had been told to hold with our engines running. About the time we were becoming concerned with overheating the engines, 'Darn Thing' tower advised Army 428 to turn right and taxi to a hard stand in the parking area. As we cut the engines and opened the hatches and doors, a weapons carrier drove up and a man climbed out. He limped up to the plane and said, "Alright, everybody get his personal gear and leave everything else just where it's at. Do you have any tools in there?"

I responded, "And who are you?" He wore no identifying insignia or rank, not even a cap.

"I'm Bernie Cohen, and I'm the line chief. We need this airplane pretty quick and need to start working on it. So, get your stuff and clear the airplane." Not far in the future we were to discover that Cohen was a legend. He could have been released from the service years before because of severe arthritis in his hip, but he refused to leave. He stayed with the group through the entire war. The man was a mechanical genius. Each plane had its own crew chief and they, in turn, answered to Cohen who was line chief for the entire squadron. As line chief, he made all the big decisions on plane repair and maintenance. Decisions that had to be made quickly and well. He was on the go all the time. We quickly learned that what he said went. You didn't argue with the line chief, even if you were an officer.

"Yeah," I said, "there's a box of machine tools there. Where are we anyway?"

"You're in Amendola. You're now at the Twentieth Bomb Squadron parking area of the Second Bomb Group.[16] That's the Ninety-seventh over there," as he pointed across the runway. "I assume you're gonna be assigned to the Twentieth and this is the Second Bomb Group area." With that we removed our gear and ourselves from #428.

We were struck by the grimness we saw on their faces. Ground crewmen were standing around quietly talking to each other. All the hard stands, except where a few airplanes were being repaired, were empty except where we had parked. If this was a sample of combat, we thought, there was no joy here.

Finally, one of us asked a nearby ground crewman about Cohen. He was the line chief, they said, and we'd have to forgive him. Everybody was hurting. An hour earlier they'd just been notified that the Twentieth had been shot down to the last plane. That day, on Mission 263, in the Twentieth alone, they had had seventy casualties. With that sobering news, we boarded the truck and proceeded the few miles to the olive grove, which was home for the Second Bomb Group.

Mott Prather, the first crew chief assigned to #428, later told me, "We were grieving so about the Twentieth, but I said to another ground crewman, 'We may have lost the Twentieth, but they've sure replaced them with some mean, fighting SOBs. They won't even let us have our airplane!'"

Upon our arrival we were met by Tiny Atkerson, a very impressive first sergeant. He was another Fifteenth Air Force legend, as we soon discovered. His office wasn't much, just some boxes with records and files. Everything seemed old and worn, but it was very serviceable and immaculate. The minute he walked into the office I decided to retire my clipboard.

He greeted us with, "Welcome to the Twentieth Bomb Squadron, Second Bomb Group. We're upset and grieving over the loss of that squadron. Normally, new crews are not greeted and handled as you have been. We're not yet prepared for you. We haven't cleaned out your tents as we have just received word that the Twentieth was wiped out today. They were apparently shot down in Czechoslovakia near the Polish border at an oil refinery target."

From his manner, you could tell Atkerson was a steel fist in a velvet glove. Very pleasantly, he told us that if we had any problems to talk to him. If we needed money, we were to come to him, and since this was a combat unit, drinking to any kind of excess while on flight alert would not be tolerated. That was his only negative comment. It would not be easy and we would have to make do for a while. He admonished us to keep our eating utensils clean because of the danger of dysentery. Everything the Italians raised was grown in soil fertilized with human excrement—a centuries old custom. For that reason, we were not to eat any fresh fruit, nor buy anything from peddlers trying to sell produce over the fence. About three days later, despite the warning, I bought a watermelon. Was I sorry! Even apples gave you dysentery.

Before he dismissed us, he apologized for the condition of our living quarters. "We're sorry, but you'll have to use the tents in their present condition. The personal effects and uniforms of the previous occupants are still there. We'll get you new blankets before you proceed to your tent. Drop off your bags and then return here for additional briefings."

This was our first look at what would be home for the next few months. The officers were assigned to one tent, and the enlisted men to another. Our home, which we soon dubbed the 'Amendola Ritz,' was the last tent in an olive grove and placed next to a stone wall. That was the ugliest tent I'd ever seen. It was covered with patches of different colors. Later we learned it had come from Africa with the Second Bomb Group. Inside we placed our bags on unmade bunks that looked as though the occupants had just left. Rings, wristwatches, fountain pens, change, and personal effects were clustered in a pile on each bunk. Before leaving on a mission, you placed your personal effects on the bunk and no one ever bothered them. After this brief examination, we returned to the Twentieth Bomb Squadron area.

Thirty minutes later we were undergoing a hastily put together briefing and orientation. Some of the personnel had tears in their eyes. We asked the group squadron commander how they knew what had happened, since the survivors had not yet arrived. He replied that the news about the Twentieth going down had been radioed, probably by wireless, to the Fifteenth Air Force headquarters in Bari, then passed to the Group, and then on to the Squadron. Each B-17 radio operator had a wireless key which he used for long-distance communication. After each mission, the group leader also wired results of the bomb strike. It was a sobering time for the remnants of the Second Bomb Group and our enthusiasm was considerably dampened.

During that afternoon's orientation we were introduced to Atabrine. Since air crews could not take quinine for malaria, we had to take Atabrine tablets each day with a cup of water. We were to drink only from the Lister water bags hanging in the area, and to take the Atarbrine when we drank it. One of the side effects of Atabrine is that your skin turns a yellow or orange, as though you had a case of bright yellow jaundice. The resulting deposit on your skin could be scraped off by fingernails. They laughingly described how becoming it was when the whites of our eyes also took on a yellow or orange cast.

We were shown the mess hall where we could eat that evening if we wished, and where breakfast would be served the next morning. At 0830 the next morning we were to report for an additional briefing. Because the Twentieth had almost no crews left, they believed it wouldn't be too long before we'd be flying our first mission.

Among the do's and don'ts was an admonition about water usage. All water was hauled in, therefore, it was rationed. With that knowledge we soon learned to shave out of a steel helmet and bathe in five gallons of water a week. Later that situation changed for the better.

After the briefing and all the caveats, we entered the battered, canvas-roofed, but spotless, mess hall. In the briefing we had been cautioned about cleaning our eating utensils very, very carefully to avoid dysentery. As we walked into the nearly empty building, the few occupants were quiet and talking in small groups. Some had tears in their eyes and a few were openly crying. Even a few of the Italian prisoners of war who assisted the regular cooks were showing open displays of grief. It was unnerving to see a grizzled crew chief wiping tears from his eyes. As we were going through the line, one cook asked, "You're new guys aren't you?"

"Yes."

"Tough luck today with the outfit. Just eat everything you want because we got too much. We got seventy missing tonight, so there's plenty of everything."

Then we were introduced to Twentieth Bomb Squadron coffee. Once the coffee was made, it was poured into a small barrel that had previously contained hydraulic oil. A fire under the barrel kept the coffee hot. When we complained about the oil film, they told us, "Just brush it aside." The oil imparted a funny, shiny color to the coffee. That coffee was scalding hot. By the end of my tour I believed that coffee didn't taste like coffee unless it had been flavored with a little oil boiled out of the pores. About the time the oil was completely boiled out, the bottom of the barrel had burned out and they had to break in a new barrel.

Around 1515 that evening, the remainder of the group finally arrived, dead tired. The Second Bomb Group's toll for that mission was ninety-two casualties. The sound of all those engines roaring over the field as they straggled in was awesome.

We were a subdued crew, harboring an uneasy feeling about Mission 263. Rumors said the squadron had been faked out, but nobody knew exactly what had happened. What we did know was that if Fenstermaker had not banged his head back in Gander, we would have flown this mission with this squadron, and we, too, would have been killed or shot down. Some of the planes which took off without us that day in Gander had been with this squadron. This included many of the men with whom we had trained. It was a sobering introduction to the war.

Finally, we returned to our tent and climbed into beds that we could imagine were still warm. That was our welcome to the Twentieth Bomb Squadron, Second Bomb Group, Amendola, Italy, on 29 August 1944.

The next morning after breakfast we were sitting in our tent. Two men from the Graves Registration Unit entered. They wore neckties and knew their job. "We need the personal effects from the crew that was here," they announced upon their entrance. They spread six white sheets outside the tent, one for each bunk, and started packing the personal effects in them. While they were packing, they asked us to go through the gear and remove anything their families shouldn't see—classified material, escape material, or anything of a personal nature that might embarrass their families. They carried a list and checked it against the effects which had been left. We were impressed with their efficiency. I went outside when they had finished packing the sheets, and, while they were wrapping up the sheets, I looked at the tents in the area. It was scary. Every tent had six bundles in front of it, filled with personal effects. Everywhere I looked, there were those white bundles. The men finished wrapping up the sheets, and loaded them from every tent into a truck. When they left, the truck was almost full.

After their departure we were told to report to the squadron orderly room where they took our names and collected the files we had brought with us. They logged us in, looked at our shot records, made sure our names were spelled correctly, asked whether or not anybody was sick or having any problems, and the last time we'd been paid. These preliminaries completed, they enrolled us in the Twentieth Squadron. Now, we were officially part of the Twentieth Squadron.

Our second day at Amendola began an intensive three-and-a-half-day orientation. The orientation officer, in his first set of comments, said we could not write home and give our location, other than we were 'somewhere in Italy.' All mail was censorerd. All references to casualties, targets, etc., would be eliminated by the censors. We were to be very general in our letters, as the Germans had a bad habit of intercepting out-going mail.[17] Their regular spy system could obtain vital information from reading even casual comments. He cautioned us against being cute to avoid the censors.

Next on the agenda was a lesson on the geography of our area. He pointed out the distances to the Adriatic, the Yugoslav coast, and to the heavy fighting on the front to the north of us (the Gothic Line).

During the lecture, he mentioned that we shared the field at Amendola with the Ninety-seventh Bomb Group, our sister group. They lived about three miles down the road from us, near the entrance to our air field. A very special relationship had grown between the Second and the Ninety-seventh, and we were not to do anything that might damage that relationship. The association began with the Allied landings in North Africa, and the two groups had been together ever since. They were two of the four Groups that furnished B-17s for the African Campaign.

The admiration was mutual. Ground crews from one group, hearing about the other group's special problems, always pitched in to help. If one Group was short an airplane, the other loaned them one, if one was available. They loaned each other parts and tools. In short, they looked after each other. Close friendships had evolved during those many months of fighting. The mutual good feelings extended beyond the ground crews to the flight crews, as well. By way of illustration, he told us about the following incident which had occured the previous February.

He began by saying we had a very able and wily opponent in a Luftwaffe general named Huth. Major General Joachim Huth was the commanding officer of Southern Germany's air defense command, and long an arch enemy of the Second and Ninety-seventh Bomb Groups. Huth was a disciple of Adolph Galland,[18] who believed in concentrating large forces against individual squadrons and groups until they were eliminated. On several occasions, he had almost succeeded in eliminating the Second and the Ninety-seventh Bomb Groups.

That morning of 24 February, it was the Second Bomb Group's turn. The Ninety-seventh was leading the strike force with the Second flying rear guard in the low box. One hundred miles from the target, Huth sent twenty 109s against that low squadron. The fight continued for a hundred miles until they reached the IP[19] to bomb Steyr. The only respite the Second Bomb Group had was during the bomb run over that day's target, the heavily defended Daimler-Puch aircraft components factory. Once the Second was off the target, Huth slammed approximately 110 single and twin-engine destroyer fighters into the Second.

Even though he was engaged and had eighteen of his bombers damaged, the Ninety-seventh's group leader directed his arriving fighter escorts to the rear where he knew the Second was being annihilated, fourteen of whose aircraft were already down. The last squadron of the Second was completely gone. The remaining fourteen bombers in the Second were exhausting their ammunition and had dead and wounded aboard. Those damaged aircraft had possibly ten minutes left before they, too, would be no more.

While their attention was riveted on the final and complete destruction of the Second, P-38s[20] from the Eighty-second Fighter Group, and units from two other fighter groups, piled into the attacking fighters like an avalanche. The Germans lost several aircraft during that surprise pass and the survivors scattered and headed for home. This courageous decision by the Ninety-seventh's commander was not lost on those of us in the Second. The Ninety-seventh had our eternal gratitude for that action.

Chapter 4

[1] By the end of 1940, Britain was low on hard currency, but still very much in need of material assistance to continue its war against Germany. In response to Churchill's desperate requests for assistance, President Franklin Roosevelt pushed through Lend-Lease legislation in March 1941, enabling Britain to obtain war material and pay when the war was over. These same provisions were eventually extended to China and the USSR. The bill to the United States at war's end was about four and a third billion dollars, of which Britain owed three and three-quarters billion dollars. John Keegan, *The Second World War.* (New York: Penguin Books, 1989), 21; Mayer, ed., 151.

[2] The Azores are a cluster of small islands approximately 900 miles west of Portugal and about the same distance northwest of North Africa. When the war began, Portugal controlled the Azores Islands. The Allies wanted

use of the islands for a forward base against German U-boats and started negotiations to install a naval facility there in May 1941. The British finally gained use of the airstrip in Terceira in October 1943. The U.S. Navy was granted rights to use the same base in January 1944.

[3]In twenty-five years of professional flying, McGuire recalls only two other occasions of going through weather as bad as that day.

[4] An electrical discharge during thunderstorms that looks like fire and appears on the tops of tall objects such as masts, trees, and towers, and on the nose and wingtips of aircraft. Mediterranean sailors consider it a sign of protection from their patron saint, Erasmus or Ermo.

[5] A Gibson Girl was a small, portable radio operated with a hand crank like old-fashioned telephones. It put out an SOS signal which rescuers could home in on. It had a very limited range, but saved many airmen's lives during the war. Several crews that flew over the Mediterranean and the Adriatic used the Gibson Girl very successfully when they were forced to ditch their airplane. It was mounted in a flotation collar.

[6] 1 November 1943, the Twelfth Tactical Air Force was split. A strategic air arm, the Fifteenth, initially comprised of six heavy bomber groups, four groups of B-17s and two of B-24s, in addition to four fighter groups, was given the task of joining the Combined Bomber Offensive against Germany being conducted by the U.S. Eighth Air Force and the Royal Air Force. Later in the war, the Fifteenth Air Force fielded fifteen Groups of B-24s, as well as seven Groups of fighter escorts comprised of P-38s, P-47s, and P-51s. Kenn C. Rust, *Fifteenth Air Force Story* (Terre Haute, Indiana: Sunshine House, Inc., 1976), 4-5, 18.

[7] Flak was the term coined for anti-aircraft (AA) fire. One of the significant difficulties that anti-aircraft defenses confronted was hitting distant airplanes that could maneuver rapidly in three dimensions. The tactic that all forces in World War II used was one of throwing up barrages of time-fused shells in front of bomber formations. Direct hits were desired, but shells were designed to fragment at pre-set heights, with the hope of damaging nearby aircraft. The German Luftwaffe controlled all aspects of AA ground defense, including guns, radar, and searchlights, deploying these defenses in depth around targets of Allied strategic bombing. See Chapter 9 for a more detailed description of the various types of flak.

"A visual image of encountering flak during a bomb run is to imagine yourself running across a football field with three hundred spectators throwing grenades at you." (McGuire)

[8] During World War II, the French Navy had the dubious distinction of being the target of both Axis and Allied forces. From the beginning of the war until June 1940, when France surrendered, the French fleet cooperated with British naval units. Under the control of the collaborationist Vichy government, the fleet came under attack by British and American forces in North Africa. Elements of interred and colonial ships (four battleships, nine cruisers, eleven destroyers), in turn, fought against Germany under the Free French Government until the end of the war. It was this small fleet which probably fired on McGuire's formation.

[9] The German 88mm was one of the most dreaded guns of the war. A high-velocity weapon, it was originally designed as a heavy anti-aircraft weapon, but its efficiency against tanks as well was first demonstrated by Rommel in the campaign against France in 1940. It was an awesome and effective gun when employed in static anti-aircraft defense. Its major disadvantages were its weight, lack of mobility, and high profile. Hans von Luck, *Panzer Commander.* (New York: Dell Publishing, 1989), p. 41; Wheal, et al., 154.

[10] Axis forces surrendered Tunis 13 May 1943, and 275,000 soldiers were made prisoners of war. At that date it was the largest capitulation of men and matériel in the war for the Axis. Keegan, 343.

[11] Foggia, with its nearby airfield complexes, was a prime objective of the British Eighth Army when it landed at Taranto on 9 September 1943. The airfields were captured and occupied by the Thirteenth Corps on 1 October 1943. The following month the Fifteenth Air Force was created to take advantage of the air bases, as their capture enabled the opening of the strategic bombing campaign into southern Germany, the Balkans, and southern Europe. The British commander, Harold Alexander, resented the subsequent strain on his supply services in keeping the airfield complex running because targets for the Fifteenth were generally not in Italy. Keegan, 353; Wheal, et al., 168.

[12] At Amendola the airplanes were parked in the open. To provide a more dust-free environment for the mechanics who worked on the aircraft, hard stands were created from Marston matting embedded in the soil and then soil and matting soaked with oil.

[13] The ME BF-109, along with the Boeing B-17, was considered one of the two truly great planes of the war, admired by friend and foe alike. It came into German service in September 1935, and served until the end of the war. It first saw military action in Spain with the Condor Legion. It was propelled by a 1,475-hp Daimler-Benz engine, and could reach a top speed of 386 mph at 22,640 feet. It had an effective range of 650 miles, and was armed with three 20mm cannon and two 13mm machine guns. It was a very agile airplane and could operate effectively at altitudes up to 40,000 feet. Bailey, 203; Caiden, 54; Wheal, et al., 301-2.

[14] A two-place, twin-engine, medium-range fighter, the ME-210 was designed as a replacement for the ME-110. Numerous accidents, primarily because of serious instability, caused production to cease in April 1942. Only 352, of an original order of 1,000, were built. Its maximum speed was 385 mph and was armed with two cannon and two forward-mounted and two rear-firing machine guns. Parrish, 402.

[15] One historian labeled the Junkers JU-88 as one of the most versatile military machines ever produced by any nation. The defensive fighter version was heavily protected by armor plating and flown by a three-man crew. Initially designed as a transport plane, it was modified as a night fighter against the nocturnal British bomber streams and also equipped with primitive radar. It served Germany formidably in this role. It also saw much use against American daylight formations and was most effective before long-

range fighter escorts were available. It was powered by two 1,340-hp Junkers Jumo engines, and had an operating radius of 1,230 miles. It was armed with five 20mm cannon and four machine guns, and could carry rockets, cables, and aerial bombs. Bailey, 201; Caiden, 55.

[16] The Second Bomb, or Bombardment, Group was formed near the end of World War I in Lille, France. It was the first bombing arm of the U.S. Army. In 1937, the U.S. Army B-17s were delivered to this group. During the late 1930s, the Second Bomb Group was most instrumental in integrating the capabilities of the B-17 into the strategical framework of the U.S. Army Air Corps. Jablonski, 13-16.

[17] McGuire was extremely surprised about a month or so after his arrival in Italy, when his parents wrote telling him exactly where he was located. His father had been talking to a German prisoner of war that had been involved in the heavy fighting at Foggia against the British and later captured north of Anzio by the Americans. German POWs were working on farms in the Hatch area. The POW even correctly identified McGuire as being with the Second Bomb Group. In his next letter home, McGuire wrote, "You are correct about my location."

[18] Lt. General Adolf Galland began his flying career as a glider pilot, joining the unofficial Luftwaffe in 1933. He volunteered for the Condor Legion in Spain in 1937, and when he left Spain as a flight commander, he had over 300 sorties to his credit. He became the commander of JG.26, the much feared 'Yellow Noses,' during the Battle of Britain. He was an excellent pilot and a farsighted commander. In 1942, at the age of 30, he was appointed General of the Luftwaffe Fighter Arm, which made him the youngest German general. He served in this capacity until January 1945, when he was summarily dismissed by Goering. From 1942-45, his innovations and suggestions for improving the efficiency of the fighter arm were constantly overruled by both Goering and Hitler. From January 1945 until the end of the war, he was commander of a crack ME-262 jet fighter squadron. After the war he became a consultant to the German aerospace industry. For more about Galland, read his book, *The First and the Last.* (New York: Ballantine Books, 1954)

[19] The IP, or Initial Point, was the point where the bombers committed to a specific target and began the bombing run. Pilots turned control of the bomber over to the bombardier who flew the plane with the aid of the Norden bomb sight so the approach would be as level and precise as possible. Because the bombers flew so straight and level, they were extremely vulnerable to flak from the IP to the target.

[20] The P-38 Lockheed Lightning, a twin-boomed fighter, was introduced into the U.S. Army Air Force in 1941 with great expectations which were never completely fulfilled during the war. The Lightning fought in every theater of the war, but it was not one of the great planes of the war because it lacked maneuverability as a fighter, especially in comparison to the P-51, the Japanese Zero, or the German Focke-Wulfe 190. It did journeyman work as fighter escort and reconnaissance, however, for the Allied Forces wherever it was assigned. A flight of P-38 Lightnings in the Pacific Theater,

for example, flew an extremely long distance and shot down Admiral Yamamoto's aircraft when he was inspecting his forward bases. The Lightning had a speed of 414 mph, ceiling of 40,000 feet, range of 2,260 miles, and was armed with one 20mm cannon and four .50 caliber machine guns. Wheal, et al., 349.

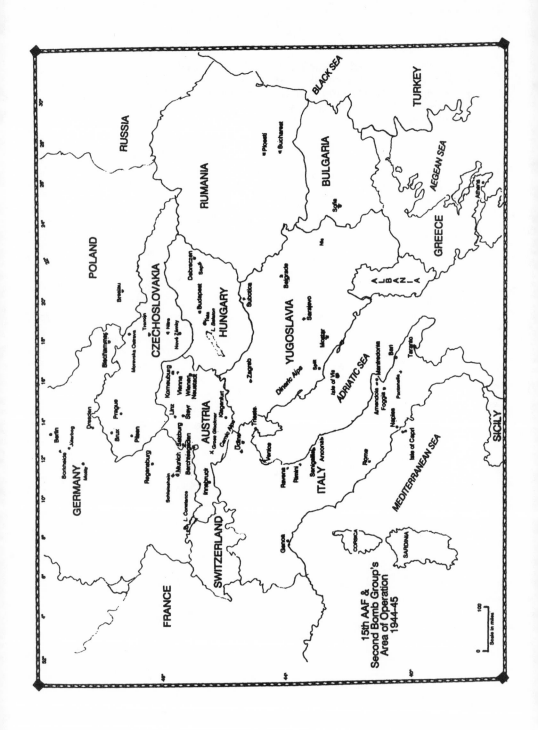

15th AAF &
Second Bomb Group's
Area of Operation
1944-45

Scale in miles
0   100

Mission 263

29 August 1944. Someone was roughly shaking him as a voice kept repeating, "Sergeant Martinez, wake up. Sergeant Martinez, wake up, wake up please. Please, Sergeant Martinez wake up."

Vicente Martinez[1] struggled from a deep, deep sleep into reality. It was pitch black in the tent. "I'm Martinez, what do you want?"

"Sergeant, the Operations Officer of the 429th (Squadron) sent me down to tell you that you have to fly today. You're filling in for a ball turret gunner that the flight surgeon has just grounded. He says he's sorry."

Martinez groaned. "There has to be a mistake. I've flown four days in a row. Last night they told us we would have two or three non-operational (non-flying) days. I'm bushed. I've got to have some rest."

"I'm sorry, Sergeant. The Operations Officer apologizes too, but says he has no choice. You're to fill in on #915, and the pilot is John Fitzpatrick. Here's the scoop on it," as he handed Vicente a slip of paper. "You're going to have to get up now. They're still serving breakfast but it's 0400 so you don't have much time. Transportation is 0515. If you have trouble the Operations Officer said he would send you down in a jeep so you could get there on time. Get out of bed now. Don't go back to sleep on me."

Vicente groaned, cussed his luck, and wearily climbed out of bed. His body ached all over. Four days in a row riding in that cramped ball turret was man-killing work. Two of those days had been to Blechammer and Vienna. He was beat mentally and physically, but managed an ice cold shave in a helmet. Since he was prone to airsickness if he ate breakfast, he confined himself to a cup of hot tea.

He was finished in time to catch the truck to the equipment room to draw his equipment and an escape kit and then walk to plane #915. The other gunners had already finished their pre-flight checks and were outside putting on their flight gear and other equipment. Vicente spoke to them but didn't have time to be sociable as he needed to pre-flight the ball turret. He was getting into his gear when the pilots, bombardier, and navigator arrived.

They gathered around the side of the airplane and the pilot told them their target would be the oil refinery in Moravska Ostrava, Czechoslovakia. A crew member groaned and asked, "Where the hell is that, Lieutenant?"

"It's on the far side of Czechoslovakia. It's a long haul and right on the Polish-Czech border. As a matter of fact, when we come off the target today and make our turn we will be over Poland. We're supposed to be flying at 26,500 feet, but don't count on it because the weather is broken, layered clouds. We could be bombing at a much higher or lower altitude than that and our en route altitude may vary considerably because of the clouds. We're due over the target at 1102."

Mission 263

HEADQUARTERS
SECOND BOMBARDMENT GROUP (H)
Office of the Operations Officer

APO 520,
29 August 1944.

OPERATIONS ORDERS)
:
NUMBER........263)

1. This Group will furnish twenty-eight (28) aircraft to bomb and destroy PRIVOSER OIL REFINERY & MORAVSKA MAIN M/Y, CZECHOSLOVAKIA. Alternate Targets: (1) INDUSTRIAL AREA of MORAVSKA OSTRAVA on PFF. (2) SZOLNOK M/Y. (3) SZAJOL M/Y. (4) CZEGLED M/Y.

2. Rendezvous: AMENDOLA; 12,000 feet; 0807B.

3. Route Out: BASE to KEYPOINT to PITOMACA (45/58N 17/14E) to ERSEKUJVAR (47/59N 18/10E) to HOR LIDEC (49/11N 18/04E) to IP to TARGET.

4. Route Back: RALLY to HATVAN (47/40N 19/40E) to NJEGO-SEVAC (45/34N 18/12E) to DAVOR (45/07N 17/31E) to KEYPOINT to BASE.

5. IP: NEUTITSCHEIN (49/36N 18/01E).

6. Bombing Altitude: 26,500 feet.

7. Bomb Load: Twenty (20) 250 pound GP bombs, one tenth second nose fuse, twenty-five thousandths second tail fuse.

8. Escort: Six (6) groups of the 306th Wing will provide penetration, target and withdrawal cover for the 5th, 55th, and 304th Wings.

9. Communications: VHF Channel "B", Call-sign Freezol 16.

By order of Colonel RYAN:

JACOB W. BIGHAM JR.
Major, Air Corps,
Operations Officer.

-1-

<u>BRIEFING NOTES & FORMATION</u>

TARGET: <u>Priveser Oil Ref., Czech.</u>

BRIEFING	0415
TRANSPORTATION	0515
STATIONS	0545
TAXI	0615
TAKE-OFF	0625
BOMB LOAD	20 X 250
ASSEMBLY	0710 Amendola 5,000'
BASE ALTITUDE.	26,500
I.A.S.	150
I.P.	Neutitschein (49/36N 18/01E)
AXIS OF ATTACK	30
TURN AFTER BOMB RELEASE	Left
T.O.T.	1102
T.R.B.	1420
COMMUNICATION	Channel "A"
ESCORT	
COMMANDER	Col. Cunningham
DEP. C.O.	Capt. Redden

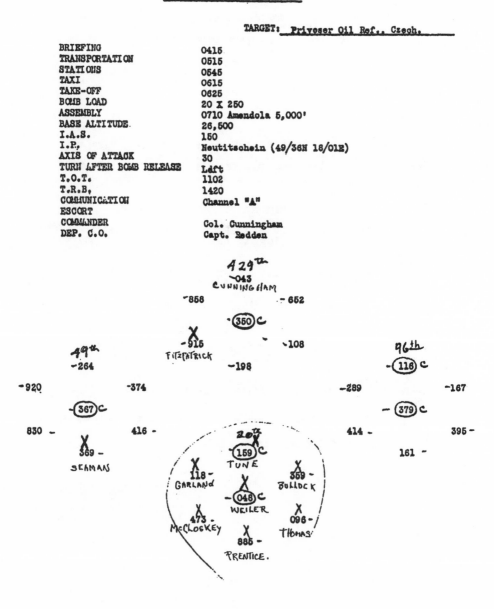

<u>ESCORT:</u> Six (6) groups of the 306th Wing will provide penetration, target and withdrawal cover for the 5th, 55th, and 305th Wings.

The bombardier said, "If you haven't noticed, we're carrying twenty 250-pound bombs. We're not after the buried stuff today. We're looking at cracking plants, oil storage tanks, tank and boxcars, and things like that. Some of the group will be hitting the marshalling yards and the refinery. The Moravaska Ostrava refinery and marshalling yards are adjacent to each other."

They were flying #6 position in the lead squadron. Lieutenant Colonel J. S. Cunningham was that day's group leader and Captain G. A. Redden would be the deputy group leader. On their right flank they would have the Ninety-sixth Squadron and on the left the Forty-ninth, with the Twentieth flying the low squadron and tail-end-charlie, the last squadron in the formation. The Ninety-seventh Bomb Group would be about three miles ahead

#1
(squadron leader)

#3   #2

#4

#6   #5

#7
('tail-end-charlie')

Position numbers in a
B-17 squadron.

of them. The entire Fifth Wing would be active on this mission and the 306th Fighter Wing would provide the penetration, target and withdrawal cover for the Fifth. Two B-24 wings, the Fifty-fifth and the 305th, would also be working in that area. There would be six groups of P-51s[2] that day. Some P-38s might be out earlier, but not in the target area.

The co-pilot said intelligence wasn't sure how many guns would be on the target, but they didn't expect too many, as there hadn't been the last time they visited Moravska Ostrava. Heavy German fighter concentration was available to the area. The layered clouds they should encounter that day created ideal ambush weather, so they were to keep their eyes open.

Vicente didn't recognize any of the other crew members, but it was difficult to see in the early morning light, especially when they were wearing helmets and goggles. At least they weren't a new crew. He was already missing his own crew. They had been together throughout the fighting in July and now most of August. July had been a rough month. The Fifteenth Air Force had suffered more casualties that month than during any other month in its existence—318 bombers, roughly a third of their entire bomber force.

Fitzpatrick announced, "Our taxi time is 0615 so we'd better get aboard and do our last-minute checks unless there are any other questions." With that they boarded.

The Ninety-seventh took off first. As soon as they had cleared the runway, Colonel Cunningham, leading the Second Bomb Group, started his take-off run. The first squadron off was the 429th, followed by the Ninety-sixth, the Forty-ninth, and finally the Twentieth. It was the custom in the Second Bomb Group that ground crewmen moved forward to the edge of their hardstands to watch and intently listen as their charges thundered by. This was their final check on the color of smoke and flames coming from the exhaust stacks and to observe any sparks or unusual sounds. Many offered silent prayers that their crews would take off without incident and come home safely.

After the last aircraft had roared by and faded into the distance, one crew chief turned to another, "Let's go get some breakfast and some sack time. I've been up all night and I'm bushed." The other replied, "I'll have breakfast with you but I'm coming back and sleep under a wing someplace. The squadron is due back at 1420 and we should be here in plenty of time, so notify your bunch." They wearily walked to the trucks for their ride to breakfast.

Shortly after 0700 the Second Bomb Group fell into their position behind the Ninety-seventh and the rest of the Fifth Wing and headed across the Adriatic toward the Balkans, still climbing to reach their designated altitude of 26,500 feet. Everything was going smoothly in spite of a heavy haze and clouds. Off the coast of Yugoslavia, they wired the Fifteenth Air Force's headquarters in Bari that they had just passed over three small naval craft, probably German E-boats headed west at flank (maximum operating) speed. Radio and intercom chatter in the Fifth Wing had been minimal and very quiet.

However, this was not the case at Major General Huth's 7 Air Division bunker in Schleissheim, near Munich. This huge, underground complex was a beehive of activity. In the center of the very large war room was a detailed frosted-glass map of southern Germany and the satellite countries. Behind it sat rows and rows of telephone operators, each one connected to a radar warning center, lookout station, ground observer corps, fighter base, or a flak base somewhere in southern Germany or the surrounding countries.

Spies located in Italian farmhouses and at listening and radar posts all over German-occupied territory were feeding information to Huth's headquarters. Because of their sophisticated electronics, the Germans had the ability to listen in on all conversations between the various Allied aircraft and the aircraft and their headquarters. From the time we began our radio checks, they monitored our transmissions. Within a few minutes after take-off, they knew the size and probably destination of any Allied strike force.

In two large rooms, electronic spies wore headsets to monitor information received from these radio transmissions, radio checks and activity at the Fifteenth's bomber and fighter bases. Information received was scribbled on note pads. Those E-boats had already relayed word that a wing of B-17s had passed overhead headed in the general direction of Vienna. Radio transmissions from strategically placed fishing boats in the Adriatic added to German data regarding American activities.

On a balcony overlooking the general war room, General Huth and his staff of analysts, strategists, intelligence, and language experts kept track of all information relayed to this center. Each person analyzed the scraps of paper handed to them and then placed this information on that giant glass map. By 0745 Huth had already notified his flak and fighter commands about what he believed was the intended route of three bomber wings—one B-17 and two B-24s—and the possible routes of fighter groups that apparently were departing to furnish escort. From this information, Huth decided the regular targets of Vienna or Wiener Neustadt were not that day's destination for this American task force. He called his counterpart at the 8 Air Division bunker in Berlin. Several of these bunkers were strategically placed throughout Nazi Germany and the countries they controlled. These bunkers, called 'Opera Houses' by regular Luftwaffe personnel, were the nerve centers of German air defenses.

About 0845, General Huth asked an intelligence officer, "What do we have at Moravska Ostrava other than the oil refinery and marshalling yards?" A few minutes later the officer returned with the answer. "We have approximately fifteen hundred units of rolling stock being made up to be taken to Moravska Ostrava and loaded. In another area we're going to have about a thousand tank cars to move out to Moravska Ostrava. We also have four big squares of supplies, all designated for Budapest and the Russian front. Several trains will be made up in the Moravska Ostrava marshalling yards today. It's a huge shipment."

Huth groaned, "The damn Yankees know." With that he picked up the phone and called his counterpart at the 8 Jagdgeschwader Fighter Command near Berlin. The time was 0900. Huth said, "If they go to Moravska Ostrava today, we'll be waiting."

At 0902 the scramble alarm sounded at the Borkheide Luftwaffe fighter base. Twenty ME-109s started their take-off runs at 0905 and three minutes later they had cleared the field, assembled, and were headed for Dresden. At Jüterbog forty-two more aircraft began leaving the ground at 0904. They assembled at 0912 and were joined by those from Borkheide. At Mörtitz twenty-seven more ME-109s assembled at 0911, also headed for Dresden. All together, Huth had gathered a force of sixty-five ME-109s and twenty-four Focke-Wulf-190s with some Storm Fighters[3] interspersed in the FW-190s. This force of eighty-nine fighters landed at Dresden, topped off their fuel tanks, made last-minute checks, and were airborne a few minutes later.

The Luftwaffe battle commander divided his forces that day. Forty-six ME-109s were sent south of Trencin, and twenty-four FW-190s and nineteen ME-109s were positioned north of

Trencin. These units could conveniently hide in the clouds and haze. With that General Huth turned to his staff, "Well, we have the Flying Coffins taken care of. Now let's plan something for the Furniture Vans."[4]

The British knew Huth very well. They remembered him when, as a Lieutenant Colonel commanding Z JG. 26, he turned his heavy fighters lose on the boats and the British and French soldiers struggling to evacuate Dunkirk. They remembered him for his escort missions with twin-engine fighters during the Battle of Britain. The Fifteenth Air Force command structure, and particularly the Second Bomb Group, knew General Huth well. Several times before, Huth's forces had marked the Second for extinction, the last time being the previous February, when he almost succeeded.

Mission 263's route would take them over the middle of Lake Balaton, home to three major German fighter fields. It was truly one of the largest fighter complexes in Eastern Europe. These fields were manned by veteran Luftwaffe pilots from different Jagdgeschwaders, including a squadron of JG. 26 Yellow Noses. Daily, they encountered both Americans and Russians, fighting them from Ploesti back to the Lake Balaton area in Hungary. Lake Balaton was definitely not a place for a squadron to straggle.

That day the Fifth Wing figuratively thumbed their noses at the Germans and crossed over the heart of their defenses. The Fifth Wing seemed to be in very good shape, except for the Second. Colonel Cunningham, in the 429th Squadron, had one aircraft starting to straggle. The Forty-ninth also had a straggler, and uncharacteristically, the Twentieth was straggling badly.

William Tune was a very competent and able squadron leader, but seemed to be having problems in his squadron, too. The Twentieth would close up until they were almost in their normal position, as close as five hundred yards, and then they would fall back as far as two thousand yards. Possibly some of his aircraft had developed ailing engines which couldn't hold the necessary high throttle settings. In spite of their problems, he was keeping them in good formation. The meager official records from this mission do not explain the reason for the Twentieth's uncharacteristic actions. All aircraft had checked out fine when they left Amendola. The ground crews would never have allowed a sick airplane to be flown, nor would the air crews have been expected to fly such an airplane. Whatever the problem, it had developed en route. Colonel Cunningham knew, and probably the other squadron leaders as well, but any conversations were not included in the official written records. Bill Tune stubbornly kept them in formation within themselves and they continued to the target.

At 0947 gunners from the Second reported three cruisers or skulkers flying several thousand feet below and shadowing them. The skulkers[5] turned with them on every course correction, so they knew information was being fed back to General Huth's headquarters and other area Luftwaffe units. The Second passed over Nové Zámky about 1028. One minute later reports were coming in from the various squadrons to the leaders and others in the group that two FW-190s were paralleling their course, staying out a little more than a thousand yards away. The Germans called these skulkers 'Wooden Eyes.' Their primary duty, aside from giving locations of the bombers and directing oncoming fighters, was to ensure that German fighters concentrating on a fight were not jumped by enemy fighters. Even with the Wooden Eyes serving as lookouts, they continued to be hit by enemy fighters. Disgusted German fighter pilots said they had about as much vision as a wooden Indian, therefore the term Wooden Eyes came into use in the Luftwaffe.

In the area around Nitra, the Luftwaffe commander placed his forty-six ME-109s from south of Trencin in the front of that German formation, having them assume the 'fingers-four'[6] position flown by American air escort, rather than their normal line abreast, gaggle-type formation. Nineteen more ME-109s, plus twenty-four FW-190s from north of Trencin, he moved back into position to strike, out of sight of the bomber formation.

In Trencin, Juraj Rajnenick, a fourteen-year-old lad heard the sound of approaching bombers. He hastily ran into the house for his father's binoculars and returned to the front yard to watch as the Ninety-seventh Bomb Group flew over with the Second Bomb Group behind them. He witnessed most of the subsequent fight between the Second and Huth's forces.

At 1040 Cunningham notified the squadron leaders that their P-51 escort which would provide penetration, target, and withdrawal cover was due to arrive in the next two or three minutes, and to caution their gunners not to fire if some of the P-51s dropped out of the clouds near them.

After Fitzpatrick, in #915, had relayed this to his crew, the tail gunner said, "Lieutenant, there's a big group of fighters coming up at six o'clock. In this haze I can't tell whether they are friendly or enemy, but they are flying American-type formations and I would assume they're ours." This same information was being repeated by nearly every other crew in the Second.

Fitzpatrick called back, "Keep your eyes peeled. We need to know whether they're friendly or enemy as soon as possible."

All over the Twentieth gunners, already expecting their escort, relaxed a bit with the word that those fighters were flying American-type formations. They believed these to be their P-51 escorts.

Those who were fooled by the oncoming formation should not be faulted too much as it is almost impossible from a head-on position, particularly under hazy conditions, to distinguish between a P-51 and a ME-109. About the only visible difference at that angle is the very small radiator hanging below the belly of a 109 that is different from the air scoop on the belly of a P-51. From a profile, the difference is obvious.

Just south of Trencin the German battle commander shouted, "*Horrido. Horrido.*" (German battle cry when they were going in to attack.) The 109s approaching from behind, came in firing rockets, 20mm cannon, and machine guns, and cut through the Twentieth like a huge scythe. Seconds later the group hidden north of Trencin followed them, also firing rockets, cannons and machine guns. In the 429th Squadron, the tail gunner on #915 shouted, "Lieutenant, they're enemy and they're all over us!" By the time they were recognized as enemy fighters, the attackers were about two-hundred yards, and sheets of flame erupted from Twentieth Squadron machine guns—but it was too late. The formation was shredded. Robert McClosky in *My Baby*, #473, was burning and spinning down. Merrill Prentice in *Tail-End-Charlie*, #885, was burning and going down. J. A. Weiler, flying *Queen*, #048, was also smoking badly and going down.

The first element of attackers continued their sweep on through the rest of the group, attacking the other three squadrons of the Second Bomb Group. The surviving aircraft of the Twentieth Squadron, were immediately hit by a second wave. Those were the 109s and 190s from north of Trencin. They hit the Twentieth from the three and nine o'clock positions, coming in V's of eight to ten airplanes and criss-crossing back and forth across the remaining planes of the Twentieth.

Bill Tune, in #159, went down. Thane L. Thomas, in #096, finally took a hit in the bomb bay, probably by a rocket, and exploded into a thousand pieces. Bill Garland, in #118, and William Bullock, in #359, were desperately trying to fight through the melee to form a small element. The carnage in Bullock's airplane must have been terrible. The German battle commander designated four or five of his airplanes for each crippled Twentieth Squadron aircraft still in the air. They made repeated passes as the survivors fought desperately. With the first attack, it was obvious that this was a fight to the death, so conservation of ammunition was not foremost in their minds. Their only thought was to hang on until their escort arrived. Only their escort could save them, so they fought and they fought. Finally, Bullock's plane went down.

Garland fought his *Snafuperman* for many miles. My heart goes out to them as I can imagine the carnage, death and destruction inside that fatally hit airplane, but they fought valiantly. At last, overwhelmed, the venerable old *Snafuperman* went into a spin over the little town of Metylovice. Charlie Beecham,

Mission 263

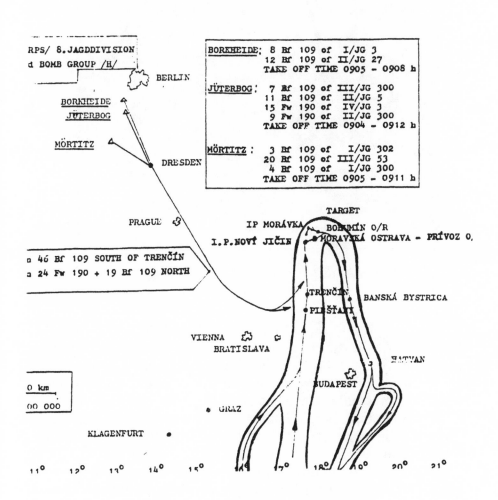

RPS/ 8.JAGDDIVISION
d BOMB GROUP /H/

BERLIN

BORKHEIDE
JÜTERBOG

MÖRTITZ

DRESDEN

BORKHEIDE:	8 Bf 109 of I/JG 3
	12 Bf 109 of II/JG 27
	TAKE OFF TIME 0905 - 0908 h
JÜTERBOG :	7 Bf 109 of III/JG 300
	11 Bf 109 of II/JG 5
	15 Fw 190 of IV/JG 3
	9 Fw 190 of II/JG 300
	TAKE OFF TIME 0904 - 0912 h
MÖRTITZ :	3 Bf 109 of I/JG 302
	20 Bf 109 of III/JG 53
	4 Bf 109 of I/JG 300
	TAKE OFF TIME 0905 - 0911 h

TARGET

PRAGUE

IP MORÁVKA   BOHUMÍN O/R
I.P.NOVÍ JIČÍN   MORAVSKÁ OSTRAVA - PŘÍVOZ O.

□ 46 Bf 109 SOUTH OF TRENČÍN
□ 24 Fw 190 + 19 Bf 109 NORTH

TRENČÍN   BANSKÁ BYSTRICA
PIEŠŤANY

VIENNA
BRATISLAVA

HATVAN

0 km
00 000

BUDAPEST

GRAZ

KLAGENFURT

11°   12°   13°   14°   15°   16°   17°   18°   19°   20°   21°

German Battle Plan for Mission 263

107

My Baby, #473, piloted by Lt. Robert McClosky on
Mission 263. *(Courtesy R. Bischoff)*

a Twentieth Bomb Squadron pilot had photographed *Snafuperman* during a run over Budapest. Years later, he immortal-
ized that B-17 in his painting, "Second Bomb Group over
Budapest." *Snafuperman,* a cross between "Snafu" and "Super-
man," is prominent on the nose of #118.

The Twentieth Bomb Squadron had ceased to exist. All that
was left was smoke from their wreckage spread over a thirty or
forty-mile area.

The best descriptions of the fight come from a ball turret
gunner and a tail gunner from the Ninety-sixth, whose squadron
was hit a few seconds later. Their signed, joint statement said:

> The Twentieth Squadron of seven airplanes was
> attacked by sixty-five enemy fighters. ME-109s in
> waves of about twenty-eight each, continually pressing
> attacks from between five and seven o'clock, breaking
> off to the left and right. I saw two B-17s in flames from

the attacks. The formation was broken up and four or five ME-109s would concentrate on each B-17 of the Twentieth Squadron. I saw no 'chutes out of any of the planes. Enemy fighters were attacking our squadron at the same time so I was unable observe what finally happened to each plane of the Twentieth Squadron. This was from 1046 to 1053 hours."

GEORGE C. HOWE, 37030442,
S/Sgt., AC.

WILLIAM K. FOLEY, 32863885,
S/Sgt., AC.

From the official debriefing reports, another observer stated that he saw six of the Twentieth's airplanes go down in a small area: one smoking, but still fighting. Another eyewitness reported he saw the Twentieth shoot down five enemy aircraft before he, himself, was covered up with enemy. Two or three seconds after sweeping through the Twentieth, the 109s and 190s struck like an avalanche on the tail of the other three groups. The unit that hit the 429th was obviously going for the group leader, Colonel Cunningham, and they almost succeeded.

The Group was engaged from 1041 until 1103. The Ninety-sixth took a full load on the first pass. Lieutenant Arnold Kwiatowski's (#161) tail gunner, Staff Sergeant John A. Lamb, was hit by a 20mm cannon shell in the shoulders and face, which also created severe damage in the tail section and shot out their mechanical and electrical linkage rods to the bomb racks. Because of the loss of the linkage rods, Staff Sergeant James O'Grady, bombardier/togglier, dropped their bombs by hand all the way from Moravska Ostrava to Yugoslavia.

Lieutenant Henry Wallet, in #379, acquired a two-foot hole in his plane's tail. A hit in #915's #3 engine also resulted in a huge hole in the wing with several other large holes around it. The pilots had difficulty feathering the damaged engine, and the fire extinguishers would not extinguish the fire. The gunners had quit calling out "attacking airplanes." There were simply too many. Every man prayed for the escort to arrive as that was their only hope of salvation. They also quit worrying about conserving their ammunition and simply tried to stay alive until the 51s arrived.

The attacking aircraft almost came through their windows before breaking off their attack. Vicente would fire at one airplane, and as soon as that one had passed by, another took its place. #915 began straggling. At the head of the formation, Cunningham's airplane was severely damaged in that first pass from several hits by 20mm cannon. His left elevator was shot off, the left aileron and flaps shot out, and the #2 turbo was gone. The airplane almost looped when it took this series of hits. Cunningham fought it back into a level position the best he could, even though he was losing altitude. By then, even though

Vicente Martinez' regular crew: *(back, l. to r.)* Ray Lavadie (engineer), (waist), (radio), Gilmer Hawkins (tail), Sgt. Webb (waist), and Martinez (ball turret); *(front, l. to r.)* Lt. Pierce (co-pilot), Lt. Kertuba (bombardier), Lt. Fowler (pilot), and Lt. Horowitz (navigator). *(Courtesy V. Martinez)*

the squadron had lost its cohesiveness, he managed to bring them back together. So far he had lost only one, #915, from the squadron's formation.

Back in straggling #915, Vicente, assisted by another gunner, had just finished shooting the wing off an ME-109, when he looked down and saw a 109 at point blank range hanging on his prop just below the turret. Suddenly the airplane lurched—like a car hitting a curb—as the fighter opened up with his cannons. Vicente had him framed in his sight and thought to himself, "He's mine. I have him. I'm going to put this right between his eyes." As he pulled the triggers, all he heard were the clicks of the solenoids that activated the trigger mechanisms, and not a sound from the guns. He was out of ammunition. Although out of ammunition, Vicente stayed in his turret and moved it around hoping to bluff the Germans into thinking he was still operational. Most of the other gun positions had also exhausted their ammunition.

The Forty-ninth Squadron was faring a bit better. Duane Seaman, in #369, took a number of hits from cannon and machine gun fire, and fell back because of numerous holes in his wing and a smoking engine. As he straggled out of the formation, he was hit again. Apparently Seaman was trying to join up with two surviving Twentieth Squadron airplanes to form a fighting element. Several of the Forty-ninth and 429th gunners saw him as he crossed underneath. One reported many holes in the wing—one very large—one engine burning and one smoking. Another said the wing was beginning to turn red. #369 was headed down toward the undercast. They had previously jettisoned their bombs.

Forty-eight years later, Tim Reidy, the ball turret gunner on #369, wrote an article for the Second Bomb Association newsletter, and explained what happened that day. When Seaman reached the clouds the plane was burning so badly he gave the order to bail out. The crew succeeded in parachuting safely to the ground, but were immediately captured and spent the rest of the war in a Stalag Luft. The last they saw of #369, it was burning furiously.

In #915, Fitzpatrick was still having difficulties feathering his #3 engine and extinguishing the fire. A second engine was out. In desperation, he dived the aircraft hoping to blow out the fire. It worked. Down in the undercast, realizing that his airplane probably wouldn't stay in the air much longer, Fitzpatrick gave the order to jettison the bombs and throw everything possible overboard, to lighten the aircraft. Vicente immediately set to work to drop the ball turret. Next the guns, freq (frequency) meters, and everything else that could go overboard went except their shoes, parachutes, and escape kits. There was nothing left to do but pray.

Five minutes after Fitzpatrick entered the undercast, other crews heard him call Colonel Cunningham and report that he was hit and needed an escort if he was to make it home. No more was heard from #915 until 1230 when two aircraft, again, picked up signals stating that #915 was thirty-five miles northeast of Lake Balaton and needed an escort. He was having great difficulties. That was the last radio communication from #915.

With target visability very poor, Cunningham ordered a second run over the target, coming from a different direction. This time they approached from Poland, using the PFF (radar). Fortunately, the flak was not very accurate. As the Second Bomb Group left the target area at Moravska Ostrava, they could see many fires and much smoke. Their bomb results had been good. Colonel Cunningham gathered his remaining three squadrons and headed for the rally point. Trying to keep his cripples with him, they were flying in the twelve thousand to eighteen thousand foot area, ordinarily much too low to fly in the slow B-17 as you were then within reach of even light flak. They did encounter flak fire twice en route back to the field. The weather continued to deteriorate.

The war is full of half-told stories. We would see something one day that peaked our curiosity. The next day we faced another set of problems, and never knew the answer to the first question. Most of your energy was focused on trying to stay alive over some other target. You only ever knew half of what had happened.

Navigator's logs and the debriefing notes are rife with untold stories about the day Cunningham brought the remnants of his three squadrons into Yugoslavia. The Ninety-seventh reported a B-17 down in a pasture. A few minutes later Cunningham's group reported a B-17 parked in a pasture in Hungary. This caused much consternation about who's B-17 was that? When escort fighters saw a bomber go down, they usually went down to take a close look, assess the damage and see if there were any survivors. After a bomber had been on the ground for even a short time, it was too dangerous to get too close. The Germans used these downed bombers as decoys and moved mobile flak batteries in to attack any fighters coming to look. The photographs of this downed B-17 were taken from extremely high altitudes and could not reveal the craft's identity. Therefore, for years, the identity of that bomber was a matter of speculation.

In a very few minutes Martinez observed two crippled B-24 stragglers which had been in a terrible fight themselves that day. The first report came as they watched a B-24 crash in Yugoslavia. They swung out of their way and took pictures with their target cameras. A moment later another B-24 came by. Seven parachutes came out, but fifteen minutes later the airplane was still flying. Two or three minutes later Second Bomb Group personnel reported enemy aircraft landing on a little field nearby. One parachute came out of a B-24 and the airplane crashed in the field. One enemy aircraft had been circling these stragglers. Fighters along the route home had been picking them off. It wasn't a good day to straggle.

Later, at 1433, gunners and personnel in the Second again reported a B-17. This one, skimming the wave tops and going in the wrong direction, had just passed under them. Over Split, Yugoslavia, they reported three to four freighters loading or unloading in the harbor.

*   *   *

Meanwhile, at Amendola the ground crew that had left the hardstands for breakfast and sack time had rested and lunched. As they turned off the road onto the field at 1330, the crew chief said, "I don't like the looks of this. Not at all. There must be something wrong in the squadron." They craned their necks to see what was happening. In the Twentieth's area they could see Bernie Cohen and the engineering officer standing in the back of Bernie's weapons carrier with men gathered around the vehicle. Two men were off to one side consoling another that was apparently crying. Some walked off by themselves, looking at the ground. Vehicles from all the other squadrons were parked by them. Two vehicles crossed the field from the Ninety-seventh Bomb Group's side, headed for the Twentieth's area.

After observing all this, ground crewman continued, "It doesn't look good. I'm afraid something's happened to the Squadron." As they turned on to the Twentieth Squadron's hardstand area, one said, "Look what we got while we were gone. Man, she's a beauty!" They turned to see the object of his admiration. On one of the Twentieth's hardstands stood a gleaming, new B-17G, tail numbers 428—the Ralph Chambers crew had just arrived.

About an hour earlier, Bernie Cohen and those ground crewmen who had remained at the hardstands had heard the grim news relayed from the Fifteenth's headquarters: The Twentieth was gone!

A little after 1515, Cunningham fell in behind some of his aircraft in the traffic pattern to land at Amendola. Two fired flares for wounded. Many were shot up. His ship was badly damaged. Finally, nineteen surviving aircraft had landed. Lieutenant Colonel John S. Cunningham cut his engines at 1522 and wearily climbed out to examine what remained of the left side of his airplane. Ailerons, elevators, flaps, controls, turbo, and everything else on that side had been shot off. He watched the ambulances leave. The Twentieth Squadron crew, stunned by the news, simply stood around. Except the crew putting battle markings on a new B-17 with tail numbers 428, no one was working.

A ground crewman asked Cunningham, "Colonel, what happened?"

Cunningham replied, "Well, I left with twenty-eight airplanes this morning and I only brought nineteen home. The Second Bomb Group took ninety-two casualties today. Everybody in the Twentieth went down."

Crash site at Krhov, thirty-nine years after Lt. J.A. Weiler's B-17G-35-BO, Serial No. 42-32048, crashed. The wooden cross holding this placard containing the names of Weiler's crew was still standing in 1983. The cross is placed directly on the site where the Fortess crashed on 29 August 1944.*

---

* The photographs on this and the next three pages are courtesy of Ralph Bischoff. They have quite a history of their own. Juraj Rajnenick was a fourteen-year-old Czechoslovakian boy who witnessed the fight between the Second Bomb Group and the attacking German fighters. These photographs are from his collection. Some he took himself, and others he obtained years later from German archives and other sources. Most of the data for the picture captions come from what Rajnenick wrote under his photographs. He sent copies to Mrs. Tiny Atkerson when he learned of Sgt. Atkerson's death. She donated them to the Second Bomb Group Museum, and Mr. Bischoff purchased copies from the Museum.

(above) Conqueror and his victim. FW-109A-8 pilot, Oberfeldwebel Nowak of II.Sturmgruppe Jagdgeschwader 300, poses over the burning engine of 2Lt. J.A. Weiler's B-17. Nowak apparently landed nearby very shortly after the crash as he is still in his flight gear and holding his coordinates.

(below) A German intelligence officer examines the engine of 2Lt. T.E. Thomas' B-17. The bomb bay exploded from a direct hit and parts were scattered over a wide area. Intelligence officers determined the effectiveness of the attack and searched for data in the wreckage.

(*left*) German soldiers from the army garrison at Slavicin unceremoniously drag the body of a member of 2Lt. T.E. Thomas' crew away from the crash scene.

(*below*) A little-known face of the air war. German soldiers at Sanov, of Jagdkommando "Ruhsam," pose over the body of a member of 2Lt. T.E. Thomas' crew.

(above) Cemetery at Nova Bosaca on 29 August 1946. The reburial ceremony of four members of 2Lt. McCloskey's B-17G *My Baby* crew. Note the U.S. flags on the coffins.

(below) The four flower- and flag-covered coffins contain the bodies of Sgt. Charles A. Munden, right waist (Dallas, Texas), S/S Harold Schirmer, left waist (Southgate, Kentucky), Sgt. Elmer J. Pruitt, Jr., tail (Clair Shores, Michigan), and S/S Edwin R. Everett, radio operator (Scranton, Pennsylvania).

Crash Sites for Mission 263

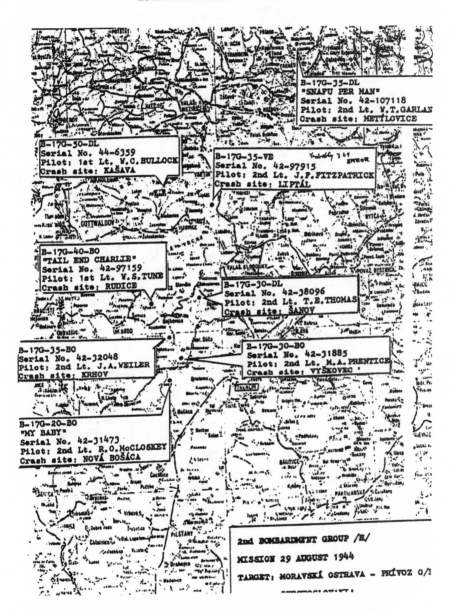

B-17G-35-DL
"SNAFU PER MAN"
Serial No. 42-107118
Pilot: 2nd Lt. W.T.GARLAN
Crash site: METÍLOVICE

B-17G-50-DL
Serial No. 44-6359
Pilot: 1st Lt. W.C.BULLOCK
Crash site: KAŠAVA

B-17G-35-VE
Serial No. 42-97915
Pilot: 2nd Lt. J.F.FITZPATRICK
Crash site: LIPTÁL

B-17G-40-BO
"TAIL END CHARLIE"
Serial No. 42-97159
Pilot: 1st Lt. V.S.TUNE
Crash site: RUDICE

B-17G-30-DL
Serial No. 42-38096
Pilot: 2nd Lt. T.E.THOMAS
Crash site: ŠANOV

B-17G-35-BO
Serial No. 42-32048
Pilot: 2nd Lt. J.A.WEILER
Crash site: KRHOV

B-17G-30-BO
Serial No. 42-31885
Pilot: 2nd Lt. M.A.PRENTICE
Crash site: VYŠKOVEC

B-17G-20-BO
"MY BABY"
Serial No. 42-31473
Pilot: 2nd Lt. R.O.McCLOSKEY
Crash site: NOVÁ BOŠÁCA

2nd BOMBARDMENT GROUP /H/

MISSION 29 AUGUST 1944

TARGET: MORAVSKÁ OSTRAVA - PŘÍVOZ O/I

Barwick

INTERROGATION SHEET
HEADQUARTERS
SECOND BOMBARDMENT GROUP (H)

A/C No. 043   SQUADRON 429th DATE 8/29/44   MISSION NUMBER 263

Bomb Load 20 X 250   Target Chart No. _____   Primary Tgt. Privoser O/R

1st Alt. _____   2nd Alt. _____   3rd Alt. _____ O...

Pilot: Lt.Col. J.S.Cunningham   1st Lt. H.P. Niehaus
Co-Pilot: 2nd Lt.D.R.Stuckey   Right Waist: Pvt. J.Kakatolis
Navig: 1st Lt.J.S.Merritt   Left Waist: S/Sgt. E.DeLorenzo
Bomdr: 1st Lt. H.Safer   Tail Gunner: S/Sgt. B.O.Clarke Jr.
Upper Turret: T/Sgt. S.C.Bushy   Radio Gunner: T/Sgt. R.R.Hindert
                        Observer:

FORMATION: _____ WAVE **1** SQDN. **1** ELEMENT **1** NUMBER

EARLY RETURN: Turned Back at _____ hrs. at _____ H _____ E.

Reason:

Time: Engine On **0614** Engines Off: **1522** Bombs Away **1113**

Bombs Dropped: **20 X 250#** Bombs Jettisoned: _____ Bombs Returned

Formation: Wave **1** Sqdn. **1** El. **1** No. Bomb.Alt. **23000**

Photos: **No Camera**   Heading 175 True / Course 184

Weather Enroute: Clear. Hazy **0-10**/10 cloud coverage at **15000** ft.
Weather at Target: Clear .Hazy **5/6**/10 cloud coverage at **15/18000** ft.

Results of your own Bombing: *Bombing by PFF synchronous - Industrial Area of Mintalan*

Results of other's Bombing: *Couldn't see - (Saw some oil storage hit)*

FLAK   None   Slight   Good   Good
at   Heavy   Moderate   Accuracy(Alt.): Fair   Deflection: Fair
Target Light   Intense   Poor   Poor

FLAK Description: -

Length of time in FLAK: FLAK ELSEWHERE: None
Flak Damage to your A/C: None   Flak in distance @ 4552,1800 -
Location of FLAK Batteries: Slight Heavy - Vhaeglo
  On Target Chart No.   1251-15,200 ft

OBSERVATION OF E/A: Time **1043-48** Hrs. Place 4850X1752 (4905X1751) Your Alt. **26,500** ft.

Number **70-85** Type Me 109s (and) FW 190's **5-7** o'clock High Open/Close Closed to **100** yds.

Actions: shooting mostly 20 mm - (and rockets) -

Enemy A/C Damage to your A/C: Various — 1st bunch 10105-1030 Place _____ Type P510
ESCORT: 2nd bunch 1048 - drove enemy fighters away

NICKELS DROPPED: None

TARGET CHARTS RETURNED: ✓

INJURIES: NAME   RANK · SERIAL NO.   TYPE INJURIES:
          None

John S Barwick
(Interrogating Officer)

****PUT OBSERVATIONS ON REVERSE SIDE****
(Number, Time, Place, Alt. Observed, etc.)

120

Mission 263

HEADQUARTERS
SECOND BOMBARDMENT GROUP (H)
Office of the Intelligence Officer
APO 520

SPECIAL NARRATIVE REPORT:
MISSION: 29 August 1944 - PRIVOSER OIL REFINERY, CZECHOSLOVAKIA.

I. ENEMY RESISTANCE

A. **Fighters:** Fifth to seventy (50/70) Me-109's and Fw-190's, mostly
Me-109's, attacked the formation, starting at approximately 1041 hours at 49
deg 05 min N, 17 deg 55 min E and continued to approximately 1100 hours in
the vicinity of the Initial Point. Attacks were made between 3 and 9 o'clock,
high, low and on the level. Most of the attacks were concentrated on the last
squadron, which was the 20th Squadron, and on one B-17 from the 49th Squadron
and one B-17 from the 429th Squadron, which were lagging far behind their
respective squadrons. The E/A were exceptionally aggressive, making numerous
passes and coming into as close as 20 yards, then going right through the formation, firing rockets, then following up with 20 mm., and machine guns. The
attacks were made by the E/A in line abreast in 4's and up to 10's staggered up.
Some of the E/A also attacked in "V" formations of 10/20 E/A. It was also reported
that two Fw-190's were acting as spotters, circling the formation, out of range,
before the attacks were made. It was also reported that the M/A, while in the
distance, and before forming for the attacks, assumed the formation usually flown
by the P-51's, which led them to believe they were friendly escort. After attacks
were made, the E/A left. It was generally believed that no friendly escort was in
the vicinity when the E/A were attacking, but one crew said that 5 P-51's were
observed to come down from above, and went after the E/A below our formation.
The entire last squadron of the formation which was the 20th Sq, consisting of
seven (7) B-17's, plus one B-17 from the first and third squadron, were lost to E/A.
Claims: 8 Me-109's destroyed, 1 Fw-190 destroyed; 4 Me-109's probably destroyed;
1 Me-109 damaged and 1 Fw-190 damaged.

SEE ATTACHED DIAGRAM OF OUR FORMATION AT THE TIME OF THE ATTACKS

B. **Flak:** Over the target this group experienced slight, inaccurate,
heavy type flak.

II. SIGNIFICANT OBSERVATIONS

A. **Ground:** A smoke screen was observed at 47 deg 10 min N, 19 deg 48 min E
at 1215 hours from 20,700 feet.

B. **Communications:** Observed a M/Y with 800/900 wagons at 49 deg 14 min N,
18 deg 45 min E at 1131 hours from 21,500 feet.
Observed a M/Y with 1,200 wagons at 47 deg 40 min N,
19 deg 40 min E at 1207 hours from 19,000 feet.

- 1 -

C O N F I D E N T I A L

CONSOLIDATED EYE-WITNESS DESCRIPTION

COMPOSED BY

THE INVESTIGATING OFFICER

30 August 1944.

Findings and conclusions re: loss of seven (7) B-17's (entire squadron), comprising the fourth squadron of the Second Bombardment Group (H) formation which was flying on a combat mission to Moravska Ostrava, Czechoslovakia on 29 August 1944.

This Group was heavily attacked by E/A from 1041 to 1100 hours. From 50/70 enemy aircraft took part, coming in aggressively to as close as twenty (20) yards from three to nine o'clock, concentrating on the rear squadron. Because of fighters also attacking other squadrons in Group, careful interrogation throughout the returned crews showed that attention was so engrossed, each in meeting their own attackers, that coherent accounts as to specific detail of just how any one or more of the planes in this squadron were lost is unobtainable.

However, after careful interrogation and subsequent evaluation and synthesis of reports, it was ascertained that the formation of this squadron was first dispersed by action of waves of enemy fighters (Me-109's and FW-190's in W-formation, ten (10) to each formation). Then, groups of four or five enemy aircraft attacked single B-17's of the squadron.

This action was observed to occur between coordinates of 49 deg 05 min North 17 deg 55 min East to 49 deg 36 min North 18 deg 01 min East, and between hours of 1041 to 1100 from an altitude of 23,000 to 26,000 feet. The fourth squadron at this time was approximately 1,000 to 2,000 feet below and 500 to 2,000 yards behind Group formation.

Two aircraft of the fourth squadron were observed to go down in flames; observation of what happened to other aircraft was not possible as Group continued, minus last squadron, to target. The largest number of chutes observed in the area of enemy attacks was three (3).

George B. Sweeney

GEORGE B. SWEENEY,
Captain, Air Corps,
Investigating Officer.

C O N F I D E N T I A L

-1-

C O N FI D E N T I A L

EYE FITNESS DESCRIPTION

Interviewed by
Investigating Officer
on 29 August 1944.

1st Lt. Charles E. Crafton, O-753618, pilot of B-17 No.
858, 429th Squadron which was flying in the first wave, first
squadron, first element, third plane.

B-17 No. 915 called at 1230 hours stating that he was
approximately 25 miles Northeast of Lake Balatin and was calling
escort for protection. I did not see fighters attack No. 915
but only heard them give their position.

CHARLES E. CRAFTON,
1st Lt., Air Corps.

Charles E. Crafton 1st Lt A.C.

The Mystery Explained

Flying #915 beneath the undercast, Fitzpatrick encouraged them to look for anything else they could toss that would lighten the load. By then he had managed to pull the plane fairly level, but was still slowly losing altitude. As they were crossing the White Carpathian Mountains, he was hoarding all the altitude he could get. The crew unbolted and threw out a piece of armor plating and then there wasn't anything to do but sit and sweat. Other than prayer, they were utterly defenseless. Fortunately, they encountered no enemy aircraft. Fitzpatrick nursed that stricken aircraft for almost two more hours. Since no escort was to be furnished, he plodded along, straining to keep his plane in the air. They passed Lake Balaton. The Alps were ahead and they couldn't cross them. The airplane was beginning to fade and they were losing altitude faster and faster.

Finally, he called the crew. "This is the pilot. We're not going to be able to make it. We can't keep this thing in the air much longer. Anyone who wants to bail out now can, while we still have altitude. This would be a good time. I see what looks like a cleared wheat field ahead that I'm going to try and set this thing down in it. If you want to ride it down with me, go ahead. If you want to bail out, it's up to you."

The crew members huddled for a bit and said, "Lieutenant, we'll take our chances and ride it down with you."

"I'm going to try and make that field dead ahead. Maybe we can get into it without getting hurt."

The back crew all went into the radio room, wrapped coats around their heads, and braced themselves for the worst. But for a row of trees just before it, Fitzpatrick would have made the field with only minimal belly damage. The big Boeing snapped branches and broke trees as they hit and began sliding. Parts of the bomb bay were torn away when they hit the trees. Dirt came into the bomb bay, and the ball turret cavity also scooped up dirt. It was impossible to see. After a bit, the airplane slid to a halt.

This was the mystery B-17 which had landed in that pasture. Somebody yelled, "Get out. Get out!"

The dust and dirt were so bad in the fuselage that Vicente could only grope his way to the waist door, which he opened and went out. Technical Sergeant Eugene Moriarty, the flight engineer, joined him and said, "Let's get away from this thing before it blows up."

They ran a short distance and waited. Through the dust, Vicente could see some of the crew coming out the front hatch. They could also see soldiers and peasants coming from different directions. Moriarty told Vicente, "Let's get the hell out of here." They began running. The field was thick with chest-high weeds. The soldiers fired and shouted at them to stop, but they kept running. Finally, the soldiers running, out of patience, began shooting in earnest. By that time Martinez and Moriarty had split. As the bullets barely missed him, Vicente realized that further attempts to escape were impossible, so he laid down on the ground and stretched his arms above his head. A second or two later he had the shock of his life.

A very muscular soldier, stripped to the waist with his shirt tied around his hips and a rifle with a bayonet on it, was cursing him. He was obviously very irritated that he'd had to chase Vicente so far in such hot weather. One of the soldiers surrounding him looked exactly like Adolf Hitler, right down to the mustache. For a second or two Vicente thought, I've been captured by Adolf himself! They jerked him roughly to his feet. After they searched him, they tied his arms and wrists with cords. About that time he was joined by a captured Gene Moriarty. The two men were trussed like pigs going to the market—hands-to-feet—and thrown into a motorcycle sidecar for a very long ride to headquarters at Tata, Hungary. There they were separated. Then the interrogations began.

He told them he didn't know the pilot or any of the crew. They were used to dealing with captured American airman and refused to believe that. Vicente explained that he wasn't a regular member of that crew and the only person he knew was the one they'd captured, and he didn't even know his name. He tried to explain that he was just filling in that day, but the inter- walked in. He didn't know if the newcomer was German or

Hungarian, but he kicked Vicente in the back and struck a vicious blow to his kidneys with his fist. A former track star, Golden Gloves boxer, and baseball player, Vicente was very muscular and athletic.[7] As he came out in a fighting position a ranking officer appeared. The rough interrogation stopped.

The new officer asked Vicente if he was thirsty. When he replied yes, they gave him some local wine. The officer apologized at great length for its lack of quality. They seemed to be very proud of their wine and blamed the poor quality on the water. It tasted great to Vicente. He was then moved to a little jail, where he spent the night.

The next morning Vicente and about twenty-five other prisoners that had been captured the day before were loaded onto a truck for the long trek to Budapest. At Budapest each POW was put in solitary confinement. Food was a thin, watery soup of dehydrated vegetables and two slices of hard bread. That was their daily fare. One day after he had finished his soup, he looked in the bottom of the aluminum bowl and some American had scratched, "No wonder they call this damn place Hungary!"

After two weeks in solitary, a truck picked up a large load of American airmen POWs to deliver them to a German train. The POWs had to stand in the back of this flatbed truck, accompanied only by a driver and one guard. They were to be loaded into boxcars and taken to a Stalag Luft someplace in Austria. As they drove through the heart of Budapest, when the driver turned the vehicle in one direction, the Americans in the back leaned in the other. After each incident the guard and driver threated them, but they were willing to do anything to create chaos and inhibit their progress.

The truck had a flat tire, and when the guard demanded they patch the flat, they all pointed to their arms. Each was a sergeant. Under the Geneva Convention, they were not required to do manual work. Cursing soundly the driver changed the flat himself while the other stood guard over about twenty-five POWs. The townspeople, curious as to what was happening, came up to talk to Vicente and the others. One kindly gentleman offered Vicente some cigarettes. He didn't smoke, but took them rather than hurt the man's feelings. He would give them to somebody else. This fraternization was making the guard nervous, so he took his charges into the lobby of a large hotel where he could see each man. When the flat was finally fixed, Vicente and his fellow POWs climbed back onto the truck and continued across the Danube to the marshalling yards where they were loaded in the boxcars destined for Austria and the Stalag Luft. Then they had German guards and life became much more grim.

Vicente survived the war, but it was very grim toward the end. In December the Germans announced that, due to Russian advances, the camp inmates were to be moved five-hundred miles to northern Germany. Transportation was not available and they would have to make the move on foot. Vicente was a member of the European Death March called the Black March. They walked across Germany during one of the coldest Decembers on record without proper clothing and shoes. They were furnished no food supplies and forced to live off the land. If they couldn't find a barn, they slept in the open in the rain and snow. Most of the airmen completed the march, but the survivors still suffer health problems as a result of that brutal treatment.

In an ironic twist of fate, they were liberated in May 1945, by elements from the Canadian Army, but the Canadians had no way of getting the POWs to the American side. The two Allied forces were separated by an SS division. Freedom meant three more days of walking around that German unit, even after they had been liberated.

Chapter 5

[1] This description of Mission 263 has been pieced together by McGuire from declassified Allied and Axis reports, an eyewitness account from a fellow New Mexican, Vicente Martinez, and from a manuscript written by a Czechoslovakian historian who, as a teenager, personally observed a portion of the Twentieth's unsuccessful fight for life on that day.

[2] The P-51 North American Mustang was introduced into battle in October 1941 when approximately 200 were delivered to the Royal Air Force. As it was initially designed, the engine was considerably underpowered. The British installed a Merlin engine into the American airframe, and one of the most effective fighters of the war was born. The hybrid version was introduced in March 1943. Its subsequent ability to fly long distances caused an immediate strategical reversal of advantage between defense and attack. With Mustangs as escorts, Allied bombers could penetrate deeper into the continent with greater safety from German fighters. The hybrid version had a cruising speed of 437 mph, ceiling of 41,900 feet, range of 2,080 miles, and was armed with six .50 caliber machine guns. Keegan, 430, 432; Wheal, et al., 349.

[3] See Chapter 14 for a more extensive description of Storm Fighters.

[4] Contrary to most American airmen's belief, it was the B-17 and not the B-24 that the Germans named the 'Flying Coffin.' In the early days of the war the British purchased twelve of the earliest B-17s. At that time the British were not familiar with tight formation flying, and used them in a single-ship attack format, rather than in formation where the guns overlapped. Once the Luftwaffe discovered the B-17 was defenseless from below and from the six o'clock position, because there were no guns underneath and in the tail, an officer commented that the Americans had built a flying coffin. After the Luftwaffe examined a B-24, with its slab-sided and clumsy square look, someone remarked, "It looks like a furniture van." Thus the nickname for the B-24. Our escort fighters were nicknamed 'Indians.'

When the United States entered the war and began using the B-17s, they immediately replaced the British .303 caliber machine guns with the heavier Browning .50 caliber gun. Two new gun positions—tail and ball turret—were added for additional protection, and each equipped with two .50 caliber machine guns. Later, the G Model added a chin turret with two .50 caliber machine guns, replacing the hand-held nose gun. A former Luftwaffe pilot said it best, "Jumping on a B-17, with their thirteen heavy-caliber guns, was like grabbing a mad porcupine."

[5] See Chapter 14 for more information about skulkers.

[6] The best way to visualize the 'Fingers-Four' formation is to hold your hand out level, with the thumb folded under. The fingers illustrate the positions of fighters in this formation.

[7] After his liberation, Martinez became a teacher and coach in New Mexico schools. His teaching and coaching career was cut short by ill health. He had to move from his beloved Vallecito, New Mexico to Los Lunas, New Mexico to be near the Veteran's Hospital in Albuquerque. He has a lovely home in Los Lunas and his wife is a librarian at the public library. They have three sons: one is a pharmacist, another is a geologist, and the youngest is a student at New Mexico Tech.

'Flak Holes'

#428 was quickly pressed into service and we didn't see it again for several days. When we next saw it, #428 proudly bore the colors and insignia of the Twentieth Squadron, the Second Bomb Group, and the Fifth wing. A large, black "Y," signifying the Fifth Wing, had been painted on the upper part of the horizontal stabilizer. The black ring surrounding it identified it as belonging to the Second Bomb Group. These markings were black to contrast with the aluminum color of #428. Camouflage painted planes had white markings. The tips of the rudder and horizontal stabilizer were a bright yellow with the rudder painted black. The wing tips were also bright yellow, with two broad, black stripes across the wings. In time, we learned to identify all aircraft in the Fifth Wing by their markings. This was extremely important during take-offs in cloudy conditions, when you were attempting to locate and join your squadron.

Army 428 was then christened, Tweet Tweet, the Twentieth Squadron identification call sign. Added to Tweet Tweet was the call sign for whatever position in the formation she was flying on that particular day—for example, Adam, Baker, Charlie, David, Edward, Frank. Every time we saw her a lump formed in our throats as we remembered the love and attention we had lavished upon her in Lincoln.

We didn't fly any missions for about four days after our arrival, but spent our time in orientation classes and being introduced to the squadron.

The day after our arrival we were informed of a meeting at a big cave near our group quarters. The wing commander, the Second Bomb commander, and the Twentieth Squadron leader would all be there. A huge place, the cave was more of a cavern that had been in use since Roman times, and contained a church, as well as an auditorium. It was also very cold. Throughout the cave, highly visible signs proclaimed, "Gunners, learn to lead. Gunners learn to lead." As we left the cave one near the exit admonished, "Lead, lead, lead." These were reminders to the inexperienced about the importance of leading the target. Even after we had learned this lesson from first-hand experience, our first encounters with jets were to be rude awakenings.

The group commander welcomed us and said we would not fly missions immediately, because there weren't enough planes or personnel. They would use the time to teach us as much as possible before flying our first combat mission. Our instructors would be fellow air crewmen who knew what they were talking about because they'd been doing the fighting. It was important to listen to them and take their lessons to heart. Those lessons might save our lives.

The next day we went down to the flight line bringing with us our new equipment—oxygen masks, clips, parachutes and parachute bags. Part of our tour of the Twentieth Squadron facilities was to the equipment shack. In this fascinating building, each airman had a storage bin for his equipment. The equipment shack personnel went through everything we had, checking to make sure it was serviceable. Somehow I acquired an extra parachute bag, kept it, and later put it to good use. All the flight equipment we had been issued in Lincoln was stored there between flights. Upon returning from a flight, if our suits needed cleaning or drying, they were cleaned and then hung up to dry. The equipment crews inspected our parachutes after each flight, and the remainder of the equipment was inspected as time permitted.

Before each flight, when they called your name, they handed you your parachute bag, your personal medical kit, and you drew the proper escape kit[1] for whatever area you would be flying over. These escape kits were very valuable and you had to sign for them. It was their responsibility to see that we took everything we needed for each flight. The co-pilot received and signed for the big medical kit.

Following the tour, they announced we were about to inspect the plane we would fly in combat the next day.

That's when we met *Flak Holes.*

After we had climbed out of the truck that delivered us to the flight line, all we could do was stand and stare when they told us that this plane was to be ours. It was the ugliest B-17 I had ever seen in my life. We all thought somebody was playing a practical joke on us. It looked like a great big green Dalmatian, if you can imagine one. Nothing on it was the same color. There seemed to be holes in every square inch, and most of the holes had been patched with what looked like lids off food or Spam cans. Even the wings were painted different colors. The only recognizable things on it were the squadron and group markings, a big white "Y" in a white ring, with the yellow wingtips and black stripes on the wings.

It had no nose art, but after a close inspection one of the crewmen managed to read the faint lettering on the nose: 'The world's largest accumulation of flak holes.'

After one look, I turned to Chambers, "Lieutenant, do we have to fly that ugly thing?"

Someone else commented, "It looks like one big flying flak hole," hence its name. To me it was always *'Old Ugly.'*

Chambers looked on it as sadly as we did and said, "Looks like that's what we're assigned to, boys. Let's go in and take a look at it."

We were curious to see what a combat-veteran aircraft looked like on the inside. I had anticipated everything would be nice and oiled, serviceable, but that was not how *Flak Holes* looked on the inside. It seemed like everything was jerry-rigged. The cable wires looked old, but they were not frayed. The plexiglass was scarred and the vision plate on the ball turret was scratched. The plane simply looked like it didn't have too long to live. I swore one wing actually drooped. *Flak Holes* had come from Africa with the Second Bomb Group. It was a conversion model, which meant the chin turret had been added since it had left the factory.

It was one of the few olive drab airplanes in a sea of aluminum, and did it ever stand out in the crowd. When clowning around, we often improvised skits and pretended we were German pilots.

"Say, Hans."

"Yeh, Fritz."

"See that funny colored one? Let's pick on it."

"No, it ain't got long to live. Let's leave it alone."

They put us through intense training sessions for the next several days, cramming in the information. We listened to armorers, radio operators, navigators, and gunners. The gunnery classes were taught by experienced gunners who had been up there and knew what they were talking about. They tried to teach us as much as possible before we flew our first combat mission. We were a well-trained crew by then.

Chapter 6

[1] Each kit contained $2,200-2,700 in various currencies. Before each mission, airmen signed a statement of charges when assigned the kit, and had to pay for it if it was lost.

First Mission

Each squadron headquarters posted mission lists, also called loading lists, the day before a mission. Personnel clerks typed the number of each plane in the squadron and the crew assigned to it. These lists were posted at headquarters, and it was the responsibility of the crew to know with whom they were expected to fly the following morning. The evening of 3 September I checked this loading list and discovered our first mission would be the next day. All of our crew were scheduled to fly, but on different airplanes and with veteran crews. My ship had three veterans on it. The brass purposefully attempted to keep a mixture of veterans with green crewmen on their first mission to provide some stability and experience and also to evaluate the performance of the new men. Graham and Scofield were assigned to another aircraft in our squadron. I particularly hated to see Graham assigned to another airplane; this meant I'd have a strange right waist gunner behind me.

I didn't sleep at all that night. Lying there in bed, I wondered if I could take the pressure. Conversely, I was excited and confident I would perform well under fire. When the Charge of Quarters (CQ), the man responsible for waking and insuring the appropriate crews were up and at it, came by about 0215 or so I was awake and waiting.

Every mission we dressed the same. Our clothing was layered for warmth. Next to the skin we wore woolen long johns and the wool shirt was lined with either silk or nylon so our necks didn't become chafed from contact with the wool. Pure wool chafed your neck from the constant turning of your head as your eyes moved looking for fighters. Then came the regular woolen pants and shirt. The waist and tailgunners often wore two sets. The ball turret gunner was severely restricted on the amount and type of clothing he could wear because of the cramped quarters in the ball turret. Fur boots were our flying footwear. Flight coveralls went on over the pants and shirt and, in winter, a leather, sheepskin-lined B-3 jacket and leather gloves completed the outfit we wore until flight time.

Just before flight time, the coveralls were removed and replaced with a heated suit and heated socks. The suit and socks had thin electric wires embedded in them, just like an electric blanket. The cord came out of your hip and plugged into the aircraft. This heated suit was stored in our parachute bag between missions. Fur pants, called shearlings, went on next with the wool towards our body. Added to this bulk were the Mae West, parachute harness, knife, pistol and escape kit. I preferred to put my escape kit in a hip or leg pocket, where it was handy. It also prevented myself or anyone else from stepping on it and breaking the more fragile contents. Everything on our legs was stuffed into the boots to help seal in body heat.

Finally, we put on the mufflers and three pair of gloves—nylon or silk, wool, and the top glove was leather and went halfway to our elbows. We wore silk scarves or G.I. mufflers to protect our throats and necks. The mufflers and scarves helped keep body heat in and prevent moisture from your oxygen mask from draining onto your throat and freezing on your skin. Frostbite on the throat was a serious threat.

(left) Lt. Ralph Bischoff models what the well-dressed pilot wore at -70° while en route to the target.

(right) From the IP through the target, a steel helmet and flak vest were added to Bischoff's dress. The small snap on the right shoulder is like the one on McGuire's vest hit by flak. *(Courtesy R. Bischoff)*

Our G.I. boots we tied together by the laces and hung on the parachute harness. You couldn't walk very far in the fur boots without rubbing your skin raw, so if we were ever shot down we could wear the G.I. boots once we hit ground. It was neither fashionable or flexible, but warmth was our primary concern.

I didn't eat much for breakfast. My stomach churned from nervousness; my eyes burned from lack of sleep. We were briefed, and I hitched a ride to the flight line. I was issued my parachute bag, escape kit, and oxygen mask and then reported to my aircraft. I was determined to be as professional and business-like an airman as possible, and that included a thorough pre-flight check. After chinning up into the aircraft, I stowed my parachute near the left waist position and started my pre-flight check.

Another gunner, was also doing his pre-flight check. He introduced himself. I'd observed him as he walked up. He was so pale I had the distinct feeling that he'd just checked out of the hospital. Several men in other crews looked as pale as he did. I'm sure it must have been difficult to put together a full squadron after Mission 263, when the Twentieth lost every plane and crewman. That morning I noticed several planes, with other squadron markings on their tails, parked on the hard stands. The Twentieth Squadron had either borrowed, traded, bargained, or stolen them to equip a full squadron for this mission. Later we heard they had pulled everyone off R&R (Rest & Recreation)[1] and grabbed whoever they could from hospitals in order to fill the seventy plus crew positions needed to fly a squadron of seven planes. My fellow crewman was obviously one they had pulled from the hospital.

We both attended to our pre-flight checks. I immediately discovered problems with the talk switch on my throat microphone and jumped out of the plane to ask the crew chief for another. He yelled at someone and said they would get another as quickly as possible. Shortly afterwards one of electronics crewmen came out and checked the intercom lines, verifying the faulty talk switch. He issued me another throat mike.

136

While I was completing my pre-flight, I felt my fellow crewman watching me carefully. Exchanging casual conversation as we worked, we began warming up to each other. Obviously a veteran, he must have appreciated my attention to my job, and perhaps my solemnity, for he took me under his wing and gave me some good advice.

When I had completed my pre-flight, he said, "McGuire, you'll still be in the Army Air Corps for World War III if you lose that escape kit. Those things are expensive, and if you have to bail out of this plane, you'll need it badly and you won't have time to start looking for it. If I were you, I'd put that kit in one of your pockets, zip it up and forget about it. That way you won't break anything in it by stepping on it, and it will be right there for you when you hit the ground. You'll have enough to think about if we have to get out of one of these things.

"Another thing," he continued, "if you don't mind, I'd like to point out that your G.I. shoes are not tied correctly to your parachute harness." We were taught to clip our G.I. shoes onto our harnesses. Our fur-lined flying boots were not made for traveling on the ground, so if we had to bail out, we had to change shoes upon landing. "You have," he continued, "too much slack. With your shoe strings that loose, when your 'chute opens you'll get these right in the teeth, so let me show you what to do." He retied the shoes onto the harness in the correct fashion. He was very nice and polite as he gave me this advice. I appreciated and needed all the advice I could get.

After completing my pre-flight, I again swung back to the ground. Now that I had a little time to think about this first mission, I realized my palms were sweaty. The break gave me time to wonder whether or not this mission would be a milk run[2] or one of the many tough ones I'd been hearing about.

By this time the other crewmen had arrived. There was not much talking going on among us. I didn't know anyone there. The officers—pilots, navigator, and bombardier—arrived. The pilot briefed us about the raid. Our mission that morning would be against the U-boat pens and harbor at Genoa, in northern Italy. It was the home base for the Mediterranean U-boat fleet.

The plan was to fly over the middle of the Mediterranean as if we were going to attack targets in southern France, then turn over Corsica and take a straight run at Genoa. We could expect moderate and accurate flak. The flak batteries around Genoa were good. We could also expect fighter opposition, as there were several bases in the immediate area, including Udine and Klagenfurt, in Austria. The Italians in northern Italy were still fighting for the Axis,[3] and Faschisti Italian fighter pilots were flying at least twenty-two Macchi 202[4] fighter planes based in Milano.

After the pilots' briefing we boarded the airplane. My heart beat faster than usual, my stomach felt queasy, and I perspired too much. I was absolutely determined to do nothing to embarrass the crew or myself. I would not let anything get to me, or bother me. In spite of all the unknowns facing me, I was cocky and thought I'd do well under fire. I would soon find out.

Fear came early that morning. As we started taxiing off the hard stand, I looked back and to my horror saw another B-17 one yard behind our rudder and horizontal stabilizer. We moved forward a little bit, they moved forward a little bit, brakes squealing like a thousand hogs. I gulped and looked forward. We were about one yard from the tail of another B-17. That scared me. If a hydraulic line busted, or if any brakes went out, or if a throttle was pushed too hard, or not hard enough, the plane behind us could chew us up very quickly. That was the day I discovered takeoffs were almost as bad as the bomb runs.

Every plane from all squadrons of the Second Bomb Group—my Twentieth, the Ninety-sixth, the Forty-ninth, the 429th—taxied nose-to-tail until we were cleared to take off. The Ninety-seventh Bomb Group shared the same field as the Second Bomb Group, so they had to keep all the airplanes closely packed on takeoff.

We were the second plane in line. When we saw the green flare indicating that it was clear for take-off, the plane ahead of us turned to the left while we turned to the right. Both planes took off at the same time. As we rolled down the field, the two planes behind us started their takeoff. With this first takeoff, as with every other takeoff, it seemed like the airplane would never get airborne. I knew they were overloaded; we always flew far over the gross weight allowance. That day we ran, and ran, and ran, and I began to think the wheels would never leave the ground. Finally the Fort[5] bounced a little, bounced a second time, then smoothly left the ground. We flew about two miles at what seemed to be just a little above stalling speed while the wheels came up. That takeoff, and every one thereafter, seemed to take an eternity. I never learned to like takeoffs.

My second scare of the day occurred when our squadron went into a defensive box formation.[6] One of the first bits of information that we learned after our arrival at Amendola was that pilots of the Second Bomb Group, and especially the Twentieth Squadron, were famous for flying tight formations, but I couldn't believe what I was seeing. When I peered out the left waist, it looked as if the wings of the seven aircraft were overlapping each other. I'd been told German fighter pilots would pass up a tight bomber formation because there were no holes for them to get through. They preferred loose fighting formations, and given the choice, they would hit those units.

Our squadron then joined the other three squadrons to form a Group formation.[7] As soon as the last aircraft from our Group was airborne, the Ninety-seventh Group started taking off. Our two Groups eventually joined with the Ninety-ninth, 301st, 463rd, and 483rd Groups to form a huge strike Wing: this was going to be a major effort. Every B-17 the Fifteenth Air Force could rake, scrape, patch together and put in the air, about 167, were pitted against a single target. It was a big show. The groups flew about two to three miles apart. We were prepared to drop 490 tons of bombs on the target.

After the formation was formed, the pilot said the B-24s of the Fifteenth would be ranging up and down Yugoslavia, principally targeting marshalling yards, railroad bridges, and viaducts, as a diversion for our raid. Later we learned that B-17s seldom bombed in Italy. Most of our missions were against Germany, France, Rumania, Austria, and Czechoslovakia.

So far everything seemed to be going as scheduled. We hit our first landfall over Sardinia. Looking back I saw an airplane from another squadron peeling off and returning to base, one engine smoking and its prop feathered.[8]

We hit our second landfall, Corsica, and turned straight for Genoa. The weather was good, with the usual ocean haze, scattered with broken clouds.

We reached our IP (Initial Point) and began the long approach to the target. I heard the bomb-bay doors open. Suddenly, black puffs appeared almost in the formation—my first, but definitely not my last, look at German flak. Each black cloud burst around a large, red kernel of explosives. It looked nasty, even from a distance. I just knew they were 88s. We had been told a well-trained 88 crew could fire about twenty rounds a minute. I made some quick mental calculations and figured each gun would be throwing up 850 pounds of scrap iron and explosives at us during the run. I wasn't really that scared. In fact, I was almost enjoying it. I didn't yet appreciate how good those German batteries were firing that day. The first shells which broke in the formation were fired by tracking batteries.[9] I thought the flak was heavy that day, but changed my opinion after crossing targets over Vienna, Blechammer, Munich, Regensburg, Brux, and Linz.

This flak may not have been that heavy, but they were, as ever, accurate. While I was peering out the waist, a shell broke a few feet off our wingtip. Something jerked me around a little bit and I turned and saw something white standing in the air. After looking at it for a few seconds it finally dawned on me that a piece of my sheepskin-lined jacket had been torn off. There was a hole in my collar about the diameter of a pencil. Then I noticed a very small gash in my goggles. I was quite proud of those English glass goggles.

At the time I was quite proud of that little hole in my collar. It hadn't yet occurred to me that if I had been standing a few inches to my left the flak would have gone through my throat.

As we approached the harbor and our target, a variety of ships and boats milled about, scattering like so many bugs on a pond. It appeared that we had surprised them, even though their flak batteries responded quickly and accurately. The sub pens, the object of our mission, were plainly visible and several subs were in their slips. The flak became a little heavier over the target and my respect for them increased.

We dropped our bombs and turned right to the rally point.[10] The right waist gunner behind me suddenly called, "They're dropping out!" I looked out the left waist port and saw Graham and Scofield's airplane. Previously, it had been flying directly across from ours. Earlier, before the run to target, I had waved at Graham at the right waist gun. Their plane plunged out of formation in a steep dive, then leveled off around fourteen thousand feet. I watched them pull far ahead of us as they lost altitude, making a bee-line for home. They flew out of sight. Tears welled up as I thought of Graham and Scofield going down someplace, or crashing. The war had started working on me.

I took one last look at the target before we, too, flew out of sight. Even from that altitude you could tell it had changed shape from the force of the tons of bombs.

No fighters met us on that raid. Except for worrying about Graham and Scofield, the trip home was uneventful. I needn't have worried. We landed without any problem, and as we taxied in, I looked out and saw Graham and Scofield standing at our hard stand, both grinning from ear to ear. Their oxygen system and turbochargers had been shot out over target, and after dropping their bombs, the pilot had to quickly drop to a lower altitude and run for home. On their way home they were approached by four fighters, which could not be identified. The gunners on the 17 fired several bursts across their bows to tell them to keep their distance. The four fighters turned away from the bomber, and when their profiles were presented, they were identified as P-40s.[11] The fighters escorted the lone bomber out of the combat area.

I was exhausted and admit to being a little shaken, but nonetheless was proud of myself as I left the plane. I hadn't done anything embarrassing. From that point I believed I would do well under fire.

As we left the plane, some of the brass drove up in a jeep. They said something to the squadron leader, and soon everybody was grinning and slapping each other's backs. I knew something good had happened. The debriefing officer[12] later told us we'd sunk numerous submarines and other vessels as well as considerably damaging the harbor. Forty-nine years later, while researching information for this book, I discovered we had sunk seven submarines that were almost ready for commissioning, plus four more assorted vessels, including a huge cargo submarine (the Germans called them cow submarines), designed for hauling supplies to a submarine fleet. We also destroyed the harbor, which had been a major base for the U-boat flotillas in the Mediterranean.

It was ironic that the Second Bomb Group had participated in the destruction of that fleet. The Second had been Billy Mitchell's group in the 1920s when he proved air power, by itself, could sink ships of war.[13]

Back in our tent, I again fingered the hole in my jacket and the gash in my goggles. It came to me with a start that somebody had tried to kill me, and I became very indignant. From then on I understood with startling clarity—I was trying to kill them and they were trying to kill me! I decided it would be wise to change to rubber Polaroid goggles which wouldn't shatter. I didn't want glass flying in my eyes if my goggles were hit.

That was our first mission. Compared to most of our other missions it was a milk run. It was unusual in that we immediately knew what impact our bombs had on the target. The remainder of the time we seldom knew the results of our strikes.

From then we flew on almost a daily, regular schedule. I wore that same flight jacket with the hole in the collar during my entire tour. It became a good luck charm. By the end of my tour, when I turned it in, it looked very ratty. One sleeve was burned and all of the sheepskin was burned off both cuffs. I was secretly proud of it. It was fun to wear to impress the rookies.

My manhood had not been too heavily challenged on this mission. My outlook on World War II was to change drastically, however, when, in seventeen short days, we hit Debreczen.

First Encounter with German Fighters

I didn't encounter German fighters until my fourth mission. Four FW-190s, coming directly at us, tried to break up our formation but didn't succeed, so they swept past and hit the group behind us. It happened so quickly, I couldn't believe how fast they were. Leading them with my gun was like trying to catch a weasel. They dived at us in a curving attack from twelve o'clock high, four abreast, wing to wing, in what we called a pursuit curve. This was a downward, three-dimensional curve to the inside until they suddenly went under us and away from the formation. Because of the nineteen-foot tail on B-17s, they were forced to curve under us, thereby losing some of their effectiveness. They much preferred the B-24, because with its shorter tail they could curve over the top, which gave them an advantage. Closing speed was the sum of the speeds of both aircraft. Because of the 190s' faster speed, closing speeds could be close to six-hundred miles per hour. They still reminded me of *banderilleros*, running toward a bull at an angle, and then sticking in the blade before twirling out of his way. I aimed and shot at one in the middle, thinking if I missed him, I might hit the others, but I was too slow and didn't hit anything. Calculations ran through my head as I tried to figure the angles in that curve.

After they passed, I had a sinking feeling in my stomach. Nothing I had seen in gunnery training had prepared me for that kind of speed. We had received the best training in the world, but the sinking feeling came from knowing I wasn't trained to hit anything going that fast. I had to revise my thinking.

143

Chapter 7

[1] Rest & Recreation spots for the Fifteenth Air Force in Italy were generally the Isle of Capri, Naples, or Rome. Rome was considered the choicest location.

[2] The term connotes a mission with little or no enemy opposition.

[3] The Italian ruling class formally arrested Mussolini on 25 July 1943, and sought alliance with Allied forces between that time and the beginning of September, a move prompted by the threatened invasion of Italy. An unconditional armistice was signed on 3 September, almost one year before McGuire's first mission. German forces rapidly reinforced existing divisions in the Italian peninsula, and, with the support of hard-core Fascisti military units, stubbornly contested the Allied advance up the peninsula to the very end of the war. Keegan, 347-353.

[4] Italian Macchi C200 series fighters were very fast and maneuverable fighters designed from a line of racing seaplanes. The fighters were single-seater aircraft. They could reach speeds of over 350 mph at a ceiling of 34,500 feet. The Macchi was an elegant aircraft, another model of Italian industrial craft, but its radial engine proved relatively weak and the airplane was somewhat under gunned. It was armed with two 12.7mm machine guns and two 7.9mm machine guns. Wheal, et al., 285.

[5] Airman slang for 'Flying Fortress.'

[6] A tightly formed squadron could protect itself with a total of ninety-one .50 caliber machine guns; a tight group with 364 machine guns.

[7] Bomber formations were huge pyramids of aircraft designed to construct defensive fire screens, as well as to concentrate bomb weight and bomb pattern on the target.

[8] If an engine went out, the pilot had the ability to "feather" it by turning the leading edge of the propellers into the wind. This was done to reduce drag as well as to eliminate vibration from a damaged engine which might weaken the plane's structure.

[9] Germans fired both tracking and barrage flak. Tracking flak was fired by batteries outside the target area, aiming at formations as they passed nearby or overhead, literally deflection shooting, which was very difficult. Barrage flak was fired by flak batteries in or around the target; the aim being to throw up concentrations of flak in spaces through which the attacking bombers had to fly to hit the target.

[10] All formations loosened up somewhat from the IP to target to lessen the effects of flak. After dropping their bombs, all formations turned toward a rally point several dozen miles from the target and in the general direction of their home field.

[11] The Curtiss P-40 Warhawk entered production in 1939. Various models were sold to England, France, Russia, and China during the first part of the war. Distinctive shark-tooth markings were painted on the noses of the P-40s flown in China by General Claire Chenault's American Volunteer Group, the Flying Tigers. The Warhawk was easy to fly, durable, sturdy

and adaptable, but it was not a popular pursuit plane because it did not match the performance of other fighters in the European theater, especially at high altitudes. It did find a valuable niche in the war, however, as a close group-support weapon, largely in the Pacific. P-40s were introduced into the Mediterranean Theater in November 1942, with the Allied landings in North Africa. P-40s were no match for the Luftwaffe, however, and were replaced as soon as possible in the U.S. Army Air Corps with P-38s. The last of 13,738 P-40s were produced in December 1944. The planes observed by elements of the Twentieth Bomber Squadron on this first strike were probably flown by Commonwealth Air forces, as over 3,000 P-40s were delivered and saw service in North Africa and Italy. The P-40 was fitted with numerous engines, but the most common was the Allison 1,200 hp. It had a range of 750 miles, ceiling of 30,000 feet, reached speeds of 343 mph. It was armed with six .50 caliber machine guns and could carry a bomb load of 1,500 pounds. Omar Bradley, *A Soldier's Story*, (New York: Henry Holt and Company, Inc., 1951), 22; Wheal, et al., 348-49; Parrish, 469; Mayer, 192-93.

[12] At the end of every mission, each airman was interviewed by a debriefing officer for target results, enemy opposition—both from flak and fighters—as well as information on observed friendly casualties.

[13] William 'Billy' Mitchell was America's first and foremost proponent of air power. The son of a U.S. Senator, he was born in Nice, France in 1879. He was the first commander of the Air Service arm of the U.S. Army in World War I, and in that capacity he personally led strategic strikes into Germany in 1918. As Air Service Chief, on 21 July 1921 he led a squadron of bombers which sank the repatriated German dreadnought *Ostfriesland*. This was the first naval vessel ever sunk by aircraft and the action created a sensation around the world. Mitchell pushed for an independent air arm, and upon getting no response from the Navy and War Departments, publicly accused these departments of incompetency and treasonable administration. He was court-martialled and resigned from the service in February 1926. Before he died in 1936, he continued to be a prophet of the efficacy of aeronautics, warning, among other admonitions, of the potential air threat to Pearl Harbor. He was posthumously awarded the Congressional Medal of Honor. Mitchell was also a member of the Second Bomb Group. Richard Marshall, ed., *Great Events of the 20th Century*. (New York: The Reader's Digest Association, Inc., 1977), 202; Anthony Bruce, *An Illustrated Companion to the First World War*. (London: Michael Joseph Ltd, 261; Randal Gray, *Chronicle of the First World War*. Vol. II, 1917-1921, (New York: Facts on File, 1991), 310.

− 8 −

The Kalamaki Strike

Sept. 15: *Bombed airdrome just outside of Athens,*
Greece. Our Group did not get into any flak.
Bombs hit good.

Wayne Lesher
Navigator's Diary

Intelligence discovered, in early September, that on the 15th a German SS Division was to be moved out of Athens from the Kalamaki Airdrome and, because Germans always did things on time, they planned to strike them. The intention was to strike when they were out on the airdrome, in the open, loading into air transports.[1]

For that strike we loaded our bombers with white phosphorus incendiaries and fragmentation bombs. The fragmentation bombs were small, and very sensitive. They were very small, antipersonnel bombs. When they exploded, they scattered shrapnel. The incendiaries and bombs were cluster-loaded in the racks. The clusters were bound by straps to the rack, and when released, the freed incendiaries and fragmentation bombs fell individually like emptying a box of matches. At least that was the way the system was supposed to work.

The entire Fifth Wing, armed with a mixture of bomb types, took off and headed for Greece. It was an easy eight-hour mission. In order to surprise them, we flew in from the Turkish side of the Dardanelles, which added miles to the flight. As we approached the target from the Straits, we saw two German warships about sixty miles offshore. One was towing the other.

Since we thought our element of surprise was over and their defenses alerted, we flew straight for the air base. Our plane wasn't the first over the target. The Germans had managed to start the smoke pots, but their flak batteries were not yet operational. Through the smoke below, we could see many JU-52 transport planes lined up on the airdrome. We dropped our clusters. It was a good strike with much fire showing through the smoke pots.

After the bomb bay doors closed, the radio operator reported over the intercom that a rack hadn't dropped right. One rack of incendiaries and fragmentation bombs was partially stuck crossways and some were lying loose on the bomb bay doors. The pilot opened the bomb bay doors while the bombardier and I raced to the bomb rack and worked frantically to them them, by hand, out through the open bomb bay doors. The last thing you want is incendiary bombs exploding inside your airplane. While we struggled to release them, Chambers straggled a bit from the formation so we wouldn't be a hazard to rest of the squadron. Finally, they fell, but it was anyone's guess what that last rack load hit. The rest of the Wing was certainly on target, though. We could see transports burning as we left the area.

Flak Holes flying over Kalamaki Airdrome, Athens, Greece. The multitude of different-colored patches is very obvious. Smoke billows up from the bomb strike and the smoke pots, which were the only defensive measure the Germans had time to activate. A sharp eye or a magnifying glass will show German fighters still on the ground with several trying to take off or in the air. *(Courtesy Kenn Rusk, photo by Twentieth Bomb Squadron)*

That was our easiest mission. There was no opposition, but we did have a few uncomfortable minutes trying to clear the bombs from the plane. A camera plane above us photographed the airdrome being hit, and the picture included *Flak Holes*. It's the only known picture of her. The plane looks serene and peaceful, but inside we were working frantically to clear the bombs.

The Fifth Wing returned via Albania, Sarajevo, Yugoslavia, and over the Adriatic to Amendola. Shortly after the Fifth Wing had departed the area, several wings of B-24s hit Eleusis and the Tatoi Airdromes, destroying many enemy aircraft at those locations.

Years later, the Greek Government awarded the Freedom Commemorative Medal to all participants in this raid.

Chapter 8

[1] Germany had conquered Greece in April 1941, but by early fall 1944 their strategic position in that area was being threatened to the north by the Russian armies advancing into the Balkans. It was decided to begin evacuating their forces in Greece beginning 12 September. That evacuation was completed by the end of October 1944. Keegan, 158, 364, 508.

Flak

We *hated* flak, and always took a beating from it.

Flak was the shrapnel from an anti-aircraft artillery cannon designed to shoot aircraft down. Its projectiles were like a huge hand grenades. The little, black puffs of smoke we flew through were exploded flak projectiles. Once the projectiles had exploded, they weren't dangerous. Generally, when you were hit you never saw it. You might have seen the flash in the core when it exploded, but then it hit you at the same time.

Flak came in different sizes from so small you could hardly see them to those that were bigger than a man's hand. These jagged pieces of metal were designed to rip through and destroy vital parts of an aircraft, and kill personnel. A tremendous explosion threw shrapnel in every direction. We called the flak cannon 'guns' and indicated the size of the defense by saying there were a specific number of heavy guns on the target.

The Fifteenth Air Force and the other tactical air forces that flew up to thirty thousand feet dealt only with the heavy flak. The German Flak 41 model, 88mm, was one of the finest anti-aircraft guns in the world, and probably one of the finest guns ever made. It was sighted like a rifle. Model 41 was the one we faced day in and day out and was the mainstay and backbone of their ground defense. It was a huge beast and weighed almost nine tons when set up to fire with a barrel twenty-one and a half feet long and a muzzle velocity of more than 3,282 feet per second. The projectiles weighed over forty-two pounds each.

A good crew could fire it twenty times a minute. It was, undoubtedly, one of the finest weapons in World War II. It could fire higher than we could fly and as it was accurate up to thirty-two thousand feet, we were never able to climb above it. The gunners aimed using visual, radar, infrared, and sonar methods, so they didn't have to see us to hit us. Towards the end of the war we thought they were using proximity fuses.

All anti-aircraft guns were under the Luftwaffe's control. Goering insisted that anything to do with aircraft be in his purview, so most of the batteries we faced were manned by Luftwaffe personnel assigned to defend specific targets. The guns were so versatile they assigned flak batteries to the Wermacht (German ground forces) and mechanized divisions, to protect them against air attacks. The 88 was used in some tanks as an anti-tank weapon. German infantry also used it with deadly effect.

They also had mobile 88s. The guns on the Flak 18 model weighed less. The barrel length was only sixteen feet, two inches, and fired a projectile that weighed slightly less than the 41 models, but being mounted on wheels, they could be moved from one site to another on short notice. Each unit weighed about eleven thousand pounds when ready to fire. These mobile units were used with great success for ambushes. Their range was as high as the other guns. As we threaded our way amongst the defended areas of Europe, following our usual tracks, overnight they would move guns into an undefended area. When we encountered these unsuspected ambushes, they inflicted serious damage.

Flak was white-hot when it went through the airplane's skin. Then it quickly turned to cherry-red like a blacksmith's anvil and finally, back to a gray-black. It could, and did, start fires. It also caused puncture wounds and burned the inside of the wound. It didn't take much to nick a fuel, oxygen, or hydraulic line, or damage a wire connection, or control cable. Unnoticed, a small hole expanding and contracting and at the higher altitudes on future flights could cause serious problems. Even a minute nick in a nearby line could be an accident waiting to happen. It was important that crew chiefs discover any holes or nicks in something vital, such as an oxygen system.

Another gun we dreaded was the 105mm. When set in place and ready to fire it weighed eleven and a quarter tons, and its projectiles contained fifty-seven pounds of scrap iron. Its muzzle velocity was an unbelievable 2,900 feet/second, although the rate of fire was less than for the 88. A hit by a 105 generally inflicted very, very extensive damage. Smoke from an exploded shell was gray in color rather than the usual black from the 88mm.

Finally, the grand-daddy of them all was the Flak 40 model. A 128mm, it weighed almost twenty tons in the firing position. Its muzzle velocity of 3,280 feet/second could really slam that 105-pound projectile at you. The rate of fire was slower, but the explosion covered a wider area, and the flak pieces were larger. It could shoot projectiles 48,500 feet into the air. The whole sky shook when the 128mm went off. One of those projectiles, fired into a formation, could wreck havoc with a thin-skinned bomber. Someone once asked about the thickness of the skin on a B-17. "Just thick enough to keep out the rain," was the answer. It didn't do anything to keep out the flak. Smoke from a 128mm was white.

German cordite stank. If you were near a burst, the propellers drove the rotten-egg smell back into the airplane. It burned your eyes and assaulted your nose. Smell was another way you could tell the nationality of the flak coming up at you.

Fascisti flak in Italy didn't stink, nor did our flak, and we were shot at a time or two by American gunners. We could tell the size of the gun by the color of the smoke from the flak. When they burst, it looked as though the clean blue sky had developed a nasty rip. The Germans cleverly used colored smoke in another way. Whenever they had finished firing at a formation, they fired a red round. This was the signal to their fighters that the shooting was over and it was safe for them to attack. That was when we were the most vulnerable as we were scattered and many had engines feathered.

The Germans were excellent marksmen, and they became better as the war progressed. We never knew how many guns would be on a target, especially after the Russians began moving into Rumania. From that time on we would encounter areas where the defenses were almost unbelievable. As the Germans retreated westward, their guns were moved back and compressed more and more into places like Vienna. When we started concentrating on the oil refineries in an effort to cut off

A squadron from the Second Bomb Group flying in close formation. Bomb bays have not yet opened. Gray and white flak bursts are visible throughout the formation. *(Courtesy M. McGuire)*

their gas and oil supplies, it didn't take us long to discover that all along they had known how vulnerable these areas were, so they heavily protected them. I don't want to demean the sacrifice made by those British cavalrymen in Tennyson's 'Charge of the Light Brigade' as they journeyed through that Valley of Death, but in a waggish moment I once stated, "If those guys had to ride with us on missions to Blechammer, a bunch of them would have been AWOL."

Flak batteries had a distinct advantage. We had to start our bomb runs from a known point. Even though we tried to vary it, we had to have land marks from a known point, the IP. From the IP the bomb bays were open and from that instant, the Germans knew the identity of our primary target. They simply drew a straight line from the IP to the target. All they had to do was figure our height. They knew we made most of our bomb runs at 150 mph on the pilot's air speed indicator and a head wind meant that your track across the ground was even less. Therefore, they had the luxury of knowing our exact track. Diversionary tactics to throw them off seldom worked well. We would rather bull through and get good results so we didn't have to come back on another day.

Would I take flak over fighters? If we'd faced fighters on most missions, I'd take flak. Fighters were the most deadly enemy we had. Along toward the end of the war some fighters carried as many as four to six cannon, as well as rockets, and were armor plated. The pilots we faced toward the end were coming up almost into the airplane. In that case, flak was preferable. Fortunately, we didn't face fighters that often. We frequently saw them when they were concentrating on a group or squadron and trying to wipe it out. If you were selected, it was a foregone conclusion that, without an escort you would go down to their attack.

All things considered, when we did face fighters I felt better for then I was earning my money. We could fight back and get even for those minutes and hours of running the flak gauntlet. Fear was not as much of a problem during fighter attacks as during flak barrages, perhaps because we were actively occupied. Flak seemed to be harder to take if you were a gunner as you had nothing to do during the approach to the target. The pilots and bombardier were busy with the bomb run; the navigator, if he was a good one, never looked up from the charts on his table; the engineer was busy watching instruments and looking for fighters; the radio operator was on the telegraph key reporting bomb damage or monitoring the radio frequencies for battle orders. Because enemy fighters generally held back when flak was flying, the gunners just had to sit there and take it. We knew we would face flak every time we went out.

Bomb runs were generally from twenty-five to fifty miles in length. The winds aloft could change by one-hundred eighty degrees, so in order to get good bomb strikes, windage and visibility at the target had to be considered, as all of these factors affected the bombs' performance. We tried to place the bombs precisely on that target. In order to do that, the plane had to be as straight and level as a carpenter's level. All the bubbles in the airplane had to be level. Evasive action was not an option as it would affect the effectiveness of the bomb run. Bombardiers couldn't take time out to fire at fighters as they were totally involved in the dropping of those bombs. As a bombardier you had to ignore shattering glass, the sudden appearance of holes and the sound of metal tearing, and concentrate solely on putting the bombs on the target.

On one mission we were to hit a major target in the Munich area. Munich was a big railroad transportation center and fuel storage depot. Bombing Munich was never a picnic as it was one of the most heavily defended targets in Germany. Normally, we faced from three to five minutes of flak as we approached the target. On this particular mission, we encountered flak for at least fifteen minutes.

The lead bombardier couldn't acquire the target on our first approach. It was obscured by smoke and he wasn't satisfied so he told the formation leader he couldn't drop the bombs. The formation leader pulled around Munich for another try. That was the first five minutes.

We were going to have to go through that again. Flak tracked us all the way to our new IP which we approached at 145 mph. The Germans continued to throw flak at us. By the start of the second run, my knuckles were white. Flak was exploding all around us. They had our exact range and altitude. Every round appeared to be a hit. You could hardly see for the smoke. Survival seemed impossible. Over the target, the lead bombardier again announced he could not locate the target, and unbelievably, once again the leader announced we had to turn away for a third run. That was the second five minutes.

In we went again as the flak pounded us. I was terrified and began praying aloud to myself. "Lord, let me off this mission alive. Let me off this mission alive even if I become a prisoner of war. You can put me behind barbed wire. Just let me and my friends live through this." I have always been ashamed of this because, somehow, I had unknowingly pushed the intercom button and everybody on the airplane heard me praying. The co-pilot yelled, "Get off that intercom whoever is making deals with the Lord!" No one answered. Every man thought he was the one guilty of voicing his thoughts. Somehow we survived that third run over Munich and successfully dropped our bombs. Strangely, the third run didn't seem as bad as the first.

Later, when they discovered I was the one making deals with the Lord, I received no end of ribbing about making arrangements with God to have us made POWs. The worst part was sitting there and taking that awful pounding and knowing there was nothing you could do. It was like being in a boxing match where you were not allowed to hit back.

The tail and ball turret gunners had the best views of the target and could observe the results of the bomb strikes. One day Scofield was in his ball turret watching for strike results. We were, as usual, encountering heavy flak. Suddenly, we heard over the intercom, "I'm hit." Somebody asked who it was and the voice came back, "It's Lou." Then he added in a very relieved tone, "Never mind."

While watching the ground, he'd been hit by a piece of flak which blew out his entire view plate, the piece of plexiglass and metal which was directly under him. The spent piece of flak, and it was a big one, hit his flak suit at his stomach. Fortunately, it hit flat instead of edge-wise, otherwise it could have cut him in half. White hot when it hit, it began burning but remained on the outside of his flak suit. He was relieved to know it hadn't penetrated, but it certainly got his attention for a few seconds and he sported a beautiful bruise on his midriff for several days.

As previously mentioned, the Second Bomb Group was famous for its tight formations. Close flying was the best defense against fighter attacks. As a protective measure, the formation spread out at the start of a bomb run. If a ship was hit while flying in a very close formation, it could crash into another airplane and create a pinball-type chain reaction.

The last thing we wanted was a fighter attack, but strangely, my memories, my nightmares were always of flak. I don't remember that much about fighter attacks. It was the flak that featured in my nightmares, particularly during the first two years after my return home. Our most harrowing thought was that, once again, we were going to have to run that gauntlet for the next twenty-five or fifty miles. You prayed to come out alive on the other side of that living hell. This is what wore you down. You couldn't fight back. You could only sit and take it.

Many airmen were hit by flak, although much of it was such tiny shards you were unaware of being hit. The sting of flak when it hit your body, even the very small pieces, was extremely painful.

World War I flak was called Archie. One source stated, that in that war, it took approximately three thousand rounds to shoot down one airplane. They were highly inaccurate unless the airplane got down into the small arms fire. Aviators from World War I used the locations of Archie batteries for navigation.

When I think of war, I think of flak.

– 10 –

Debreczen

21 Sept.: *Bombed Debreczen Marshalling Yards*
(Hungary). Flak was very accurate. All ships
were hit. We had about 17 holes. Weather
very bad too.

> Wayne Lesher
> *Navigators' Diary*

By 20 September, we had settled in with the squadron and
were well-acquainted with the rest of the Second Bomb Group.
We had even become half-way comfortable in the Amendola
Ritz, situated in an olive grove about four or five miles from the
airfield. We were also getting to know our squadron mates,
some of them on a first-name basis, including most of the pilots
as well as most of their crews. We also became acquainted with
some of the airmen from the Ninety-seventh Bomb Group, who
lived down the road and across the field.

Debreczen

By late September we had several missions under our belts. Several were decidedly milk runs. Some weren't so easy. We'd flown to Munich once or twice, and those Munich trips were never picnics, but we had returned safely even though the opposition was tough. Those missions served us well, however, because we were feeling increasingly confident in our ability as a crew. We'd dealt with our initial jitters, faced some heavy flak, or what we thought at the time was heavy flak, as well as some fighters, and we were beginning to trust not only our individual abilities, but the abilities of the other crewmen. A mutual respect was growing among us. We weren't scared mentally or physically. With every mission, however, we started understanding the odds we faced, and we knew there weren't many more milk runs coming up for us in the future. We hadn't yet reached the point of believing we wouldn't survive, or that anything bad would happen to us. We were very confident and cocksure. That was about to change dramatically, and during the course of a single raid.

We'd had a day off and were standing down. It was raining and the clouds were low. Although we didn't think the weather would be good enough to fly the next day, several of us walked over to the headquarters mission board to see what was planned for the next day. We put on our raincoats and walked over. Surprisingly enough, we were scheduled to fly the next day. The next morning at briefing we discovered the target was a city I will never be able to get out of my mind because of what we went through: Debreczen. We unknowingly mispronounced many German and Czechoslovakian proper names and Debreczen became 'Debraken.'

That evening we went through the normal motions of preparing for the next day's raid. It was important to be as clean as possible despite all the mud around us, so we spit bathed, shaved and went to bed early. That night's sleep was, for many of us, the last peaceful sleep we had over there.

The CQ awoke us at 0230. Church services would be at 0330, briefing at 0400, and take-off was 0630. We proceeded as

159

usual to prepare for the flight. The CQ volunteered the information that the weather was continuing to get worse.

We were waiting at the flight line around 0600 when the officers showed up after their briefing. Fenstermaker had found something not quite to his liking with one of the engines, and he and the crew chief were fussing over it before everything finally checked out. We were flying *Flak Holes* that day. It was still raining and we didn't believe the weather was going to be good enough to fly. The ceiling was very low. Chambers, Karsten, Lesher, McDonnell, and Sutton got out of the truck and walked over to us. Sutton carried his little bag with identification colors of the day and the code and frequency books which he would need to radio information back to the base.

Chambers asked if everybody was all right, and, receiving an all-around affirmative, asked everybody to gather around him at the waist of the ship, as we always did. We were anxious for information about the target. In a measured voice, with his smooth Southern accent, Chambers started talking. "Whether or not the mission is still planned is in question because of the weather conditions, but if we go, it's Debreczen today. We won't have to fly very far for this one, only about a thousand-mile round trip.

"Debreczen is an important target. The B-24s have been hammering the Orient Express Railroad lines, knocking out the big bridges and the train yards in Yugoslavia, however, most of the supplies for the German Eastern Front are coming through the marshalling yards at Debreczen. It's in Eastern Hungary, near the Rumanian border. The particular marshalling yards that are targeted for us today carry the largest amount of these supplies, so this is a very important target. The Germans are painfully aware that we have been looking them over, so I suspect we'll have a fight on our hands today.

"The weather will be very bad, and we'll be forced to fly low under the clouds in order to access the target. Also, because the weather is bad, we'll have to make an instrument take-off. I would advise everybody to snap his chest 'chute on because we'll be climbing in heavy weather, and there will be a constant danger of collision. If we hit anybody we'll have to get out of the plane in a hurry. We will be in bad weather the entire trip. Good luck, let's do our jobs the way we're supposed to. Karsten will give you the scoop on the intelligence reports."

Our co-pilot then spoke. "Alright fellows, the Germans have been real active lately in this area. They are reinforcing their fighter forces and anti-aircraft weapons. We really don't know exactly what to expect by way of opposition. We know they have moved a lot of flak guns back from the Eastern Front, but we don't know what kind and how many. We do know they have been adding to their coastal defenses in Yugoslavia, so we can expect some flak when we come off the Adriatic. They have also moved in some mobile weapons, and we don't know where those are located.

"We can, of course, expect fighter opposition. We'll be running the gauntlet of fighters stationed out of Sarajevo, Zagreb, even Belgrade. The German fighter squadrons have been moving around a lot to confuse our escort, so we don't know where to expect them. In the Lake Balaton area, however, they have built three new fighter fields and they've flown in additional fighter squadrons, including one squadron of Yellow Noses. So we'll probably get fighter opposition today, and it could be heavy. Keep your eyes open and your guns ready. They told us in briefing to expect moderate to intense flak, but we just don't know. We do know that they have a lot of warehouses there filled with desperately-needed supplies, so I look for us to have a good fight."

He finished and Lesher spoke up. "Our trip today will be a little over a thousand miles as it is almost right at five hundred miles from here to Debreczen. Our course will take us past Sarajevo to our rally point at Subotica. After we cross the Alps on the Adriatic we will be flying mostly over plains all the way to target. Debreczen should be easy to see. We have a very long IP, which will start over Sap. After hitting the target, we will again rally at Subotica. The weather will more than likely be overcast at the target, so we'll be forced to fly a little lower than

161

usual. Report anything you see to me in the way of convoys or maritime shipping. Sarajevo will be the first place that is easily identifiable once we cross the coastline."

Chambers then asked McDonnell to show us a photograph of the target so we could identify it. The marshalling yards were easy to spot on the photograph, and they would be even easier to spot if we were flying in at twenty thousand feet instead of our usual twenty-nine thousand to thirty thousand-foot altitude.

After we studied the photo for a few minutes, Chambers said he was going to say a prayer, and anybody who wanted could join him. We knelt and prayed silently, each of us praying the way we thought best. When finished we drifted away. Thompson and I walked quietly back by the tail, which, by then, had become our routine. The two of us prayed again, this time together, and he gave me a very short Bible lesson. While in Italy, I became very interested in learning more about the Bible. Suddenly, we heard much noise. Jeeps and trucks started roaring up the flight line. The mission was on.

When it was time for takeoff we all climbed in the ship. At exactly 0615 all engines in the Second Bomb Group started simultaneously. The entire group eased nose-to-tail on the muddy airfield. The 429th Squadron taxied ahead of us. They would fly lead squadron. The Ninety-sixth was next, followed by the Twentieth. The Forty-ninth brought up the rear. Brakes squealed, mud flew, water splashed. The pilots were having difficulty with forward vision because of mist clouding the windscreens. Finally, the 429th got the green flare, and in a great spray of mud and water its planes quickly took off, one after the other, followed by the Ninety-sixth.

Planes from the Twentieth started taking off. That day we were tail-end-charlie in our squadron and by the time it was our turn, the air was very turbulent. As was our custom, those of us in the back braced ourselves in the radio room during the takeoff. We considered that the safest place during takeoffs and landings because there were three ways to exit in the event of a crash. I also developed a habit of taking a small fire extinguisher from the waist position with me to the radio room. Being trapped in a burning plane was the worst of my nightmares. The plane lurched through mud and water, and we breathed a sigh of relief when we were airborne. We quickly moved back to our position as the plane disappeared into clouds and rain. It seemed for a moment that we lost power in one of the engines, but then everything was fine and we started climbing. (Refer to the Battle Order and Briefing Notes & Formation report on the following pages for the location of all planes participating on this mission. The Special Narrative Report, Confidential Mission Report, and eight debriefing reports are included at the end of this chapter.)

I was nervous. It looked like we were climbing through a bowl of milk. The airplane in front of us had simply disappeared, but we knew he was out there somewhere. Sutton called over the intercom that all aircraft from the squadron had taken off without incident. Immediately we had a call from Karsten, cautioning us to keep close watch as the sky was full of airplanes and if they weren't holding assigned altitudes, positions, and headings, there would be a big problem. After what seemed an eternity in that milk soup, we finally broke out into scattered clouds, and were startled to see a B-17 flying just a few feet behind us. It was a Fort from another squadron. With better visibility because of the clearing weather, he quickly moved back to his assigned squadron. The Second Bomb Group, twenty-eight planes strong, circled back to Amendola for our rendezvous. It looked like one or two planes were having mechanical difficulties, and for that reason we always flew a couple of spare aircraft. At Amendola we meshed with the other squadrons. The skies were full of colored flares as we fit together into fighting formation and headed toward the Adriatic Sea and Yugoslavia.

Immediately after joining the Group we all heard a string of profanity from Scofield. He had lowered himself into the ball turret to discover it was covered with mud. Before takeoff the armorers had cleaned his view plate and port hole to perfection, but the takeoff had caked it with stinking, pudding-thick, Italian mud. Potentially, this could be a deadly problem. He left

Bloody Skies

Battle Report

✓

APO 520,
21 September 1944.

OPERATIONS ORDERS)
                    :
NUMBER........279)

1. This Group will furnish twenty-eight (28) aircraft
to bomb and destroy DEBRECZEN M/Y, HUNGARY. Alternate Targets:
(1) NOVI SAD M/Y. (2) BROD M/Y.

2. Rendezvous: AMENDOLA; 10,000 feet; 0755A.

3. Route Out: RENDEZVOUS to Keypoint to DRINJACA (44/18N
19/09E) to control point SUBOTICA (46/06N 19/40E) to SZARVAS
(46/53N 20/32E) to IP to Target.

4. Route Back: RALLY to SUBOTICA to PODGORA (43/14N
17/06E) to BASE.

5. IP: SAP (47/16N 21/21E).

6. Bombing Altitude: 20,500 feet.

7. Bomb Load: Twelve (12) 500 pound RDX bombs, one tenth
second nose, twenty-five thousandths tail fuse.

8. Escort: The 15th Fighter Command will provide strong
close escort for the 5th Wing.

9. Communications: VHF Channel "B", Command 6440 kcs.,
Call-sign Reckless 2.

By order of Colonel RYAN:

HAROLD L. THAYER,
Captain, Air Corps
Operations Officer

Debreczen

TARGET: <u>Debreczen M/Yds Hungary.</u>

BRIEFING	0430
TRANSPORTATION	0520
STATIONS	0550
TAXI	0620
TAKE-OFF	0630
BOMB LOAD	12 X 500
ASSEMBLY	0715 Amendola 5,000'
BASE ALTITUDE	20,500
I.A.S.	150
I.P.	Sap (47/16N 21/21E)
AXIS OF ATTACK	35
TURN AFTER BOMB RELEASE	Right
T.O.T.	1107
T.R.B.	1350
COMMUNICATION	Fighter "A", Bomber "B"
ESCORT	P-51's
COMMANDER	Major Bedgood
DEP. C.O.	Lt. Donovan

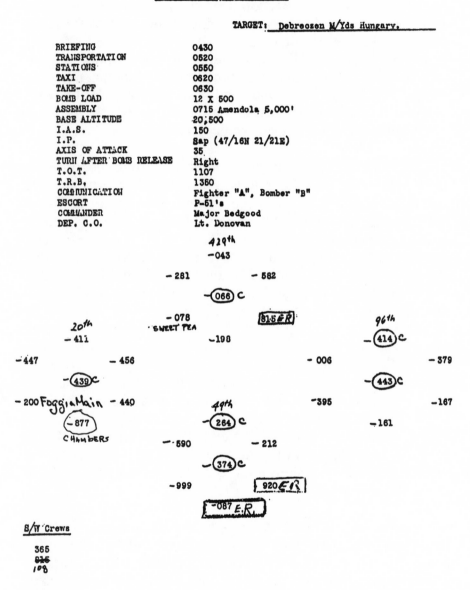

S/W Crews

365
~~816~~
108

ESCORT: 15th Fighter command will provide strong close escort for the 5th Wing.

NICKELS: None

the turret and started cleaning it off as best he could by reaching out through the inspection hole in the bottom of the waist near the turret, and using rags to wipe off the mud as far as he could reach. It was a tough job. Graham and I helped. Scofield grumbled about how the mud made the turret stink, and we kidded him that we didn't realize the smell was coming from the mud. Even though the clouds had broken up a little, the rain was still falling heavily. By rotating the turret into the rain, he got it clean enough to provide some visibility.

We were unaware that shortly after the Group mobilization over Amendola, the Fifteenth Air Force issued orders to cancel the mission. South of us, in the Taranto-Bari area, our B-24s were based. While their arm of the strike was taking off there had been some collisions and a lot of near misses. Weather conditions there had been much worse, so headquarters canceled the mission. All the B-24s got the word, and most of the B-17s, but not the Second Bomb Group. We never received the cancellation notice, and, in the muck of the storm, the other B-17 groups in our wing turned back. We flew onto the target alone, believing there was an entire air force behind us.

The Second Bomb Group, as usual, was flying in a defensive box. The weather was so bad, however, that we were flying in a spread formation, bad-weather formation, and keeping in sight of one another if we could. Sometimes we lost sight of the other squadrons. We did notice a plane in the 49th Squadron dropping out, radioing about problems with one of his superchargers. One of the spare ships took its place. We crossed the Alps at the Adriatic coast.

The Eighth Air Force in England had fog and bad weather to contend with, the Fifteenth Air Force in Italy had the Alps. Much friendly rivalry has developed between former Eighth and Fifteenth Air Force members. The Eighth Air Force has a well-documented history because of its earlier origins. The Fifteenth was a war-time creation and its members did not have the luxury of time to create a written history. Obviously, the

Eighth attributes our lack of history to a lamentable lack of literary ability. We contend that, for each ten men, the Fifteenth had nine men fighting and one writing; the Eighth had one man fighting and nine writing, which is why they have so much history.

Another on-going debate between the two groups is over the relative difficulty of their respective routes. The Eighth claims theirs to have been the more hazardous route because of their need to cross the English Channel and the dangers of ditching in that cold water. The Fifteenth's standard response was, "Have you ever tried ditching in the Alps?"

Each airplane carried a tremendous amount of weight on missions—twelve 500-pound bombs, ten men, and a full compliment of ammunition, plus a few extra belts carried by the gunners. Much of the time those planes flew weights the manufacturer considered impossible. Those Wright Cyclone engines were always straining on take-offs. Then, we had to climb the Alps.

It was a continual climb from take off until we reached our targets in Germany or southern Europe. This climb was necessary to clear the Alps, which were from ten thousand to fifteen thousand feet above sea level. If you weren't high enough when you crossed, the turbulence would bring you down. Also, there was always the danger of heavy icing during the crossing. During the winter the Alps were generally covered by clouds. Sometimes you couldn't see anything but the clouds beneath you, but you knew the Alps were sticking up somewhere in all that white fluffiness and you had to get over them. The Alps were a tremendous barrier for us, and always a major consideration on most of our raids.

The turbulence that day was bad, as usual. Luckily, we encountered no flak. As we crossed the Alps, Lieutenant Joe McCormick, flying #815 for the 429th started throwing oil and turned out. We were down to twenty-six aircraft. Immediately after McCormick dropped out our base reported that weather conditions had socked in the field. We would have trouble landing on our return.

As we crossed the Alps, we were scattered out, but it didn't take much time to fall back into a tight defensive formation once we were all on the other side. As we flew over the Hungarian plains, I counted the planes in our formation. There were now only twenty-five ships.

Leaving the Alps, we encountered better weather. We were in a high state of alert because we would have been easy to spot. Tail winds had put us about fifteen minutes ahead of schedule. We kept looking for our escorts. Karsten had told us earlier that we would pick up a strong escort that day. When we didn't spot any fighters coming over the Alps, we knew they must have been having a tough time in there.

It wasn't long before we hit our IP at Sap, fifty or sixty miles from our target. Our approach paralleled one of their big highways which the bombardiers used to correct our drift. Our formation was very, very tight that day, but the overcast made us drop lower and lower as we approached the target. Any second we could start picking up flak.

Normally the ranging rounds of the flak batteries would be a little out of our formation, but not today. The first burst hit right in our formation. That was scary. Then I heard somebody say, "My God." What I saw when I looked out at the formation ahead of us was difficult to describe. Their gunners were leading us perfectly. I had never seen anything like it. The sky had simply turned black ahead of us. A big, black box of solid flak burst immediately ahead of us, and we were flying into it. The black box was not much wider than our formation. Perfectly timed, and perfectly aimed, it looked like we were flying into a big, solid black wall, sparking with nasty red flashes. It was as though a great hand had torn the sky apart, exposing its bloody interior.

With a sinking feeling, I thought, "None of us can get through that alive." I looked out the waist and saw the 429th directly over the target. I could barely see them through the smoke and fire. Every plane appeared to be taking hits. The sky filled with pieces of airplanes. Engines smoked. Someone reported the airplane flying #6 position in the 429th rearing out of formation and falling off to the left. They, apparently, had taken a direct hit.

Then it was our turn. We were flying tail-end-charlie in the third wave (squadron) that day. Pieces were flying off our airplane. It looked as though every plane in the Twentieth Squadron was hit at the same time. The flak sounded like hail smashing onto a tin roof. The noise was deafening. Concussions from near-hits rocked the plane. I curled myself into as small a target as I could. Reports were coming in over the intercom at a rapid pace, identifying planes on fire, pieces falling off or engines smoking. From my position, every plane in the Twentieth appeared to have at least one engine feathered, or pieces flying off, or portions hanging down. I didn't think we could stand it for another minute and was convinced that every airplane in that group was going down. The flak was too accurate, too intense. Every round they fired seemed to be a hit. The air was black with smoke. The air stunk like rotten eggs from the German cordite. My eyes burned. There was no way to survive. I prepared myself to die, and did a lot of praying.

Someone noticed plane #078 from the 429th. It was *Sweet Pea*, flown by Lieutenants Guy Miller and T. M. Rybovich. *Sweet Pea* had taken a direct hit right in the waist just as it was dropping its bombs. It was flying just ahead and to the right of us when hit. Then it wandered in front of us and back over to our right before the pilots could correct its flight. That's when I had a good look at it. There was a huge hole in the waist. It looked like it was mortally hit, but miraculously *Sweet Pea* stayed in the air. Somehow the pilots managed to get it under control, and they desperately tried to keep up with the group. I believed *Sweet Pea* would never return to the field. It wasn't my job to watch *Sweet Pea*, though. Our formation was really taking it on the chin. We were in the tail end position, and it seemed like every German gun in Debreczen was firing at us. An oil inspection door whipped past us. Our squadron leader, Lieutenant E.C. Blanton, took a hit and feathered an engine.

Blanton's crew lived next door to us in Amendola and we considered Sergeants Kelly, Bajorn, Slivka, Dikes, McGeary, and Dexter good friends. Our squadron maneuvered to avoid all the debris from the 429th Squadron. We still headed for the target. Blanton was leading us right into that inferno, bad engine and all. Another plane, flown by Lieutenant L.S. Malik, had an entire wingtip shot off, and was fighting to stay in formation. They had also lost some of their superchargers. Without superchargers you can't maintain an altitude above fourteen thousand feet.

To protect myself, I wore anything that had steel in it, and kept all fingers and toes crossed. Right over target we encountered a burst that must have been less than five feet outside my waist window. The concussion slapped me in the face like I had been hit with a fist. I was stunned and my head rang like a cow bell. I don't know how we avoided any of that flak, but didn't see any new holes in the plane caused by this blast.

Malik started losing altitude. Blanton was falling back. The entire squadron was scattered at different levels. We could see that Malik was hit hard. While scattered, Lieutenant T. H. Hancock, flying in the #3 position, took a hit which completely blew off one of his engines. Hancock fought desperately to hold his altitude. About that time I began seeing many holes in our airplane, but strangely, no one on our crew had reported any personal injuries.

Another ship in our squadron, flown by Lieutenant W. J. Warren, was hit, and hit badly. He had one engine completely knocked out. Another engine was on fire but still running. My head was still ringing, and I was numb all over. Warren started down, losing altitude. Just as he started down, the plane in front and to our right, flown by Lieutenant Ralph Bischoff, received a hit as he swerved to avoid pieces of *Sweet Pea* which were still dropping. It looked like Bischoff had two engines knocked out. His #4 engine looked terrible. The cowling on #2 was shot up, smoking and losing oil, but still running. The beating we were taking was unbelievable. After what seemed an eternity, McDonnell finally called, "Bombs away!" It felt so good to be rid of those bombs in the middle of that flak. Somehow we made it over the target. All airplanes dropped their bombs on the target.

The above events took place over a twenty to thirty second time period. Total time in the flak was five minutes. The destruction and confusion during this period are almost impossible to describe. It was like a walk through hell!

Sweet Pea started straggling badly out of the formation ahead of us. I took a closer look at it from the waist. It looked horrible. From my vantage point it looked like the entire waist had been shot out. I could not believe a plane in that shape could fly. I don't know how the pilots kept the trim on it. A .50 caliber gun hung from the hole in the waist, dangling by its bungee cords and ammunition guides.

By then the Germans had their smoke pots going full blast and covering so much of the target that it was difficult to tell how effective our bombing had been. One of our squadron tail gunners did report some of our bombs right on target.

Lieutenant Ralph Bischoff, pilot of aircraft #440 on the Debreczen mission. Photo taken in Italy in 1944.
(Courtesy R. Bischoff)

We came off the target, regrouped, and headed to our rally point at Subotica. We were now able to take stock of what had happened. It looked and felt like our squadron had been shot to pieces, but we were all still in the air and still in rough formation.

Lieutenant J. G. Tulley was flying ship #200 in the #6 position in our formation. His bombardier, Lieutenant E. W. Henderson, had been hit badly in the leg, and they thought it was broken. Because of flak damage, Tulley was having problems keeping up with the formation and was forced to fly low.

Later, the crew claimed they were low enough to cut weeds in the fields they passed. Because of their low altitude, Tulley's crew spotted a dummy airfield established by the Germans to trap Allied fighters. This particular field contained fifteen dummy airplanes. It was customary for our fighter escorts, while on their way to meet bomber formations, to strafe any small airfields they might see and thereby disable any fighters on the field and prevent them from coming up to intercept the returning bombers. The Germans set up dummy fields using airplane shapes made from wood and cardboard. As the fighters swooped down on their strafing run, hidden flak batteries would open up on the unsuspecting fighters with intense small arms fire. In this case, it was the Germans who were surprised to see a B-17 fly over their decoy. This information was duly reported at the debriefing.

Warren was straggling. Malik was straggling. Bischoff was straggling. Hancock had dropped down. Blanton was straggling. We hit cloud cover and the group leader told us to scatter and get home the best way possible as the weather was too bad to hold a formation. When we emerged from the clouds, Malik, Tulley, Bischoff, and *Sweet Pea* had disappeared. It appeared every plane in the Second Bomb Group had an engine feathered, or pieces missing. My ears were still ringing so loudly I couldn't hear anything over the intercom. It looked like a long trip back to base.

For the return trip we had to cross the Dinaric Alps, the mountains on Yugoslavia's central western coast. Thank goodness they weren't as high as the Italian or Swiss Alps. The formation crossed successfully and then dropped altitude, skimming the Adriatic on our approach to Italy. Warren was still straggling badly, but managing to stay on the fringes of the formation.

What was left of the formation finally approached Amendola where the weather had improved slightly, and the field was visible through a hole in the clouds. We got into our landing pattern. Flares were fired from several airplanes as they approached, signaling wounded aboard. Ships with wounded received landing priority. At 1500, our ship landed. We were safely home with only seventeen holes, and no injuries in our crew other than our feelings and my ears. Everybody stood around the landing field, watching, waiting, hoping the others would make it back. They came in one by one—each from a different route.

One of the first in was Lieutenant Joe Carpenter's ship, #920, from the 49th Squadron. Carpenter had developed oil problems and dropped out of the formation before Debreczen, and instead went to the secondary target at Subotica. He conducted his own war with the marshalling yards in Subotica, making a single bombing run and registering good hits.

After Carpenter landed, we received a report that Tulley had flown into Foggia Main to deliver his bombardier to the hospital there. After he had lost the formation that day he had been jumped by two ME-109s. The 109s made four passes at him from the tail position. Not having any success from that angle, made four attacks from the three o'clock position, again without success. The attacks lasted about ten minutes. Tulley came out of the fight with only a couple of holes in his rudder, and his feathers ruffled.

Then Malik arrived. He had sustained serious damage to his ship. The ball turret vision plate had been blown out by flak, seriously wounding his ball turret gunner in the eyes. On his way back, Malik also played hide and seek with several ME-109s.

Warren made it. He, too, had lost many sacred things to flak. His #2 engine was on fire and another shot out. We counted eighty-five holes in his ship. On his return he had to drop to fifteen thousand feet because he had lost his oxygen system, and had inadvertently flown directly over a small flak battery of about five guns. Those guns stung him some more, but still didn't bring him down.

Hancock made it. He had sixty holes in his ship and one engine shot out. He, too, had run into more flak on the way home. Several planes crash landed while we were waiting for the others to show. Everybody was a fireman that day, getting a bucket or a hose. In one crash landing a co-pilot, Joseph McCullough, was seriously hurt.

Following several of the crash landings, Bischoff flew in with major damage to his aircraft—one engine out and one smoking. He came in on three engines, and they couldn't understand why one of those was still running. He had numerous small holes in his ship, and ten large enough to throw your hat through. Miraculously, there were no wounded. He had crossed the Alps with five hundred feet to spare, and received a bad surprise when a battery of flak guns opened up on him at this altitude. He didn't think he could make Amendola, and was prepared to ditch his ship in the water. Weather reports were that visibility was zero at the field, so he planned to follow the coast line and ditch in the water near Manfredonia and skid onto the beach. He was ready to put it in the water when the weather unexpectedly cleared at the field and he was able to get a fix on their location and land back at Amendola.

All this time we had heard nothing from *Sweet Pea*, no radio reports or sightings from any of the other ships. After about thirty minutes, we had given up expecting her. There obviously wasn't any hope of the ship even being able to fly, let alone return to the field. We all stood close to the runway, waiting, helping out where we could.

Then somebody saw her. *Sweet Pea*. Flying low and slow, she fired three red flares. Three wounded aboard. It looked physically impossible for her to be flying at all, with her entire waist section cut out. I honestly couldn't tell what was holding her together. Miller and Rybovich had to be fantastic pilots to have

Sweet Pea of the 429th Squadron, Second Bomb Group. Lieutenants Miller and Rybovich flew this damaged B-17 525 miles through inclement weather, across the Alps and the Adriatic after taking a direct hit on a mission to Debreczen, Hungary. All crew members from the waist back were either killed or wounded. *(below)* In this close-up of the damage to *Sweet Pea's* waist, look closely at the upper portion of the hole and you can see light coming through from the other side. *(Courtesy Fifteenth Air Force Association)*

brought her back. She was dragging things under and behind her. They put her down in a perfect landing, but upon hitting the ground she popped open like a ripe pea pod. Many of the spectators ran out before she stopped rolling. I joined them as several of the crew were good friends and I wanted to help. We all wanted to help.

Before I reached *Sweet Pea*, others had made it and turned back.

"How bad is it?" I asked.

"Mack, you don't want to go out there. It's real bad; you don't want to see it."

I walked up anyway. It was a mess inside. Everybody from the radio man back to the tail gunner had either been hit or killed. They had no intercom, radio, or oxygen. They had been hit just as they were releasing their bombs. The racks were hit so badly that four of twelve armed bombs remained stuck in the bomb racks. Twenty-nine minutes after they'd been hit, Staff Sergeant R.M. Mullen, the togglier, had crawled back into the open bomb bay and released the four bombs, one at a time, with a screwdriver. I lost some friends in that ship that day.

Transportation equipment quickly rolled up and hauled it away. I didn't think *Sweet Pea* would ever fly again, but she did. They cut the ship immediately behind the radio room by the back of the bomb bay doors, took the tail from another damaged B-17, and welded them together. *Sweet Pea* never flew combat again, but hauled cargo and supplies, although it didn't survive the war. One day, it caught fire over Bari and plunged to the ground.[1]

By the end of that day we were all exhausted and stunned. We had crossed the target with twenty-five aircraft, and twenty-two came back to the field, most with damage. Although all aircraft in our squadron returned, many were unserviceable for combat after that Debreczen raid.

That mission changed my whole outlook on the war. Before Debreczen we'd hit a few difficult and dangerous targets, like Munich and Budapest. We'd also had some milk runs. Over Debreczen, however, I didn't think we would come off that target. The war became more serious when I realized what the Germans could do with those guns. They were superb gunners. They knew what target we were heading to, they knew the weather conditions, and they knew where to expect us. When they cut loose like that, it was as if they had torn a big gash out of the sky, and then painted it black—and we had to fly right through it. It made me realize how vulnerable we were. I was acutely conscious of being in a little aluminum cylinder with a skin less than a thirty-second of an inch thick, held up by one hundred and four feet of aluminum wings, carrying nine or ten tons of extremely volatile high-octane gasoline, and freighting twelve five-hundred pound bombs and thousands of rounds of ammunition.

That's when the "dreads" started. That's when the post-briefing medical whiskey started tasting good. That's when I started smoking. That's when the war started getting grim, and it never let up.

About ten days after the Debreczen mission, I received a letter from my parents. They had enclosed a newspaper clipping. I kept that clipping for years because it made me so furious. I even memorized it. Released by either API or Reuters, it originated from the Mediterranean Allied Air Force Command Headquarters. That very short, bland clipping read:

> Today Fifteenth Air Force Flying Fortresses bombed marshalling yards in Debreczen, Hungary. Pilots reported visibility of the target was obscured by smoke. They were unable to ascertain how much damage was done, but they thought it was extensive. All airplanes returned safely.

This clipping made that mission sound like a trip to the drugstore for a short beer or a cup of coffee. I've been mad all these years because of that news release. Many people died or were wounded that day, and their sacrifices deserve a better epitaph than "all planes returned safely." If I ever had an opportunity, I swore to rectify that article.

Nine of the returning aircraft were unfit for further combat. To my knowledge, this was the only Group to fly a mission intended for an entire air force. On this day, 21 September 1944, I was paid $4.98, and earned every penny.

The following special narrative report is the initial report and was subsequently updated several times. Aircraft debriefing reports for the Twentieth Squadron and Second Lieutenant G. M. Miller's *Sweet Pea*, are also included.

NOTE: Colonel John Ryan, who issued the Operations Orders on page 160, was known to Second Bomb Group personnel as 'Three Finger Jack.' On one mission, because of poor visibility, he took the Group across the target three times before he was satisfied with the visibility over the target. During one of the passes he lost part of one finger, hence the nickname. Ryan later became a member of the Joint Chiefs of Staff and also served as Chief of Staff of the U.S. Air Force.

Chapter 10

[1] The photograph of *Sweet Pea* on the Amendola airfield, used on the cover of this book, as well as in this chapter, was proudly displayed at the Boeing plant during and after the war as a symbol of the B-17's excellent aeronautical engineering.

Debreczen

HEADQUARTERS
SECOND BOMBARDMENT GROUP (H)
Office of the Intelligence Officer
APO 520

SPECIAL NARRATIVE REPORT:
MISSION: 21 September 1944 - DEBRECZEN M/Y, HUNGARY.

I. ENEMY RESISTANCE

A. **Fighters:** None.

B. **Flak:** Over the target this group experienced intense, accurate, heavy flak.

Slight, accurate, heavy flak was also experienced enroute at 44 deg 54 min N, 18 deg 49 min E.

II. SIGNIFICANT OBSERVATIONS

A. **Ground:** A M/T convoy, one mile in length, was observed heading S.E., at 1126 hours at 46 deg 15 min N, 21 deg 08/10 min E, from an altitude of 16,000 feet. (Phoned into Wing A-2 as Flash News).

III. CONCLUSION

A. **Total Losses:** None.

B. **Damage:**

From Flak	22	(13 minor, 9 severe)
From Fighters	0	
Other Reasons	0	

C. **Victories:** None.

D. **Corrections on Telephone Mission Report:**

(1) Para. 4 - Time over target to read 1050/1053 instead of 1050/1052.
(2) Para. 4 - Altitude over target to read 20,000/23,900 feet instead of 22,900/23,500 feet.
(3) Para. 6 - Add 1 others, as described in Para. 6, Mission Report.
(4) Para. 12 - To read seven (7) casualties instead of two (2).
(5) Para. 14 - Weather Enroute to read 0/10/10th's cloud coverage from 2,000/22,000 feet instead of 0/10/10th's cloud coverage from 3,000/20,000 feet.

- 1 -

1522

1. UNIT **2ND BOMB** GROUP **(H)** TIME **1552** DATE **21 SEPTEMBER** 1944

2. **25** OFF TO ACTUAL TARGET **DEBRECZEN M/Y, HUNGARY.**

3. **5** EARLY **25** SORTIES

4. **25** OVER TARGET AT **1050/1053** HOURS, AT **20,000/22,200** FT.

5. **25** DROPT ON TGT **73.5** TONS **500** LB. **RDX** BOMBS **.1 nose; .025 tail** FUSING

6. **1** OTHERS B-17 No. 920, jettisoned 4 X 500 RDX's at 45-12N, 20-00E, at 1010 hours, from 20,000 feet. 8 X 500 RDX's were dropped on Subotica M/Y, Yugoslavia, at 1027 hours, from 18,000 feet. Results - a good pattern in choke point.

7. **None** E/A SEEN

8. **None** ENCOUNTERS, TIME, PLACE, ETC

9. **0** DESTROYED

   0 PROBABLE

   0 DAMAGED

10. **I-A-H** FLAK AT TARGET **S-A-H** FLAK AT **44-54N, 18-49E**

11. **0** LOST, REASONS

    0 MISSING, LAST SEEN

    0 AT FRIENDLY FIELDS

12. **7** CASUALTIES **2 killed; 1seriously injured; 4 slightly injured.**

13. **6** A/C TAKING PHOTOS

14. ROUTE AS ORDERED **Yes** BASE TO **Except for flying around weather.**

FIGHTERS RENDEZVOUS AT **1008 hours** AT **47-10N, 22-00E - P-51's.**

FIGHTERS LEFT AT **1008 hours** AT **Unknown**

WEATHER ENROUTE **0/10/10th's cloud coverage from 2,000/22,000 feet.**

WEATHER AT TARGET **Clear - hazy.**

15. TYPE BOMBING **Visual** RESULTS **Target area well covered.**

16. NICKELS DROPPED **None.**

RECEIVED BY _____ AT _____ HRS.

PHONED TO NUTMEG BY _____ AT _____ HRS.

•••SEE REVERSE SIDE•••

180

Thomas

INTERROGATION SHEET
HEADQUARTERS
SECOND BOMBARDMENT GROUP (H)

A/C No. 078 SQUADRON 429th DATE 9-21-44 MISSION NO. 279

Bomb Load 12 x 500 Target Chart No. 12-24-NA Prin. Target Debreczem M/Y
Hungary

1st Alt. ____ 2nd Alt. ____ 3rd Alt. ____

Pilot: 2nd Lt. G. M. Miller Lower Turret: Cpl. W. F. Steuck
Co-Pilot: 2nd Lt. T. M. Rybovich Right Waist: S/Sgt. J. F. Maguire
Navig.: 1st Lt. Theodore Davich Left Waist: Cpl. J. F. Totty Absenced
Bombr.: S/Sgt. R. M. Mullen Tail Gunner: Cpl. E. H. Buss Absenced
Upper Turret: T/Sgt. G. E. McGuire Radio-Gunner: Anthony Ferrara, S/Sgt.
Observer:

ROUTE FORMATION: WAVE 1 SQDN. 2 ELEMENT 3 NUMBER ____

EARLY RETURN: Turned back at ____ hrs. at ____ N. ____ E.

Reasons:

Weather Enroute: Clear Hazy 19 his -10 miles 10 cloud coverage at 12,000 ft.
Weather at Target: (Clear) Hazy 10 cloud coverage at ____ ft.
Time: Engines On 0610 Engines Off 1530 his -12 miles Bombs Away 1049

Bombs Dropped: 6x500 Bombs Jettisoned: 6x500 Bombs Returned ____

Bombing Formation: Wave 1 Sqdn. 2 El. 3 No. Bomb.Alt 23,300 ft.
Course: 355 True

Results of your Squadron's Bombing: ____
Results of other Squadron's Bombing: Not observed

Photos: None Charts Returned: ____

FLAK None Slight (Good) (Good)
at: (Heavy) Moderate Accuracy(Alt): Fair Deflection: Fair
Target Light (Intense) Poor Poor

FLAK Description: Tracking FLAK ELSEWHERE:

Length of time in FLAK: 3 min
Flak Damage to your A/C: ____
Location of FLAK batteries:
On Target Chart No. None

OBSERVATION OF E/A: Time ____ hrs. Place ____ Your Alt. ____ ft.

Number ____ Type None o'clock High Low Level Closed to ____ yds.

Actions:

Enemy A/C Damage to your A/C: None
ESCORT: Rendezvous ____ Type None Time ____ Place ____
Departure ____ Type ____ Time ____ Place ____
NICKELS DROPPED: None

TARGET CHARTS RETURNED: 3 3 photo

INJURIES: NAME RANK SERIAL NO. TYPE INJURIES:

T/Sgt. J. F. McGuire
S/Sgt. Anthony Ferrara

(Interrogating Officer)

****PUT OBSERVATIONS ON REVERSE SIDE****
(Number, Time, Place, Alt. Observed, etc.)

Cpl. J. F. Totty
Cpl. E. H. Buss

A/C NO. 203   SQUADRON 20th.   DATE 9/21/44 MISSION NO. 279

Bomb Load 12 x 500   Target Chart No. 12-24-"A Prin. Target Debreczen M/Yds M...g

1st Alt. _____   2nd Alt. _____   3rd Alt. _____

Pilot: 2nd Lt.J.G.Tulley
Co-Pilot: 2nd Lt.S.A.Townsend
Navig.: 2nd Lt.R.E.Fisher
Bomdr.: 2nd Lt. E.W.Anderson ✓
Upper Turret: Sgt. S.C.Lewis

Lower Turret: Cpl. D.B. Foley
Right Waist: Sgt. XXXXXX D.B. Tomaro
Left Waist: Sgt. J.L. Welborn
Tail Gunner: Cpl. A.S.Czulada Jr.
Radio Gunner: Sgt. A.L.Hosberg.
Observer:

ROUTE FORMATION: 1 WAVE 3 SQDN. 2 FLIGHT 3 NUMBER

EARLY RETURN: Turned back at _____ hrs. at _____ N _____ E.

Reasons:

Weather Enroute: Clear   Hazy   8/10 cloud coverage at 35M 20 km ft.
Weather at Target: Clear   Hazy   6/10 cloud coverage at _____ ft.
                                   Vis. 15 mile
Time: Engines On 0620   Engines Off 1120   Bombs Away 1047

Bombs Dropped: 12   Bombs Jettisoned: _____   Bombs Returned _____

Bombing Formation: 2 Wave 1 Sqdn. 2 El. 3 No. Bomb.Alt. 22 m ft.
                                                 Course: 36 True

Results of your Squadron's Bombing: Couldn't see for smoke was there
Results of other Squadron's Bombing:

Photos: _____   Charts Returned: _____

FLAK   None   Slight   _Good.   _Good
at   Heavy   Moderate   Accuracy(Alt.): Fair   Deflection: Fair
Target Light   Intense   Poor   Poor

FLAK Description: T/B   FLAK ELSEWHERE:

Length of time in FLAK: 5 minutes
Flak Damage to your A/C: 16 holes
Location of FLAK batteries:
         On Target Chart No. ——

OBSERVATION OF E/A: Time 1815 hrs. Place 4606N/1940 Your Alt. 68000 ft.

Number 2   Type ME 109's ; ;   o'clock High Low Level Clsed to _____ yds.
Actions: 2 planes made 4 attacks came from 6 o'clock from 30 yds, bro! and closed to 300
            " "   " "   3 o'clock and don't john and firing.   to 100 15 minutes
Enemy A/C Damage to your A/C: 2 bullet holes
ESCORT: Rondezvous _____   Type _____ Time _____ Place _____
         Departure _____   Type _____ Time _____ Place _____
NICKELS DROPPED: _____

TARGET CHARTS RETURNED: 47/cs 3 perline

INJURIES: NAME   RANK   SERIAL NO.   TYPE INJURIES:
Broken Leg E.W.Anderson 2nd Lt.   heftly cut very badly; may
                                                    be broken.
                                                    W A Hallba...
                                                    (Interrogating Officer)
                                                    1st M AC
****PUT OBSERVATIONS ON REVERSE SIDE****
  (Number, Time, Place, Alt. Observed, etc.)

serious flak - slight F/a

INTERROGATION SHEET
HEADQUARTERS
SECOND BOMBARDMENT GROUP (H)

A/C NO. 877   SQUADRON 20th   DATE 9/21/44   MISSION NO. 273

Bomb Load   12 x 500   Target Chart No. 12-24-HA   Prim. Target Debreczon M/Yds Hung.

1st Alt. _____   2nd Alt. _____   3rd Alt. _____

Pilot: 2nd Lt. R.E.Chambers   Lower Turret: Sgt. L.H. Scofield
Co-Pilot: 2nd Lt.J.W.Karsten Jr.   Right Waist: Sgt. J.J.Graham
Navig.:   2nd Lt. W.E.Lesher   Left Waist: Sgt. M.W.McGuire
Bombr.:   2nd Lt. J.J.McDonnell   Tail Gunner: Sgt. J.W.Thompson
Upper Turret: T/Sgt. J.J.Fonstermaker   Radio Gunner: Sgt. J.A.Sutton
                                        Observer:

ROUTE FORMATION: 1 WAVE 3 SQDN. 3 ELEMENT 1 NUMBER

EARLY RETURN: Turned back at _____ hrs. at _____ N _____ E.

Reasons:

Weather Enroute: Clear Hazy   9/1/10 cloud coverage at 120,00 ft.
Weather at Target: Clear Hazy   0 /10 cloud coverage at _____ ft.
                                   Vis: 8/10 miles

Time: Engines On 0618   Engines Off 15h   Bombs Away 1056.30

Bombs Dropped: 12   Bombs Jettisoned: ——   Bombs Returned ——

Bombing Formation: 2 Wave 1 Sqdn. 3 El. 1 No. Bomb.Alt. 2150 ft.
                                              Course: 354 True

Results of your Squadron's Bombing: Could't see due to smk

Results of other Squadron's Bombing:

Photos: _____ Charts Returned: _____

FLAK   None   Slight   Good   Good
at   Heavy   Moderate Accuracy(Alt.): Fair Deflection: Fair
Target Light   Intense   Poor   Poor

FLAK Description: Barrage   FLAK ELSEWHERE:

Length of time in FLAK: 3 minutes
Flak Damage to your A/C 17 holes - minor
Location of FLAK batteries:
        On Target Chart No. ——

OBSERVATION OF E/A: Time _____ hrs. Place _____ Your Alt. _____ ft.

Number _____ Type _____ : o'clock High Low Level Clsed to _____ yds.

Actions:

Enemy A/C Damage to your A/C:
ESCORT: Rendezvous _____ Type P-51's Time 1144 Place 46 10 N 1940 E

        Departure _____ Type P-51's Time 1145 Place ''   ''
NICKELS DROPPED: _____

TARGET CHARTS RETURNED: 37/6's; 1 portion

INJURIES: NAME   RANK   SERIAL NO.   TYPE INJURIES:

None.

F

W.A.Wallback
(Interrogating Officer)
1stHA.C

****PUT OBSERVATIONS ON REVERSE SIDE****
(Number, Time, Place, Alt. Observed, etc.)

INTERROGATION SHEET
HEADQUARTERS
SECOND BOMBARDMENT GROUP (H)

A/C NO. 440   SQUADRON 20th   DATE 9/21/44   MISSION NO. 279

Bomb Load 12 X 500   Target Chart No. 12-24-HA Prim. Target Debreczen M/Yds Hungary

1st Alt. _____   2nd Alt. _____   3rd Alt. _____

Pilot: 2nd Lt.R.F.Bischoff   Lower Turret: Sgt. M.J.Halfi
Co-Pilot: 2nd Lt. J.Molslag   Right Waist: Sgt. R.W. Finch
Navig.: 2nd Lt.J.J.Meade   Left Waist: S/Sgt. S.A.Krajczynski
Bombr.: 2nd Lt. J.R.Myers   Tail Gunner: S/Sgt. J.T.Griffin
Upper Turret: T/Sgt. L.L.Chambers   Radio Gunner: S/Sgt. J.I.Cahh
    Observer:

ROUTE FORMATION: 1 WAVE 3 SQDN. 2 ELEMENT 2 NUMBER

EARLY RETURN: Turned back at _____ hrs. at _____ N _____ E.

Reasons:

Weather Enroute: Clear Hazy.   8/10 cloud coverage at _5m/82m_ ft.
Weather at Target: Clear Hazy   0/10 cloud coverage at _____ ft.
    Vis: Unlimited

Time: Engines On 0615 Engines Off: 1550 Bombs Away 1051

Bombs Dropped: 12   Bombs Jettisoned: ----   Bombs Returned -- -

Bombing Formation: 2 Wave 1 Sqdn.2 El.2 No. Bomb.Alt. 22m ft.
    Course: 355 True

Results of your Squadron's Bombing: Couldn't See due to smke

Results of other Squadron's Bombing: _____

Photos: _____   Charts Returned: _____

FLAK	None	Slight		Good		Good
at	Heavy	Moderate	Accuracy(Alt.):	Fair	Deflection:	Fair
Target	Light	Intense—		Poor		Poor

FLAK Description: T/B   FLAK ELSEWHERE:
Length of time in FLAK: 3/4 minute   3/4 gun 4438/1822E 1217hr 14m
Flak Damage to your A/C: 10 hole- major   -H-1-S-1-H
Location of FLAK batteries:
    On Target Chart No. — - · —

OBSERVATION OF E/A: Time _____ Hrd. Place _____ Your Alt. _____ ft.

Number _____ Type _____ _____ o'clock High Low Level Clsed to _____ yds.

Actions:

Enemy A/C Damage to your A/C:
ESCORT: Rendezvous _____ Type P-51's Time 1105 Place 4720N/2150
    Departure _____ Type P-51's Time 1215 Place 4525N/19¼
NICKELS DROPPED: - ·

TARGET CHARTS RETURNED: 47/cb:1 picture

INJURIES: NAME   RANK   SERIAL NO.   TYPE INJURIES:

_____ (Interrogating Officer)

****PUT OBSERVATIONS ON REVERSE SIDE****
(Number, Time, Place, Alt. Observed, etc.)

INTERROGATION SHEET
HEADQUARTERS
SECOND BOMBARDMENT GROUP (H)

A/C NO. __447__ SQUADRON __20th__ DATE __9/21/44__ MISSION NO. __279__

Bomb Load __12 X 500__ Target Chart No. __9/3/44__ Prim. Target __Debreczen M/Yds__

1st Alt. _____ 2nd Alt. _____ 3rd Alt. _____

Pilot: 2nd Lt. T.A. Hancock   Lower Turret: Sgt. J.V. Melandes
Co-Pilot: 2nd Lt. S.C. Bender   Right Waist: Cpl. T.V. Fletcher
Navig.: 2nd Lt. C.W. May   Left Waist: S/Sgt. R.E. Henry
Bombr.: 2nd Lt. J.B. Atkins   Tail Gunner: Sgt. C.A. Summerfield Jr.
Upper Turret: T/Sgt. J.E. Butler   Radio Gunner: Sgt. J.H. White
                                    Observer:

ROUTE FORMATION: __2__ WAVE __1__ SQDN. __1__ ELEMENT __3__ NUMBER

EARLY RETURN: Turned back at _____ hrs. at _____ N _____ E.

Reasons:

Weather Enroute: Clear (Hazy)   C-10/10 cloud coverage at __18000__ ft.
Weather at Target: Clear (Hazy)   __/10 cloud coverage at _____ ft.

Time: Engines On __0617__ Engines Off: __1450__ Bombs Away __1050½__

Bombs Dropped: __12__ . Bombs Jettisoned: _____ Bombs Returned _____

Bombing Formation: __2__ Wave __1__ Sqdn. __1__ El. __3__ No. Bomb. Alt. __20000__ ft.
                                                      Course: __351°__ True

Results of your Squadron's Bombing: __Smoke__

Results of other Squadron's Bombing: __Good (hits__

Photos: _____ Charts Returned: _____

FLAK None Slight   (Good)   (Good)
at   (Heavy) Moderate Accuracy(Alt.): Fair Deflection: Fair
Target Light (Intense)   Poor   Poor

FLAK Description: Tracking Barrage FLAK ELSEWHERE:

Length of time in FLAK: __4 min__
Flak Damage to your A/C: __Serious__   engine out feathered
Location of FLAK batteries:
      On Target Chart No. _____

OBSERVATION OF E/A: Time __1450__ hrs. Place __45.20N 19.00E__ Your Alt. __1600__ ft.

Number __2__ Type _____ O'clock High Low Level Closed to __500__ yds.

Actions: __No Attacks__

Enemy A/C Damage to your A/C:
ESCORT: Rendezvous _____ Type __P-51__ Time __1125__ Place __46-10N 20-15E__

          Departure _____ Type _____ Time _____ Place _____
NICKELS DROPPED:

TARGET CHARTS RETURNED: __3 T/c + 2 Photo__

INJURIES: NAME   RANK   SERIAL NO.   TYPE INJURIES:
                None

                                    George B. Sweeney
                                    (Interrogating Officer)

****PUT OBSERVATIONS ON REVERSE SIDE****
(Number, Time, Place, Alt. Observed, etc.)

INTERROGATION SHEET
HEADQUARTERS
SECOND BOMBARDMENT GROUP (H)

A/C NO. 439 SQUADRON 20th DATE 9/21/44 MISSION NO. 270

Bomb Load 12 x 500 Target Chart No. 12-24-W Prin. Target Debrecen M/Yds Hungary

1st Alt. _____ 2nd Alt. _____ 3rd Alt. _____

Pilot: 1stl Lt. W.J.Warren   Lower Turret: S/Sgt. A.J.Ulrich
Co-Pilot: 2nd Lt.J.J.Hickey   Right Waist: S/Sgt. A.J.Shepard
Navig.: 2nd Lt. R.J.Galattly   Left Waist: S/Sgt. A.A.Gailey
Bombr.: 2nd Lt.G.A.Wyman   Tail Gunner: S/Sgt. J.A.Cox
Upper Turret: T/Sgt. F.Pinto Jr. Radio Gunner: T/Sgt. W.Anderson
                                Observer:

ROUTE FORMATION: 2 WAVE 1 SQDN. 2 ELEMENT 1 NUMBER

EARLY RETURN: Turned back at _____ hrs. at _____ N _____ E.

Reasons:

Weather Enroute: Clear (Hazy)   0-10 Vis'a cloud coverage at 16000 ft.
Weather at Target: (Clear) Hazy — /10 cloud coverage at _____ ft.

Time: Engines On 0610 Engines Off: 1555 Bombs Away 1049

Bombs Dropped: 12   Bombs Jettisoned: _____ Bombs Returned _____

Bombing Formation: 2 Wave /Sqdn 2 El No. Bomb.Alt 22000 ft.
                                        Course 204 °True

Results of your Squadron's Bombing: Into Smoke .
Results of other Squadron's Bombing: T/a

Photos: Took Charts Returned: _____ Excellent

FLAK   None   Slight   (Good)   (Good)
at   (Heavy) Moderate Accuracy(Alt.): Fair Deflection: Fair
Target Light (Intense)   Poor   Poor

FLAK Description: Tracking & Barrage FLAK ELSEWHERE: 1215 45-03N 18-38E
Length of time in FLAK: 7-8   5 guns accurate 15 sec
Damage to your A/C 1 Engine at #2 on fire
Location of FLAK battery: #3 out 85 knew T/S.G.
        On Target Chart No.

OBSERVATION OF E/A: Time _____ hrs. Place _____ Your Alt. _____ ft.

Number _____ Type _____ o'clock High Low Level Clsed to _____ yds.

Actions:

Enemy A/C Damage to your A/C:
ESCORT: Rendezvous _____ Type P-51 , Time To dg Place T/a .
        Departure _____ Type 51 , Time _____ Place Coast .
NICKELS DROPPED: _____

TARGET CHARTS RETURNED: 3 H & Photo .

INJURIES: NAME   RANK   SERIAL NO.   TYPE INJURIES:
                None.

George B. Sweeney
(Interrogating Officer)

****PUT OBSERVATIONS ON REVERSE SIDE****
(Number, Time, Place, Alt. Observed, etc.)

INTERROGATION SHEET
HEADQUARTERS
SECOND BOMBARDMENT GROUP (H)

A/C NO. 456   SQUADRON 20th   DATE 9/12/44   MISSION NO. 279

Bomb Load 12 X 500   Target Chart No. 12-24-14   Prin. Target Debreczen M/Yds Hungary

1st Alt. _____   2nd Alt. _____   3rd Alt. _____

Pilot: 1st Lt. E.S.Malik   Lower Turret: S/Sgt. E.J.Levin
Co-Pilot: 2nd Lt. J.C.Campbell   Right Waist: S/Sgt. F.J.Terrio
Navig.: 2nd Lt. A.L.Skinner   Left Waist: S/Sgt. T.J.Gronski
Bombr.: F/O W.D.Stricklin   Tail Gunner: S/Sgt. A.L.Hunt
Upper Turret: T/Sgt. E.T.Knitter Radio Gunner: T/Sgt. S.J.Laraccio
                                  Observer:

ROUTE FORMATION: 2 WAVE / SQDN. / ELEMENT 2 NUMBER

EARLY RETURN: Turned back at _____ hrs. at · _____ N _____ E.

Reasons:

Weather Enroute: Clear (Hazy)   Vis :15   0 - 9/10 cloud coverage at 20000 ft.
Weather at Target: (Clear) Hazy   — /10 cloud coverage at _____ ft.
                                                          Hi Stratus,

Time: Engines On 0615 Engines Off 1455 Bombs Away 1050

Bombs Dropped: 12   Bombs Jettisoned: _____   Bombs Returned _____

Bombing Formation: 2 Wave / Sqdn. / El. 2 No. Bomb.Alt 22100 ft.
                                              Course: 155 True

Results of your Squadron's Bombing: On T/c .

Results of other Squadron's Bombing: T/c

Photos: _____ Charts Returned: T/c

                                                Excellent
FLAK   None   Slight   (Good)   (Good)
at   (Heavy) (Moderate) Accuracy(Alt.): Fair Deflection: Fair
Target Light   Intense   Poor   Poor

FLAK Description: Tracking   FLAK ELSEWHERE: 1214 44. 5 8 - 14 - 3 7 1600
                                             4. acc
Length of time in FLAK: 3-5min.
Flak Damage to your A/C: Serious . Tokyo, Turbo.
Location of FLAK batteries:
          On Target Chart No. —

OBSERVATION OF E/A: Time _____ hrs. Place _____ Your Alt. _____ ft.

Number _____ Type _____ : : _____ o'clock High Low Level Clsed to _____ yds.

Actions:

Enemy A/C Damage to your A/C: _____
ESCORT: Rendezvous _____ Type - _____ Time - _____ Place - _____

          Departure _____ Type , _____ Time _____ Place _____
NICKELS DROPPED: _____

TARGET CHARTS RETURNED: 6 T/c + 3 Photos .

INJURIES: NAME   RANK   SERIAL NO.   TYPE INJURIES:
S/Sgt. Levin, E.J.   Poss. Piece of Plexiglass in eye.

                                        George B. Sweeney
                                        (Interrogating Officer)

****PUT OBSERVATIONS ON REVERSE SIDE****
(Number, Time, Place, Alt. Observed, etc.)

INTERROGATION SHEET
HEADQUARTERS
SECOND BOMBARDMENT GROUP (H)

A/C NO. 411   SQUADRON 20th   DATE 9/21/44   MISSION NO. 279

Bomb Load 12 X 500   Target Chart No. 12-24-HA Prin. Target Debrecen M/Y Hungary

1st Alt. _____   2nd Alt. _____   3rd Alt. _____

Pilot: 1st Lt. B.C.Blanton
Co-Pilot: 2nd Lt. H.L.Beynes
Navig.: 2nd Lt. I. L. Tharope
Bombr.: 1st Lt. Smith
Upper Turret: T/Sgt. H.S.Kelly

Lower Turret: S/Sgt. H.F. Bjorn
Right Waist: S/Sgt. K.K. Slivka
Left Waist: S/Sgt. D.W.Dykes
Tail Gunner: S/Sgt. J.S.McGarry
Radio Gunner: T/Sgt. L.K.Dexter
Observer:

ROUTE FORMATION: WAVE 3 SQDN. 1   ELEMENT 1   NUMBER

EARLY RETURN: Turned back at _____ hrs. at _____ N _____ E.

Reasons:

Weather Enroute: Clear Hazy 0-10/10 cloud coverage at 10-25000 ft.
Weather at Target: Clear Hazy /10 cloud coverage at _____ ft.

Time: Engines On 0615 Engines Off: 1456 Bombs Away 1050

Bombs Dropped: 12.500# Bombs Jettisoned: _____ Bombs Returned _____

Bombing Formation: 2 Wave 1 Sqdn. 1 El. 1 No. Bomb.Alt. _____ ft.
Distance from #159 -500# bbs. Ft _____   Course: 352 True
Results of your Squadron's Bombing: Went into smoke. Heading 353
Results of other Squadron's Bombing: Good, Acc.

Photos: None Charts Returned: _____

FLAK   None   Slight
AA   Heavy   Moderate   Accuracy(Alt.): Good Deflection: Good
Target Light   Intense   Fair   Fair
                                           Poor

FLAK Description: Tracking   FLAK ELSEWHERE: 1106-4705,2155-SAH
                                             (Radka)
                             1011-4630,2012-SIH Way(?)
Length of time in FLAK: 5 min
Flak Damage to your A/C _____ 15/20 hrs - Secors 1218-4952,1840-SAN G
Location of FLAK batteries:
          On Target Chart No. _____

OBSERVATION OF E/A: Time None hrs. Place _____ Your Alt. _____ ft.

Number _____ Type _____ : : _____ o'clock High Low Level Clsed to _____ yds.

Actions:

Enemy A/C Damage to your A/C:
ESCORT: Rendezvous _____ Type P 51 Time 1105. Place 4708,2150
                           Type _____ Time _____ Place _____
          Departure
NICKELS DROPPED: None

TARGET CHARTS RETURNED: ✓

INJURIES: NAME RANK SERIAL NO. TYPE INJURIES:
None

(Interrogating Officer)

****PUT OBSERVATIONS ON REVERSE SIDE****
(Number, Time, Place, Alt. Observed, etc.)

– 11 –

Precautions

By the end of September I was convinced I wouldn't make it home. At best, I would be shot down, so I began learning escape procedures. We had good Intelligence officers at the Group who took me under their care and spent extra time with me. I was determined to learn and do everything needed in order to escape if I was shot down in occupied territory.

The first order of business was to sharpen my knife to a razor-sharp edge. Knives were to cut parachute shrouds if you bailed out and became hung or tangled in trees. We'd been using them instead to open food cans. One squadron mechanic was particularly good at sharpening knives and he put a razor's edge on mine. I started spending more time firing my pistol–shooting with both right and left hands–and carrying an extra clip for the .45. In Germany, neither the knife nor the gun

James Thompson *(r.)* and McGuire practice shooting left-handed.
(Courtesy M McGuire)

would do me much good, but they would be helpful if I went down anywhere else, particularly Yugoslavia.

In addition to the big war, Yugoslavia was involved in a civil war. Three political groups, the Partisans, the Chetniks, and the Ustashi, were fighting among themselves. Two of them, the Partisans[1] and the Chetniks,[2] also fought the Germans when they weren't fighting each other. The Partisans were good fighters. The Allies supplied them with ammunition, supplies, and medicine, plus giving them encouragement and advice. They were Communists fighting under Josef Broz.

The Chetniks, fighting under General Draza Mihailovic, were the old loyalists and fought the Partisans as enthusiastically as they fought the Germans. The Partisans and the Chetniks were both considered excellent military groups, with stern and unforgiving discipline. Men and women both served in these groups. Women assumed the same combat roles and duties as men. We heard if a woman became pregnant they killed her. As far as soldiering was concerned, they made no distinction between men and women. After months of living and fighting in the mountains, you often couldn't differentiate between the sexes. Most of them wore sheepskin clothing, and were armed to the teeth with weapons and bandoleers. If a soldier got drunk twice, they killed him the second time. This was considered very stern discipline for irregulars, volunteers.

It was the third group, the Ustashi,[3] of which we were particularly horrified. Located in Croatia, the Ustashi fought with the Germans against the Partisans and the Chetniks. If you went down and landed among either the Partisans or the Chetniks, you had a good chance of escaping, but if you went down among the Ustashi, you had to fight to get out. That's why I wanted my knife sharp and my .45 ready. Few Allied fliers, who went down among the Ustashi lived to tell about it. Those that returned told hair-raising stories about their experiences and their captors. The Ustashi killed everybody, and you didn't die a good, clean death. Captured Allied airmen were either killed outright or tortured to death for information which they sold to the Germans. In some instances, we heard of our airmen being hung from street lamps in Ustashi-dominated towns. If I went down among them and couldn't fight my way out, I was going to kill myself rather than submit and be tortured.

They assisted the Germans in many ways, even serving as secret police. They had their own guerrilla force as well as a uniformed air force and flew ME-109s against us.

Intelligence told us to get to high ground if we went down in occupied territory. At that stage in the war the Partisans or resistance forces controlled the high ground, in Yugoslavia as well as in Italy. The Germans controlled the roads and communications. We all carried maps, particularly of the area where the Ustashi were active. This information was updated daily because of the ebb and flow of the battle in Yugoslavia. We also were given information on how to contact underground resistance groups in the larger cities if we went down near them.

Intelligence offered me some useful tips. In our escape kits we had two or three packages of American brand cigarettes, Camels or Chesterfields. These packages were covered with cellophane and tinfoil. We also carried chewing gum. While flying we couldn't eat because of the oxygen masks, so we popped gum in our mouths and threw away the foil. The Germans quickly learned about our habits, and were able to track down many airmen simply by following the trail of wrappers they dropped while trying to escape.

An American holds and smokes a cigarette differently than a European. We smoked a cigarette and threw away a sizable butt, but Europeans smoked them until they burned their lips. So, if the Germans found a half-burned cigarette, they knew an American had been there. Also, Americans eat differently than Europeans. When eating a meal in an open cafe in an occupied city, if you didn't hold your fork turned upside down in your left hand and used a knife with your right, you were immediately identified, regardless of how good your cover.

They taught me to take my shoes when I flew on missions. You couldn't run or walk very far in those fur flying boots with the heated socks which we wore on missions. After just a short walk you'd be a basket case because the fur boots would dry the oil out of the bottom of your feet. It felt like somebody had used a blowtorch on them. Therefore, we carried our shoes strapped to our parachute harnesses where we could get to them quickly. I generally tied mine close together.

Our escape kit contained a variety of useful items—soup, dried food tablets, drugs to keep you awake and give you energy, fish hooks, matches, Halazone tablets, a mirror, a small knife, appetite depressants, cigarettes, chewing gum, chocolate, and birdshot. Almost anything you would need to live off the land could be found in it. Two other very important items in the kit were maps, printed on silk with correct German place names so we could compare them with road signs, and a compass. Then there was the money. Each kit contained several thousand dollars, consisting of several hundred dollars in different currencies, including American dollars. Once, during a mission briefing by S-2, we were told what it would cost to bribe Hungarian border guards. Some of the brass complained we were paying them too much and creating an inflationary condition.

Therefore, we were told not to pay more than twelve dollars per guard. If necessary, I would have signed a note or given them the deed to the White House if that's what it took to get out. We carried these kits in a pocket so they would be on our person in the event of a bailout. I preferred to put mine in a pants leg pocket.

Also, we carried photo IDs for fake passports if we ever contacted the underground. Getting photos was difficult because the Germans controlled film distribution. That was the reason we carried our pictures with us. The Gestapo would still be laughing at us if they were around because of those pictures. They posed us in civilian shirts and neckties. The ties were outlandish. They looked like something out of an Alf Landon political campaign, with big Kansas sunflowers on them. The pictures all but had "American" written across our chests. Those photos, and the fact we airmen in the Fifteenth Air Force were a nice, bright yellow or orange from the Atabrine, would make it difficult to escape except for a lot of luck.

Additional protection came in the form of four stove lids about the size of coffee-can lids. I had obtained them from an airman named 'Forty Rod' when he landed in the hospital. Being cast iron, they were heavy. In that extra parachute bag I had acquired, I put a horsehair pad from a seat chute (generally issued for the Pacific campaign). In place of the machete and other items which were usually in the horsehair pad, I placed those four cast iron stove lids. This extra 'chute bag offered me added armor protection, especially when flying togglier and sitting in the plexiglass nose. In addition to the stove lids I carried bandages, a very slender, two-foot-long, high-grade steel, chrome-plated crowbar, pliers, a long-handled screwdriver, and head-space gauges for adjusting the guns.

That little crowbar, with a screwdriver on one end, always accompanied me on all flights. I had to be very careful never to get it around a compass as it would cause compass drift, but that crowbar was a vital tool if I had to pry bombs loose, trip shackles, or pry a turret loose. It was a very practical tool.

I also carried a pocketful of Italian nickels. They came in handy when loosening bomb shackles. The cocking levers had releases on top and when they froze you were supposed to use a screwdriver to release them. Italian nickels were about the same size as American nickels and were exactly the right size to fit the slots in the release screw. Besides, they were easier to carry in your pocket than a screwdriver.

Fortunately, I never had to put any of this knowledge to use, but it did provide some measure of comfort.

Chapter 11

[1] The Partisans were led by Josef Broz, aka Tito. They were Communists as dedicated to fighting loyalist Chetniks and pro-axis Ustashi as they were to fighting Germans. After September 1944, all British and Yugoslavian logistical support was sent to Tito's Partisans and withdrawn from the Chetniks. The Partisans and Chetniks, approximately 100,000 strong, engaged thirty Axis divisions in Yugoslavia. Keegan, 156, 362, 492-93.

[2] The Chetniks were resistance fighters loyal to the deposed King of Yugoslavia. They were led by Draza Mihailovic. The word Chetnik is a Serbian term meaning 'opponent,' a term coined during the Turkish occupation of the area. Although the Chetniks initially fought with the allies, they ran into disfavor when they signed a separate peace with Axis forces in the area so they could concentrate their forces in battle with the Partisans. Keegan, 492.

[3] The Ustashi were right-wing nationalists, Croatians, who proclaimed an independent state on 6 April 1941, coincident with the German invasion of Yugoslavia. Some Ustashi even battled with the Germans against Yugoslavian forces. The military value of the Ustashi forces was of such dubious quality, however, that Germany did not send them into major fronts, content to leave them in Yugoslavia to aid the Axis divisions employed in internal security operations against the Partisans and Chetniks. Keegan, 156, 363, 492.

We Can't Make It Back

23 Sept.: *Bomb Brux Bergius Synthetic Oil Refineries*
in Brux, Czechoslovakia. Flak very
heavy. Got 2 large holes in wing and a
small one in the nose. Landed at a British
fighter base 18 miles from front lines
with only 10 gals of fuel left.
Wayne Lesher
Navigator's Diary

It was 23 September, shortly after sun-up. Little black balls of clouds, whipped by the wind, crossed over the field as we stood around the tail of that mission's plane, awaiting the day's briefing by Chambers and the up-front crew. Our faces were still raw and blistered, as we weren't used to wearing those oxygen masks for five to six hours at a time. This caused some discomfort. Chambers gathered us around the tail and said, "Today our target is the Bergius Synthetic Oil Refinery in Brux, Czechoslovakia."

I groaned inwardly. A 'groaner' was our name for a long haul or a vicious target. When the briefing officer mentioned a particularly hated target and pointed to the end of that red yarn, the assembled air crews groaned in unison. The groan was involuntary, and generally followed by a lot of profanity. Two days before we had gone to Debreczen. The day before we'd hit the Allach Bayrsche Motor Worke in Munich, and today we were going to an even worse target, a real groaner target, Brux.

Chambers continued, "It's going to be a long haul. We'll be airborne eight-and-a-half to nine-and-a-half hours, depending upon winds, route, etc., so be prepared for a long one. It's heavily defended, as you all know. We've heard about Brux ever since our arrival. This is our first time to hit it, so we're now in the big leagues. Save as much oxygen as possible. We'll go on oxygen about eleven thousand feet. I'll notify you when. Wayne will now give you his part of the briefing."

Lesher stepped up. "Our route will be up the Adriatic, cross the Alps and we'll be in Austria and Bavaria. We can expect to encounter a fast-moving cold front. In about two hours we will see the forerunners of it. They have advised us there will be severe turbulence over the Alps, with occasional bad turbulence en route, so don't lay anything down that you're going to have to reach for in a hurry because we'll bounce around a lot." He named the IP, our arrival time, and the time we expected to return home.

Watching Wayne as the rising sun was shining on his face, it occurred to me there was something wrong with his face. Finally, it dawned on me that he was a bright yellow. As I looked around, all of us looked as though we had severe jaundice. It was the first time I had noticed it. The Atabrine tablets were starting to work. From that day on we looked like we belonged; we were no longer a 'new crew'. McDonnell showed us a picture of the target map, and identified the various landmarks from the IP in. He particularly asked the ball turret and tail gunners to report on the bomb strikes if they could. Our bombing altitude would be 26,500 feet. The flight would be very cold and windy, and we might have to make two bomb runs, depending upon the weather over the target. We groaned and hoped not.

Chambers asked Karsten to give us an intelligence report on opposition. The number of guns on the target was another groaner. We could expect considerable fighter strength in that area and along our track as there had been much activity lately.

Chambers announced we would be boarding in about three minutes. Start engine time would be in about fifteen minutes. Thompson and I walked to the tail. He took out his little blue Bible and read a passage. We briefly discussed it, said a quiet prayer, then boarded the aircraft and shut the hatches. Our aircraft was relatively new. Outside of a few patches and nicks here and there, it still retained its Stateside gleam.

I remember the dryness in my mouth and imagined myself almost able to spit dirt. We were still shaken from the Debreczen raid and the day before at Munich, where we had taken another beating. Perspiration formed on my upper lip and all of us were doing some heavy thinking and breathing. A canteen of cold coffee from that morning's mess hall helped as I swished it around my mouth before drinking it. It was good to have moisture back in my mouth.

Take-off was another sweat job, but all aircraft took off safely. As we neared the head of the Adriatic, three freighters zig-zagged through the water below us, probably on a course from or to Trieste. This information was reported and immediately flashed back to the Fifteenth Air Force. In an idle moment, I thought how much fun it would be if we could drop a couple of bombs. Their zigs and zags were about equidistant. We might even get lucky if we put a bomb down the center line, although maritime shipping wasn't the Fifteenth's problem; that belonged to a tactical air force.

As we approached the Alps, that cold front came across our track. Big, black clouds that seemed to have no tops, rolled across the Alps. The portion of that mountain range that we could see was breath-takingly beautiful. Every time we crossed the Alps, my admiration for that ancient general, Hannibal, grew. Transporting elephants across that rugged mountain range was a phenomenal feat. Those peaks looked sharp enough to impale anyone who fell upon them.

Until this time the flight had been uneventful, then we hit the turbulence. Lesher wasn't kidding when he said there would be bad turbulence. In the waist, where we were standing, I felt like a spring on a diesel truck—up, down and sideways. There were some teeth-rattling motions. Everything that wasn't stowed carefully was bouncing around. It was about as bad a turbulence as I ever encountered in all my years as a pilot. Sometimes we were almost turned around, it was so vicious. As we entered a black layer of clouds, in the distance and off on our starboard wing, we heard a loud shattering blast and felt the shock wave. Each man said a silent prayer as we knew what had happened. One plane had collided with another and the bomb loads had detonated. When we had crossed the Alps and were over Austria, again we were surprised that the weather there was better than in Italy. German weather always seemed better than Italian. Layered clouds moved across our track but they were nothing like what we had just crossed.

As the squadron moved back into battle formation, after having loosened up earlier because of the turbulence and instrument conditions, Lesher announced we were running a few minutes behind schedule. This was a serious matter. By being late, you could miss your escort or arrive at the IP simultaneously with another squadron. We didn't realize then that the weather had delayed the entire Fifth Wing.

A few minutes later we saw a jet in the distance below. He wasn't interested in us. An occasional cloud of dust boiling up from the dirt fields below indicated fighters were taking off, so we could expect some fighter activity in that area. Those dust clouds were our clue as to whether the fighters were taking off or landing. There was little dust when they landed.

About ten minutes before the IP turn, we donned our flak vests and steel helmets. I helped Scofield with his gear as it was very difficult for him to put his on while sitting in the ball turret without disconnecting his oxygen system or one of his umbilicals. It was very cold and our heated suits were on the high position. Looking over Graham's shoulder as we turned on the IP, I could see the group ahead of us being pounded. I became nauseated and was afraid I would up-chuck. We were all mentally preparing to run the gauntlet at that place we had heard so much about. Now, I could see why.

Thirty seconds or so off the target, an 88 shell exploded off the left horizontal stabilizer. I had been bending over the gun, using it for a shield, when my leg kicked up like a can-can dancer's. Simultaneously, I was slammed into the other side of the airplane, disconnecting my throat mike. For a few seconds I was numb, particularly in my arm. Graham said, "McGuire's down." As I struggled to regain my footing, another explosion on the opposite side slammed me chest first back into the .50 caliber. Again I landed in a crumpled heap while trying to assess what was wrong. The pain in my right arm led to me believe I had been badly hit. In the process of trying to get to my feet, I looked down. There, beneath my feet, was a huge gash. It looked two feet long, but actually was only about six to eight inches long. My arm still felt numb, as did my hip. Checking for damage, I felt inside my clothes but couldn't find anything in the vicinity of my right shoulder until I saw the fastener on the flak vest. Its disfigured and distorted condition indicated a hit. Ordinarily, I only fastened the right shoulder snap, to quickly remove the jacket in the event we bailed out. Once I could move my hand a bit, I checked my foot. My right foot, which had been directly over the gash had a furrow in the boot heel. Deciding my injuries weren't fatal, I tried to determine the extent of the damage. That is when I discovered my mike had become disconnected. I hastily retrieved the cord and reconnected.

Both blasts sounded and felt like we were flying in a tin barn. The aircraft had jerked, slewed, and sounded like it was flying through a heavy tin obstacle course. A few seconds later the bombardier called, "Bombs away. Bomb bay doors coming closed. Somebody check."

Another announcement warned us to stand by for the turn to the rally point.

Chambers' very calm voice came on. "Would everybody check in? Let's see if we have any casualties."

Thompson reported, "This is tail, I'm not hit but I've got lots of holes back here. There's holes every place."

I said, "This is left waist. I don't think I'm hit. We've got holes all over. I can see daylight every place."

And Graham said, "I'm OK, but we're losing fuel out of #4. We've taken two bad hits in the starboard wing."

Scofield reported, "I'm alright. We've got some holes down here. One of them bounced off one of the guns, but it seems to be alright. I'm OK."

Sutton said, "I'm alright. I've got holes all over the place. The hatch even has holes in it."

"I've even got holes in the turret," commented Fenstermaker, "but I'm going to start transferring fuel immediately. We have a bad fuel leak out here, Lieutenant. I think you should give that #4 engine a shot with the fire extinguisher, just in case." Apparently Chambers and Karsten were trying to feather the #4 engine.

Karsten continued the check-in. "We're alright up in the cockpit, but we've lost the #4 engine. Don't know if we can get it feathered. We're losing fuel."

Lesher said, "We only have one hole up here."

Then McDonnell concluded with, "I'm OK."

We settled down to watch for fighters. Fenstermaker came over the intercom, "Graham, take a look. Can you see the hole from your position?"

Graham replied, "There's one at the base of the #4 fuel cell, a big one, and apparently, although I can't see it, there is another one close to the #4 tank that is also good-sized. We've got holes every place."

Chambers said, "Scofield, can you see out to the #4 and determine what we've got out there."

In a moment Scofield answered, "No, lieutenant, I can't."

Graham announced he was disconnecting to check our control cables. He picked up an emergency oxygen bottle and walked along the cables, feeling the top and bottom as he walked. At the tail he checked on Thompson and then came down my side, still checking cables. After checking the radio room and the bomb bay, he reported, "Right waist to pilot. None of our control cables have been bothered, but we're carrying a bunch of holes. The tail wheel appears to be alright, but we've got holes in the horizontal stabilizer and the elevators."

Thompson added, "We've got some in the vertical stabilizer as well. Just about every place you look there are holes."

Fenstermaker then said to Graham, "We've got to start transferring this fuel. I'm going to be overloading the generators, so would everybody turn his heated suit off? I know it's rough, especially for Scofield and Thompson, but turn them off now." We turned off everything electrical. Scofield turned his turret down and came up with his head inside the plane.

It was quiet for a bit, then Chambers asked Fenstermaker, "How are we coming?"

"The pumps are transferring alright, but it looks like we've lost a lot of gasoline out of #4, and it's still coming out."

I looked out over Graham's side. The wing was wet with fuel spraying back from the base of the engine nacelle. John reported, "I can't tell whether the cell has been holed, but I suspect it has. I'm trying to get what's left transferred as fast as possible. Let's hope nothing happens to the pumps. I'll be out of the turret."

My heart was in my throat. I was still exploring to see if I had really been hit. My arm continued to hurt. Finally, I decided I was uninjured. My biggest worry was standing over that hole and the possibility of my foot going through it if I put weight on it. I carefully avoided that spot.

Suddenly, I realized we were no longer in formation. It was disappearing in the distance. I thought, "My God, we're straggling!" This was our first time to straggle and I knew Amendola was at least seven hundred miles away, across a very, very dangerous area. Whenever you discover you are alone, it is a shock, especially when it is your first experience. I wanted to holler, "Wait for us," but the rule was inexorable; you didn't slow the majority down to wait for one. Slowing down for one straggler was a good way to lose all aircraft. We were on our own—a long way from home.

At my position, I thought, "If I were Chambers, what would I do?" Soon after that he called, "Pilot to navigator. Let's not worry about the rally point. Give us a course for the straightest, quickest point home."

Lesher responded, "You're on it. You'll have to detour once or twice around the heavily defended areas like Prague and Pilsen, but stay with the course we've got and we should come out at the base of the Alps at the Berchtesgaden. We've still got some winds bothering us a little, but it seems like they're swinging around a bit to the corner for us. If this keeps up, pretty soon we'll have a tail wind. Let's hope for that."

Karsten, Chambers, Fenstermaker and Lesher conducted a lengthy conversation. The rest of us were in a high state of alert, looking for fighters. Suddenly, I saw a glint or flash of light, watched it a second before calling, "Unidentified aircraft at about eleven o'clock low. I don't know what it is, but it's paralleling our course." Soon McDonnell identified it as another B-17, also straggling home at a much lower altitude. We were slowly overtaking him, so we knew he was probably fatally hit. We were both on the same course, heading for the Alps and trying to hit them in the Berchtesgaden area. Tears came to my eyes at the thought of what was going through their minds. As slow as we were going, if we were overtaking them they probably had two engines out, but the distance was too great to tell. We watched them until they finally disappeared under some lower clouds. We never knew their group or if they had bailed out, were shot down, crashed, or managed to land.

Graham called Fenstermaker, "John, we've quit losing fuel. The wing is a little damp, but there is no more spray. Either it's getting empty or you're getting it out."

During one of his communiques to the pilots, Lesher said, "We've lost about two hours fuel, and there's no way we're going to make it home."

A sudden quiet descended upon the back for about the next thirty minutes. Fenstermaker finally told Scofield he could operate the ball turret, so he went down and began helping on the lookout. Without the heated suits we were shivering and trying to still our chattering teeth. Prague was on our port side and we gave it a very wide margin to avoid flak. Soon we would be seeing Pilsen on the starboard. We were splitting the difference between those two hot spots.

The pilots took advantage of an overcast by closely hugging the underside. If jumped, we could quickly duck into it. About then Thompson called, "Tail to crew, we have a bunch of bogies at about five o'clock. It looks like they're going to parallel us. I don't know what they are." Soon he added, "I think we have about twelve or fifteen back here. They're coming up real fast. They're not pointing at us and look like they're going to fly parallel to us and they're level with the cloud base." We had a chance against two or three, but not against that many. Fenstermaker returned to the top turret and we prepared for the worse. Then Thompson said, "I believe they're P-51s, but I'm not sure yet."

John Fenstermaker, flight engineer, by his top turret.
(Courtesy M. McGuire)

The unknown aircraft passed by on our starboard wing and four peeled off to move closer to us. We were prepared to fire when they presented their profile and rocked back and forth. Sutton acquired radio contact and said, "They're ours. They have the right call sign." About that time we could see that big star on the wings and side. Very carefully they slid in toward us as they looked us over and waved. One radioed, "Big friend, the area is full of EA (enemy aircraft). Keep your gunners awake, they might have to earn their pay. You have other cripples coming behind you. We've stayed as long as we could and are cutting our fuel pretty thin, so we're on our way home. Good luck." With that they rocked their wings and faded into the distance. For a short time we felt good.

There was still much conversation going on between the upfront crew. John asked Lesher for some calculations. Between the Regensberg-Munich areas, I'd been watching a group of bombers off in the distance underneath us. Flashes from cannon fire and tracers indicated they were heavily engaged and we'd seen parachutes of both colors. At least the white ones were easy to see.

"Left waist to tail, are those B-24s at about 6:30 now?"

Thompson replied, "I believe so. I can't see a big tail, so they probably are B-24s."

Scofield chimed in from the ball turret, "Roger, they're B-24s. I've been watching them. They're getting the hell shot out of 'em. I don't believe they're ours."

"No," I said, "it looks like they're heading for France or Belgium. Also looks like they're losing the fight."

Scofield added, "There've been several parachutes since I've been watching. They're giving a good account of themselves. I hope those fighters don't see us."

I watched until they faded into the distance. They were heavily engaged, but it was difficult to see details of the fight other than bright flashes, tracers, and smoke. It was one hell of a fight. We decided they were Eighth Air Force going home through France.

Later Chambers said, "You fellows in the back end, I'm sorry to keep you in the dark. I know you are dying of curiosity. I don't have anything real good to tell you, but I can tell you this much. We're not going to get home with the gasoline we've got, although we're not sure how far we can go. We've figured it every way we could. Do any of you back there have any suggestions? Mack, what do you think?"

"Lieutenant, will this thing clear the Alps?"

"I believe so. I don't think it will be a problem getting across the Alps unless we get into heavy icing or it gets too wild."

"Well, Lieutenant, Switzerland is just off our starboard side right now. We could go there. We would have to fight standing patrols all the way in, but we have lots of ammo. If we're lucky, we can be interned. I don't want to be interned, unless that's our last resort. If we bail out here we'll be prisoners of war and the areas where the partisan underground are active are behind us. This is the way I feel, we can cross the Alps, hug the Italian coast line, and then go until we run out of fuel. We can bail out or ditch while we still have some power. We had white caps this morning so it will be rough ditching. Maybe we will get lucky. Can we make Ancona?"

The Eighth Air Force had problems similar to ours.
(Courtesy Lassiter Collection)

"No. We've looked at that possibility."

"Lieutenant, I'm pretty sure I either heard on the radio or read in yesterday's *Stars and Stripes* that the British Eighth Army has captured Rimini."

Lesher interjected, "Rimini is about sixty miles from Ancona, Ralph. From my bomb line coordinates, it doesn't show our line that far up."

I said, "I'm positive I heard on the radio that the British Army did capture it. If that will help, let's go for broke. I don't want to be a prisoner of war and I want to stay out of Croatia. I propose we go for it, hug the Italian coast line, go as far as possible and hope air-sea rescue can get to us before the E-boats. Maybe later we can drop turrets and guns over board to pick up some speed. I'd hate to do that now because we have EA around us. They're having a hell of a fight behind us with some B-24s. If they discover us, we're going to need everything we have. Otherwise, without guns we're going to be another oakleaf cluster on some Kraut pilot's Iron Cross."

Chambers laughed and said, "I reckon with you."

Scofield ran his turret up and waved his approval. Graham turned around and gave me the thumbs up signal and Thompson said, "This is tail and I'd like to see us go as far as we can. I agree with Mack."

"I'm glad you fellows feel that way because that's what we'd already decided to do. Maybe we'll get lucky. We've got a quartering wind now, and a tail wind would help us squeeze out a few more miles. Keep your parachutes handy. If I ring the bell once, get your 'chutes on. If I ring it twice and leave the bell on, that means salvo the hatches and bail out. If I'm able to give voice commands I will. We had decided to go whole hog, go for broke, so you fellows say your prayers."

My blood felt as though it had turned to ice water. Those were words I had hoped never to hear. Deep in thought, I was feeling sorry for myself, but also highly alert. A fighter attack, if it came, would come quickly. Then there wouldn't be much time for thinking.

Busy formulating an escape plan predicated on getting out on the Italian side, I had forgotten the cold. If we jumped, I was heading for the high ground. The Gothic Line was stalemated, with possibly the exception of the break through to Rimini, so there wasn't much chance of escape there. The intercom was quiet as everybody was occupied with their own thoughts.

Noise from the intercom was beginning to irritate me. The Germans had been jamming it all day, they always did. I hadn't paid that much attention to their efforts before, but that awful 'O-ring, O-ring, O-ring' (some airmen swore it was 'Goering, Goering, Goering'), got on your nerves after a while, especially when you were listening as hard as we were. I looked at Graham and could see his eyes crinkle as he smiled. He always made me feel good and helped me relax, and that was a tense time. As we approached the Alps, the heavy clouds were no longer the threatening dark type we'd seen that morning. Maybe we'd get lucky there. Dropping the ball turret and then trying to ditch was a hazardous way to land. When you ditched with the gaping hole where the ball turret used to be, the airplane came to a screeching halt with that hole acting as a giant scoop, filling the waist with water or sand. The pilot had to drag the tail to keep the nose out of the water as long as possible to keep from diving into the water. Ditching would be tough on us in the back and about the only thing we could do was get go to the radio room, open the radio room hatch and hope it wasn't damaged so badly we couldn't exit from there. The only thing left was to sweat and pray.

Fenstermaker's voice came on and I jumped about a foot because it was so unexpected. "Lieutenant, I think I'd better transfer some fuel from the #2 engine into the #3. It's getting a little low and the cylinder heads are getting a little too hot. We can't afford to lose two on one side, so I'll transfer a little bit of the fuel now." Chambers told him to go ahead. It was a good idea as we certainly didn't want them all out on one side.

Surprisingly, the trip across the Alps wasn't bad. It was instrument flying weather–turbulent and a little icing. Shortly Lesher said, "We're clearing the Alps and are now abeam of

Udine." I was feeling better every minute. It was like being in a crap game for your life. In desperation and helplessness we were talking to the airplane. "Come on Baby, you can make it. Another hundred miles," and similar words of encouragement. Once, I even discovered myself standing on tip-toes to try and lighten the airplane. By then Chambers and Karsten had the nose down and we were running between layers of clouds. The shore line was obscured. Chambers asked Lesher for a course that would keep him ten to fifteen miles offshore. That told us we were over water.

During our gradual descent we had picked up speed. Chambers was on the radio to 'Big Fence,' that Allied lifeline of DF (Direction Finding) stations that had saved the lives of countless Fifteenth Air Force airmen. Big Fence knew we were trying for Ancona, but didn't have enough fuel to make it. We asked for verification that Rimini belonged to our side. Big Fence replied, "Indeed it does. They are still fighting in that area, so I would suggest you move closer to shore. Keep in contact. I know your problem and I'll tell you when to turn."

With every revolution of those three props our chances were improving, but a miss was as good as a mile, as I reminded myself. We had increased our speed considerably. At twenty-four thousand feet the pilots lowered the nose to pick up speed from the lower altitude, so my prayers, and everybody else's I sure, were intensified. We were so close, so close. Finally Lesher said, "I've got us abeam of Ravena, that's seven miles offshore. That's the best I can do fellows. We're abeam of Ravena."

"Where's that," Chambers asked?

"It's about twenty-five to thirty miles, I believe, from there to Rimini."

About that time the #2 engine started banging and Karsten said, "The stand pipes are up (above the level of gas in the tank). Let's rock it a little and see what we can do." This procedure kept it running for a short time, but then, with a bang, the #3 engine cut out.

With that loss Chambers again called Big Fence. "Big Fence, give us a steer to the nearest friendly field. We're running out of engines fast. We're losing what we've got left."

Big Fence came back and said, "Tweet Tweet Charlie. Hold what you've got and in a minute or two I'm going to tell you to turn." We held our heading until Big Fence came back on and gave us a particular heading. You have a British field eighteen miles dead ahead of you, which you should be seeing it any time now. You're still over enemy lines." Because of the danger from friendly fire, we had made sure our IFF (Identification Friend or Foe) was back on.

On those instructions we dropped out of the last layer of clouds and directly on top of a very startled line with Germans running every place. It must have been quite an apparition; a B-17 coming out of the clouds with its engines banging and popping. The Germans were so dumbfounded that, even though we weren't very high, we didn't receive any ground fire. By then the #2 engine was feathered.

Chambers said, "I don't see a field."

About that time McDonnell said, "I can see a Hurricane fighter[1] coming out of that field right dead ahead of us. It looks like it's just a few miles ahead."

Chambers took the frequency furnished by Big Fence and called. "Mayday, Mayday. This is Tweet Tweet Charlie. I'm out of gas and losing engines. Please clear us for a straight in approach. This is a Mayday."

A British voice came back very quickly and said, "Tweet Tweet Charlie, you're not cleared to land. DO NOT LAND. There is an operation going on at this time. You're not cleared to land. We suggest you land on the beach. You are not cleared to land at this installation. Do not attempt to land at this installation."

About that time engine #1 started banging and popping and Chambers said, "You go to hell. We're out of gas and full of holes. Get out of the road."

We were horrified. It was an unwritten law that an airman or aircraft in distress would be given priority over almost anything. We'd have let Hitler land if his intentions were good and he had been in a crippled airplane. These were our allies and they weren't going to do the same for us. Chambers took a look at the field and racked the plane around to take the longest portion. I swear the landing gear had just snapped into place when we touched. We didn't run too far and our passage put deep ruts in the soft earth. A nearby tetrahedron (a sheet iron wind tee) set a few feet above the ground lost its encounter with our wing. Other than a deep dent in our wing and destroying the tetrahedron and putting ruts in their field, we inflicted no real damage. With brakes locked we came to a stop not far from a large gasoline dump area which probably contained a thousand barrels of fuel. Each barrel proclaimed, 'Texaco. Made in USA. Lend-Lease. Aviation Fuel.'

After I opened the waist door and jumped to the ground, my legs were shaking so badly they would hardly hold me. The others joined me and Chambers came down the waist, checking the damage inside the airplane.

About that time we spotted a vehicle with a long antenna and flag coming across the field. We had removed our fur gear and fur boots and were wearing our G.I. shoes, but we still wore our Mae Wests, sidearms, and parachute harness. Chambers joined us and we were congratulating each other when this vehicle drove up and stopped. There were three officers in the vehicle. The one with three 'pips' on his shoulders appeared to be the commanding officer. He was a smallish, insignificant individual that needed a haircut, and was wearing a purple, polka-dot ascot. The one in back was wearing a red beret and could have been a military police officer. He was a big man.

Chambers and Karsten moved forward a few feet to meet them. Once their vehicle stopped, the one that appeared to be the commander stood up and shook a stick at Chambers. Livid with rage, he shouted, "You have landed at a British military installation after receiving express orders not to. You have halted an important military operation. You have destroyed Crown property, and I intend to impound this aircraft and place you and your crew under arrest."

For a moment Chambers could only stare at him. About this time Karsten uttered an expletive deleted type of comment. Chambers looked at the Britisher and very calmly said, "Mister, we're sorry that we've destroyed Crown property. We're sorry that we've halted a military operation, but you listen to this. I said we were out of gasoline, NOT ammunition. This airplane belongs to the Fifteenth Air Force of the U.S. Army Air Corps. I took it out this morning and I'm taking it home, and nobody, but nobody, is going to arrest any of my crew."

With Chambers' pronouncement Karsten twirled around and ran back to the airplane. I wondered why. Then we heard the master switches come on and a few seconds later the top turret rotated around with the guns pointing into the gas dump. That action certainly wasn't lost on the other two British officers who said something to the first officer. Then he looked up and saw the guns. His glance went back to Chambers very coolly standing there with his hands on his hips. The rest of us took our cue from Karsten and returned to our gun positions. That is, all except Fenstermaker and Graham who were working around the #4 engine. One was holding the other up so he could have a better look at the nacelle on the #4 engine.

The officer with the red beret said, "These guys are going to fight. You had better make a phone call." After a quick conference, the commanding officer sent a short radio message and announced, "We'll be back."

Chambers said, "We'll be here. We need fuel and must make some repairs if possible." The man glared at him and left. Chambers had not raised his voice. He just stood there with his hands on his hips.

It wasn't long before I noticed three truck-loads of British soldiers that had driven up and parked on a little knoll not far away. One truck had a .30 caliber machine gun mounted on the vehicle, but they weren't making any threatening moves. The ball turret slowly rotated toward them. I didn't want to kill anybody, but it would take only a second or two to chew up those trucks. I did wonder if they had mortars. All day we had been trying to stay alive and, now, to face this from our Allies!

We were still incensed by their rudeness. Perhaps they had a right to be mad, but we had a right to stay alive.

In a short while, the three officers returned. Their commander said, "Alright, how much gas do you have to have?" Graham had measured the remaining gas. Since all the stand pipes were above the fuel level, there was probably ten gallons or less in the entire airplane. We had gone just as far as it would go.

Fenstermaker said, "Lieutenant, I believe we can make repairs on that #4 engine. It looks like the main fuel line has been shot in two. There's a little problem with the tank that could be fixed if we have lots of tape, screwdrivers, and tools. Also, I need some tin snips."

The Britishers listened carefully and the commander said, "I will notify the RAF." Apparently, these were British engineers who had just opened this operation. We were still a short distance from Rimini, and this field was right on the beach. The commander spoke into his radio again and soon the trucks left. We hadn't been bluffing and were certainly prepared to shoot if Chambers had said, "Fire." Our fire power could have destroyed that whole operation in less than ten seconds. We had won that battle.

Soon, some unarmed soldiers wandered over. They walked around the airplane admiring it, counting the holes, and oohing and ahhing. One walked up and, in his almost incomprehensible accent, said, "I heard you chaps were prepared to fight."

I responded, "Yeh, we were fixing to clean this place out." Two others were helping Karsten count holes. Some said we had 192 holes. Two were very large—one in the wing and the one under my feet. Everything from the bomb bay back had been punctured, however there was nothing we could do other than try to repair the #4 engine.

RAF mechanics drove up in a truck with tools, tape, and ladders. Fenstermaker and Graham, with help from some very good and affable RAF men, started to make the repairs. The RAF men thought the situation extremely hilarious. In the meantime we were standing close to the airplane in the event we had to get inside it quickly, but there was no longer any hostile intent on their part. A D8 Caterpillar was parked close by and Scofield thought he could repair the damage we had done to their field in ten minutes, but they had already begun shoveling dirt into the ruts so their operation could continue.

The Hurricane carried a bomb between its landing gear, so it only cleared the ground by an inch or two. If they had hit a rut it would hit the bomb, flip the airplane, and probably detonate the bomb. There was a legitimate reason for their concern and anger. The RAF types seemed very understanding.

We relaxed somewhat and speculated about our situation if we had to leave the airplane there. It would need to be towed out of the way and we'd have to get transportation from an American unit. Our problem was solved when Fenstermaker said, "We can do it, Lieutenant. It isn't going to hold for very long, but if we can get five hundred gallons of gas we can make it home. We will just put a little in #4 and when we get off the ground we'd better feather it as that tape will not hold it for very long. That is the best we can do under the circumstances."

The British CO returned as we were getting the cowling closed. "When are you going to get your aircraft out?"

Chambers replied, "We've just finished the emergency repairs and will be leaving in a few minutes."

Meanwhile their gas buggy had fueled us with exactly five hundred gallons. As the gas buggy drove off, the British commander said, "And who is going to pay for this?"

Chambers looked at him and very coolly said, "Mister, you just send me the bill." We don't know if they ever sent a bill or not.

We rutted their field again as we jockeyed into position to take off from the longest portion of this short field. The take-off was easy as we were without bombs or a full load of fuel. Once airborne, we turned and came back over the harbor and then headed for Ancona.

After we landed, I was sitting across from Chambers on the drive to the debriefing. He was exhausted mentally and physically. I pondered the many decisions that he'd made that day, and every one had been right. He must have felt me looking at him because he turned around. I grinned and he grinned back. "Well, old buddy," he said, "we earned our pay today."

I said, "Yes, sir, we won't have to back up to the paymaster this month."

That mission bonded our crew.

Chapter 12

[1] The Hawker Hurricane entered RAF service in December 1937. A single-seat fighter propelled by a Rolls-Royce Merlin liquid-cooled engine, it was the first British fighter to fly faster than 300 mph. By the Battle of Britain, 7 August 1940, 2,309 Hurricanes (thirty-two squadrons) were available to meet the German air blitz. The Hurricane provided the backbone of air fighter defense against the Germans. It was rugged, hard-hitting, more maneuverable, under 20,000 feet, than the German ME-109, and its metal tubing and fabric construction made it easy to repair. McGuire's crew probably noticed the Mark IV Hurricane, which was built as a ground-support weapon with a universal armament wing which could mount guns, bombs, or rockets. The fighter was operation until 1947. A total of 14,000 Hurricanes were built before production stopped in 1944. It was powered by a 1,030-hp engine, could reach speeds of 318 mph, and had a ceiling of 36,000 feet and a range of 460 miles. Its primary armament was eight .303 machine guns. Simon & Schuster, p. 290; Wheal, et al., pp. 208-09; Rand-McNally, p. 124.

− 13 −

Hollywood Meets
The Amendola Ritz

Before one mission I noticed a flare as I entered the plane. Not knowing who had put it in there, or why, I was suspicious, since I had never seen one exactly like it. Perhaps it was a white phosphorous flare dropped for Pathfinder missions,[1] so I stowed it−a decision I would regret.

Because of sabotage, we were very suspicious of strange objects in airplanes. At a nearby field we had recently lost four B-24s to sabotage. Somebody had placed a pressure bomb, set to detonate at a certain altitude, on one of the planes. When it exploded, it set off the bombs in the 24, and took with it three other planes from the formation. Therefore, we were sensitive about the possibility of sabotage. For a while a man slept on every airplane even though guards patrolled around them to make sure nobody put anything aboard.

Sabotage was a rare thing, but it did happen, and was one of the things we looked for before each mission. This threat made me suspicious of this strange kit. I didn't know who had put it in the plane, or for what reason, even though we carried a lot of flares.

Most flares were signal flares stored in the pilots' cockpit. Each day's mission had its own flare color codes. On one mission we might fire two reds and a green which meant, "I'm Twentieth Bomb Squadron, I'm lost, and where's Mama?" The rumor was that firing a white flare and lowering your wheels meant you were surrendering.

On that particular mission I stowed this strange flare kit somewhere in the waist compartment once I had determined it wasn't a pressure bomb. As the mission proceeded, I forgot about it.

As usual we ran into heavy flak that day and after flak had come through the plane, one of the crew called over the intercom, "Fire in the waist!" We all feared burning to death in one of those airplanes and had seen planes plummet in flames to the ground. My frequent nightmares about our plane catching on fire came true on that day.

I was at left waist gun that mission. This plane came with plexiglass enclosing the waist gun position. Plexiglass had its advantages because you didn't get so cold, but a speck on the window looked like a fighter coming at you. When somebody yelled fire, I looked from the waist gun into the compartment and saw flames, smoke, and burning phosphorus from that flare kit I had stowed. The smoke and fire were moving from front to rear. I quickly ran over to it. Evidently the flare had been set off by white-hot flak and it was burning brightly. That flare had to be removed from the airplane or we'd catch fire. Airplanes are extremely vulnerable to fire because of the numerous oxygen and gasoline lines, leaking hydraulic lines, as well as the gun oil, and gun oil soaked rags we carried for cleaning. Oil-soaked rags did not freeze as easily.

Immediately, I grabbed the burning flare and raced to our camera well, but then remembered we had a camera aboard that day and there wasn't an available hole. Since I couldn't throw it out of the waist gun position because of the plexiglass, I raced back to the inspection plate near the ball turret.

That day I was wearing three pairs of gloves—heavy leather, heavy wool, and the inner, heated silk gloves. In my haste I accidentally disconnected the umbilical cord containing my oxygen hose, mike cord, headset cord, and heated suit cable. Lack of oxygen was making me light-headed. I opened the inspection plate to stuff that burning flare through the hole. It did not want to go out. As I pushed and pushed, the fire burned through all the gloves and started on my hands. The flare still did not want to go out. The pain was extreme.

Graham, at the other waist gun, kicked me to get my attention since I was no longer on the intercom. Somehow he had opened the waist door, and managed to hold it open with a belt or strap. The fire continued to eat into my hands. Scofield came out of the turret. I picked up the burning flare and raced back to the waist door, still dragging my umbilical connections behind me. Finally, I reached the waist door and tossed it out. The flare disintegrated and exploded just as it left the plane, displaying the full magnificence of the flare. I worried about the planes underneath us, but my first concern was to get that burning flare out of our plane. The entire incident seemed to take an eternity, but probably was only about twenty seconds.

The others poured gun oil on my hands which weren't hurting too badly at that moment, but the pain was very bad by the time we returned from the mission. In addition to battling the hurt, I hid my condition from Chambers and the others in the crew. Chambers would have sent me to the Flight Surgeon, who would have grounded me for some missions. If that happened, the crew would get ahead of me in missions and I wouldn't be able to fly with them anymore. Staying with my crew was very important to me.

After the mission I casually strolled over to the flight surgeon's office in the hospital clinic and asked a medic for some burn ointment. I made very light of it.

The attendant looked at my hands. They didn't look too bad at the time, so he applied ointment and bandages and gave me some to take back to the tent. He didn't ask how I had acquired the burns, and I didn't volunteer any information. He probably thought the burns had been caused from lighting our tent stove, as that was a common occurrence. I didn't want anybody in our crew to see my hands.

We didn't fly the next day, and I was by myself in our tent, lying on my cot with all this stinking stuff on my hands. By then they were extremely painful. There I was, with my hands wrapped and stretched out so I wouldn't touch them, and wearing only my loose-fitting G.I. shorts with gaposis in the front. A soldier I had never seen before came into the tent and asked, "Are you McGuire?"

I said, "Yea, what do you want?"

He said, "Would you like to meet Madeleine Carroll?"

I said, "No, but if you've got Betty Gable out there, you can let her in." I thought he was being a smart-aleck. Before I knew it, Madeleine Carroll was standing in my tent!

Imagine! There I was, lying on my bunk wearing only my G.I. shorts with the gaping front, and holding my hands up in the air. I looked up and there she stood, a beautiful woman dressed in some kind of Red Cross outfit.

She looked down at me, gaps in my shorts, hands in the air, and said, "You have a very strange name for your street here."

Near us were four latrines, and if there had been a fifth, it would have been in the same spot our tent occupied, so the designation on the map used by the Charge of Quarters read, "End of Outhouse Row."

I didn't know how to respond, so I didn't. She talked for a few minutes, then, seeing that I was extremely embarrassed, wished me a speedy recovery and left. She was a very nice person.[2]

Why was I selected for this visit? On my visit to the clinic the day before I had signed in as required. When USO representatives arrived at any field they generally checked with the clinic for any sick or injured men. The clinic had provided Madeleine Carroll's guide with my name and the location of our tent.

For the remainder of my tour I flew with burned hands. The skin was deeply seared and it hurt to fire my machine gun, but for the balance of my tour I took my licks and kept on flying. Even today the palms of my hands are still red from those phosphorus burns and I have never been able to form callouses on the them.

Chapter 13

[1] Pathfinders were lead planes equipped with look-down radar enabling formations to bomb above cloud cover. When operated by an experienced crewman, this type of bombing could be effective. When the radar indicated they had reached the mean point of impact, the bull's eye, the operator fired a flare and the entire group released their bombs simultaneously.

[2] In 1944 when the thirty-eight-year-old Carroll was visiting McGuire as part of a USO tour, she was a well-established radio, screen and stage star. Perhaps her most notable role was in Alfred Hitchcock's *The Thirty-Nine Steps*. David Regan, *Who's Who in Hollywood*. (New Rochelle, NY: Arlington House Publishers, 1977), 75-76.

− 14 −

Shooting Up The Russian Convoy

Generally, we could easily identify the Eastern Front boundary from the location of the Russian artillery.[1] From the air it looked like they were plowing the earth with it. However, we had a very difficult time trying to determine friend from foe after the Russians broke through the German front in the Balkans.

One mission, while we were flying home after a bombing run on Vienna, we looked down and saw a huge caravan; a hodgepodge of mostly military vehicles, going down the road. The caravan appeared to include every kind of vehicle in the world: ox carts, German and Russian tanks, captured trucks with every kind of marking imaginable, motorcycles, coal and wood burning cars of both Russian and German make, and, for all I could tell, bicycles, roller skates, burros, cows, and elephants as well. The caravan had traveled about forty miles beyond where the bomb line was supposed to be (the moving line on the map, indicating occupation by Allied forces, where we were not allowed to bomb). From the markings on the vehicles it looked like a German convoy. We thought they were retreating German troops with their numbers swelled by camp followers and refugees bringing all their livestock with them. They bore no resemblance to any kind of military formation. Our fighter escorts radioed the group commander and requested permission for half of the escort to go down and work it over. Permission was granted.

Our P-51s dived and really destroyed that convoy, stacking them up like cord wood. The next morning we learned they were Russians.

The Russian Army was so disorganized, and fought in such compartmentalized units, that this particular unit had made a breakthrough into undefended territory and nobody knew anything about it. They were forty miles behind the German front and headed to Berlin when the 51s stacked them up. Even the Germans were unaware of their presence.

The next day we crossed that same spot and encountered intense, accurate flak. Russian flak. We weren't that friendly with anybody but our own side.[2]

Chapter 14

[1] By the end of 1943 Russia had concentrated a vast artillery arm: six artillery corps, twenty-six artillery divisions, forty-three regiments of self-propelled guns, twenty artillery brigades, and seven divisions of Katyusha rocket-launchers. Keegan, 474.

[2] McGuire witnessed an international incident. The Russian column was attacked near Nis, Yugoslavia. The Allied fighters killed the commanding officer of the column, a general, and two other officers and six enlisted men. After this attack the Russians prohibited Americans from flying into their zones of control without prior clearance. Jablonski, 237.

− 15 −

The Rosarius Flying Circus
And Other German Defenses

The Germans even fought us with our own airplanes.

On a flight over Czechoslovakia, I looked down and was startled to see several B-17s and B-24s parked on an airfield. They were some of our aircraft which had been captured. During the war the Germans captured almost every aircraft the Allies had. One German strategy was to fly groups of captured planes around to the various fighter bases and let the German pilots examine and fly them, in order to determine how to best fight us. They called this traveling group the Rosarius Traveling Circus.[1]

They also flew these captured planes against us as decoys. One of our B-24 formations was approached by a straggling B-17. The straggler, crewed by Germans, was admitted into the formation because they thought he was a cripple. Once inside the formation, it then shot down many of them.

Once we were aware of this ploy, anything that turned its nose toward us and did not identify itself, Allied aircraft or not, was quickly shot. It was Air Force policy that *any* aircraft, enemy or friendly, coming into our formation with his nose pointed at us was a target and we acted accordingly. This precaution was primarily because of the Rosarius Flying Circus. Every mission used a unique code name and colors for identification purposes.

We were very leery of strangers. Once we were approached by a B-24 flying straight and level toward us, looking like it was going to the corner grocery store. We turned our guns on it while trying to make radio contact. After a closer look we noticed the waist door and several hatches had been salvoed. Apparently no one was on board, and it was heading straight and level for Italy. The crew was either dead or gone. Our escorts went over for a closer look, flying so close they were almost touching it, trying to see inside for signs of life. They reported to headquarters and received word to shoot it down. Every plane carried classified materials: Maps, codes, and other items that shouldn't fall into German hands. The escorts shot it down as ordered. We prayed there was nobody aboard, lying on the floor wounded and unable to bail out.

On one mission a crippled P-38 flew up to our formation. He'd been shot up and had an engine feathered. Flying on only one engine he obviously needed protection. Following procedure, he cautiously flew up to the formation and turned sideways so we could read his numbers. The pilots radioed in and identified him. That crippled P-38's approach reminded me of a cat walking in front of a bunch of dogs. After he was properly identified, he eased himself into the formation.

As he was easing in, a gunner from another ship in our formation suddenly opened up on him. That gunner, for whatever reason—using the relief can, not paying attention, or wasn't plugged into the intercom—suddenly came to life and let that P-38 have it. Whoever he was, he was a good shot. Out went the P-38's good engine. The pilot quickly pulled away, unfeathered his bad engine, and disappeared.

Later, after landing at our field, to our surprise and astonishment, that same P-38 landed behind us. The pilot cut off his engine, jumped out of the plane, and stormed over and angrily asked who had shot at him. He was directed to the guilty B-17. He walked to that plane and inquired about which gunner had shot him. When the gunner spoke up, that pilot hit him in the mouth, hard, returned to his plane, and on that bad engine flew back to his own field.

The P-38 was a dirty word to the Eighth Air Force in England, but we loved them in Italy. Most of the earlier problems with the P-38 stemmed from not knowing how to fly them. Pilots in the African Campaign had learned how to handle them and they became an important part of the African, and later the Italian-based U.S. forces. The Eighth Air Force gave most of their P-38s to the Fifteenth and those planes formed the core of the Fifteenth's P-38 strength.

Fighters In General

We feared the Focke-Wulf-190 the most. It was armed with four cannons and two heavy machine guns., Additionally, it sometimes carried six to eight rockets slung under the wings. Those rockets were deadly. A hit by one in a key spot could take out an entire squadron. The FW-190s were also heavily armored on the bottom. We were told it was three-eighths inch armor plating, thick enough to repel .50 caliber rounds. We also heard that the canopies' half-inch-thick plexiglass could withstand a hit from a .50 caliber. The German pilots were also protected by the plane's big engine. You could shoot large pieces off the Focke-Wulf and it would still fly.

It could take a lot of punishment and still fight, and was more savage because of it. The earlier model, however, had a problem fighting any higher than twenty-seven thousand feet. It's performance declined radically above this height, and the

B-17s climbed higher and higher to get away from them. Later models corrected this defect. Therefore, during the early stages of the war, most of our fights at extreme heights were with ME-109s. The Focke-Wulf worked over the B-24s because they flew several thousand feet below us.

Focke-Wulfs were also flown as 'Storm Fighters,' the German equivalent of kamikazes. Storm Fighter pilots were usually radical Nazis. Encouraged by the success of the Japanese kamikazes, some German leaders organized kamikaze-like units. Galland, and even Goering, were appalled by this tactic as it was offensive to their idea of warfare when the pilot wasn't given the option to return. Storm Fighters were even more heavily armored than the regular Focke-Wulfs. They were built not for dogfights but for ramming bomber formations in order to break them up, permitting other fighters to jump on the stragglers.

One day while returning from a run we saw a B-24 group below us. They must have been with the Eighth Air Force out of England because their course was different from ours. We regularly crossed with the Eighth around Munich and Regensberg. On this occasion we saw a large group of enemy fighters approaching them. A Storm Fighter flew into the group and rammed the lead 24, resulting in a terrible explosion. This precipitated a savage fight between the 24s and the fighters. From our vantage point, the battle resembled an old-fashioned, Wild West gun fight. Fully half of the 24s went down while we watched. With all of the parachutes blossoming around the fight, it looked like a paratrooper invasion. Different colored parachutes were visible, for many Germans were shot down as well as B-24s. The burning 24s continued to fight as they flew out of our sight, leaving only trails of smoke.

Next to the Focke-Wulfs, the twin-engine fighters, the destroyers—ME-110,[2] ME-410,[3] or JU-88s—also scared us and were extremely effective against us. They flew just out of gun range and lobbed rockets at our formations.

German fighters were most effective when they attacked us in group strength, anywhere from fifty to seventy-five fighters in

(above) While the Fifteenth Air Force was having their own troubles, the Eighth Air Force wasn't getting off scott-free. Something went wrong during this mission. Note the bombs dropped by a higher airplane are about to hit this one. One bomb is over the fuselage and another is about to strike the stabilizer. *(below)* A bomb has torn off the horizontal stabilizer, which is hanging by a slender piece of metal. The top bomb missed. A close examination reveals nine bombs falling through the air below the plane. *(Courtesy Lassiter Collection)*

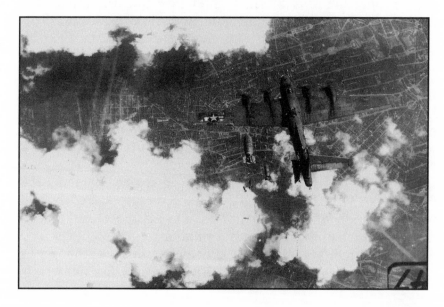

staffels, of around twelve fighters each. On many missions we observed these large groups, and always hoped they weren't headed for us. They used dirt landing strips, and from our vantage point we often saw their dirt trails as they took off.

German fighters first looked for stragglers, crippled or shot up bombers which couldn't keep up with the formation. Stragglers were a hot lunch for the German fighters. If there were no stragglers, they then observed the formations. If a formation was intact, with no damaged planes, and certainly if the formation was tight, they'd generally go hunting elsewhere. B-17 crewmen had a grisly and ongoing joke: The best enemy fighter protection B-17s had was flying with B-24s. Enemy fighters preferred to hit them rather than B-17s because their formations were often less tight. This was through no fault of the B-24 pilots, as the B-24 was more difficult to handle than the B-17, and required more maneuvering space, thus making it difficult to fly in compact formations. Another reason for the preference for 24s was the height of the B-17 tail. That nineteen-foot tail robbed German fighters of their ability to break high at the end of their pursuit curve. When breaking low they presented a better target for B-17 gunners.

If no other options were available, enemy fighters flew directly at the formation, trying to break it apart. German pilots were not stupid. Nobody in his right mind wants to attack a formation of twenty-eight B-17s with anywhere from 224 to 280 .50 caliber machine guns firing at you. If they could break up the formation, then the real fight began. Playing 'chicken,' they generally flew directly toward the formation, hoping some pilots would flinch and pull away. This knocked a hole in the formation. Green bomber pilots were more likely to flinch and break formation than experienced ones.

Their favorite time to attack was after a bomb run when the 17s were re-forming for the return flight. Another favorable time was after a lead plane had been knocked out and before we had re-grouped. It could take four or five minutes to re-organize, and during that time they would attack.

The 49th Squadron of the Second Bomb Group with other Groups from the Fifth Wing flying in formation below and in back. This is a good example of close formation flying.
(Courtesy R. Chambers)

Like lions hunting prey, they cut out the crippled, the hurt, the oldest, the sickest, the weakest. One of the reasons I'm alive today is because the pilots of the Twentieth Squadron, Second Bomb Group flew formation so tightly we were not as vulnerable. Our battle formation was beautiful, almost wingtip to wingtip, and when German pilots saw us, they gave us wide berth.

Before the B-17G[4] model was implemented—the one with the chin turret on the nose—their favorite angle of attack was straight in at twelve o'clock. Attacking from this angle, they tried to knock out the formation's group and squadron lead planes. The most dangerous angles of attack for them were coming in at six o'clock toward the tail, or at three or nine o'clock at the waist, as we could bring more guns to bear on them at those angles.

Gunners continually moved their heads, necks, and eyes in the constant search for enemy fighters. We all had excellent eyesight, and the longer we were there the better we became at spotting them. If you lived long enough, you could see them twice as far away, twice as fast. As a gunner, I observed a curious phenomenon. The fighters attacked extremely fast, but, conversely, it seemed like everything happened in slow motion. In almost every move or action, I had time to weigh the pros and cons of the situation. This same slow motion review later served me well in state police work and probably saved my life on several occasions. This time-lapse phenomenon permitted me to make many good, instant decisions. I also learned something about myself; in dangerous situations I wasn't frightened or scared into inaction. The shakes and fear didn't start until the mission was over and I was back at the field.

Between the fighters and the flak, the Fifteenth Air Force was losing the equivalent of at least a squadron a week, a group a month.

Too Close For Comfort

We all had close encounters with the enemy, but one November morning I had a very close look at an enemy fighter pilot, too close a look for comfort.

That mission I was flying togglier in the nose over the chin turret and was exercising my turret to keep the oil hot so that my guns would be able to swing on target quickly. We had just passed over the Alps through some very bad weather, and I was ready for whatever when we popped out into the sunlight.

Looking to my right, I almost jumped out of my seat when tracers passed directly under our nose. They were our tracers! Who in our formation was shooting at us? When I turned to find the culprit, I couldn't believe my eyes.

Below us, and unknown to us, a Focke-Wulf was involved in a fight. He was equally unaware of our presence. After his attack on the airplanes below, he flew upwards and into our formation. He was totally absorbed in watching the formation he had attacked and was readying for his next strike. He was headed directly at our plane, directly at the nose, directly at me, and he hadn't seen us yet. His wingtip was less than ten feet from our wingtip and engine. Again, everything seemed to happen in slow motion as I turned the chin turret toward him. That 190 couldn't have been more than fifty yards away. Then that pilot looked up and saw us flying immediately beside him. Although he was wearing an oxygen mask, I could see his eyes get about as big as baseballs.

How he kept from slamming us is a mystery, but he maneuvered out of the formation. As he dived away I finally brought my guns to bear on him and started firing. Every other gunner in the formation was firing at him, too. How those other B-17 gunners kept from shooting us down, I'll never know. Strips of aluminum blew off his wing as the plane dived away from us.

That German certainly wasn't attacking us, but he was in the wrong spot at the wrong time. The memory of those eyes will stay with me forever—big as baseballs.

Victims of Vertigo

The Germans continued to use Galland's theory of attack. Hit us with a large enough force, up to seventy-five or more fighters, to destroy a unit. Pitted against one squadron of seven or eight bombers, it was an extremely effective tactic when our escort was not around. As a result, we were facing fewer small numbers of fighters, but dreaded the large forces.

One late October morning we'd had a rough take-off and climb-out from Amendola on a mission deep into Germany. On climb-out, the inside of the airplane frosted over like an old-fashioned refrigerator. We were in heavy icing for some time. Icing posed a problem as the de-icing boots on our B-17s had been removed to allow us to carry additional bombs. We had heavy ice accreation on the climb-out and several planes returned to the field because of the icing. Suddenly, we broke out into bright sunshine. As we progressed into the mission and reached our assigned altitude of twenty-eight or twenty-nine thousand feet, we were so high the solid undercast totally obscured the ground. Germany was completely socked in that day.

Several thousand feet below us, about 8:30, my attention was attracted by a flash that heralded the beginning of a fantastic and terrifying show. Two airplanes seemed to have collided, exploded, and gone down. My first thought was of our escort as they appeared to be single engine aircraft. It was too great a distance to tell. I called the tail, "Jim, can you see down there about eight o'clock? What's happening?"

About then, aircraft began popping up like popcorn from the undercast. We could see flashes or fires and the cloud tops contained smoke, but neither of us could distinguish what they were. Whatever they were, there were about forty or fifty. They would emerge from the clouds in rows, then turn and re-enter the clouds.

Jim believed they were single-engine fighters. I concurred, but mentioned that none were aluminum colored. All were dark colors—gray, black, or green—which lead us to believe they weren't ours. Our escort would have had natural aluminum finishes. A few fighters and bombers were still painted the old olive-drab, but the new aircraft were natural aluminum which had a tendency to sparkle and shine in the sunlight.

Those airplanes disappeared almost as soon as they had appeared. Three or four even started back in the direction we had just come. We dutifully reported unidentified aircraft at seven o'clock low at cloud top.

Since talking with former Luftwaffe fighter pilots and reading Adolf Galland's *The First and the Last*, this is probably a reasonable explanation of that display. Due to fuel shortages in the latter part of 1944, Germany was unable to provide their new pilots with instrument training, other than on simulators. Even though their planes carried adequate equipment for instrument flying, many of their pilots were not trained to use them.

If their pilots encountered frosting and heavy icing inside the canopy, the ice would stick to the windscreens. When they popped out into the bright sunshine, all those frozen crystals acted like a thousand prisms and reflected the sunlight. The resulting dramatic increase in the light level induced extreme vertigo. The vertigo caused them to lose their orientation. One second they were racing at us from below, and the next they were spinning, colliding, weaving, falling, and running into one another. In the mistaken belief they were flying level, they would go into steep dives and tear the wings off their airplanes. While in a spin-out, if they could regain their orientation with the ground, they could level off and save themselves. If they couldn't, the result was chaos and probable destruction of the entire fighter group. The Luftwaffe lost many, non-instrument-trained pilots to this type of vertigo.

The combination of the weather and their own inexperience probably saved us that day. Evidently they had scheduled the Second Bomb Group to be hit by one of their Wolf Packs. That group of fighters had been vectored onto us by radar and were waiting to hit us the moment we topped the Alps.

As a pilot, this condition happened to me on many occasions. Fortunately, I was trained to ignore my senses and trust the instruments. Those German pilots didn't have that luxury that day.

Machine Guns

Although the effective range of the .50 caliber was eight hundred yards, I was confident I could hit a German fighter at a thousand yards.

I didn't like tracers, and thought those who shot them were wasting their time. Tracers, containing manganese or another chemical, quickly burned out and became progressively lighter as they burned. They did not hold their trajectory and floated back and forth. Their only benefit, in my opinion, was to let the Germans know something was still coming out of the gun. Whenever possible I asked the armorers back at the field to change the ratio of tracers from every fifth to every seventh round when they prepared my mixture of rounds. In addition to tracers there were ball rounds, the old standard anti-personnel round, as well as armor-piercing and incendiary rounds. Armor

(above) Undercast over the Alps. This is the type of cloud formation that could bring on vertigo in pilots emerging from the clouds into the bright sunshine. (below) Crossing the low part of the Lower Alps. This is close to the 'bolt hole' used by Allied aircraft trying to evade enemy aircraft and get back to Italy. These are not the high, sharp Alps, but the Yugoslavian Alps. (Courtesy R. Chambers)

rounds would sometimes pierce the armor-plating on enemy fighters. The tips of the rounds were painted different colors so we could differentiate between the various types of ammunition.

Before every mission we squeezed as many rounds as possible into the plane for each gun—generally five hundred rounds per gun position, and we shot thirteen guns on each B-17. Later, the B-17G model fired a chin-turret gun, which replaced the single nose gun with two guns in the chin-turret. That was a tremendous amount of firepower for one plane. When that plane was part of a tight formation of a squadron of B-17s, German pilots were wise to be wary. The rounds were stored in belts or canisters equipped with rollers to prevent belt-jamming. Early in my tour, I decided if the armorers removed the rollers we could store more ammunition. Did this cause jamming? Yes, but the occasional jam was worth the increased quantity of ammunition and we needed as much ammunition as possible, especially on the longer missions.

Some missions were over eight hundred miles long. There were times we fought German fighters for over three hundred miles. That is equivalent to fighting the entire distance between Los Angeles and Phoenix. A gun could be emptied in just a little over a minute and a half. If you had an excitable, untrained gunner, he could fire half his ammunition and burn out the barrel in no time at all. The best technique was to fire short bursts, generally no more than three to five rounds per burst. If you didn't make your rounds last, you were in big trouble.

Our armorers were very innovative. One of the first things they did when the Fifteenth arrived in Italy was discard all manufacturer's specifications on the head space of the guns. This enabled us to better seat the guns in the frame. Those specifications worked in North Africa, but they were not valid in Europe. The colder temperatures we encountered in flying over the Alps made the mechanisms freeze, therefore, they needed to be much looser than indicated by the factory specs. Feeler gauges were designed for making those adjustments, but we learned to determine the proper seating by the sound of the gun as it fired. We eventually had them so loose they were 'just right' if they rang like a bell when fired. The slack was necessary because they had a tendency to tighten up when fired. With the 'proper' head fittings they jammed, or the cycle of fire went down. We also removed some of the oil from the buffer units. Oil had a tendency to freeze, and if we removed oil from the buffer units, it improved the fire cycle. Our armorers experimented with different types of oil in the turrets and eventually selected a brand refined by the British. Even that oil did not work well at sixty below zero.

Knocking Off the Skulker

I know for certain I knocked down one enemy fighter. There were probably others because I was a good shot, and had confidence I could hit my target, but because we were flying and shooting in a defensive box, many other gunners were shooting at the same plane or planes. That's the beauty of the box formation. There are generally seven planes in a squadron, and perhaps a fourth of those ninety-one guns are covering any attacking enemy fighters. Two or three streams of tracers would converge on a fighter, and it would suddenly blow up. If you had been working on him, you could say, "I got him," but dozens of gunners in that same squadron had the same thought. It wasn't worth an argument. You never received a cigar for knocking down a fighter. Or a promotion either. Attacks generally came fast and went by fast, but by the end of my tour I firmly believed I could hit anything.

Our formations were constantly plagued by lone enemy fighters. We called them skulkers. When our escorts weren't present the Germans assigned a lone aircraft to dog our formations. These were generally twin-engine fighters who flew alongside us, relaying our altitude, heading, and speed to the flak batteries waiting for us, or directing other enemy fighters to us. If one of our planes was hit by flak, or damaged and had to drop out of formation, these skulkers quickly jumped them. Their principal duty was to serve as spotters on our formations.

It was aggravating to see them flying near us, as they were careful to fly more than a thousand yards from us; just outside the maximum range for a .50 caliber. This one skulker, an ME-109, had been with us for sometime on this particular day. He was flying absolutely even with our plane, opposite my position at the left waist. We figured he was eleven hundred yards away. I had become very good at estimating range and had been looking at him through my gun sights for about fifteen minutes. A 109's length was just a few inches over twenty-nine feet. I estimated his range to be about eleven hundred yards using that sight and kept him within that sight. He never moved.

Even though he was just a shade out of effective range, I couldn't stand it. I wanted to shoot at him so badly, but we had been ordered not to fire at planes outside of gun range as we didn't have that much ammunition to burn. For fifteen minutes I computed and re-computed, measuring the distance and calculating the ballistic drop. Nobody else was firing on him. My calculations indicated that I needed to shoot at a spot ahead of him and about eighteen feet above him in order to score a hit. The lead wasn't all that bad because his speed was the same as ours. He was absolutely even with us. Finally, I thought, I'm going to try this.

I fired a short burst and the first round was a tracer, which flew out about five or six hundred yards and boat-tailed. One of the shots must have hit, because, to my astonishment, the canopy blew off. My figures were correct. The canopy in a 109 is hinged at the bottom and folds over and to the right. The cockpit is a very strong cage. One of my rounds must have hit that cage, because the canopy flew off, cartwheeling backwards over the plane. As the airplane jittered back and forth, I could tell something had happened when it began a very gentle downward glide. It flew a little ahead of us and we watched him for many miles, flying at that slight angle until he was a speck and no longer visible.

Immediately after firing my short burst I was chewed out by the co-pilot who had heard my gun but could not see the result.

Over the intercom he said, "Come on now, that thing was over a thousand yards out. Stop wasting rounds." That made me mad. After all, I had hit the plane and probably decapitated the pilot.

Jets

In early fall of 1944 rumors began circulating that the Germans had built new super-fighters. That made us nervous. We first encountered jets that November and flew against them for several weeks before I ended my tour.

We didn't know what they were when we first saw them. Our first reaction was they were V-1s, the rockets Germany used for bombing England. We saw many jets in the Munich area, as well as back toward Lake Constance or Frederichsha-fen. They flew at far higher altitudes than we flew. You could easily spot them because of their thick smoke trails. During one of our briefings, we were told rocket fighters on training flights trailed black smoke, and attacking rockets white smoke. The difference was explained, incorrectly as we later discovered, that training flights used a cheaper fuel which burned black.

The Germans were flying several types of jets, and the early ones, which we encountered, were later identified as Komet rocket fighters.[5] A short time later we started seeing the ME-262s.[6] Those jets were big trouble.

On one occasion three ME-262s made passes at us, but didn't inflict any damage. They were so fast we couldn't lead them properly. In December, we began hearing of outfits decimated by them. The word spread quickly—when jets got on you, you were in big, big trouble. Conventional guns could hardly hit them, plus they had terrific fire power with so many cannon, machine guns and rockets aboard.

In addition to their speed, they had the capability flying straight up from the ground. One day a jet flew past, and about fifteen seconds later a flight of P-51s flew past at full speed, trying to catch him. We knew it was impossible for the 51s to catch them. They were almost one hundred miles per hour faster than the P-51s.

Rockets

They shot ground-to-air rockets at us in late December 1944 while we were bombing Wiener Neustadt. It was clear that day and I was sitting in the nose, looking down. All of a sudden, I saw some unusual, very long fiery flashes that appeared to come from their gun positions. The big flames were actually from rockets leaving their launching pads. At first they appeared to be going away from us, but when they arced back and headed towards us, we could see the fiery contrails on their fins. This particular volley missed the formation, but certainly got our attention. You could feel the air changing temperature as they flew past.[7]

I never saw many planes hit by rockets, but occasionally the Germans were lucky. The rockets were eighteen to twenty feet in length and carried a tremendous amount of explosive. Some were set to explode at a pre-set altitude, others exploded on contact. A hit by one of these rockets was worse than a 128mm flak hit. A rocket hit could cause a chain reaction and eliminate a formation.

It was always a chilling experience when they fired rockets. At this point I began sitting on my steel helmet rather than wearing it and those stove lids offered additional protection.

They also fired guided rockets from twin-engine fighters. During one mission I was in the chin-turret/togglier position in the nose and saw something flash past, tracking on us from a nine to three o'clock position as it whooshed by immediately under my section of the plane. It looked like a big black telephone pole with some kind of writing on it, burning at one end. "A telephone pole with fire in its hind end just went under us," I reported. It missed us by six inches and we could feel the heat it generated. Somewhere out there was a ME-410 or a JU-88 guiding it in. It was probably another of their radio-controlled weapons.

They used everything they had: Rockets, cables, smoke pots, even our own aircraft. On the ground they even camouflaged defense areas of big cities so our navigators couldn't recognize landmarks. They created fantastically realistic camouflage from wood, cardboard and netting and placed these enormous designs over their industrial areas. From our airplane, the three-dimensional figures of cars, trucks, etc. placed on it made it look as though it was just another suburban area. Bridges or distinctive curves in rivers were disguised in the same manner in the hope that the loss of a familiar landmark would confuse our navigators. Their ingenuity was incredible.

Chapter 15

[1] General Adolph Galland called this the 'Rosarius Traveling Circus,' although Allied airmen usually referred to it as the Rosarius Flying Circus. It was initially comprised of a flight of every captured Allied aircraft that could still be flown. The original Circus was flown to various Luftwaffe units so their pilots, by personally flying these aircraft, could judge their strengths and weaknesses. Later in the war, any German unit flying Allied aircraft against Allied bomber formations was generically labeled by this term. One Luftwaffe unit, I/KG200 actually flew captured B-17s with German markings during a phase of the western desert North African campaign for the purpose of dropping clandestine agents behind Allied lines. Adolf Galland, *The First and the Last*. (New York: Ballantine Books, 1954), 155; Mayer, 22.

[2] The Messerschmitt-110 was powered by two 1,475 Daimler-Benz engines, but could only reach speeds of up to 342 mph at 22,900 feet. It had an operating radius of 1,305 miles with extra fuel tanks. It was armed with four 7.9mm machine guns, two 20mm or 30mm cannon and two light machine guns. It was served by a crew of two, and was initially equipped with primitive radar, which effectively cut its speed. The ME-110 and ME-410 were vulnerable to fighter escorts, but when the escorts were not around, these twin-engine fighters were murderous to B-17 formations because of the rocket batteries and bombs with which they were armed. Caiden, 55; Bailey, 201.

[3] The ME-410 Hornisse (Hornet) was an improved version of the ME-210. It was a two-seater heavy fighter, used most successfully for night bomber raids over England, night interception of British bomber streams, anti-shipping, and reconnaissance. The ME-410 first saw combat in May 1943. The airplane could tear up unescorted formations of B-17s, but it was no match for P-51 escort fighters in daylight. It was powered by two 1,750 hp inverted V-12 engines, had a top speed of 388 mph, a ceiling of 32,800, range of 1,491 miles, and was armed with four forward-firing 20mm cannon and

two 7.9mm machine guns. Additionally, it was armed with a unique system of two remote-controlled, backward-firing 13mm machine guns. Parrish, 402; Wheal, et al., 302-03.

[4] The first of the 8,680 G Models was produced in September 1943; the last in April 1945. In addition to the chin turret, the G Model was built with wider propellers which increased the altitude capability of the airplane. Many E & F models were converted by adding chin turrets. Jablonski, 37.

[5] The Messerschmitt ME-163 Komet was the only fighter plane of the war powered by a rocket motor. The squat, barrel-shaped fighter was first flown in early 1941. Its first operational flight was in July 1944 against B-17s. Powered by a 3,750-pound thrust rocket engine, it had a top speed of 596 mph and a climb rate of sixteen thousand feet per minute. On one occasion it was timed reaching thirty thousand feet in 2.6 minutes. Armed with two 30mm cannon, it could carry twenty rockets. Parrish, 402.

[6] The Messerschmitt ME-262 was the world's first operational jet fighter and fighter-bomber which saw action in World War II. The 262 program, beset by official indifference from its inception, began in 1938. The first prototype, powered by piston engines, was delivered in April 1941. By July 1942, a craft powered completely by jet engine power was delivered. The first operational flight against Allied forces occurred in September 1944. The development of this aircraft was slowed by German officials who, early in the war, saw no need for a craft of this type. Only in November 1943 was full-scale production sanctioned. By the end of the war only 1,433 ME-262s had been built, and of this number, approximately fifteen percent were used against the Allies. This was a fortunate twist of fate for the Allies, for even with its many technical difficulties, it was arguably the most formidable fighter of the war. It was powered by two 1980-pound (900 kg) thrust Junkers Jumo 004B turbojets, could fly 540 mph, and it was armed with four 30mm cannon and carried twenty-four five-cm rockets. This plane destroyed over five hundred Allied aircraft. One 262 unit, JV-44, in one month, flying six aircraft, shot down forty-five Allied planes. Mayer, 171-72; Parrish, 402.

[7] McGuire's formation was probably shot at by batteries of *Rheintochter* missiles. This rocket was developed by the Rheinmetall-Borsig Company beginning in 1942. Tests began in August 1943. It was propelled by a solid-fuel motor, with a solid-fuel booster unit for initial launching. It was guided by radio and optically tracked by observing flares attached to the fins. It carried a 330-pound warhead and was detonated by an acoustic proximity fuse. Initial prototypes had limited ceiling of eight thousand feet, so beginning in the summer of 1944, company engineers began work on a model with booster motors which gave the missile a much higher altitude. The control system was not perfected by the end of the war, negating the missile as a factor in World War II but, nonetheless, it presaged the modern air battlefield. Mayer, 211.

– 16 –

Amendola and the 'Ritz'

Home was a faded, brownish-green pyramid tent with a pole in the center to hold up the roof. The sides rolled up for ventilation in hot weather, but during the early months there we only rolled up one side. Three colors of canvas patches decorated the various holes created whenever our stove exploded. Whenever we burned a new hole, 'Omar the Tent Maker' was called to repair it. He always came while we were gone so how he managed his repairs always remained a puzzle.

This twelve by twenty foot tent had come with the Twentieth from North Africa. Our original floor was that gooey, Italian mud. To escape the mud, we scavenged wooden boxes and installed a floor. It didn't work as well as we had planned because during each rain storm, the tent flooded and our floor became a raft floating on a sea of mud. With the coming of cold weather, we staked the sides down and covered the bottom edge with mud in an attempt to keep out some of the cold.

Inside were two sets of bunk beds and two single beds. Graham and I had the singles and mine was located next to the door. The stove occupied the center of the tent. There was a small rack for clothes and we each had a metal box on our footlockers for storage of our folded clothing and personal items. Candles and lanterns provided us with light until the tents were wired for electricity. Italian light bulbs were not compatible with our electrical system, so my parents sent light bulbs in my goodie bags. Row after row of tents covered perhaps forty acres in that olive grove. The officers had similar quarters about six rows from us. This was the accommodation we dubbed 'The Amendola Ritz.'

When we arrived, Amendola had a severe water shortage and water supplies were trucked in from some distance. The situation improved while we were there, but it seemed there was never enough fresh water for bathing. At first we had only five gallons of water per week in which to shower. The water was saved and we all shaved in the left over water. Pity the last man to shave, as the poor wretch used that whisker-laden water. We were each issued one package of four Gillette blades per month. I spent much time bathing in the nearby Adriatic, even though it was filled with the poisonous Portuguese Man-o-War and pollution from the local fishing fleet that went out daily despite the war. At least the sea water was wet and allowed us to remove the grime. If we could shower the same day in fresh water, we felt content.

Our days off were spent sleeping, writing letters, reading the *Stars and Stripes*, *Yank* magazine, and any other newspapers or mail we'd received. Reading material was never discarded and each piece re-read dozens of times. There was no PX, but when a shipment came in we could have three sodas or two beers. The only problem was a lack of facilities for cooling the drinks.

The Amendola Ritz crew was like a family of brothers. We didn't socialize much, but when we did it was generally to visit other squadrons in the Group, most of whom we at least knew by sight. Why it was so important, I don't know, but we all wanted to know where the others had been born and raised. Perhaps we were looking for someone from home.

We spent much time keeping up our gear. Many crewmen played cribbage, pinochle, or poker, but I didn't. The more missions I flew, the more sleep I needed. While the rest of the crew participated in social activities, I preferred to stay at the tent and sleep. We weren't tourists. We all wanted to hit the high spots, such as Rome, but otherwise, I preferred to relax in my free time and prepare for the next mission.

The British Bugler

When we arrived at Amendola, we were told to ignore any bugle calls we heard. A British RAF unit was not too far away and they were strongly attached to bugle calls. They amplified their bugler's calls through a huge horn to ensure that every-body in their area—as well as everyone at our area—heard their calls. Each morning their bugler pointed that horn in the four directions of the compass, which also included our direction.

For some perverse reason, their calls, including reveille, were thirty minutes ahead of our schedule. Understandably, we were unhappy about losing thirty minutes of sleep every morn-ing. Our men were fed up with it, so somebody decided to do something about the situation. One morning the British bugler started his routine; when he pointed it towards us, someone opened fire on him with an M-1 rifle. The bugler cut short his call that morning. The next morning, the bugler again pointed his horn toward us and started bugling. Again someone opened fire on him. Once again, reveille abruptly ended. By the third morning, the bugler had it figured out, and skipped blowing the bugle in our direction. From then on we got that extra thirty minutes' sleep every morning.

Rats

Fall came quickly enough for us at the beginning of our tour. We could tell winter would not be too far away, as the weather began cooling off in 'sunny Italy.'

One non-op day (a non-flying day) I seized the opportunity to catch up on my rest. While asleep in our tent on this particu-lar afternoon, I heard a peculiar noise and thought some of the

The 'Boudoir' for the Amendola Ritz with Charles Graham using a steel helmet as his washbasin. The stone wall was behind the Amendola Ritz. McGuire's helmet is in the foreground, resting on a bomb fin. A Sterno can inside the fin provided the heat to boil water for shaving and washing. This ritual was followed every evening before a mission. A clean shave was necessary as the oxygen masks fit so tightly. After wearing one for six and a half hours, your face would be terribly chafed and would be even more so with a beard. The half of a 55-gallon drum in the background was what remained of the tent stove after it had exploded. Two holes are visible in the right side of the can. *(Courtesy L. Scofield)*. *(below)* The Amendola Ritz. *(l. to r.)* Sutton writing letters, Chambers and Scofield in the doorway. *(Courtesy J. Fenstermaker)*

(upper l.) McGuire *(l.)* and Sutton heading for the shower on their day off. *(Courtesy L. Scofield)* *(upper r.)* Thompson returning to the tent after a bath in the Adriatic, a walk of four to five miles. *(Courtesy M. McGuire)* *(lower l.)* A day off! McGuire enjoys the Amendola Ritz patio furniture. *(Courtesy L. Scofield)* *(lower r.)* Chambers caught in his long johns (flaps down) after the first snow. *(Courtesy W. Lesher)*

crew had returned. I awoke in time to see one of those infamous European sewer rats. They were huge, tough, and defiant things about the size of a half-grown cat. Most had been eliminated from the area, but occasionally one came in, we think from the Foggia sewers which had been destroyed by Allied bombing.

The rat, perched atop some of my belongings, was moving things around in his search for food. I quickly picked up a boot and threw it at him. He squealed and ran out of the tent with me following, but I couldn't find him. Several crewmen were standing around. When I told them about the rat, a ground crewman gave me several rounds of .45 caliber birdshot. Every escape kit contained a few of these rounds in case we needed to shoot birds for food. Birdshot wouldn't blow them to pieces like a regular .45 round. The range also was limited because they didn't contain a full powder charge. We found these rounds to be very effective against rats as well as birds. I kept them in the tent, handy for future use.

Occasionally we'd do some recreational rat hunting, but usually with little success. They always appeared in the tents when you least expected them, and when you weren't prepared for them.

A few days later I was on my bunk when I heard that rat, again rummaging through my clothes. I quietly and slowly loaded one of those birdshot rounds in my .45 and waited for him to get away from my things, as I didn't want to shoot holes in my overcoat. When he left my clothes, I let him have it. He squealed, turned a cartwheel, and raced out the way he had come in. We covered the hole he had dug under the tent. That was one tough rat.

Several days later in a nearby tent, several crewmen had returned from a day off in Foggia. One was quite drunk when he climbed into his bed. His engineer, who had not been with them in Foggia, returned from a trip to the latrine, dressed only in his long johns. Just at that moment, a rat crawled into the tent. The inebriated crewman, having had his fill of the intrusive rat, pulled out his .45, loaded it with birdshot, and took aim at the rat. The more he aimed, the more the gun wavered. He finally pulled the trigger and hit his engineer somewhere between the knee and the derriere. The startled man jumped over the top of his cot and plowed into the tent side, up-rooting several tent stakes. The engineer went for his own .45 to avenge the insult, but the rest of the crew managed to restrain him. It was always dangerous shooting at rats inside a tent.

Scofield and the Stove

Italy was bitter cold in the winter and the only heat we had in the Amendola Ritz was a rigged-up stove which burned high-octane aircraft gasoline. Our stove was a fifty-five-gallon oil drum cut in half, set in a box of sand, with a copper line leading into it. The copper line was connected by a rubber hose to a P-38 belly tank mounted outside the tent. A valve controlled the flow of gasoline into the stove.

Lighting the stove was a tricky business due to the volatility of the gasoline. The stoves had to be relit every morning because the commanding officer, after we began running low on aircraft gasoline, ordered them turned off during the night. We drew straws each night to see who would light the stove the next morning because it was so dangerous. Whoever lit the stove had to open the valve very carefully and let in three, and only three, drops of gasoline into the stove and then quickly put a match to it before the fumes could rise. Once you had a little fire going you opened the valve and had a hot, roaring fire. Each morning you heard a symphony of explosions from all over the area as the stoves were lit. Few of us in the Second Bomb Group had any hair on our arms and we constantly singed nose hairs and eyebrows during the morning stove-lighting ritual.

One night, after it turned really cold, Scofield drew the short straw. The CQ came by our tent at 0215. Still in my sleeping bag just inside the door, he awoke me to awake the rest of the crew. Everybody yelled at Scofield to get up and light the stove to warm the tent so the rest of us could get up comfortably.

He finally got up. Having slept in his underwear, he was shivering and trying to put on clean underwear before lighting the stove. Clean underwear was very important. If we were hit on the mission, then no dirty fabric would be carried into the

247

wound. As he struggled, we continued to yell at him to get the stove started. "All right," he finally said, as he jumped into his fur flying boots, grabbed some matches, and headed for the stove. He wore nothing but a scowl and his boots.

From all over the area we could hear stoves exploding. You could almost track the Charge of Quarter's progress from the explosions. Meanwhile, Scofield, teeth chattering, was bent over our stove. We covered our heads, anticipating the explosion. The three drops went into the can but he was shaking so from the cold that he had trouble getting a lit match into it. We all knew the fumes had started building. Finally the lit match made it into the stove.

It was a Hiroshima-sized explosion, immediately followed by Scofield's screaming and yelling. We jerked our sleeping bags back and saw Scofield dancing around like an Indian at a War Dance, holding his crotch. Even in the dim light we could tell he had turned a nice pink color. He did not have a single hair between the top of his fur flying boots, which were smoking, to above his eyebrows. He did have some hair left on his head. Everything else on the front of his body was smoking furiously, absolutely everything. Every hair was either gone or burning and he was slapping out fire all over his body. When he was finished, the only hair on his body was on the back side. He had absolutely zero hair on his front side. He smoked for several minutes.

That galvanized us into action and we quickly discovered he wasn't severely burned. He was lucky. We dressed and went to breakfast. Scofield was not burned badly enough to require taking him off the mission, but he was uncomfortable for the next few days. He was a beautiful pink and absolutely hairless. He reminded me of Rosita, my aunt's Chihuahua. We called him 'September Morn' after de Kooning's painting. The crew next door picked up on his bloodcurdling screams and circulated a rumor about a wiener roast in our tent.

Thompson and 'Dawg'

We had just finished mess after a mission and were walking back to the Amendola Ritz, when we noticed a white, spotted dog sitting near a hole in the fence. Thompson walked up to him and started talking. The dog seemed interested in what he had to say. Thompson rubbed his head and scratched behind his ears as he spoke to him. After a few minutes, the dog left. The dog impressed us with his air of having to attend to much important business. Thompson, a Hoosier from Indiana and raised in a rural environment, also received much pleasure from his encounters with this animal.

As the months passed, 'Dawg,' as we called him, often came by the tent to visit, but only if Thompson was around. Jim would squat in front of 'Dawg' and rub his ears and we swore the two were actually communicating. The animal seemed to have a sixth sense as to when Thompson was at the tent. 'Dawg' absolutely refused to have anything to do with the rest of us; he was only interested in Jim. 'Dawg' always gave the impression that he had taken time from his busy schedule for this short visit with Thompson.

Their visits developed into a pattern. 'Dawg' dropped in about once every week or ten days, but only when Thompson

James Thompson and his new friend, 'Dawg.' This was the only dog McGuire saw during his entire time in Italy. *(Courtesy M. McGuire)*

was in or around the tent. They would talk for a few minutes, with Thompson scratching 'Dawg's' head and ears, and 'Dawg', of course, wagging his tail. Then 'Dawg' would mysteriously depart for parts unknown. 'Dawg' never honored the rest of us with even the slightest notice. We never knew to whom he belonged, from where he came, or where he went. He did, however, look like a busy animal who couldn't afford to spend a lot of time at the tent with Thompson. Obviously, the two had a good relationship. We kidded Jim about their conversations. This was the only dog I recall seeing during my tour in Italy.

The Children

Sadness was common to that war, as it is to every war, but there was one particular aspect to this sadness to which I never became accustomed—the children of Italy. It was heartbreaking to see them. They were everywhere. Anytime you left our immediate area you saw them. Most were bare-footed, dirty, hungry, and had runny noses. Many of their homes had been destroyed, and many were orphans, or only had one parent. Children labored in the fields to make money to eat. They'd speak to you in pidgin English: "*Mangiare*, Joe"; "Something to eat, Joe"; "*Sigarette*, Joe." It broke my heart because I knew they were hungry, and in the winter they were cold.

One cold morning I awoke to hear sniffling behind our tent so I went outside. There, a little fellow huddled next to the tent wall covered with only a piece of cardboard, waiting for the sun to come up. He had come all the way from the mountains to peddle postcards and rosaries to the Americans. The only protection he had from the cold was a linen coat. Somewhere along the way he had acquired an Italian soldier's cap that he pulled down around his ears. He was wearing short pants. He had no shoes. His buttonless shirt was pinned together by a German Iron Cross. He'd come a long way from his home in the mountains, and he was lost. We bought some of his postcards and one of us bought the Iron Cross and gave him safety pins for his shirt. A few of the Catholic men bought some of his rosaries.

I was on my way to the mess hall so I told him to wait, since he was obviously hungry. On my return I brought him some breakfast. The way he ate made me think that was the first meal he had eaten in a long time. We scrounged a heavy shirt and sweater to protect him from the cold. Someone else found an old, discarded G.I. wool knit cap and he quickly put that on. Someone found a pair of shoes that had been turned in as unsalvageable. They were much too large for him, but he was so proud of them he stuffed rags inside to be able to keep them on his feet. On the next trip back home the village cobbler repaired them. Gregorio kept them clean and polished and they were pride of his wardrobe. He walked like a duck because they were so out-of-proportion to his body. His family had sent him down to the airfield to sell us knickknacks, believing that our guards wouldn't shoot children. Gregorio said his father had been an Italian soldier who was killed in Africa.

That was our introduction to Gregorio. Gregorio was an interesting little guy, probably about ten or eleven years old. It was difficult to judge their ages because of their poor nutrition. He took good care of his family, supporting his mother, grandmother and siblings. He believed all life in the United States originated and centered around Chicago. His driving ambition was to get to the United States, particularly Chicago, and become a gangster. When I asked why, he said, "Oh, much money. All to eat that you want. Drive a big car. Get a big pistola, many women." All he talked about, and probably all he thought about, was going to Chicago and being a gangster. It was quite comical to listen to his description of gangster life and then ask us whether or not it was true.

When I tried to explain where New Mexico was, all he wanted to know was how far it was from Chicago. I finally said it was near Texas, and that interested him a little, because he'd heard of cowboys and Indians.

I'll never forget the last time I saw him. He came by every week or so. The last time was near the end of my tour, and I told him I would be leaving. He never could say "Mack." He always said "Moc." "Moc," he said, "are you going back to

America?" When I confirmed that, tears welled up in his eyes. He was still wearing that pair of shoes that we had given him which he kept shined, despite the mud. And he was wearing the same clothes, layers and layers of clothes with that wool knit cap. He was so very proud of that cap which we'd given him on that first day when we found him crying behind our tent.

We met another Italian boy, twelve-year-old Antonio. Neatly dressed, his clothes were always clean and pressed. He was from an upper middle-class family living in Manfredonia, the little fishing village near the group. Antonio was a little business man. He came around the camp on a regular schedule and picked up our clothes. His family did our laundry whenever we gave them half of a bar of soap. They also developed our photographs. Antonio walked back and forth, eight or nine miles a day, to tend his business. Antonio was an extremely bright child, and he more or less adopted us. He considered himself a part of the Second Bomb Group.

During a conversation, I discovered he occasionally visited his brother, who was still serving in an anti-aircraft battery with the Axis forces in Milano. I was astonished that anybody could get across No-Man's Land (Gothic Line) there. The war was stalemated in that section of the Italian front, and it looked like the trench warfare and barbed wire of the First World War. I was under the impression that a lizard couldn't crawl through the front. Additionally, the distance was several hundred miles, but Antonio said he had made it, and I didn't doubt his word because he was a very capable lad.

Gregorio and Antonio became good friends. I wouldn't be surprised if Gregorio is now a Chicago gangster. Several years after my return to New Mexico, I saw a movie newsreel clip on the Marshall Plan in Italy. One of the young men helping to organize a soup kitchen under the Marshall Plan, I am positive, was Antonio. Lesher received a letter from Antonio after he returned to the States. As it was several pages long and written in Italian, Lesher asked an acquaintance, an Italian airline pilot, to translate it for him. Unfortunately, the pilot was involved in an automobile accident and the letter disappeared. What Antonio had to say will never be known. Where is Antonio today? My guess is he is probably a very successful Italian businessman.

The Virgin

There was little available in the way of recreation, and we had even less time and energy to pursue it, but occasionally we had spare time to spend improving our lives and the lives of our friends.

One of our friends in the squadron, we discovered after we'd been in Amendola a few months, was a virgin and didn't have the remotest idea of how the birds and bees pollinated the flowers. A number of us cooked up a plot to help our friend lose his virginity.

He was a tough guy, but very naive. Previous to our intervention, he had gone on R&R to the Isle of Capri. Upon his return, he developed a terrible itching in his crotch and went to see the flight surgeon. The flight surgeon knelt with tweezers and a magnifying glass and asked our man whether or not he had been flying. He answered in the affirmative. The surgeon asked him how high. The answer was, about thirty thousand feet. The surgeon replied, "Well, that just goes to prove that altitude does not kill these bastards." Our friend was horrified and indignant. He swore up and down he could not have crabs, but crabs he most certainly did have. How he had acquired them, since he was still a virgin at the time, he didn't know, but finally decided they had come from an infected blanket he had borrowed from sailors at the naval installation on Capri where he had stayed. We gave him a hard time about being a member of the walking plague.

Antonio and his family were some of the few Italians we knew. He knew us all, and we became well-acquainted with his family. The entire family was very intelligent. There weren't many girls around Amendola, as previously mentioned, and since Antonio and his family knew everybody in the vicinity, we incorporated Antonio into our plot. At twelve years old, he was horrified that a man of twenty could still be a virgin. Our opinion was that Antonio must have lost his when he was five or six. We asked Antonio to find a nice girl for our friend. Antonio promised to get together with his family and come up with someone.

He did just that. His aunt was widowed when her husband was killed in Africa some time ago. She needed a husband. All of Antonio's family agreed she needed a man, but they didn't want her to shame herself. She was obviously a woman of some class and taste. Antonio told us she was self-supporting and owned her own home in a town nearby. We suggested she rent a room to our friend for a few days as he liked to fish. He would bring the food if she would do the cooking.

Antonio came by the next morning to tell us he had arranged for them to meet that evening. The timing was perfect as we were facing a four-day break from missions. All the plotters enthusiastically donated items for the meeting: chewing gum, K-rations, several packs of Kools, and a can of Vienna sausages and other food stuffs. All told, about fifteen men contributed to this war chest, which we smuggled to the aunt. We urged our friend to see the sights and go fishing. He could even rent this room from one of Antonio's relatives. The aunt was equally unaware of the plot.

The two met and they hit it off famously. Nature took its course. We thought! After 52 years we learned what actually happened. The weather was windy and rainy, and the Portugese Man-of-War and the white shark were out, so no one went fishing. Lesher had met an old football buddy and went with him to deliver orders. All these years we have snickered behind our hands about something that never happened!

The Unsung and
Forgotten Heroes

I don't think much of heroes because we were all just doing our jobs, but most of the true heroes in Italy were the ground and support crews. These were the fliers' heroes. They labored twenty-four hours a day to keep our Forts in the air. They fought their battles not against the enemy but against time, equipment and the elements. The war was physically and emotionally hard for them, and long. Ground crews were not rotated after so many missions like the flight crews. Most had started with the Group in North Africa and remained there for the duration of the war.

The pressure was especially strong on our mechanics and the other ground crews. They knew if they made a mistake, lives could be lost, planes could be lost. A B-17 was crewed by ten men who were totally dependent upon the ground crew. If a ground crewman made a mistake that caused a mechanical malfunction which resulted in the loss of airmen, he was generally never in a position to know this. So, he gave it everything he had to ensure he wasn't deficient or delinquent in his duties. He lived with the fear that he might make a mistake and overlook something.

It was easy to make a mistake because the B-17 was an extremely complex instrument. Every nook and cranny was crammed with equipment. Almost every inch of the aircraft had some function, and it was the job of the ground crew, the mechanics and armorers, to make sure all of that equipment was functioning properly on every mission. Every plane had its assigned ground crew, supervised by a line chief. We had met our line chief, Bernard Cohen, on that traumatic first day in Amendola. Italian weather was not kind to Cohen's arthritis and we admired the courage with which he coped with his disability and refused to take a medical discharge. Cohen seemed to be every place, all night, all day. If an airplane returned from a mission with rough-running engines, instantly you would see him drive up in his jeep and ask the crew chief: "Sounds like you have a problem here. What seems to be the problem? What do you think?" Whenever the flight engineer on the aircrew discovered something he wanted redone, there might be an argument. If the crew chief wasn't amenable, Cohen was always the final judge as to what was to be done.

I don't know when they slept. Their job started when the airplanes returned from the daily missions. When you landed, generally the first person you saw was the crew chief. Very quietly he asked, "How was it? Did everything work well? Is there anything wrong? How bad is that hole? Did the shrapnel knock out anything important?" They began their work while the aircrews were de-briefed. If an airplane was badly shot up and had barely made it back to the field, or if it bellied in, it sometimes was a write-off. Instantly, every crew chief swarmed over that airplane like a pack of wolves feasting on a deer, cannibalizing it for parts to improve his own airplane. While the aircrews ate supper and went back to their tents, or prepared for the next mission, the ground crews worked. They worked throughout the night. By midnight, asleep in our tents we could hear the sound of engines being run up and tested. Some of us were "pulling missions," having nightmares. Others were peacefully snoring. As long as the engines checked out and ran smoothly, the snoring continued. But the instant an engine had a mag drop, the snoring stopped. Even in our sleep, we knew when an engine had a magneto problem, and thought, "That guy has only a couple of hours to get that corrected." When an engine ran roughly, you were instantly aware of it, and even in a deep sleep it made you uncomfortable. The sound of a smoothly running engine was as good as a lullaby.

While the mechanics patched the frames and worked on the engines, the armorers and technical crews also were hard at it. The armorers loaded the bombs, which was extremely hard, dangerous, physical labor. They generally loaded each aircraft with six 1000-pound or twelve 500-pound bombs. The mechanical hoists could only get them up so high; then it required muscle power to maneuver them into the shackles of the bomb release. Next they checked and re-checked the arming wires and fuses, because if an arming wire came off in flight and the small propeller on the fuse started running in mid-flight, the bomb would explode prematurely. It was a tough business. You could tell who, among the ground crew, were the armorers. They generally had fingers and toes missing, or bandaged feet or hands from being smashed by inert and heavy bombs.

When they finished loading the bombs, the armorers went over the aircraft checking for the "witches and gremlins," as we called the small problems and considerations that could end a mission as certainly as flak or enemy fighters. They diligently checked and cleaned everything in all defensive weapons systems, loaded every ammunition cannister and ensured that the ammo would come out evenly and smoothly. *Flak Holes* had seen a lot of flight-time, and had problems that never seemed to get fixed. As mentioned earlier, *Flak Holes'* bomb rack always gave us problems. Everything humanly and mechanically possible was done to correct it. Before a mission we would test-fire the racks before they were loaded and they worked fine. Once on the mission, they wouldn't work. Perhaps they were susceptible to freezing in the extreme temperatures at the altitudes we were flying. The armorers continually changed the wiring and tried everything imaginable, but could never solve the problems. Gremlins were credited for this unsolvable aggravation. Someone drew a picture of a gremlin. It had the body of a leprechaun and a devil's face, with lightening bolts coming from his body.

On a mission the rack was set to drop the bombs either in salvo or in train. When you set the bombs to drop in train, they would fall at pre-determined intervals, one at a time. The salvo setting would drop the entire bomb load in one operation. Salvoing made the pilots unhappy because the sudden loss of six thousand pounds caused the plane to jump and it was difficult to maintain formation. *Flak Holes'* pilots were usually unhappy because our rack never worked well, and the bombs seldom dropped in train. It was the bombardier's and mine, as AG, to be sure the bombs left the airplane, and more often than not, they didn't drop in train. When that happened the bombardier had to hit the salvo switch.

While the armorers worked, the technical people were also busy, generally trying to get the radios working properly. Their biggest headache was making sure the radio systems were right. They also had to devise measures to keep our radios from being jammed by the Germans. They had their nightmares as well.

The ground crews lived and worked in extremely rough conditions. Most of them had joined the Second Bomb Group when it was in North Africa, and followed it to French Morocco, Algiers, then Tunis, and Italy. The Second Bomb Group was a gypsy organization, moving with the ebb and flow of the battle in North Africa. They never had adequate personnel, parts, equipment and very few of the niceties of life. There they were always out in the open desert where they endured searing heat in the day, sometimes as high as 120 degrees, followed by ice-cold nights. Tools would be red-hot from lying out in the sun. Dust storms and scorpions added to their torment. Everything they ate was gritty with sand.

Italy was a little better, even though the odor from emptied slop jars and centuries of fertilizing the soil with human excrement were omnipresent. Amendola was close to Foggia, which had been almost destroyed by Allied bombing a few months before our arrival. Hundreds of civilians had been killed in the fighting and bombing. On hot days the smell of unburied and poorly buried decomposing bodies permeated clothing, food and everything around us. The sewer system had been destroyed, so that smell also penetrated your clothes and your taste buds. At least in Italy, they didn't have to eat sand. In Italy they ate mud. The best description of Italian mud is smelly chocolate pudding. It stuck and stuck.

The ground crews worked on the planes outdoors, with no hangars or any form of shelter. Their faces were sun and wind-burned like leather from working out in the open, under those primitive conditions. Their hands and arms were covered with burn scars. Frequently, their ears were scarred and bloody from crawling around the interior of the airplanes and bumping into sharp-cornered equipment. No matter how cold the weather, our ground crews were constantly using their bare hands to clean parts in carbon tetrachloride. As a result, their hands were always split, cracked, and bleeding. You could always spot a ground crewman simply by his split and cracked fingers and knuckles. Their clothes were always soaked in mud, carbon tet, and gasoline. They always seemed tired, their eyes bloodshot from loss of sleep. Even in the mess hall, two or three would be together quietly discussing a technical problem that one had on an airplane—what they should do and how another had solved a similar problem. I don't know when they slept.

While we slept, others in the support groups labored. The clerical personnel made sure crews were available, kept track of sick leave, and those of us on R&R, and made sure a full complement of airmen was present to make a mission the following day.

Intelligence personnel always stayed busy. Their work began by de-briefing every airman at the end of each mission. Valuable mission information on enemy aircraft concentrations, size and type of flak, as well as bomb results had to be gathered and disseminated. They had to reassess the changes in flak gun positions along the mission route, as flak batteries moved constantly. Some airman might report that a squadron of German 109s had moved from one area to another, or a new enemy airstrip had shown up on the latest intelligence films along the way. Intelligence personnel assessed and reassessed information all night as this new data had to be ready for mission briefing the following morning. This, too, was an all-night job as they poured over damage assessment reports to determine the effectiveness of that mission. Photo reconnaissance pictures were also evaluated.

Our intelligence officers spent many hours poring over reports trying to keep track of the German fighter units and flak units, where they had relocated, and where we were apt to stagger across them unawares. There was plenty of midnight oil burned trying to figure out what the opposition would be en route, to provide us with the best route to miss that opposition. They also labored to give us the best escape routes, the best way to get out if you were shot down over a certain area, or how to contact the underground to try to come home. They tried to tell us what our best chance was for survival, four or five hundred miles from home: what plan of action to take and where we should go to miss heavy concentrations of German soldiers. Giving us evasion information was an especially difficult task for our Intelligence people because the Fifteenth Air Force ranged far and wide—across Greece, Russia, Rumania, Yugoslavia, Poland and Hungary, in addition to Italy, France and Germany.

Meteorologists were another group of unappreciated heroes of the war, as far as I'm concerned. Meteorology is still not an exact science, but what we have today is a vast improvement over what we had in the 1940s. Correct meteorological data was very important to us. Meteorologists working with the Eighth Air Force in England always had to contend with fog. In the Fifteenth, our weathermen had to contend with a tougher prospect, the Alps. The Alps were a constant headache. Would there be heavy icing that day? Would the turbulence over them be bad? Could we climb over the thunderstorm build ups? What would the winds aloft be? Although we generally had better weather conditions in Italy, we still had to contend with thunderstorm build-ups. Accurate weather forecasting was even more important for the slow B-17.[1] It was very important to know the wind speed over target. If our bomb group was headed into a fifty mile per hour wind, that effectively reduced our ground speed by fifty miles an hour. At those speeds they could almost kill you with a BB gun. You were a sitting duck. A wrong meteorological reading could get your group knocked out very quickly. On a maximum range mission, head winds or a jet stream could deplete your fuel supply and force a landing behind enemy lines. It was also important that bombers did not stay too long on any particular bomb run from the IP to the target area. Another factor meteorologists had to consider was the direction and speed of ground winds because the Germans were expert at covering large areas with smoke pots. All these considerations kept the meteorologists busy throughout the night preparing for the next mission.

Ground support crews that weren't in on the pre-mission briefings could generally guess from the type and number of bombs and fuel loads we were carrying whether it was going to be a deep penetration. If we carried a heavier load of bombs but less fuel, a shorter mission was planned. They had an instinct for targets, too.

When we returned from a mission—if we were lucky enough not to have to fire the flares on landing, signifying that we had injured or dead on board, or we were in trouble of some kind—it gave us a terrific feeling to come back and see our ground crew standing there when we taxied up. We could give them a thumbs up, meaning everything looks pretty good. It was pleasant to see our crew chief, who was normally so serious, grin from ear to ear when you told him everything had gone smoothly, everything worked right, the airplane was in good shape. Maybe it had a hole in it over there but he could stick a rag in it, jokingly of course. You could see him swell with pride.

Our jobs were tough as well. We took casualties, were shot down and either died or became prisoners, but we got it over with one way or the other. We completed our missions and it was finished with us. We could go home. The ground crews stayed until the war was finished. There was no rotation for them. The war was hard and long for those men. Many were married men who had not seen their families for several years. During that time they missed seeing their offspring change from babies into children. Wives would write about Little Johnnie being in the hospital and it might be two weeks before the next mail delivery brought the welcome news that he was now doing fine. Theirs was a lonely, stressful life.

They genuinely cared for us, but they avoided us socially and didn't want to know us all that well or have much personal contact. All they wanted to know was how well we did our job. Upon my arrival in Italy, I tried to be friendly to our crew chief, Sergeant Hart. He was from South Carolina, about 27 years old, although you couldn't tell it because he, like all the rest, always had a gaunt, tired, grease-smeared face, covered with beard stubble. One particular day, after I had struck up what I had wanted to be a friendly conversation, he turned to me.

"McGuire," he said, "you seem to be a nice person. You've got a good crew. You take care of the airplane. All of you seem to be business-like, no big problems. But I don't want to get to know you socially. If you are lucky enough, you get to go home when you finish your missions. I've got to stay here for the rest of the war. When this is all over, I'll get to go home and I don't know when that's going to be." He kicked the ground a little bit before he continued in a choked voice, "You're the seventh crew I've served, and I don't want to get that close to you. I've had my heart broken enough times. I've shed enough tears. So you mind your business, you tell me what's wrong and I'll fix it. You take care of my airplane."

That was the general attitude. They didn't want to be friendly. You knew they cared because if you had a casualty, they were there. They would walk into the tent or come up to you on the line and say, "I'm sorry about so and so, he was a good man." So you knew they cared, they just didn't want the heartache of seeing more friends go down. When told I was leaving, it was difficult to keep from going up to Sergeant Hart and hugging him. He had thawed some and I knew he was genuinely happy that I made it and was going home, but he also knew that he had to work until the end of the war. And, he had another green bunch of airmen that was now his eighth crew.

So far as I know, our ground crew served the unit until the war was over. Very few of them were rotated. They simply stayed until the war was over—from the time they got there until the time it ended. I can't praise our ground crew enough. They served quietly, without fanfare, without medals, without kind words or clean clothes or a lot of R&R. Everyday, as we flew off we would see those gaunt, dirty, oil-soaked men, who gave their all every day and every night. You don't easily forget people like that.

Two years ago I attempted to find that crew chief at a Bomb Group reunion. I was surprised and delighted to see Cohen, our line chief, and asked him what had happened to Sergeant Hart. I wanted to see him, thank him, hug him. Cohen didn't know what happened to him. Hart took his discharge in Italy and simply disappeared. A staunch Baptist, rumors had filtered back to Cohen that Hart had entered the priesthood at the Vatican, and was now serving in a seminary. Someday I would like to write and thank him for all the hours he put in, and for the deprivations he endured to keep our aircraft flying.

Chapter 17

[2] Cruising speed of the B-17G, the model flown by McGuire's crew, was 160 mph. Jablonski, 311.

– 18 –

Togglier &
Chin-Turret Gunner

In mid-November I began to receive occasional duty as chin turret gunner, a position where I also had the responsibility of being the togglier. At that time, navigators were in short supply, and since bombardiers were cross-trained as navigators, they became substitute navigators. A togglier served in lieu of a bombardier and was generally the armor/gunner since he was acquainted with the electrical and mechanical systems that had to do with the bombing and also had rudimentary training on the Norden bomb sight. Each squadron generally had two toggliers.

Before they built the G-models with chin turrets under the nose, B-17s were extremely vulnerable to frontal attacks. The .50 caliber machine guns on the sides of the nose weren't effective in preventing frontal attacks. It didn't take the Luftwaffe very long to determine the nose was the most effective point of attack. Even after chin turrets were installed, German fighters continued to attack the nose. Attacking from that angle, they were not so exposed to fire from the defensive boxes, and the closing speed of attack was higher.

We needed good shots in the nose, and I often flew there, firing twin fifties. I liked the chin turret, with the bombsight in front of me and the turret's bicycle handlebar-style firing controls. The remote gunsight dropped from the ceiling and, because of my armorer training, I knew how to set it to shoot exactly where I pointed the guns. The chin turret gunner's seat was above two .50 caliber guns which were hung in a revolving turret, or 'tub.' The chin turret was exposed to freezing air, and had the bad habit of freezing if you weren't careful. During the flight, the operator constantly moved the turret, exercising it every few minutes to keep the oil hot. If you didn't keep the turret warm, it was impossible to track a fighter; it would not move fast enough. Also, it was imperative to keep the nose plexiglass immaculately clean, otherwise a little spot of oil or mud could suddenly become a fighter with crosses painted on it firing at you.

I liked shooting from the chin turret. Shooting an extra gun was good for my morale. If I had had ten guns, I would have used every one. The chin turret fit the airplane well, but it was a little off-center. The pilot knew the instant I fired. The chin guns were only as accurate as the gunner operating them, but they seemed to be more effective because there were two as opposed to only one in the waist. They were absolutely necessary for meeting nose attacks.

We were taking heavy losses in all categories of airmen, but especially among navigators. Lesher had his table and calculations shot up several times, an occurrence which rendered him quite vocal. Navigators were crucial to our task, as well as to a plane's survival. The navigator in each plane had to know its precise location at all times, because if you were hit and had to drop out of formation, the squadron navigator wasn't any help to you. The navigator was busy all the time, working from the start of a mission to its finish. Every little turn you made to dodge a flak battery, or avoid a defensive area, he had to note. There was no such thing as flying in a straight line to or from a target.

Effective bombing was to drop our bombs on the target in as concentrated a circle as possible. Our bombs were never big enough, so we used a bombing technique called the LeMay System, where a designated group bombardier led the group into the target area. When he dropped his bombs, bombardiers on the other planes dropped their bombs at the same time. They picked the best bombardiers for lead bombardiers, the same as they picked the best crews for lead planes in the squadrons.

A perfect bomb strike over the marshalling yards in Budapest.
(Courtesy L. Scofield)

Three in the Second Bomb Group competed for that lead position. During that competition, one bombardier put a bomb in a twenty-foot-square pond at twenty-three thousand feet. He became the group bombardier.

During bomb runs, the other bombardiers watched the lead ship. When its bomb bays opened, that was the signal to open ours. Nearing the target, all the other bombardiers watched the belly of the lead plane. When you saw the fin on that first bomb, you dropped yours. Hopefully, the whole squadron dropped simultaneously with the group bombardier. If everything worked well, those bombs weren't scattered, but concentrated for maximum damage. Intervelometer settings—the rate bombs came out of the racks—were set the same throughout the group.

That is, this was true for every plane but *Flak Holes*. The bomb racks were temperamental and never worked correctly on that plane. We always dropped our entire load at the same time, and probably made the biggest bomb craters in Europe.

Six gunners in our group, including myself, were assigned as toggliers/ gunners. We had received rudimentary training on the Norden bomb sight in the event we were forced out of formation and had to drop on the target on our own.

– 19 –

Flying With Other Crews

A Check Ride

It was in the late fall, sometime after my thirtieth mission. My crew and I were enjoying a stand-down day by sleeping late, doing laundry, or writing letters home. It seemed we never got enough rest. Fenstermaker approached the tent. "Alright, troops," he said, "We're on the board to fly tomorrow. McGuire, you're flying with another crew, and we are getting the left waist gunner of that crew. They're all new to me. Apparently they were in the bunch that came in three or four days ago."

Because I had flown more missions than the rest of my crew and had previously flown with new crews, someone had put in my personnel folder that I was good with new crews, tolerating no sloppiness, and was a good instructor. I often cussed the guy who put that notation on my record, because it meant that now I had to take another green crew up and evaluate them.

No veteran liked to fly with green crews. That's how you could get killed easily. They made mistakes. Green pilots often straggled, got out of formation, or could not take head-on attacks without flinching and breaking formation. Green gunners were very noticeable to enemy fighters. Veteran gunners burned the Luftwaffe at long distances, hitting them accurately and at distances out to a thousand yards. When you hit them the moment they turned in, and if the fire was accurate, German pilots generally looked for somebody else. Many green gunners couldn't hit accurately, or to any distance, so their fire was wasteful. Enemy pilots knew immediately when a plane was flown by a green crew. That plane would be a hot lunch, and they worked it over.

Obviously, I wasn't too happy about the assignment. I asked Fenstermaker if he knew the name of the pilot flying this crew. The name he mentioned made me feel a little better as he was an old-timer in the squadron. If I had to fly with a green crew, it wasn't so bad if the plane was flown by an experienced, seasoned aircraft commander. I left the tent and walked to squadron headquarters, checking out the schedule for myself. Sure enough, the following day I was assigned to fly with a brand new crew, so new I hadn't even heard of their names. They had come in three or four days earlier and had spent their time orienting and getting settled. Their A/C was flying as co-pilot on that mission, and I double-checked to make sure Fenstermaker was correct. Yes, an experienced squadron pilot was scheduled to fly as commander. I returned to the Amendola Ritz and enjoyed the rest of the day off, getting to bed late that evening.

By the time the CQ came around a little after 0200 I was already wide awake listening to the aircraft on the line about four or five miles from us. The running engines all sounded good. We had our usual breakfast of powdered eggs and powdered milk. Our cooks were also enthusiastic about green peas and gravy. And marmalade. I hate marmalade!

Since I was flying with a new crew, I decided to arrive at the line early. Our takeoff was scheduled for 0630, and I wanted to get my own pre-flight checks out of the way and watch the new crew do theirs. Transportation dropped me off at the equipment shack. I checked out my gear carefully, and then walked the short distance to the aircraft.

After lifting myself into the airplane, I used my hand-cranked flashlight to check out the oxygen equipment and the fire extinguishers. By then I could hear the new crew walking up, so I got back out of the airplane. The officers—pilots, bombardier, and navigator—were still in briefing. They would arrive in about twenty minutes.

I watched the new crew for a few minutes and was encouraged. They looked very business-like and seemed to have the makings of a good crew. There wasn't a lot of horseplay, but then there never was before the first mission. If you tried to tell jokes your voice might crack and betray you. Watching them, I knew what was going on in their minds. It was what went on in anyone's mind before his first mission. You wondered if you can take it. You wondered if you would do your job and not let your crew down. You also wondered whether or not you had the courage to face fear, possible wounds, dismemberment, or death. I knew their stomachs were churning. After a while you learned to control those feelings. Then panic turns to dread.

Trying to identify any natural leaders, I quickly spotted one, the flight engineer/upper turret gunner. He was the oldest of the bunch, apparently in his late twenties, a short, stocky man. He was already a buck sergeant, but wasn't wearing combat promotion stripes, so he was obviously Regular Army. Most crews coming from the States held the rank of corporal and received their sergeant's stripes while in Italy. I liked him. He was very quiet, deep-voiced, all business.

I also watched for any signs of weakness: loud voices, men trying to laugh when they didn't feel like laughing. One had a loud voice—he turned out to be the right waist gunner. I could tell another guy was hurting. White-faced, shaking hands, and sullen, he continually looked at the ground.

My initial feelings about this crew were good. I had a little time to talk to them. As crew leader on this mission, maybe I could tell them some things that would save all our lives.

Asking them to gather around, first I asked whether anybody was from New Mexico, and nobody was. Then I began talking. "We've got plenty of time to get ready for this mission right now, so I'm going to give you some hard-bought tricks of the trade. What I'm about to tell you might keep you alive. It might help you. It certainly won't hurt you. As you make more and more missions, you'll develop your own style, but let me say right away I know you're worried about whether or not you can take it. Get it out of your mind. We have had only a few people who can't perform in combat. You've been well-trained. You knew what to expect when you signed up. Now it's time to earn your keep, and it's too late to worry about whether or not you are man enough to take it, or doubt your ability to perform under fire. You're going to be alright. I know you're scared. I'm scared right now. You'd be an idiot if you weren't scared. The important thing is to learn to perform well under fire, and keep your wits about you. If you can do this, you'll be alright. Some of you may even enjoy it. I immensely enjoyed my first mission until I got a hole shot through my collar—after that it ceased being funny."

At that point one man asked how many missions I had flown, and I told him over thirty. I also told him it seemed like a million, but I had made it so far.

"Don't worry about the worst but prepare for it. Now listen carefully. The first thing you should check is your oxygen mask. This is the most important piece of equipment you've been issued. It's been custom-fitted to your face. A lot of time has been spent making sure it is the right size and doesn't leak. Every time you return from a mission, clean it carefully. Every day we're flying at altitudes between twenty-eight and thirty thousand feet. If you lose oxygen because your mask is functioning improperly it will only be a few seconds before you pass out, and in a few minutes you'll be dead. So this is the most important piece of equipment you have. I always examine mine in the equipment room where I have plenty of light. I look for cracks in the rubber because these things go through tremendous temperature ranges. These masks are all that connect you with life until the plane is back to under fifteen thousand feet, so take care of it, clean it, and always check your connections. Also, keep the drain on it clear. Moisture from the mask condenses and ices up, so every once in a while reach up and squeeze that little outlet and you won't get frostbite on your throat.

"Another thing about your oxygen. Check all valves and connections very carefully, before and during the mission. The ground crews are supposed to make sure they work, but sometimes they will overlook a connection or a valve. Also know where all the walk-around oxygen bottles are located. They aren't in the same position on all models of B-17s. Never, ever use one of these bottles except in an emergency! These bottles will give you a few minutes to perform any emergency work that needs to be attended to away from your oxygen connection. The other day one of our pilots lost his oxygen on the run from IP to target. He flew the mission to target hooked up to the emergency bottle until they could get some other system fixed up. You never know when you'll need one, so don't misuse them. Also, keep a constant check on your oxygen connections after you've put on your flak vest. The vest sometimes will yank a connection loose. Learn to keep an eye on the other guy's connections as well. When the pilot tells you to put on your oxygen masks, put them on and don't take them off until he tells you to do so. There will be no smoking at any time on a mission.

"One other thing before I leave the subject of oxygen masks. All of you are scared to death. Your stomachs are churning. Some of you might get airsick. If you feel that you have to throw up, don't choke it down. Go ahead and get it over with. You'll notice tins that have been placed in the aircraft. That's what those tins are for. Get it over with, because if you foul up your oxygen mask with that mess you'll be in big trouble. We have no way to clean it up there, and if you have to take it off you'll start

272

losing oxygen and you'll get your face frozen. If you can help it, don't throw up in your cloth helmet or your steel helmet. Whatever you do don't throw up in my steel helmet. That's the quickest way to get a concussion. I plan to use mine to cover my head when the shooting starts. Anyway, don't fight the nausea. Go ahead and get rid of it when we're not getting shot at.

"Keep your muffler around your neck at all times. We wear them, not because they're fashionable, or because that's what airmen wear, but because they will save your throat from frostbite. When we're up there, you need to keep your eyes and head moving all the time, just like you've been trained. Those German fighters can be on you in a flash, so keep your head constantly moving, and if you wear a muffler around your neck it won't get raw from the motion.

"When you've finished checking your personal equipment inside the aircraft, inspect your immediate surroundings. Know where the emergency exits and fire extinguishers are located. Get to the point where you can automatically turn and have whatever it is you need. Always have your flak vest handy, because you never know when you'll need it. Normally, you can expect flak over the target, but lately we've been running into many mobile flak batteries that the Germans run under us when we're not expecting it. They'll put these batteries under us and ambush us, and when the flak starts hitting, you need to be able to just reach over and put on your vest.

"The waist gunners have the responsibility of looking after the ball turret gunner and the tail gunner. Make sure the latches on the ball turret are closed securely after he goes down into it. Make sure his oxygen connections are good after he puts on his flak vest, too. We lost a ball turret gunner about three months ago. He threw his flak vest on and, unknowingly, pulled his oxygen connections loose. He died. Also, occasionally the waist gunners need to check on the tail gunner. He's back there all by himself most of the trip.

"You turret gunners, keep your turrets turning. Exercise them to keep the oil hot. They will freeze at high altitudes.

"If everything else fails, we'll have to bail out, so take very good care of your parachutes. Before every mission check them out carefully in the equipment room where there is plenty of light. Check the pins. Guys on the ground don't have time to repack every 'chute after every mission. Our ball turret gunner once got a call from the equipment room. They showed him that some flak had hit his parachute and cut several shroud lines, yet you couldn't see the flak hole from the outside. If he had to bail out, he would have made a pretty streamer all the way to the ground. So make sure you look for flak holes in your parachute when you turn it in. When you pick up your 'chute bag in the equipment room, make sure you have the 'chute assigned to you. Don't get somebody else's. If you get hold of my 'chute, I'll knock holes in your head because I take good care of mine. I examine it regularly, even before I turn it in. Take good care of it when you're taking it to the airplane. Don't set it in down in pools of oil or water. Put it in a bin in the airplane where you can just turn around and snap it on." Except for the pilots, the crew wore chest parachutes. We always wore the harness. The parachute had rings that snapped onto the harness. With practice, you could snap it on in one easy motion.

"Have a plan in your mind," I continued, "about what you'll do if we have to bail out, which escape hatch you'll use, how you'll get to it. You won't have much time to think things through for the first time when, and if, you get into trouble up there. If you have to bail out, know exactly how many steps and where you'll get out. Long ago I decided if I had to jump out, I was going to jump out of the waist. If I couldn't get out of the waist, I planned to drop out of the bomb bay. The important thing is know where you'll get out.

"When you jump, don't be in a hurry to pull the ripcord. I've seen a lot of guys jumping from airplanes who pulled the ripcord while they were still in the plane. They're now dead. Watch out for the horizontal stabilizers when you jump. Make sure you at least clear the plane, and then the formation before you pull the ripcord. Try to wait until you are under fifteen thousand feet before you pull the ripcord, so you can breathe.

"Keep a razor sharp knife with you in case you have to cut your shroud lines if they get entangled in trees or wires. I also keep a .45 pistol handy, in case I have to land in Ustashi (Croatian) territory. I've decided I'm either going to kill myself or die fighting if I land there. Start to learn geography in case you have to bail out, and stay on top of escape and evasion techniques.

"Don't put your fur flying gear on too soon. In a few minutes you're going to be colder than you've ever been in your life. You don't want to get hot on the ground and then in an hour start freezing. Put your furs on last, then put on your parachute harness and Mae West. You'll need your Mae West because of the Adriatic. Make sure it's in good shape, and that it's fastened right.

"Your A/C is an old-timer. He's been here a long time. He's a very, very good man. He's easy-going and pleasant, but if you want trouble, don't try telling jokes or singing or having idle conversation on the intercom. In combat that is not a party line for your enjoyment. It is used only for business, and we're very sensitive about the use of the intercom. The intercom should be kept open at all times. For one thing it is the only way that we can be sure that several positions—the radio operator, the ball turret gunner, and the tail gunner—are still functioning. This pilot will skin you alive if you misuse the intercom.

"If you have anything to report, do so in a calm voice. Don't screech or yell into the intercom. You can create panic in an airplane very easily by screaming an identification. Immediately report any enemy fighters that you see. Report them as 'bogies,' and their location using the clock system. Try to identify how many of them as well. We've been getting hit by larger and larger numbers of them."

I had been talking for about ten minutes, but they all seemed to be concentrating on my words. Their attention picked up even more when I started telling them about the enemy fighters.

"The Fifteenth is really hammering Germany hard.[1] We are bombing their fuel production and transportation systems. Our bombing raids are breaking their backs and cutting their throats. We are bringing them to their knees, but there are still plenty of fighters around. The Germans have always been good, but lately they are getting more and more fanatical. Those fighter pilots are good, and they are motivated because we are now bombing their homeland. We are killing their industries and bombing their homes, families, and friends.

"You may not see more than five or six fighters for several missions, then you might get jumped by a group as large as two-hundred and fifty. They are concentrating their fighters, selecting and taking out entire squadrons. The day my crew joined the Twentieth here at Amendola, they had shot down every plane in it.

"The Germans know we're coming two hours before we get there. They can see us on radar when we leave our rendezvous because we have to climb so high to cross the Alps. From the time we get over the Adriatic, we can expect enemy fighters from Italy and Yugoslavia. We can expect enemy fighters all the way to and from the target, so conserve your ammunition. We only have about one minute's worth of ammunition at each gun, so fire short bursts. If a fighter comes at you, don't hose him down. You've got to make the ammunition last. On the way to target, when the pilot orders us to test fire our guns, don't fire more than five or six rounds, that's all."

I also gave them some personal observations on how I shot at fighters, along with some points on the kind of fighters, German and Italian, that we would probably encounter.

"You're here for two reasons, and the first is to protect your airplane with your gun. The second is to serve as an observer. If a plane is hit, count the number of parachutes coming out of it. Keep your eyes open for maritime shipping and for convoys going down the Adriatic. Report all sightings to the pilot. The navigator will log all sightings, and the radio operator, using his signal key, will inform the Fifteenth Air Force with what they call a 'news flash.' The Tactical Air Force will hopefully attack these targets if they're close enough. Our escorts, too, like to go down and work over these targets if any are available. Also the bombardier will show you a picture of the target so you can identify it and, after the drop, perhaps you can give us some idea of how the bombs fell."

The truck carrying the officers arrived and I concluded my comments with, "I'm only here today to give the A/C my evaluation of your performance and to pull my weight as a member of your crew.

"The officers will now give us a briefing of our bombing run today, so listen up." None of the crew had any questions for me. They seemed to have listened intently to what I had to say. Whether or not they were sobered by the information I couldn't say, but they were quiet.

The A/C walked over and told everybody to gather around. He introduced himself, and me, to the new arrivals. The crew's normal A/C, the man flying as co-pilot today, interested me. A first lieutenant, he looked like he had had some combat experience. He didn't have a fresh-faced look like the other men. I could tell that he and the engineer would team up and run that crew well.

The pilot started our briefing. "You guys are not getting a milk run to begin your combat. The target today is Vienna." There were audible gasps and groans. They had been around three or four days, and already knew that Vienna was a hell-hole. The flak there was concentrated and deadly accurate. The pilot continued, "We are going to bomb an oil refinery at Lobau, in the suburbs of Vienna. We should be over the target about eleven o'clock. It looks like the weather is going to be good. We will be flying in the high box, in the number six position with the Twentieth Squadron. We'll fly at twenty-nine thousand feet. It's going to be cold. Our call sign will be 'Tweet Tweet Frank.' I can tell from the looks on your faces that you've heard about Vienna. The only nice thing about Vienna is that it's only about a twelve-hundred mile round trip. We'll be crossing the Adriatic, so be sure you are wearing your Mae Wests. I also want you to use intercom discipline. I don't like a lot of talking on the intercom. It's for business. No joking, singing, or idle talking. Forget about your self-doubts. Look after one another, and you'll be alright. One of these days it will just be a memory. The navigator and the bombardier will show you a photograph of the target area so that you can get an idea of the location of the target. When they're finished we'll have about ten minutes until takeoff to take care of whatever business you need to tend to." He finished and went over and lifted himself into the airplane.

The navigator and the bombardier briefed us. When they finished, the crew split up. I noticed the co-pilot and the engineer huddling, talking seriously. One man went off by himself, back to the tail of the plane. He was the radio operator, the hurting one who had looked at the ground all the time. He walked back to the tail, and I walked after him. As was my custom when flying with Thompson, we went to the tail for a prayer and a short Bible lesson. That day, I, too, walked toward the tail and the radio operator. He was praying, so I kept my distance. When he turned and saw me standing there, I grinned. "It gets pretty lonesome in the radio room all by yourself, except for listening to all the conversations going on. You might open the door to the waist every now and then and let us know you're alive in there." He grinned back. Several others also joined me at the tail, and we prayed together for a few minutes. Then it was time to go.

The engineer and the co-pilot had finished talking, and the engineer went up to the hatch, threw in his parachute bag, and with one hand lifted himself into the plane. That was impressive. You had to be in top-notch physical condition to accomplish that feat.

Takeoffs were uneventful that day, if you can ever call taking off in an overloaded B-17 uneventful. We labored up to our rendezvous point and gained our altitude. Around nine thousand feet, the bombardier and I met in the bomb bay and removed the pins in the fuses. I took out the tail fuses, while he removed the front ones. I was back in position by the time we'd topped fifteen thousand feet, and the pilot told us to put on our oxygen masks and take positions.

Everything seemed to be going fine. The Wright Cyclone engines were still grinding away, taking us higher and higher to clear the Alps. By that time we were over an Adriatic dotted with whitecaps. We passed over a little fishing fleet that I often saw on missions.

We test-fired our guns. All the gunners, except the right waist gunner, fired two short bursts. The right waist fired about seven or eight rounds, which was not bad. I thought again that this might be a good crew.

About five miles off the coast of Yugoslavia, I spotted and reported maritime shipping, a couple of freighters zigzagging frantically as they headed toward shore. They had spotted us and probably thought the whole Fifth Wing was going to bomb them. I reported to the pilot and navigator that they were heading toward the Gulf of Venice, probably Trieste or some-place near there. Those freighters were making good time despite their zigzagging course. As I watched them, I felt an unexpected push from behind. It was the right waist gunner, crowding me as he too peered out the left waist. I couldn't believe this guy was away from his post *and* standing on my umbilicals, several of which he had unhooked. He turned and looked at me, smiling. I didn't say anything, but gave him a withering look and he hastily retreated to his position.

In a minute or two the navigator said we were over the coast of Yugoslavia and headed for the Alps. The weather was good that day, with scattered clouds. We started encountering the usual turbulence as we crossed the Alps.

Bypassing Zagreb on the right, the tailgunner reported what looked to him like flak over the city. We didn't know what they were shooting at. There weren't any B-17s over there. Maybe it was our escort. I asked the tailgunner what color the flak was, and he said that it was white. I reported over the intercom that it was probably big guns, 128mm. The pilot asked me how much a 128mm projectile weighed, and I told him about one-hundred and five pounds of scrap iron.

Wondering about our escort, I asked the pilot if he knew what P-51 group was escorting us that day. He said, "Roger, it's the 325th."

"Good," I responded, then added for the benefit of the nervous new crew, "they're one of the best groups we have. They're easy to identify, with yellow and black checkerboard tails. So don't shoot at anything that's got a checkerboard on it today."

The pilot then asked me about the difference between the 128 and the 88, as far as the color of the bursts and weight of the shell, and when I finished telling him, he said, "Thank you. All of that information was provided by McGuire, our in-house expert on flak."

A few minutes later the co-pilot called over the intercom. Our escorts would be joining us in a few minutes and advised us not to get excited and shoot them down if they had checkerboard tails.

The top-turret gunner called and said, "Top turret to crew. There's something going on at one o'clock high. I can't tell what it is. They're making contrails occasionally, but it looks real strange."

The co-pilot said, "I believe we've got a dog-fight going on up there. Keep your eyes peeled."

A minute later somebody reported a twin-engine aircraft going down steeply at twelve o'clock, engine smoking, heading for home. From my brief glimpse, it looked like a ME-410. He was dropping right into the rest of the Fifth Wing. Evidently he noticed that he was getting into four groups of B-17s, as he turned and headed toward Vienna, still in a steep dive.

Shortly after this the P-51s dropped some and crossed over the top of our formation. The pilot came on the intercom. "We're about five minutes from the IP, so get your gear on, put your pots on, and hang on."

On went our flak vests and steel helmets. Then we turned on the IP and started the bomb run. The bomb bay doors opened. The group below us began picking up occasional flak. The closer to target we flew the heavier, more intense, and more accurate was the flak from both barrage and tracking batteries. The air turned black along our path. Where our box was flying, however, there was little flak, but the Germans were using 88s, 105s, and 128s. Ahead and below we noticed parachutes coming from one of the lower groups, but we did not see any planes going down.

All of a sudden, our formation received four ranging bursts, very close together. I thought, 'Alright, here it comes.' One battery, apparently, had picked us up, getting our range. Three more rounds burst very, very close to us, but that was as close and as much as we got that day. For Vienna, this was a delight.

As we approached the target, I felt sorry for the groups underneath us. They were really catching it. I could hardly see them for the black smoke bursting around them. Shortly, we felt the plane lift a little and the bombardier said, "Bombs away!" As we made our right turn after passing the target, I looked back at the groups behind us. It looked like a black, vicious mess behind and below us. The target was really getting it that day, too. After two or three minutes we cleared the flak area, and all went back on alert. The pilots asked if there was any damage. Everybody checked in. The tail gunner said, "I have a big hole back here. It's about two or three inches high and about an inch wide. A piece of flak bounced off the wall and is lying here on the floor."

The pilot said, "Looks like we got a milk run out of this one today. I've never been to Vienna when it's this nice, but those other groups are catching it. Tail, keep your eyes open and see what happened to those other two parachutes."

This was a vulnerable time to get jumped by fighters, so I was keeping a pretty close watch out my waist, straining my eyes to spot any fighters in the area. A glance over at the right waist position showed the gunner wasn't there. I checked the floor, in case he had been hit. He wasn't there. I ran up to the radio room, thinking he might have had to use the relief tube, but he wasn't there. As I raced back to my position, I saw his feet sticking out of the tail. He was back in the tail with the tail gunner.

I called, "Left waist to tail gunner, are you alright?"

The tail gunner answered back, "I'm okay"

I said, "What's the right waist doing back there?"

"He said something about wanting to see my flak."

I told the tail gunner to tell him to get back to his post, but not quite that politely. The right waist gunner, who had disconnected his intercom, turned around to crawl back to his post. He was carrying one of the walk-around oxygen bottles. Back in his position, he put the bottle on the catwalk, and started hooking up his oxygen hose and communication gear. He had also thrown down his flak vest. I glared at him. He got the idea without my saying a word, and turned and started watching out his waist window.

The trip home was uneventful. When we had crossed the Alps and were over the Adriatic, we peeled off our fur gear and replaced it with our Mae Wests. We descended toward Italy, but were still on alert because of danger from fighters. As we dropped lower and closer to the coastline, the pilot told us we could take off our masks and start stowing the gear, except for the guns.

That was when I exploded. "What in the hell did you think you were doing back there? What was so urgent that it caused you to leave your post?"

He was very defensive. "I wasn't scared," he blurted. "I guess I was excited. When the tail said he had a hole and some flak, I went to see what it looked like." He added quickly, "I just realize now what a mistake I made."

"Yeah, you made a mistake. You're going to see a lot of flak before this war's over, and most of it is going to be from your commanding officer. You left your post in a combat situation without any authority. You were back there bothering the tail gunner while he needed to watch for bomb strikes. I told you this morning they like to hit us as we come off target so you needed to be on special alert right after we drop our bombs. You are in a hell of a lot of trouble."

He was white-faced and looked horrified. Tears popped into his eyes.

I didn't let up. "Read the label on that walk-around bottle."

He picked it up and read, "Emergency air supply, walk-around."

"Yea, that's right, it says 'emergency.' You were in the tail horsing around sightseeing, satisfying your curiosity. If we'd been attacked we would have been vulnerable at that point. I don't have to tell you that's a court-martial offense. The thing that bothers me more, though, is that you used an emergency bottle. You were running around sight-seeing with a precious supply of oxygen. So don't look miserable and tell me you're sorry. You should have thought of that earlier. I'll have to report this to the pilot, and I'm trying to figure out what to tell him. We're going over this again on the ground after we land, so meet me as soon as we get out of the airplane. You have probably cost your crew some additional training time."

On the way to the landing strip I could tell the word was quickly getting around to the crew. After we had rolled to a stop, I stowed my guns, grabbed my parachute bag and climbed out. The man met me back at the tail. Still white-faced, he had tears in his eyes and was shaking.

He said, "Sergeant, I wasn't scared. I just wasn't thinking. I never realized the seriousness of the situation."

I repeated that he was not a damned tourist up there, and I was going to have to report him.

He begged, "If you can let me off the hook this time, it's not ever going to happen again."

By that time, the engineer walked up, concern on his face. The others swarmed around the right waist gunner, talking to him. They were all upset. The man then had tears running down his face. The engineer took me by the arm and pulled me over to one side. He said, "Sergeant, he's a pretty good man, and this is a pretty good crew."

I agreed with him. "Yea, they are a good crew, and well-disciplined, except him. He was back there having a lark, having a good time, and he didn't understand the seriousness of the situation."

The engineer said, "Look, will you let me handle this? I will make sure he understands the seriousness of the situation." I told him that I couldn't turn the matter over to him, that I had to report it to the pilot, and if the pilot said it was all right, he could handle it. I didn't think he would ever do it again, and the engineer agreed.

After a few minutes the pilots left the plane and walked back to the tail. The co-pilot, and crew's regular A/C, looked very concerned, asked if we had a problem.

I told him, "Yes, sir, we had a little problem, but we've taken care of the matter. The engineer has asked me to let him handle it."

He said, "I'm not so sure that's the way to handle it, but I'll talk it over with the pilot. Stick around."

In a few minutes the pilot joined me, and we walked to the equipment room. "Well McGuire, we got a milk run out of Vienna. I don't believe it."

"Yes, sir, we got a milk run, but the rest of the outfit didn't. The Ninety-seventh and those other groups were getting it laid on them."

"Yeah, it was bad for them."

"Did we only see two 'chutes coming out of all of that?"

"Yes," he said. After a pause, he asked, "McGuire, did you have a problem back there?"

"Yes, sir, we did, but I took care of it."

"Was a guy sight-seeing back there?"

"Yeah, but he won't be doing that anymore. If you don't object, sir, I believe the matter is taken care of. He realized the error of his ways, and I gnawed on him pretty severely. This is a good crew, a proud crew, one of the best new crews I've ever flown with. With the exception of that one error, I'd say they were good. How was your co-pilot?"

"Man, that guy's been around. He was an instructor for a long time and has beaucoup flying hours. He taught me all kinds of things. I let him fly nearly the whole mission, and he did so without any trouble. He's going to be good. I liked the engineer and the up-front crew."

"Those were my sentiments as well, sir. If you don't mind, let me finish taking care of the matter back there."

"What did the guy do? Did he leave his position?"

"Yeah, he went back into the tail to look at a piece of flak, but he's not going to make that mistake again."

"Alright. I think the rest of them are good, and if you're satisfied that he'll come around I'll let the matter drop."

I turned and walked back to the engineer who had been watching us. He stood a little apart from the rest of the crew, who were gathered around the shaken right waist gunner. "Sergeant," I said, "if you think you can take care of this matter we're going to let it drop. Impress on him the serious nature of his offense, that all of us could have been killed because he wanted to look at a hole in the airplane and a little piece of flak."

"Don't worry, McGuire, I'll take care of it, and I appreciate your attitude. We got a milk run today after all, didn't we?"

"Yeah, but not the guys beneath us. There will be a lot of casualties in the Fifth Wing tonight."

I saw the crew several times during the next few days, waved at them and they waved back. Even the right waist returned my wave. I heard later they had been shot up after a good, long fight, and had to land on the Isle of Vis[2] off the coast of Yugoslavia, but I never learned whether they took casualties. They were as good a crew as I had ever flown with, except for that gunner.

A Green Crew and an Ass Chewing

I was convinced that I belonged to the best crew in the Fifteenth Air Force. We were well-trained and experienced and wanted to fly all our missions together, but flying with other crews was inevitable. No one liked to fly with unknown crewmen. I knew how my crew would react in the air. I didn't know how others would act. Somebody might make a mistake and everyone could die. It seemed we sustained more casualties among the inexperienced ones, the greenhorns, than the old-timers.[3] To keep the greenhorns from getting into trouble on their first missions, they generally placed an experienced crew member in new crews going into combat for the first time.

I had good work habits and maintained a good work ethic during my tour. Everything was done by the book—checking, rechecking, making sure things were exactly right, both on the ground and in the air. Our entire crew was that way, and the squadron brass must have liked that because they assigned me to break in several new crews. One morning towards the end of my tour I discovered they had assigned me to break in yet another new crew on their first combat mission.

After the briefing I hopped a ride to my assigned airplane and couldn't believe what I saw. The crewmen were evidently in high spirits. Two were wrestling with each other; another two were playing keep-away from a third by pitching his parachute over his head; one was resting calmly on the ground, hands behind his head, atop his parachute which he had thoughtlessly thrown in a pool of oil; the others were running around and playing like school kids. They were definitely not tending to business. The guns were still covered in canvas and they hadn't checked out the plane. I couldn't believe it. I became *very* upset.

Bailing out of the delivery truck like a man possessed, I started squalling. Just as I started yelling, a jeep drove up behind me. I was so upset I didn't pay any attention to them, other than assume they were mechanics driving up to work on the airplane, something mechanics were doing all the time.

My temper flared and my vocabulary became very profane. I lined them up and declared that the first one uttering a word would have his teeth spread all over the ramp. Then I proceeded to tell them what kind of dunces they were. Marching right up to their faces, I shouted that they didn't know what they were getting into, and they didn't care to find out. That parachute they were pitching around and possibly damaging, might, in a few hours, be one of their most sacred possessions. It was obvious they hadn't been inside their airplane. That angered me even more, and I let them have it. They didn't even know whether the oxygen system in their airplane was working. They had not checked their oxygen masks, or the pans, the guns, the ammunition, or the heaters. They were running around sweating and wrestling like children. In a couple of hours they were going to be colder than they have ever been in their lives, colder than they ever thought possible, and that sweat they had been working up by horse-playing would freeze solid on their bodies. They still had time to get an oxygen mask if they didn't have one, or fix an important connection if it wasn't working, but they were wasting time and they certainly couldn't wait until the shooting started to fix things.

I called them a bunch of dumb jackasses and concluded by saying I had completed forty missions. This day made my forty-first, and I would like to be around to complete forty-two, and here I had to fly with a bunch of stupid jackasses. I had the extra stripes, and they were in my territory. If I had to ride with ignoramuses that day, they were at least going to act like airmen. I really laid it on them. This started them hopping and they quickly settled down and began preparing for the mission.

The two men behind me turned out to be a general and a colonel, who had heard every remark. Horrified by the crew's antics, they had driven over for the express purpose of doing what I had done. The general later told my squadron commander that had been the best ass-chewing he'd ever heard, and he'd enjoyed being an observer.

We successfully completed that day's mission. Although we didn't get hit by fighters, the flak was bad and we developed engine trouble approaching the target. Earlier in the flight I noticed the feathering unit oil had not been checked. Oil had to be kept hot or it wouldn't work. I tactfully asked the co-pilot a leading question about how hot oil had to be going into the feathering unit. He immediately checked, started the heating process, and it worked fine. After we finished the mission he came up and said, "Thanks, McGuire, I completely forgot to watch that oil. I'll never make that mistake again." One of the new crewmen had flak come through his seat and singe the seat of his pants, but everyone came back from that mission.

After we landed, those enlisted men raced away from me as though I was about to throw boiling water on them.

Years later at a Second Bomb Group Reunion, while talking to a small group of friends, a couple of men I didn't recognize were watching and circling around me. Finally, one walked up, introduced himself, and said, "Mr. McGuire, running into you has been the high point of this meeting. You shocked us today because you seem like such a soft-spoken, mild-mannered man. The last time we saw you, you were the most terrifying person we had ever seen." These two were part of that crew. "Mr. McGuire," the other continued, "I have never been so scared of anybody or anything in my life. Even your pistol looked bigger than ours. Combat wasn't half as bad as looking you in the eye, with your finger sticking in my chest. I was more scared of you than I was of the Germans." It was hilarious.

Chapter 19

[1] Although the Strategic Bombing Offensive against Germany had been waged since January 1943 by the Eighth Air Force out of England, it wasn't until the arrival of the P-51 as a long-range escort in early 1944 that the effects of the daylight bombing campaign began to tell. Beginning January 1944, strategic planners concentrated bombing of both the Eighth and the Fifteenth Air Forces on fuel production and supply lines, with striking results. By September 1944, the Luftwaffe's fuel supply had been reduced to 10,000 tons of octane a month where the requirement was 160,000 tons. Wheal, et al, 349, 455.

[2] The Isle of Vis, situated in the Adriatic off the coast of Yugoslavia, was used by the Allies as a base of operations for Partisan activity in Yugoslavia.

[3] McGuire's perceptions about the low survival percentages of green crews is statistically correct. Bomber crews who had flown more than five missions achieved a higher survival rate than beginning crews, who figured disproportionally among the five per cent loss per mission in the Eighth Air Force. Keegan, 428.

Hanging From the Ball Turret,
and Other Scofield Stories

The most physically demanding job on a B-17, or a B-24, was that of the ball turret gunner. Ideally, he would have been a very slender midget with a mind like a computer. On a B-24 the ball turret could be retraced into the body of the airplane when it was not in use. On a B-17 it was fixed by a post mounted in the top of the ceiling and the ball turret protruded from the belly of the Fortress. With a full complement of ammunition and gunner aboard it weighed approximately a ton.

Without the two ball turret guns, it would have been impossible to survive in a B-17. One of the reasons was the nineteen-foot tail that extended upwards and discouraged attacking fighters from breaking high at point blank ranges. If they were making a head-on pass and planned to miss that tail, they had to break off earlier on a nose-on attack. During a head-on pass at a Fortress, a majority of Luftwaffe pilots liked to break low, to make their run on the nose and then break downwards. When they did that, the ball turret was in an ideal position to send them on their way, so even when they cleared the airplane they were vulnerable to fire from the ball turret. Facing that lethal turret at a slower speed, the Luftwaffe was painfully aware of the ball turret in both the B-17s and B-24s. The turret was a definite plus for us when attacks came low and from around the clock, completely around the airplane.

The sight used in the ball turret was the latest in technology. A compensating sight, it was made by Sperry and all that was necessary was for the gunner to preset the sight when he identified an aircraft. With the target aircraft framed, and the proper setting in the sight, the sight would compute for all the ballistic probables. For example, a ME-109 had a length of twenty-nine feet, seven inches and a wing span of thirty-two feet eight-and-a-half inches. The Focke Wulf had a slightly longer wing span. With these basic figures dialed into the sight's computer, the sight was extremely accurate. All you needed to know was if the aircraft was coming toward you or paralleling you. In the first instance you were concerned about the width and in the latter the length. It was a thinking man's position.

The ball turret gunner spent more time trying to survive than any other member of the crew. First, he could not wear all of the heavy clothing the rest of us in the back end of the airplane wore: leather, fur-lined pants and heavy fur-lined jackets and mufflers. Because of his limited clothing selection, he relied more on his heated suit. The turret had very little insulation and when the temperatures went down from forty-five to seventy below zero, it was extremely painful. You were not only numb, but you hurt from the cold. He had to learn to ignore that pain. It was a constant job to monitor his gauges, his connections, his umbilicals, and be extremely conscious of that precious lifeline, his fragile oxygen mask and hose.

Also, when in the turret with the turret lid closed, most of his body's weight rested on his kidneys. The design of his relief tube was very impractical, as it tended to freeze after the first use. Therefore, he had to be conscious of his liquid intake prior to a mission. With the seeping cold that came through the plastic and being bent into a position that placed so much weight on his kidneys, he exited and re-entered the turret several times during each mission.

Entering the turret was a very delicate operation. He stretched both hands up over his head and turned two handles that operated the worm gears which locked the turret door into place. The entry and exit door was his seat back. His knees were up by his shoulders and his hands were above his head on the gun handles, triggers, and push-to-talk switch. In order to see the world around him, he spread his knees and looked between his legs at the view plate, a small port hole between the guns. It was an extremely uncomfortable position. Since our missions ran an average of seven to ten hours, the ball turret gunner really took a physical beating from the extreme cold and traveling in that unnatural position. He truly earned his money.

Another problem was that he could not see nearby aircraft in order to know his relationship with the axis of his own airplane. He was in a lonely world down there. He could only see the belly of the airplane, the bottom of the tail, and the bottom of the prop arc. It was easy for him to become disoriented, so occasionally he ran the turret back until he could identify a spot on the airplane. In this way he knew what direction he was facing—six o'clock, twelve o'clock, etc. Vertigo was commonplace due to swirling clouds, snow or lack of orientation to the ground. Sound was another problem. The chambers of those big .50 caliber machine guns were just a few inches from his ears. When those guns were fired, the explosions were extremely loud and painful. The life of a ball turret gunner was a very grim one.

Our ball turret gunner was Louis Scofield. Louis should never have been a ball turret gunner. Broad-shouldered, muscular, and of medium-size, it was physically difficult for Lou to climb in and out of the turret and stay there for long periods.

One morning the weather was very cold, as usual for that time of the year, and we'd been flying in and out of clouds. Lou had been in the turret for some time and came out to use one of the relief containers and try to restore circulation in his body. That day he'd brought an extra coat along. After beating his hands together and signaling to me how cold it was down there, he put on that extra coat. I was preoccupied and didn't see Louis re-enter the turret, which he did with some difficulty. At that point we were over Bavaria. A few minutes later co-pilot Karsten called over the intercom, "Another airplane told the squadron leader that we have something hanging out of the belly of our airplane. Would you guys see if you can find out what it is? Scofield, can you see it?"

All we heard was a strange-sounding, feeble voice saying, "It's me. The door on the turret is open and I'm partially out."

With those words, the scramble was on inside the plane. I looked through the inspection plate and, sure enough, Lou had only one shoulder inside the turret and was frantically struggling and kicking his legs to get the rest of his body inside. His hands were above his head in the customary ball turret position, so he could not use them to pull himself up. In those cramped quarters it was very difficult for him to do anything. We had to reach through that small inspection plate in the floor of the waist and try to push his shoulders back into the turret. Once we had accomplished that, we then had to try to pull the door closed. We assured ourselves that he had oxygen and could hear. I removed my parachute harness and equipment and the fur-lined jacket. The thickness of the fur cuffs made it difficult to reach through the hole and then be able to see around them. A thought flashed through my mind, 'Here comes some frost-bit fingers and arms.'

In the first attempts I couldn't push hard enough on his back to do any good. To be effective I would have to reach farther down toward the middle of his back and then push. Lou kept his cool. His hand were still on the gun controls so I asked, "Lou, can you run the guns down about six or seven inches?" I held my breath as he repeated this maneuver several times until we managed to push him back inside. By then he was numb from the cold. A crowbar under his seat would have pried him up easily but, who knew what damage that would have caused to him, and the turret.

We finally managed to get his other arm and shoulder back into the turret. Also, we had worked the door up past the mid-point where the slip stream worked for us rather than against and I managed to lock one handle. Lou locked the other when he was up.

When he came up into the waist, after regaining his position in the turret, he didn't seem too disturbed about the whole thing. Scofield was rather unflappable. We were more upset than he appeared to be. We had been confident that we could extricate him, but worried about the damage we might have to do to the ball turret. He was *very* cold and stomped around and beat his arms to stimulate his circulation. That extra jacket was the culprit and he quickly shed it. After he had climbed down into the turret and reached up to lock the worm gears the material in the spare jacket had gathered around the locking mechanism and they were not properly recessed. His customary push back to settle into the seat and work himself into a more comfortable position pushed the insecurely latched door open and it went past the mid-point. Before he realized it, he was dangling from the ball turret with nothing but thousands of feet of air between him and the ground.

That incident provided much interesting conversation for our bull sessions with other crews. It also generated many recollections of other Scofield stories that, although less dramatic, were more entertaining.

We recalled the late October morning when we'd had a rough take-off and climb-out from Amendola on a mission deep into Germany. That was the mission where the Wolf Pack had been vectored on to us, but instead fell victim to vertigo. Somewhere over Bavaria, again, Scofield had come up from the turret on one of his many visits to the relief container. Watching all the activity below us, I reached over and actuated the charging handle on the .50 caliber to chamber a new round as I didn't want to be caught with a frozen, inoperable gun. Graham mimicked my action. Scofield, disconnected from the intercom, could only see our actions and the two of us peering intently over the side. Thinking he was about to be caught away from his position, panic set in. I'll leave it to the reader's imagination as to what happened in his haste to return to his position. It looked like a Chinese fire drill as he attempted to get rid of the relief container, zip his pants and re-enter the ball turret. After a frantic trip down into the ball turret, Scofield moved his gun around. When he couldn't locate any action he asked, "What's happening?"

"We had some unidentified aircraft at seven o'clock low, but they're gone now." Profanity was all we heard from the ball turret. The description of Scofield's Chinese fire drill, when he thought we were under attack, provided much future enjoyment for both the tellers and the listeners.

Then, there were his money saving stratagems. Our ball turret gunner often made sorties off somewhere by himself. We never knew exactly what he was up to except he would come out in Class A uniform and necktie, the full treatment. Lou was always raising and saving money for some project, especially when close to an R&R leave. He liked to go first-class, so we always watched these activities with great interest. We were issued about five packs of cigarettes a week and Scofield decided to quit smoking and sell his cigarettes. He also sold his candy, pop, and beer rations to add to his savings. Occasionally, he mooched a cigarette. One morning standing on the flight line before daybreak before a mission, Scofield suddenly blurted, "God, I'd give anything for a cigarette." He had no success in borrowing a cigarette. One of the crew chiefs said he didn't smoke, but he'd give him a plug of tobacco if he wanted to try that. Nearly all the crew chiefs chewed tobacco because they worked around gasoline. Scofield thought that was a wonderful idea, accepted the offer and popped the plug into his mouth and began chewing.

(above) Louis Scofield examining a hole near his ball turret after his last mission.

(right) Scofield *(r.)* while on R&R in Naples. *(Courtesy L. Scofield)*

He began working on that big chaw of tobacco. After a few spits, he commented that it was pretty good. We looked at him with great disgust. After we boarded and took off, Scofield suddenly realized he didn't have a place to spit. When I looked around, I saw him using my oily-rag can, which he used without removing my cleaning rags. I glared at him. Scofield and the tobacco got along well until it was time for him to climb into the ball turret. He picked up his umbilicals and waited until I slapped the top of the turret to indicate the doors were locked. Then it dawned on him that he was now wearing an oxygen mask and had no way to spit. He was in a fix. He couldn't crawl back and spit the plug out because, having crossed the bomb line, we were in a high state of alert and were expecting enemy fighters.

Several options were open to him: he could try to spit in the turret, but the armorers took a dim view of that, and besides, he could only turn his head a few degrees and that would result in spitting on himself. His second option was spitting between his legs if he could summon up enough velocity, but then it would splatter on his view plate and that was unsatisfactory. The only option left was to swallow the tobacco.

A few minutes later he burst out of the turret dragging his umbilicals, grabbed the can, and vomited violently. A more miserable looking person couldn't be imagined. After a few minutes back in his position, he was up again. This routine was repeated several times until everything, including last week's groceries, was gone and he was having dry heaves. Aside from providing us with some comic relief, it was dangerous for him as he could not afford to foul his oxygen mask. He was so sick that day that if the Hindenburg had been tied to our tail, he couldn't have hit it with his guns. On his last trip up, he was orange from the Atabrine, and a pasty white and a pukey green from the tobacco.

That evening after debriefing he was still sick and still heaving. He asked Sutton to accompany him to the infirmary. He went in hoping only a few a medics would be around. Doc

Ihle came out instead. He looked at Scofield and asked the obvious question, "What's wrong with you?"

"Doctor, I was hoping you could give me something to settle my stomach."

"What's the matter? Did you eat something that disagreed with you? You got the flu?"

Scofield uttered a reluctant, "No." Sutton went into spasms of laughter.

Confessing, Scofield said, "Doctor, I was trying to give up smoking and chewed tobacco on the mission. When I couldn't spit in the ball turret, I swallowed it."

Doc Ihle looked at him in disbelief. "That's the most disgusting thing I've ever heard." Doc disappeared into his medicine room and returned with a bottle. "Take this every two hours until it's gone. Also, I'd suggest that you don't use any more tobacco and I'm glad to see you quit smoking."

Fortunately, Scofield didn't have to fly the next day. He was still sick.

Again, we had much fun describing the look on Lou's face. Perhaps the best description was a cold, wet dog.

That wasn't the only time Scofield had problems with his view plate. On another mission he could not leave the turret but had a serious need to relieve himself. He had previously used the turret's unreliable relief tube and unbeknownst to him, it had frozen solid. When he started to use it again, it almost immediately overflowed. This resulted in a thick film of yellow ice quickly forming on top of his view plate, effectively blocking his view of the world, as well as any enemy fighters which might be coming his way. Scofield was nothing if not inventive. He fired three or four rounds from his twin-fifties. As the empty links fell to the bottom of the turret, he twisted himself around, how I don't know, took one of the links and spent the rest of the way home scraping yellow ice from his view port.

Perhaps Scofield's most hilarious adventure was with the stove. Thinking about that wiener roast still brings tears to my eyes.

Tuskegee Airmen
The 332nd Fighter Group

I don't remember the day, and the target was possibly Regensberg, but we had been shot up badly, again. One engine had been feathered and one was working poorly. We were in a bad way, as well as running low on fuel. The pilots decided after we passed Gross Glockner to split the difference between Trieste and Venice, and then moved a little closer to the coast-line of Italy. We were about twenty miles offshore.

The pilots saved all the altitude we could get. We were wearing our parachutes but didn't relish the thought of ditching in the cold water of the Adriatic and risk being picked up by German E-boats,[1] so we decided if the plane couldn't make it we were going to try to fly over Italy and bail out.

The fuel gauges registered empty. By then Lesher, the navigator, announced that we had passed the bomb line (were in friendly territory).

Chambers contacted 'Big Fence,' our radio-direction finding unit, with whom we had been in contact since we left Austria. They had been monitoring our progress, and knew we were in serious shape and had fuel problems. Chambers asked, "Would you give us a steer to the nearest friendly base, the quickest one we can get into? It's about all over here."

A strange voice responded over the frequency, "This is Gallant. We're right off your starboard wing, the landing strip that's right under you." We hadn't seen it. Sure enough there was a runway in the distance. Gallant continued, "You're welcome to come in here. I can see you."

Chambers immediately pulled us over and we went straight in. As we were going in, I could see P-51s sitting around the strip. They were the 'Redtails,' planes of the 332nd Fighter Group of the Black Tuskegee Airmen.[2] We had seen them very often in the air around us over Germany. Their nickname came from the very distinctive red markings on their tails. We landed and rolled toward the end of the runway. At the end of the runway, we ran out of gas. There wasn't even enough gas left to taxi in. We'd been in the air almost ten hours.

Ground crewmen ran toward the plane with fire extinguishers, and an ambulance raced up to us. Miraculously, nobody was hurt, but later we counted over seventy-five holes in the plane. We were near exhaustion and had been on oxygen around six and half hours. The deep creases in our noses and faces made that very evident. A white froth developed on your face from a mixture of the vaporization that goes on, and your saliva. Our eyes were watery and bloodshot from staring at the sun, straining to spot fighters. They packed us in the ambulance and drove us to one of the 332nd's squadron headquarters.

Arriving at headquarters, suddenly everything was funny to us. We had been very tense before landing, but afterwards the smallest remark seemed hilarious. In the CO's office at headquarters there were not enough chairs, so I sat on the desk.

Nobody else was around but our crew, and we started laughing about the mission and being brought back to headquarters in an ambulance. I was sitting on the desk laughing, and suddenly this Black major walked in, looked at me, and said, "Get your ass off my desk, will you?" I thought, "Well, this is going to be another bad incident on a completely bad day." I immediately apologized.

The major, though, turned out to be a fine and considerate man. He asked what had happened, where we had been. Evidently, he and his squadron had also been out that day escorting some B-24s that hadn't come back yet. We were quite a bit ahead of the B-24s that had started after us that morning. From his conversation, evidently his group of Redtails hadn't been engaged too heavily that day. He took one look at us and asked if everybody was all right. Did we need doctors? We told him we would appreciate a large shot of bourbon or a cup of coffee, or just anything. He said, "Well, I wanted to ask you fellows, how long has it been since you had anything to eat?"

I quickly told him, "Since 0230 this morning," and by then it was late in the afternoon.

He said, "I figured that, so I stopped by the kitchen, and the cooks are going to fix up a snack for you. They'll be ready in a little bit."

Shortly after that we heard the welcome announcement that the cooks were ready for us. That day I ate the finest meal I had in Europe. All the crew felt the same way. They did not serve us standard fare. We knew what was standard fare at any bomber or fighter mess hall. They had dipped into their goodie bag for treats they were saving for special occasions and served us pork chops, all we could eat. They wanted to make sure we didn't leave hungry.

While we were eating, the terrible screeching and banging and hollering and noises of props beating on the landing strip assaulted our ears. A P-38, either a weather or photo-recon ship, was crash-landing, a solid mass of bullet holes. Recon ships only carried one or two guns because they had to be able to outrun everything they encountered. Flying to the same

Tuskegee Airmen - Class of 45A, Twin Engine Pilots. *(back, l. to r.)* Harvey McClelland, James Kennedy, Herbert Schwing, Quentin Smith, Cleophus Valentine, Argonne Harden, Alfred McKenzie, Herdon Cummings, Melvin Clayton, Calvin Warrick, Francis Thompson, William Curtis, Rutledge Fleming, Charles Goldsby, Luther Oliver, Charles Dorkins. *(Courtesy Alfred U. McKenzie)*

targets we did, they carried large amounts of fuel and large cameras. They took pictures of the bombing patterns to enable us to assess damage, or they went ahead and announced what kind of weather was in the target area. They lived a very exciting life.

This P-38 came skidding in, stood on its nose and plopped back down. Pieces of it were strung all over the airstrip. We saw ground crewmen helping the pilot out. It wasn't ten minutes before he showed up with bloody bandages on his head. As he came through the mess hall door he announced, "They told me we're having meat." He sat down with us and helped himself to the pork chops. Eventually, he called in and told his squadron that he was at the 332nd Fighter Group, and could they send some transportation? But he was more interested in the pork chops.

Why were the Tuskegee Airmen so hospitable? Evidently, they had taken one look at our airplane sitting there full of holes, and since they knew where we had been, what had happened, and the length of time we had been out there, they knew we had had a very rough day. They wanted to make it a little better for us by fixing a special meal out of their goodie bag. We were very impressed by their hospitality. Most squadrons stockpiled some good things or materials for special occasions, but these guys were sharing them with us. I repeat, without a doubt that was the best meal I had during my entire tour in Italy. Those cooks really fixed us up. We knew we were eating somebody else's pork chops, and we ate enough for fifteen to twenty men. And that photo-recon pilot wasn't timid either when it came to eating. He was a big man. I still laugh when I think of him coming in all banged up and asking for pork chops.

That meal was just another example of the excellent outfit they were. The relationship between the Tuskegee Airmen and the bombers in the Fifteenth Air Force couldn't have been closer. They were one of the premier groups in Europe. I can't say enough good about the Tuskegee Airmen. Their boast was that they never lost a bomber they were escorting, and I believe they were right.

The Redtails escorted us many times. The fighters, called 'little friends' by bomber crews, of course, couldn't start the mission with us and fly alongside all the way. They only had sufficient fuel to escort you over the hot spots, areas where we anticipated trouble. A group always tried to be there when we started our bombing runs to target. That was when we were absolutely vulnerable. The fighters also tried to be around when we flew over the Alps in the Klagenfurt area, where many enemy fighter fields were located. The deepest fighter cover my crew ever had was at Brux in Czechoslovakia, which was six-hundred and ten miles from our field in Italy.

The Redtails seemed to fly more planes in their formations than our other fighter squadrons. When you were six hundred miles from home, those red tails looked mighty nice. I never heard any racial slurs from bomber crews directed towards the Redtails. Lord, we loved them.

Chapter 21

[1] E-boats, or *Schnellboote,* were very fast motor torpedo boats. The German navy led most of the other powers involved in the war with the design of this low-profile, powerful surface craft. It was powered by diesel engines and fired an accurate and dependable torpedo. Until 1944, with the ascendancy of radar and air superiority, E-boats were a constant thorn in the side of Allied navies as they effectively harassed shipping in numerous theaters. Wheal, et al., 487.

[2] The Tuskegee Airmen was the name given to men of the segregated 332rd Fighter Group, comprised of the Ninety-ninth, 100th, 301st, and 302d squadrons, commanded by Lt. Col. Benjamin Davis. These Black officers were trained at the Tuskegee Air Base near the Tuskegee Institute in Alabama. During their training in the States they were segregated from white facilities and all social contact was discouraged, resulting in the name they gave themselves, "The Lonely Eagles." Parrish, 639.

– 22 –

Combat Fatigue

In the beginning of the war the British had flown their airmen until they died or were shot down. As a result, some of their men refused to fly because they were too exhausted or scared, resulting in many courts-martial. Morale and efficiency suffered as their men saw no way out but death. British Air Chief Marshall Arthur 'Bomber' Harris strongly advised General Ira Eaker not to make the same mistake when he was sent to England to establish the Eighth Air Force. He recommended a policy that limited the number of combat missions an airman flew. As a result of this prompting, the American commanders set a limit of twenty-five combat missions for the Eighth Air Force. When an airman reached that limit, he was rotated home for training and reassignment.

Combat Fatigue

The Fifteenth Air Force set a limit of fifty combat missions for us. That seemed a lot. After our arrival, they told us that four to six percent casualties were acceptable losses. Outside of official channels we discovered that, in July alone, the Fifteenth had lost 318 bombers out of a total of 1,900. It didn't take a rocket scientist to figure that twenty-five missions times four percent meant there was no way you were going to make it back home, especially when you used fifty missions instead of twenty-five. We figured the only way to survive was by being lucky.

Most of us went over there cocky and feeling lucky. Nothing was going to happen to us individually. Then things started getting tougher. Flak guns were being concentrated over our targets as the Russian front moved westward, compressing the German gun batteries into tighter patterns. Every mission started receiving more flak. Larger formations of enemy fighters began hitting every mission. This made you think. Every group I knew about had suffered very severe losses. That my entire squadron was shot down on the day we arrived at Amendola preyed upon my mind. You started thinking, and that was the beginning of combat fatigue. We called it being 'flak happy.' I got flak happy like the rest.

There are classic stages. First, I wouldn't get killed—it couldn't happen to me. I couldn't handle the idea of getting killed and viewed the danger like watching a good movie. On my first mission that piece of flak which cut through my flight jacket and grazed my goggles, could have killed me. Instead of becoming frightened, I became indignant. The Germans were trying to kill me! After four or five missions, I still did not believe they could kill me, but, as the missions became more dangerous, I reached a stage where I thought there was a very good chance I might be shot down, become a prisoner of war, or be wounded. After about thirteen missions, I figured the odds and decided my chances of surviving were not that good. By the time the seventeenth mission was under my belt, I decided I probably would not make it.

All of us developed body tics or twitches. My tic appeared in one finger after about my twenty-fifth mission. To this day it still occasionally jerks. I didn't want the crew or my buddies to see me twitching, so I started smoking to hide it. We all started 'pulling missions' at night—having nightmares about the missions, reliving previous missions. You could hear men talking or screaming in their sleep. Some gave orders. We all had to talk regularly to our flight surgeon, Doc Ihle. He was a great doctor and it was his responsibility to ensure that all crewman in our squadron were psychologically fit to fly. None of us wanted to be rated unfit to fly because of combat fatigue. We considered it a personal weakness.

When airmen became flak happy they acted strangely. Some became combative, and liked to fight. Others withdrew within themselves, and spoke only when spoken to. The worse time for being flak happy was about half-way through your tour. You were not so tired, and your mind was still active so you constantly thought about your mortality. Some of the men would go to the nearest town, get drunk, and then fight. One of our airmen acquired quite a reputation for drinking, so we called him 'Forty-Rod' for the type of whiskey he drank, but nobody ever flew drunk.

People started doing weird things. We had one guy, a pilot, who used to pray aloud into the plane intercom. Unnecessary talk over the intercom was forbidden; it was strictly for business. I flew with him on a couple of missions, and he really unnerved me. He would interrupt his oral prayers to instruct the co-pilot, "Give me 2350 on number two engine," and then returned to his prayers. He believed it was his duty to confer with the Lord on the way to the target.

Nectarine Peelings

Other airmen simply snapped. Once the squadron received a shipment of nectarines. The others took a handful to eat after mess. I had learned my lesson from the watermelon and decided not to eat any fruit that I suspected could make me sick. That evening, a combat airman from a nearby tent came around. He was carrying a sack and acting rather strangely. He asked if we had any peelings from the nectarines. We said no, but we'd save them the next time. No one asked why he wanted them because we figured he planned to make moonshine. A few days later he came around again and asked if we had peelings. Again, we said no. This time, however, Scofield asked, "What the hell are you going to do with the peelings?"

The man looked suspiciously around him, and leaned toward Scofield, and, in a conspiratorial whisper, replied, "I'm going to be the richest man in the world because I've found a way to turn these peelings into gold. All I have to do is bury them. When I dig them up, they have turned into gold."

That response convinced us that he was about two or three quarts low. We surmised that he must have just been released from a hospital. Since we never saw him again, he was probably shipped home. I certainly didn't want to fly with him.

(left) The two Jims, Thompson and Sutton, eating nectarines.
(right) Charles Graham at the door of the Amendola Ritz.
(Courtesy M. McGuire and W. Lesher)

The British Soldier

Later, I was on the bad end of another psychological case. One non-op afternoon I was lying on my cot getting some well-deserved sleep. Graham and Fenstermaker were also asleep in the tent.

A strong voice with a British accent awoke me. "I'm going to get you now."

I looked up and saw a British soldier in battle dress. He was babbling. I asked, "Can I help you?"

When I raised up on my elbow, I saw he held a piece of pipe that appeared to be from a bathroom fixture. Immediately, I was fully awake, and realized he was threatening me. His words now started making sense.

"You've been shacking up with my wife in England," he said, "and you even did it while I was in Africa."

"I've never even been to England," I said, desperately trying to remove my arms from under the sheet. This man was crazy, and he fully intended to spread my brains all over the tent.

"Bloody Yanks are all the same," he continued as he lifted the pipe. I thought he was going to hit me at any second. Attempting to be calm, cool, and collected, I quickly tried to distract him before be started swinging.

"I'm from New Mexico. Do you know where that is?"

"I don't care where that is," he said, "you've been with my wife all this time."

Someone walked behind him, momentarily diverting his attention from me, so I could get out of the cot. I mentally began determining how long it would take me to grab my .45 and chamber a round. American airmen, drawn from their tents by the Britisher's rising voice, gathered around our tent. Fenstermaker and Graham, now awake, moved toward him.

"Your actions," he stated as he again moved toward me, "have caused me to quit loving my wife." He tightened his grip on the pipe, and moved closer. Others intervened. Someone gently removed the pipe from his hands, and he was led off.

I didn't sleep well that night. He could have brained me in my sleep that afternoon. It would have been horrible for my parents to receive a telegram saying their son had been killed by a British soldier wielding a bathroom fixture pipe. The entire incident was frightening.

Ensuring Luck

Everybody knew that without luck you weren't going to make it, so most of us carried something practical to increase our luck. My pilot carried an escape map of Italy with him.[1] Some flew with pictures of their wives or babies or girlfriends, placing them in their shirt pockets. Before every mission, Sutton always read a letter he'd received from his fiance. When he read that letter, it gave him strength. He carried that letter, from which he had cut out the dates and her name, on every raid. Not only were pictures and letters considered good luck, since we did not take billfolds or wallets with us on missions, they wanted to have something with them in case they were shot down and imprisoned. We all had something.

Personally, I carried my stove lids and wore an old set of wings. I left my beautiful sterling silver wings[2] on my bed before every mission. If I was ever shot down, I wanted my family to have those wings. The old pair was my good luck charm. Besides, if I was shot down, I didn't want some German selling my wings as a souvenir. Those four stove lids I had obtained, I kept in that extra parachute pack because I didn't want the pilot to know I was adding unnecessary weight to our load. One day I threw the bag containing the lids into the plane. It missed and fell back to the hard stand, making a noise like two Volkswagens having a head-on collision. When the pilot asked what caused the noise, I played dumb. I kept them near me on missions and sat on them because they could and did stop shrapnel. Everybody kept something which gave them comfort.

The strongest thing that kept us going was the bond with our crew mates, the men you had trained and fought with. You would give your life for them, sometimes without even thinking. This bond caused you to do things that you ordinarily wouldn't do. I can understand why infantrymen throw themselves on grenades to protect their friends. For example, I have acrophobia, fear of great heights, which, for some strange reason, never bothered me in an airplane, except when I looked down through open bomb-bay doors. On one mission, the bombs failed to release. Being the plane's armorer, I had to cut them loose. Taking an oxygen bottle and an axe, I walked along a slender catwalk above the open bomb bay doors. I get dizzy up on a roof, and there I was, sitting and chopping at bomb releases, seventy degrees below zero, hanging by one arm and standing on one leg, and looking at the ground thirty thousand feet below. All this was accomplished without a parachute because there was no space to wear one on that catwalk. How I did it, I don't know? But I had a job to do. Others depended on you. You acted without thinking. There was no time for feeling flak happy. No time for being fatigued or scared. All of us did it.

Pride

We had great pride in what we were doing and fought because of that pride. Pride for our country, our Group, our Squadron, and our crew sustained us during the hard, impossible, bad times. I believe everybody initially joined to fight because of pride in America. We had been attacked. Our country and the world were being threatened by the Japanese and Germans. It was not for patriotic reasons, however, that enabled a man to continue to fight and daily face the horrors and stress of air combat. It took more than patriotism to keep getting in that airplane day after day, encountering flak and enemy fighters. It was for pride—pride of your Group, your Squadron, your crew, and, perhaps most importantly, yourself.

I began to perceive myself as a little cog in a very large wheel. Teamwork is tremendously important in a bomber crew. If one member did not do his job, he endangered the plane and every member in it. I keenly felt the importance of doing the best job I could possibly do as a member of my crew, and sincerely believed the other crewmen had the same attitude. I never wanted to disappoint myself or the crew. That attitude is what sustained us despite the shakes, the dreads, the physical suffering, the constant danger. That's why we prayed for strength. We had pride in the job we were doing for ourselves and others.

We all shared a common prayer.

Let me fight well today, O Lord.
Let me do nothing to bring shame or
  disgrace on my family, my comrades,
  my group, my country.
Let me conduct myself in such a manner
  that there is no shame.
Let me not be wasted, but if I die,
  let me die like a soldier should.

Religion

Most of us felt a strong belief in God. The ones who cracked under the strain generally were those without that belief. I don't know how men survived without it. It was through my faith that I found the strength and courage to keep up the fight.

It is a cliche, but there really were no atheists over there, at least not among the men with whom I flew. Particularly not after the first couple of missions. Men constantly facing that kind of danger sought ports of refuge, and many found strength and solace in religion, if they didn't already have it. We called it foxhole religion, although we, of course, never had foxholes to protect us. I would have paid anything for a foxhole up in the air.

Religious services were held before every mission. My crew always held a short prayer service on the flight line before takeoff and then Thompson and I had our usual prayer and Bible lesson back at the tail.

Sometimes the other crew members and I talked to Ralph Chambers. In addition to being an excellent pilot, he was a very decent, religious man. He encouraged us to come by and talk if we were having problems. He always had time for us, although I don't know how because he was a very busy man. Many times these discussions with Chambers ended with him reading aloud from his Bible.

Everyone liked to think God was on his side, but I was aware that good men on both sides of the war were praying to the same God.

Asleep one night in November, about half-way through my tour, I thought I heard a voice. It was distinct and audible. Before they had been shot down, others had told me about hearing a similar voice. This phenomenon was common among men flying combat. It was a precursor to the first signs of combat fatigue. Some gave up when they heard the voice. Its appearance generally followed a rough period of fighting where you believed you had used up your luck. That night the voice simply said I was going to be killed the next day. It said, "Today is the day." I awoke and was soaked to the skin, as though someone had poured a gallon of water over me. I got up and prayed until we were called for the day's mission. I felt I was done. The feeling was that I could do nothing about it, so I was very fatalistic. I got up and shaved, put on my clothes, and went to the mission briefing.

The day's combat target was Vienna. It was going to be a tough target. Vienna and Linz were the two hottest targets. I thought, this is ironic, a kid from New Mexico gets shot down and killed over Vienna. I had, also ironically, a feeling of peace. I made my peace with the Lord. There was nothing else I could do. I wrote my parents and told them I believed I would not be back, but thought they would understand and not grieve too much. I didn't want it any other way and my conduct would be honorable and I was at peace. This letter was left on my pillow, along with my sterling wings and other personal possessions and they would be forwarded to the folks if anything happened to me. I believed in what I was doing. We were serving a good and worthy cause. I was determined that even though I was going to die, I would go on the mission and not do anything to embarrass my crew, my country, my group, and particularly my family. When the briefing was over, I grabbed my parachute bag and went out and got into the truck to be taken to the flight line.

About 0530 that morning, while waiting in the truck for the drive out to the flight line, I heard a bird singing. That was the first bird I had heard sing during my tour in Italy. He was singing his heart out. The eastern skies were beginning to lighten, and for the first time I saw beauty in Italy. I felt oddly relaxed, and by the time we reached the line, I was laughing and joking.

I was flying with a relative new crew on that mission. Everything fit if I was going to die that day. I wanted to stay and fly with my crew, but this plane was short a waist gunner. You never worried about anybody else on your crew, because you had trained and flown with them. You knew they knew their jobs. You knew the pilot and everyone else were going to do the right things. When you flew with another crew, you never knew how they would react. This was one more factor to add to the certainty that I was going to get killed. At the plane I did my best to make sure we had done everything we were supposed to do, and were prepared. It would be extremely cold because of our assigned bombing altitude. Someone on this unknown crew had not done something right to prepare for the mission, and I snarled a little. One of them said, "Don't pay any attention to him getting on you. He's a little flak happy."

Everything went well on the way to target, although I expected the worse. As we approached the target I tensed, waiting for it to happen. Nothing happened over the target. When we came off the target, I told the others, "Be alert, this is the time you generally get hit with fighters." I was determined to be a hell of a good example to the others. We braced for the fighters, and they never showed up. We had an uneventful trip home.

Coming in for a landing, we got in a traffic pattern, and I thought, well if I'm going to die today, then some nitwit is going to ram us. Nothing happened. Then when we started landing, I thought, well maybe the landing gear will fold up. We landed safely. After we landed, all I could think of was that some guy was going to shoot me clearing his guns. When that didn't happen, I was flabbergasted. I could not understand why I wasn't dead.

From that day on, I believed I didn't have a chance in the world of making it home. Not one in the world. When my fatalism didn't come true, I decided God was saving me for something else. Since then, every day has been a bonus given by God. This peace helped me through many dangerous assignments in my police work and I didn't fear death as much as other policemen. Toward the end of my tour—during my last eight to ten missions—I only wanted to get it over. The entire crew knew we were all in trouble, but we each tried to conceal it.

All of us were flying sick, and we weren't supposed to fly in this condition. I flew with burned hands and bad head colds. Chambers finished his tour flying with one arm and a hand in a cast. We had a horror of not being able to fly with our crew. None of us wanted to miss a flight and have some knucklehead replacement joining the crew and doing something to cause the plane to get shot down. Also, nobody wanted to get behind the rest of the crew in the number of missions flown. Nobody wanted to finish his tour with another crew. We were a close, tightly knit crew. We were comfortable with one another and went to great lengths to help each other. We were a family.

I didn't care whether I was shot down, captured or even killed. I just wanted to get it over with and feel no pain before I cracked up, or did something that would jeopardize the crew or the plane, or disgrace myself, my family, and my crew. On every mission, toward the end, I had to be very careful, very aware of what I was doing.

Also, I was having bad balance problems. My middle ear was acting up. I couldn't have balanced on one leg if the flight surgeon had asked me. The hearing in my left ear was noticeably affected. I had lost weight as well, dropping from around 220 pounds to 178 as the result of dysentery. All I wanted to do was sleep when we weren't flying. Even in sleep I couldn't rest because of the nightmares—pulling missions. I kept having dreams about burning to death, about fires in the plane. I'd wake up sweating.

Combat Fatigue

When writing home, I was very careful not to sound pessimistic. At that stage I no longer quoted the number of missions needed to come home. I had given up on making it. Also, for quite some time I had been fighting homesickness. I wanted to see my brother, my mother and father, and my friends. I longed to see those broad green expanses of cotton fields, the chile crops, and the trees, and do some hunting. My family had shipped me cans of chopped chile every time they had an opportunity. There wasn't much food available that really went with chile, as it didn't go well with powdered eggs or green peas and gravy. Every can of chile made me more homesick. I didn't want to admit this to anybody, or even discuss it with anybody.

During this time Uncle Johnny wrote that he still had that bottle of Scotch, and to remember we would drink it when I got home. I couldn't wait to get home, but at the same time knew I would never make it home. I was obsessed with the thought that I wouldn't make it home.

The day they told me to pack my gear, I couldn't believe I was being rotated home and a plane was waiting to take me to Naples. I could not believe I had made it and I was actually going home.

When I left Italy, I was credited for fifty missions.

Chapter 22

[1] This is the same map used in the photograph for the back of this book's dust jacket.

[2] When McGuire graduated from Gunnery School, the Commanding Officer presented the top five students with a special set of sterling silver wings, called "Chanute Wings." The story was that William Rogers' son was a pilot stationed at Chanute Air Base and he had his company make them especially for his son. Whether the story is true or not, those receiving them knew they were the finest made. When he presented them, the CO told McGuire and the other four, "Today they shine, tomorrow they better glitter."

R & R

It was about half way through my tour before I finally drew R&R. We were all tired—we couldn't get enough rest. I had drawn some two- or three-day passes when the weather was particularly bad, but they were to Foggia, and that place was in ruins. Flying togglier with different crews I had pulled more missions than the rest of my crew. One day the first sergeant, Tiny Atkerson, told me it was time for a lengthy rest. He said, "McGuire, you're getting up there in missions now, I see you've been hitting it pretty hard. You're due for some R&R. You can go to Rome, or the Isle of Capri. Knowing you, I figured you'd get a kick out of going to Rome, so I've put you down to go to Rome. There'll to be two or three other guys from the Twentieth Squadron going, along with some mechanics who also need the time off. Pack your bags and get them ready because the day after tomorrow you'll leave early in the morning." I was particularly grateful as I was starting to hurt a little bit. A deep-seated cold nagged me most of the time I was over there, and it was starting to wear me down. Also I'd started losing weight. It was past time for a break.

I was thrilled to have been picked to go to Rome. Not only was I anticipating the time off, but as a history buff, the prospect of visiting a place so steeped in history was an added bonus.

Rome had been declared an open city, and, as such, had been spared much of the destruction visiting the rest of Europe.[1] I recall only one area of the city had been hit by our bombs, and it had suffered little damage. I would finally get a chance to see Italian life.

Like any healthy American boy, I was full of hormones and vitamins, and thinking about girls as well as history. There were no girls in the vicinity of Amendola. Their absence puzzled us. The women in our area were so ugly, I could never get over it. They all seemed to have a wart with three long hairs hanging out, and about as many teeth. And they all smelled rank. Most of us didn't see any women around there with whom we'd be caught dead. I had to remind myself, though, that among the local populace soap was almost nonexistent, and water was at a premium. Even if there had been soap, they couldn't have afforded it, it was so very expensive. Therefore, at our unit we put emotions on hold. But I definitely could have been sent to the penitentiary for what I had in mind when I left for Rome.

We left before sunrise on the scheduled day. Atkerson really looked after his combat crews. As he had mentioned, several others from the Twentieth Squadron, as well as some B-24 crews, were in on the party. We created quite a convoy as we picked up men from different squadrons and groups along the way. The weather was freezing. The only vehicles they had to transport us were old G.I. trucks with canvas covers. We drove down the Appian Way.[2] Mines, cleared from the road by engineers and stacked on either side of the road looked like rock fences. They were piled higher than the truck. The sight horrified us. They had only cleared the mines from the middle of the road, and our trucks had to stay right in the middle or we'd be in trouble. Because we drank so much coffee before leaving, we frequently had to stop and relieve ourselves behind the truck, all the while being careful or we'd set off a mine. That was when I started having trouble going to the bathroom.

At one place our convoy stopped and picked up two big truckloads of American nurses going to the front. Well, this posed an additional problem—now we could no longer just fall out behind the truck and go to the bathroom. To be discreet, we'd have to go over to the side of the road. Most of us chose not to relieve ourselves because we didn't want to get killed going to the bathroom, but one soldier couldn't wait. The truck stopped and he walked over to the side of the road. While relieving himself, some others were amusing themselves by throwing rocks at a nearby sign and set off a mine. Other than gravel in his ass, he wasn't hurt. The nurses had a great time as they removed the gravel.

When we arrived in Rome, I discovered my billet was at a Fasciste aviators billet. I'll never forget walking into it and looking at the marble floors and columns. It was like living in a palace. Atkerson was really taking care of me. Mussolini had built this place for his combat pilots' R&R, and it had been used by both the Italians and the Germans. We were assigned small, individual rooms with a hot shower available on each floor. Each man paid valets to shine his shoes, and wash and press our uniforms. There was also a barbershop.

A shower was first on my agenda. We'd been allotted only five gallons a week in the field, so I decided to take a long, hot shower, and used all the hot water I could stand. I looked like a prune when I got out. I also kept noticing these funny-looking things over in the corner, and it was explained to me that those were bidets. I was really getting an education in European habits.

A haircut was next. Going immediately to the hotel barbershop, I sat down. A barber came in with a rig that looked like it belonged to a fire-eater. They used fire to cut hair, and

called them singes. I'd never heard of them. The barber attempted to cut my hair by burning it, but I quickly put a stop to
that when I started to smell like a burning dog. He was accustomed to that kind of response from Americans.

R&R in Rome didn't turn out to be at all that I had
planned. It was interesting, but I was in trouble almost from the
time I got there until the time I left.

Once cleaned, I decided to see Rome. I grabbed my musette
bag full of chocolate, K-rations, nylons, lipstick, and Kool cigarettes and gum, and started on my adventure. These important
barter items were from the supply I had purchased in Newfoundland. Italians liked the menthol taste of the Kools and you
could trade one package of Kools for three packages of regular
cigarettes. My intentions were not honorable. The Aviators
R&R home was on the far side of the Tiber River, near the
heart of Rome. As I walked over one of the bridges, I noticed
many people gathered around, hollering and screaming. Walking over to see what they were doing, I thought they were playing some kind of water sport because of the racing shells on the
river. It looked like they were using oars to bat a ball around in
the water. All of a sudden, to my horror, I discovered it was a
man's head! They had some guy in the water, and were whack-
ing him on the head with poles and oars, knocking him under
water every time that he came up. They were actually beating
him to death. The water around him was bloody.

An American captain and a group of soldiers were watching
nearby. He was an engineer from the Forty-fifth Infantry Division.[3] I high-tailed it over to him, and said, "Captain, they're
killing that guy in the water. Do something!"

He said, "Look, son, it's a political thing. You stay out of it.
Don't get caught in it. We're not supposed to get involved, so
just stay away from it and get the hell out of here." An Italian
onlooker was taking movies. Later I saw that same incident on
a newsreel. The man they were beating to death had been a
high-ranking Fascist, and they were taking out their hatred of
Fascists on him. I beat it out of there. That was my introduction
to Rome.[4]

I continued walking toward downtown Rome. It was thrilling to walk under the same archways where the Caesars and their legions had returned in triumph. I was not far from the Vatican, which, although I was not a Catholic, I wanted to see. Along the way, however, I saw a girl with a very good figure, and thought, 'I'll give it a try.

The limited Italian vocabulary I'd managed to acquire wasn't enough so I decided to sprinkle in a little of my New Mexico Spanish. The Italians back at Amendola laughed when they heard me speak, but they understood me. Summoning up my courage, and in my best combination of Italian, Spanish, and New Mexican, I asked this lady if she'd like to join me in a beer or a cocktail or something. She started laughing. Taking a good look at her, I thought she had a squirrel under each arm. Then it dawned on me that it was hair—long hair. Her legs were about the same way. I had an Airedale at home that had less hair on its legs than she did. She also needed to shave her shoulders. I had never seen such a hairy woman in all my life. Since I had made the contact, I took her to a sidewalk cafe, bought her a drink, and then took off. Besides, she smelled a little rank, too.

My journey downtown and my education continued. Those Italians were not very modest. Emptying slop jars out of the windows into the street didn't do anything to improve the smell, either. Besides, Americans took a dim view of getting hit with the contents of those slop jars.

On one street I was shocked to see a man hanging from a light pole. Looking farther down the street I discovered the entire block had men hanging from several light poles. The residents had discovered some Faschiste and deserting Nazis hiding in area houses. In amongst the hangings there was a lot of rock-throwing going on between Italians. One woman was bald-headed with a big "X" painted on the top of her head. Evidently her lover had been a German.

In the heart of Rome, close to the Vatican, Supreme Allied Headquarters had been set up in a large, very nice hotel. Hungry and looking for a good meal, I wanted a T-bone steak in the worst way. During my search for a restaurant, I saw two American infantrymen, a lieutenant and a sergeant, go into a little covered sidewalk cafe. I crossed the street to follow them. Just before I reached the cafe, a fight broke out inside it. A troop from some English regiment were in there.[5] They wore berets, and were apparently in Rome for R&R as well. From what I could hear, a good fight was in progress, and I knew Americans were involved. I didn't want to get involved because that would involve setting down my goodie-filled musette bag. Coinciding with my arrival, the American sergeant came spinning out the door. A British Redcap, a military policeman, hit him across the face and teeth with a thing that looked like a sash weight attached to a leather thong. The lieutenant was making a stand in the doorway. When I told the Redcap to knock it off, he made a pass at me with the sap. After that attack I took it away from him and hit him two or three times, still holding onto my musette bag.

About that time I heard whistles blowing, and knew I was going to be in the pokey for the rest of my R&R. At that moment, however, two or three open truckloads of GIs drove by. I shouted, "Limeys! Limeys! They're kicking the hell out of us." All the G.I.s piled out of the trucks, and proceeded to finish the fight. I beat it down the road, hoping to distance myself as far as possible from the place. Another convoy of G.I.s, back from the front, came toward me. They were muddy and unshaven. Jumping in front of one of the trucks I squalled, "I just hit a Redcap back there, and I'm going to be put in the pokey here pretty quick unless you give me a ride."

The driver said, "Hop in," and I rode with them for four or five blocks. They had been up on the line for some time and were being transferred back to Naples. This stop in Rome was to shower, clean up and get to look like humans again. A hot meal was also high on their list.

After they let me off I needed to go to the bathroom, but couldn't find any public facilities. That's when I saw my first *pissouri*. *Pissouris* come in all sizes and shapes. To my horror

This photo was taken while McGuire was on R&R in Rome, about halfway through his tour. *(Courtesy M. McGuire)*

and discomfort, I saw a man using one and a woman holding his hand while he was doing it. All of a sudden it dawned on me what he was doing. He was going to the bathroom. A group of nuns went by while he was using it, and they stopped and visited with the woman. He finished, went out, and, on the other side, the woman went to the bathroom. They had their toilet facilities right out in the open, on the street corner, like a bus stop. A waist-high panel provided the only privacy. The women's facility was a little closer to the ground than the men's. I decided I would rather die than use one of those things. It reminded me of that green outhouse my father had bought during the Depression. I would have given a whole month's pay for an outhouse at that moment.

My discomfort was creating a severe problem, so I decided to return to the Supreme Allied Headquarters and use the restroom facilities there rather than those public restrooms. A sign on the front of the building said, 'Authorized Personnel Only.' Upon reaching headquarters, I put on my best official face—wished for a clipboard—and marched in with my musette bag like I was on official business. Using headquarters restrooms was strictly forbidden. After that, my travel in Rome was limited to how far I could go and still get back to Allied Headquarters when I had to use the bathroom.

It rained the entire time I was in Rome, which limited my walking. For a package of Kool cigarettes I could ride the horse-drawn carriages back and forth on my ventures. I would make a sortie and then get back to either the R&R facility or Allied Headquarters to use the bathroom. I saw the usual tourist sites—the Coliseum, the Fountains, the Vatican, St. Peter's Basilica. My favorite spot was the balcony from where Mussolini had made all his speeches.

One evening I found myself near an opera house, and saw this very nice-looking woman coming out. I decided to give her my best shot, and again in my best pidgin Italian, asked where I could find the biggest damned steak in Rome, and would she care to come with me? I still had not found a steak, and even if I had to blow two months flight pay, I was determined to eat one.

She was a very, very attractive woman. Classy. She did not need her shoulders, or her armpits, or her legs shaved. She told me a good cafe was right across the street from the opera house. I attempted to ask her what they called a steak. After a futile attempt to explain it to me, she grabbed me by the arm and said, "I'll take you."

At the cafe, I told her I'd buy her a steak, too, if she would order one for me. The waiter had given me a menu of about five pages, and I didn't understand a single thing on it. In Rome they didn't have enchiladas or anything that humans ought to eat. I told her, "Now, I want a T-bone steak," and even drew a picture of the 'T.' She nodded and laughed. We had drinks and were getting the royal treatment from the *maitre d'*. Besides being very good looking, she seemed to be very much at home there. Things were beginning to look up. I was finally going to get my T-bone steak, and seemed to be making some headway with her.

When the meal came I was never so disappointed in my life. They brought out two or three little things that looked like fried Vienna sausages. Our meal cost me forty-eight American dollars. To make matters worse, I started feeling the urge to go to the bathroom again. Still, I thought I was making some headway, when she suddenly said, "I want you to meet my husband."

I thought, uh oh, here's trouble. He came into the restaurant from the opera house. He looked like a bowling ball with a moustache. He turned out to be a nice man, though, and we became great friends. He even ordered the wine for us, although I paid for it. I don't like wine; it always gives me heartburn. He ordered some special stuff, and I'm thinking I'm out more money for wine I can't drink and a plate of Vienna sausage.

As we ate they jibed me about eating with the wrong hand, as well as asking questions about why Americans acted the way we did. But their questions were friendly. He was a musician who had toured America in the 1930s with a symphony, and had actually spent a little time in Santa Fe and Albuquerque.

He claimed he could always tell the character of a man by looking at his shoes. "What about the shoes?" I asked him.

He said, "Well, you have very expensive shoes. Your jewelry is good, your uniform is obviously tailored, you are obviously somebody with taste." My blouse had been made by a Chinese tailor in Denver and the shoes were those purchased in Las Cruces for me by my parents. They were the best pair of military dress oxfords that Mr. Stern could order.

He said, since I was a man of taste he had some friends he'd like me to meet, but all I could think of then was having to go to the bathroom. I had already written off his wife as a nice, friendly pal, so I wanted to head back to the action. Besides, the call of nature was again driving me. The restaurant bathroom was unisex and presided over by a female attendant. Italian restrooms were notoriously short on toilet tissue. In Amendola we were all issued little, brown packets of military toilet paper. Even the security of having several of those in my pocket, couldn't overcome the drawback of the female attendant.

I hailed a horse-drawn carriage. It pulled over, but I didn't get into it. The guy driving looked sorry and surly. He wore Italian Army officer boots, and I had a feeling he was fresh out of the Black Shirts (Fascist militia). Then I looked at his horse, encumbered with about five-hundred pounds of polished brass and cockades. The horse looked as though it weighed less than the harness. It's bones were sticking out in all directions. I was upset and told the driver he ought to be pulling the carriage, not the poor horse. In the resulting hassle, I hit him. I also snatched his buggy whip and tossed it. Then I told him he ought to feed his horse.

After that encounter, I looked for another carriage, and found a good one. The driver, Adolfo, was a nice guy who had been a footman on King Emanuel's own staff. I wasn't ashamed to have his horse pull me. On the way back to the R&R home that evening, we made arrangements for him to transport me around Rome the rest of my stay. I told him when I wanted to leave, and he always showed up.

He couldn't understood my peculiar problem about the bathroom situation, but he tolerated it and always knew where I could find a private bathroom. One time he even drove me by his apartment home. It was a nice one. He introduced me to his family as his new friend, the *"Americani aviatori."* He told them *"molte bombe,"* and pointed out the flashing on my sleeve. I understood enough Italian to know they were genuinely excited. The kids would yank on my sleeve, saying, *"Carmelle,* Joe," *"Ciocolate,* Joe," and men would say, *"Sigarette,* Joe." I enjoyed visiting with them, and, in a burst of good will, I gave them a couple of K-rations and Uncle Louie or somebody a package of cigarettes. Later I was invited to dinner .

I genuinely liked Adolfo. He was an intelligent, well-informed guide and, as we toured, provided me with much information about Rome. Anything I didn't understand, he explained. More importantly, he solved my most serious touring problem, that of being unable to use the public facilities. He considered it absolutely insane that I didn't use the *pissouri* like everybody else, but I just couldn't do it and he accepted that.

I gave up trying to find a T-bone steak. It was beyond their comprehension. Most of the time I had 'Dolfo drive me by the Red Cross canteen. For a day's sojourn I generally bought three Spam sandwiches and two cups of coffee. We didn't get any Spam in my outfit, for some reason, so they tasted good to me. I'd give a couple sandwiches to 'Dolfo which he packed very carefully in the horse's oat box he carried. He'd take them home and that little piece of Spam was very important to them. It shook me up.

The night I was invited to dinner, they got me fairly pie-eyed drunk. I had a hard time explaining to them where I was from. I would tell them New Mexico, and they could not understand that at all. They would say, "How far is that from Chicago?" I'd say that it was between Texas and Arizona, and they would respond, "Ahh, Texas. All the Indians." Everybody knew where Texas was. After supper and wine, they brought in the daughter. They told me that she was of a marriageable age and could cook. We talked all night long as they sang her praises and continued to ply me with wine. Later, I realized they were waiting the arrival of a priest. When the priest arrived with all his vestments, I realized if I passed out, I could very likely wake up married. I then politely told them marriage wasn't in my immediate plans. Perhaps they thought if she married me, they could all come to America where the streets were paved with gold.

My leave lasted five days. The first three days I didn't even think about the war, but on the fourth day I came out of a building and heard a flight of P-38s going by overhead above the clouds. You could always tell a P-38 by those Allison engines. They had a deep, deep hum. The Allison made a beautiful sound. I knew it was the Eighty-second Fighter Group coming in from a mission, and a little later I heard the bombers fly overhead. First I heard the Pratt-Whitneys, followed by the Wright Cyclones, and knew they had to be the Fifth Wing. Then my conscience began bothering me. I started worrying about the guys and wanted to get back up there. I felt I was gold bricking while they were still working.

After my fourth day, I went back and spent the last day sleeping. It had been an interesting stay. When I got back I lied a lot about my exploits to the others. Where I'd planned on being the world's greatest lover, I became the world's greatest tourist. That ended my R&R. After the Rome trip I never was interested in R&R, except to take time to sleep. Most of the time we were always so sleepy. We didn't have the nightmares when we slept in the day.

Chapter 23

[1] General Mark Clark's Fifth Army entered Rome on 4 June 1944.

[2] An infrastructure of military roads built by ancient Romans from 312 B.C. to 240 B.C. that connected the major seaports.

[3] The Thirty-sixth and Forty-fifth Divisions were Texas and Mountain States formations of National Guard units mobilized for the war. These two divisions were among several outfits that were severely bloodied in the frustrating Italian campaign. Keegan, 354.

Forty-five years later, while having coffee with a group of friends McGuire related this story. One of the men in the group was Pat McClernon, the captain who had warned him to keep out of local affairs. At that time, McClernon and his unit were en route to the front to repair a water system.

[4] At this point in the war, with a surrendered country occupied by both Allied and Axis forces, the Italian populace was engaged in an open, brutal, tragic civil war.

[5] The hard, frustrating Italian campaign, which began in September 1943 and was doomed to last the remainder of the war, did not bring out the best feelings between soldiers of the British Eighth Army and the American Fifth Army. The hard feelings started at the upper levels and flowed down, as McGuire's narrative so vividly describes. Keegan, 368.

First Casualty

Nov. 19: *Winterhofen Oil Storage. Flew to Vienna and bombed oil storage tanks. Flak heavy and accurate. Co-pilot Lynch got hit by flak in the neck and I got a piece in my knee. Left oxygen system was knocked out; #2 & #4 engines were knocked out; #4 was windmilling. Just before landing the prop fell off. Landed at Ancona & went to American Hospital at Senigallia. Flak removed about 10:30 that night. 35th Field Hospital, 2nd Platoon.*

Wayne Lesher
Navigator's Diary

Sunday, 19 November 1944, was a dismal day with low clouds, scud, gray haze from the ocean, and poor visibility. It was very gloomy, and so were our attitudes. Those who had flown the day before had been to Vienna and we had just received the news that we were going back again to hit the Winterhofen oil storage depot and tanks in Vienna. No one was very happy about that. Our crew had been flying together most of the time through the end of October. We'd had some bad experiences, but our luck had held and there had been no crew casualties. We felt comfortable flying with one another. In November the Group received some new crews and the Squadron and Group philosophy was to intersperse new crews with as many veterans as possible. Not all of these were green crews. Some had only a mission or two under their belts. On this particular day, none of us were flying in the same plane. Chambers had the day off and it was Scofield's second day in a row to make the trip to Vienna. Fenstermaker had also been to Vienna the day before. The best we could do, as we boarded the truck just before sun-up that morning, was wave to one another. That day our luck ran out.

It was one of those days when everything went wrong. Our squadron taxied nose-to-tail to the point on the runway where we started our take-off run; the other three squadrons had already departed. Suddenly, a red flare came from the tower and we heard the orders, "Tweet Tweet Squadron hold your position. We have an emergency." Brakes were locked, amid much swearing.

Out of the scud came a B-17 from another squadron with one engine feathered and smoking badly. It could have been on fire. Upon losing the engine shortly after take-off, they had detoured a few miles over the Adriatic and dropped their unarmed bombs in the sea to lighten the load before returning to Amendola and landing safely and smoothly. The minute they left the runway, we received the green light and the orders, "Tweet Tweet Squadron, you're cleared to depart."

Those few minutes of delay had put us behind the rest of the Second Bomb Group and we spent all day playing catch-up, trying to regain that lost time without overheating the engines. No one had to remind us that a lagging squadron was vulnerable. It was an uneventful trip until we turned on the IP and headed for that hell hole of Vienna, one of the most heavily defended targets in Europe. Because of my previous experiences there, my stomach was tied in knots as we watched the other squadrons plowing through flak to the target. We turned on the IP. The bomb run went smoothly enough, but we were taking a beating all the way. Every airplane there had damage. I was in the first element,[1] as was most of my crew. Lesher was in the second element, in either the five or six position in the back. Everything was going well for Lesher at that time and he was busy making entries into his log and recording the bombs away time. They had just dropped the bombs and were turning towards the rally point when a shell exploded in front of them, knocking out the #4 engine. At the same time the co-pilot tried to talk. It was more of an ahhhhh, or gurgling sound, and the pilot announced, "Lynch has been hit. Lynch is hit. Help me get him out of the cockpit!"

The airplane was bouncing badly. A second or two later a second explosion slammed into the port side of the nose and fuselage and engine #2 went out. Wayne's navigation table, along with his charts and calculators and paraphernalia, disappeared in a cloud of kindling as he was slammed off his chair and against the far wall. It felt as though a red, hot poker had hit him in the knee. The pain was intense. He knew he had been hurt, but the co-pilot needed help and the engineer was trying to drag him down into the navigator's and bombardier's area. Miraculously the bombardier wasn't hit. The engineer immediately returned to assist the pilot. The pilot had used the foam fire extinguisher but was still unable to feather #4 engine. The #2 engine on the port side was feathered without difficulty. He had managed to hold some semblance of the heading, but very quickly realized the airplane wouldn't be able to cut it in that configuration with the #4 prop windmilling.

He advised the crew to throw everything possible overboard to lighten the airplane. Lesher lay on his back for a moment, stunned. He tried to tell them that he, too, had been hit as they had passed him with the big first aid kit on the their way to Lynch. Lynch had been hit about an inch from the carotid artery and the flak had come out the back of his shoulder. He was in great pain and bleeding heavily. Lesher handed the bombardier morphine syrettes from the first aid kit to deaden the terrible pain. The morphine had frozen. Lesher told the men working on Lynch to put them under their armpits. He still hadn't told them that he had been hit. His leg felt like it was both on fire and numb. Then the pilot called, "Pilot to navigator. Give me a heading." Lesher crawled over to the remnants of his table and discovered the left oxygen system had been knocked out. Everyone was then plugged into the right system. With ten men drawing on one oxygen system, it doesn't last a long time.

The pilot was still having problems holding the altitude. Lesher was able to retrieve enough portions of some of his maps, some with holes burned in them, to give the pilot the heading to the rally point.

The morphine finally thawed sufficiently to give to the co-pilot. They marked his forehead with the customary "M" and the time of the injection.

In the back of the airplane chaos reigned as they tried to drop the ball turret. The ammunition and guns had already gone overboard, along with practically everything else that wasn't tied down other than their parachutes, shoes, and escape kits. Everybody was working frantically to lighten the airplane. The pilot was still fighting the windmilling #4 engine and plugging into the right oxygen system.

Lesher's leg was now hurting badly and he considered using a morphine syrette, but realized they desperately needed him awake and alert to navigate them out of the danger areas and back home to Amendola. They were only about five hundred miles, as the crow files, from our field; however, we didn't fly like the crow. Otherwise, we would have been dead in fifteen minutes from flying over defended areas. It was necessary that he begin plotting their position and know exactly where they were. Meanwhile they flew in and out of scattered clouds. All of his instruments—compass, ADF needle, altimeter, thermometers, etc.—had been blown away, and he needed to rely on the pilot for compass readings. They had lost considerable altitude and were lower, although a little ahead of the squadron. They were beginning to slow down and straggle.

The rest of us were unaware of their problems. Every airplane that crossed the target that day had sustained some damage. Each crew was busy assessing their own and weren't aware that Lesher's airplane and one other were having problems until later when we saw them below, headed toward the rally point.

Shortly after the pilot had the aircraft stabilized he called Lesher for a steer to the closest medical help. Lesher suggested Ancona, and the pilot agreed. They still had to cross Croatia, the Alps, and the Adriatic. Ancona was not far behind the lines where the Fifth Army and the Germans were savagely fighting, but they had good emergency medical facilities and a long landing strip. The rest of the Group continued on their planned route.

Every plane had problems, but the Group's condition was not too bad. That is, other than Lesher and his crew, who were in a very precarious position—half of their oxygen system nonfunctional, two engines out, and one of those windmilling and violently shaking the plane. Because of oxygen system problems they lowered their flying altitude. Soon they would be within range of those wicked, light caliber flak batteries.

With only pieces of his maps available, Lesher had a severe problem. His leg was hurting, but he was also concentrating on his calculations. His table was non-existent so he used his briefcase and clipboard instead. Since everybody else had big problems—mashed fingers, bare flesh frozen from touching cold metal, and they were utterly defenseless in the stripped down airplane, Lesher decided his problems weren't as bad as the others'. He didn't have time to explain, and he couldn't afford to take the morphine to deaden the pain in his leg.

I don't know how long it took for that crippled airplane to cross Yugoslavia and the Adriatic and arrive at Ancona, but the log indicates that the airplane engines ran nine hours that day. Coming in to Ancona, the #4 propeller, mercifully, fell off. Airplanes, with differing amounts of damage, were landing one after another. Lesher's plane fired one flare, signifying one wounded aboard. He still had not told them that he also was

Wayne Lesher visiting the crew while on convalescent leave. This photo was taken after McGuire had returned to the States. Each bomb painted on the nose of the airplane represented a mission flown by this plane. At this point they had been flying with different crews for several months. Lesher is standing on Marston matting. *(Courtesy W. Lesher)*

wounded. He had checked and discovered a hole in the side of his knee but there was little blood.

When they hit the ground, the fire trucks and ground crew met them and led them off into a vacant area. The fire trucks left once they discovered the airplane wasn't in danger of burning. Then the ambulance arrived, and Lesher, doing his usual conscientious job, was trying to retrieve his maps, briefcase, and code books. The others helped Lieutenant Lynch out through the nose hatch and loaded him in the ambulance. As Lesher stuck his head out the airplane to call for help, the ambulance drove off with the entire crew. He was abandoned in the airplane. He decided the best way to exit was via the bombardiers' escape hatch in the nose. Even though that necessitated an eight-foot drop he decided it would be less painful than crawling through the tunnel and bomb bay and out through the normal entry and departure emergency hatch in the waist. It is a drop of several feet to the ground. Finally, he summoned enough courage to jump from the hatch and try to land on one leg. As he lay there for a minute or two recovering, he looked to see if anyone was around.

Other airplanes were coming in with problems, and nobody paid him any attention. Finally, realizing he wasn't going to get help, he took his briefcase and started hopping on one leg and falling down, then getting up and repeating the procedure. He had covered quite a distance when a British soldier drove past him. The Brit returned and pulled up beside him. "Sir, are you all right?"

"No, I've been hit and I need a doctor badly."

The British soldier put him in the truck and took him to the closest medical facility, a British first aid station. The doctor immediately checked him and put sulfa, Mercurochrome and a light bandage on it. "There's a hell of a hole in there and the flak is still in there. You're going to need surgery and we can't do it here. I'll get you transportation to the American field hospital (MASH unit) on the other side."

When the ambulance arrived at the field hospital a few minutes later they were ready to transport Lieutenant Lynch to the hospital in Senigallia, twelve or fourteen miles away. They said Lynch needed extensive medical help at a well-equipped medical facility and Lesher needed orthopedic surgery which couldn't be performed at their facility. Fighting between the Fifth Army and the Germans had been very savage that day and casualties were arriving in large numbers from the front, just a few miles away. Finally, they got Wayne into an ambulance. Because of their preoccupation with Lynch, the crew hadn't realized until then that Wayne wasn't with them. This was the first they knew about his injury.

They took him to the Thirty-fifth Field Hospital in Senigallia. The operation began almost eleven hours after he was hit. Fortunately for Wayne, the surgeon was excellent and later became one of the best-known and most widely respected orthopedic surgeons in the United States. He skillfully and successfully repaired ligament and tendon damage in the knee caused by the red-hot flak.

We were still unaware of Wayne's problem when we landed. I turned in my parachute bag and equipment and started to the debriefing. A few minutes later, while turning in his parachute bag, Scofield overheard someone comment that two of our airplanes had landed in Ancona. One, supposedly, had badly wounded men in the front section. He didn't think too much about it at the time, other than to wonder who it might be, until he reached the debriefing. When we couldn't find Lesher, we became concerned about his absence. Later that evening one of the men from operations came into our tent and said, "Your navigator, Wayne Lesher, was hit today. He's in Ancona. Don't know how badly hurt he is, but the news is that it's not life-threatening. Lieutenant Lynch was also hit. We don't know his condition either, but it was pretty serious."

As we digested this news, Chambers, Karsten, and McDonnell came in. Chambers' eyes were moist as he said, "Fellows, have you heard the news? Wayne was hit today. They say he is going to live, but don't know how badly he was hit. He's in Ancona. Apparently, they got shot up pretty good."

It was quiet for a bit as most of us thought about the long period we had gone without a casualty, the hard times we had experienced, and all the harrowing experiences. It would be a tough loss if we couldn't get Wayne back. We depended so much on him. Since he was unmarried like the enlisted crew, we had adopted him into our group and he spent much time with us. Besides being a good navigator, we were very fond of him.

We knew our crew was long overdue for someone to be hit or killed. But, when the news came it was, indeed, a bitter pill to swallow. I remembered when, a few days before, Jack Karsten had taken a vicious hit in the chest, but his vest held and he was left with nothing more than a bruised chest, ruffled feathers, and thankfulness to the Lord. That was a close one. We'd had many such experiences, but this was the first time one of us was actually down.

Somehow, I'd thought it would be me. By that time, I didn't have a lot of faith that I would finish my missions and had reconciled myself to that fact. We were very pensive that evening and spent much time by ourselves. We finally gathered together and recalled the funny things Lesher had done and the several close calls he'd had in the last thirty days. One of us mentioned his Friday the 13th mission the previous month.

That day the Fifteenth Air Force had been putting on a maximum effort. That meant every airplane safe enough to fly and for which they could find a crew, was going to go. They split us with some going to Vienna, and some to Blechammer. Lesher went to Blechammer.

It was one of those days that couldn't have been worse. At Blechammer, we hit the south oil refinery. My airplane acquired over fifty holes and one engine was shot out, but fortunately it feathered. Lesher had about thirty holes in the nose around his station. Again, he miraculously escaped injury. Two of the holes were in his astral dome and it was hanging in pieces. The astral dome is the plastic bubble on the nose above the navigator's head through which he uses a sextant to obtain navigation fixes. A piece of flak had torn the charging handles off the charging mechanism on the chin turret. And, once again flak peppered holes all over his beloved charts. There was also a big hole in his table. The concussion from an exploding shell was so strong that it almost ripped off his oxygen mask. It did numb his lips. He sounded like someone who had just returned from the dentist's office after two root canals.

Again, his navigator's table with his precious maps and paraphernalia were full of holes. He had spent hours on those maps, pre-plotting courses and emergency escape routes. It was one of the few times we ever heard him cussing. That had been one of those missions where we'd had to slip back seven hundred miles, hide, cross the heartland of Germany and their defenses, and then go for our bolt-hole in the Alps. Everybody made it back, but again Lesher had a close one.

Another crew member recalled when his E6B computer was shot out of his hand. An E6B was a navigator's slide rule marked with circular graduations and used in the same way an engineer used a slide rule.

336

*　*　*

A few days later on another mission, 17 October, we filled in for the Ninety-sixth Squadron. Just as we crossed the target, one of the airplanes ahead of us was cut in half. Most of their fuselage and tail came cart-wheeling back through the formation and barely missed us by a few inches. When he looked back, his navigator's table sported another big hole and, again, his maps were full of holes. We laughingly said that Wayne ought to be getting paranoid. It looked like the entire German military machine was personally trying kill him.

Then we recalled his courage. Wayne had always been prone to airsickness, but never let it interfere with his duties. When he became sick, he just opened the lid of a .50 caliber ammo can which he kept besides him, and never missed a beat on his calculations. That night we all agreed that Wayne Lesher was the bravest man we'd ever met.

After about three weeks at the Thirty-fifth Hospital in Senigallia, his surgeons transferred him to Rome for rehabilitation and R&R. When he was pronounced ready, he would be returned to the Twentieth Bomb Squadron. This placed him in Rome through the Christmas holidays. We were still trying to locate him, but by the time we'd traced him to the Thirty-fifth Hospital, he'd left for Rome.

By then Wayne was ambulatory and could get around rather well with a cane. He was like the rest of us and wanted to see the historic spots, so he made the most of his walking requirements for rehabilitation and spent the time sight-seeing. A two-day tour of the Vatican would provide him with sufficient time to see the historic buildings, artwork, and statutes. He timed his visit to coincide with the gathering of the masses in St. Peter's Square for Pope Pius XII's appearance on his balcony. Standing for very long on a sore leg was not a pleasant experience. Besides, the crowded conditions gave him claustrophobia. Therefore, he decided to forego the papal blessing and continue his tour.

He was particularly interested in the Sistine Chapel and the works of Michelangelo. An official let a very small group of people, including Wayne, into the Chapel. Everyone there could tell he was a wounded airman and that was probably the reason he was selected. While standing with this small group of three or four he was approached by a member of the Papal staff, "*Leutenente*, would you like a personal audience with His Holiness?" Wayne quickly agreed. He had been touched by the feelings he had felt inside this church and now he not only had an opportunity to see a great religious leader, but also a world leader. He enthusiastically responded, "Yes, sir."

Wayne wasn't a Catholic and knew very little about Catholicism, but noticed that he was the only one not carrying a rosary. He hastily went outside and found a vender and bought a very expensive rosary which contained a tiny vial filled with soil from the catacombs. He returned in time to be led with the three others into a room off the Sistine Chapel.

Shortly after they were seated in this room, the Pope was carried into the chapel in a sedan chair. He left the chair and talked, for some time, with each person there. When it was Wayne's turn, he was awe stricken. The Pope talked to him for some time. When he finished talking, the Pope blessed Wayne and Wayne's rosary. Unfortunately, it wasn't in English so Wayne didn't have any idea what the Pope said to him.

Wayne later told us that the Pope was a very nice guy and he had a good feeling in that place. "I don't know what he said, but it was very, very impressive."

Pronounced fit for duty, Lesher returned to the Twentieth Squadron around the first of the year, even though he was still wobbling. On 8 January 1945, Wayne flew as squadron lead navigator on his first mission after being wounded. It was Vienna again.

Chapter 24

[1] The first three airplanes in a squadron are the first element; the next three are the second element, and the seventh is 'tail-end-charlie.'

– 25 –

Good News, Bad News!

In the latter days of November, we were sensitive to each other's moods and emotional changes. I had been studying Ralph Chambers with some concern. He had been losing weight and seemed a little different, as though he had a big problem. You could tell it wasn't combat fatigue. What ever it was, it hadn't interfered with anything that he had been doing, but there was a subtle change in him.

Once, when walking with Jack Karsten, I asked, "Lieutenant, I'm kind of worried about Chambers. Is he sick? Is he still worrying about Wayne? Somehow he has changed."

"Mack, I'll tell you what's bothering Ralph. Yeh, he still worries about Wayne and we can't find anything about him, but that's not his problem. Rachel is at the end of her term. They have a baby due and not knowing what's happening is bothering him considerably. He's very concerned for Rachel as that baby is due anytime. He'll be alright once that baby comes."

I thought no more about it until the morning of 2 December. Nearly all our crew were aboard that day and we were en route to Blechammer. We'd been there before and weren't anxious to go back. It was about as far as our gas reserves would comfortably allow us to go and still get home. If the plane was damaged, your chances of returning were fifty-fifty at the best. We dreaded that place like poison. That morning's trip had been uneventful until we crossed the Alps. As we came into Austria, above us we saw contrails. Our escorts were involved in a dog fight. We had seen some jets in the area and that was probably the day three ME-262s made a pass at us on the way down, followed briefly by P-51s vainly trying to catch them. It was a losing proposition. They did no damage, but to our dismay they were so fast we could hardly track them with our turrets.

About ten minutes off the IP we put on our flak vest and steel helmets and I was fighting fear and nausea. My stomach felt like it held a hundred pounds of lead. Since we knew what to expect from Blechammer, we were all white-knuckle cases. We'd been to that oil refinery before and were in a high state of alert for fighters.

Suddenly an announcement came over the intercom. "Stand by for a message from the group leader." Everyone quickly changed to the command position on the radio, not knowing what to expect. This type of announcement was highly unusual, and, generally, when you received a message from the group leader, it wasn't good news. We weren't experiencing any trouble at the time so it puzzled us all the more. Soon a voice said, "This is a message for the aircraft commander of Tweet Tweet Charlie. Be advised that you are the father of a seven pound, fourteen ounce baby boy. Mother and son both doing nicely in your hometown hospital. This message is courtesy of the Fifteenth Air Force. Congratulations to the aircraft commander of Tweet Tweet Charlie. Out."

The crew quickly changed back to the intercom position. Chambers was hollering, "Yiiipee." Then the ribbing started. "Did you hear how much that kid weighed? Seven pounds, fourteen ounces. He's half grown." Someone else added, "Yeh, that Chambers is a regular Man-O-War." These quips were interspersed with demands for cigars. I suggested they name him Blechammer. Chambers quickly vetoed that. They had already picked a name for either a girl or boy and it was not Blechammer! It was a wonderful release for us and we temporarily forgot the nightmare we had to face. Fear, dread, queasy stomachs, and white knuckles disappeared in the good-natured ribbing of Chambers. Someone called from his position, "Left waist to Daddy," and similar comments. It was therapeutic and a tremendous morale booster.

Rachel's brother had contacted the Red Cross in Winston-Salem and they sent a telegram to the Red Cross Headquarters in Italy. It was quickly passed along to the Fifteenth Air Force, which relayed it to the Second Bomb Group, which then sent it to Ralph who was on his way to Blechammer. There was about a nine-hour time differential between the States and Italy.

We took our usual beating over that awful place, and came out of it with a few holes and a little older, but we survived it unhurt. The trip back was uneventful and the ribbing continued. While it wasn't an enjoyable trip, that announcement wiped away much of the tension and anxiety. It brought home a little closer to us. After landing, Ralph stood on the field with his oxygen mask dangling from one hook, while we crowded around shaking his hand. His face, deeply grooved from the mask, was lined with the usual white powder from the moisture build-up in the oxygen mask and his face deeply grooved from the mask. He was grinning from ear to ear. With that broad grin, he looked like a jackass eating briars. You could tell he had already forgotten that mission and couldn't wait to get back to his tent and write Rachel.[1]

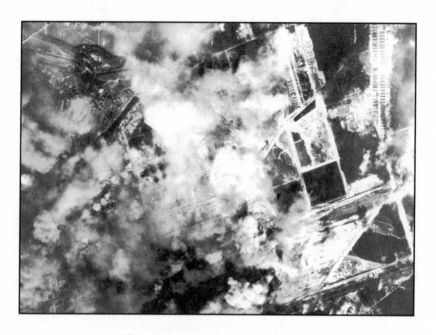

A bomb strike over Blechammer.
(Courtesy R. Chambers)

That next Sunday, no one in the Second Bomb Group church choir sang more lustily and enthusiastically than did Ralph Chambers.

December 2nd was a good day in Ralph Chambers' life.

A few days later we also received word that Ralph had been put in for his captaincy. The competition was tough with three eligible, top-notch leaders vying for that promotion. Ralph Bischoff was another who was overdue for a captaincy. We had no doubt that Ralph would soon receive his railroad tracks. That was another good day for Ralph Chambers.

Collision

Also, in late November we all almost died, not by the hands of Germans, but by the hands of an American pilot.

It was the custom on takeoffs and landings for the gunners to go back to the radio room. We figured if there was an accident on either of these occasions, we stood the best chance of surviving if we were in the radio room. There was plenty of space in the radio operator's section of the plane. He sat on his chair on the left side of the plane and operated the radio; if we were attacked by fighters, he had his responsibility as gunner as well, firing a machine gun through a clear, plexiglass hatch at the top of the fuselage. This gun was set at an angle, and was put at that spot to protect the bomber from enemy attacks along the beam of the plane, at angles of anywhere from straight above to high and to the rear. You could see clearly through that plexiglass hatch.

On landings and takeoffs we would put our backs to the radio room wall and brace one another. In any emergency where we needed to escape quickly, there were three ways to get out of the radio room. We were in that room on that day in late November, returning from a mission. Our squadron was given the signal to land, and Chambers got us in line to do so. Turning into the final approach to the landing field, we entered some low scud, which considerably reduced visibility. We gunners had, as usual, braced ourselves as we made the turn.

Looking up through the plexiglass hatch, Scofield suddenly yelled and jumped up. He lunged for the radio operator's microphone. "There's an airplane landing on top us! He's twenty-five to thirty feet above us," he yelled into the mike. Scofield's quick thinking gave the pilots this vital information which allowed them to take defensive action. I looked up and my blood turned ice cold. Above us was another B-17, settling right on top of us. All I could see was a huge, muddy tire directly above me and frightening thoughts flashed through my mind as I thought of our nineteen-foot tail sticking up. Whoever the pilot was, he hadn't seen us. He was doing just what Scofield had said, putting down right on top of us.

A bomber landing on top of another is one of the deadliest of all accidents. We'd all seen one or two. Escape hatches are mashed out of position. Props from the top airplane chew through the fuselage, pilots' compartment, fuel cells, and oxygen bottles. Both planes invariably catch fire and explode.

Chambers and Karsten, without hesitation and without verbal communication, acted as one and skidded the big bomber to one side. Chambers had just flared out the aircraft and was ready for touchdown when he heard Scofield's warning. He skidded the plane off the runway onto a vacant part of the field, and skillfully navigated the ditches, brush, ruts, and uneven terrain. How they managed to avoid a ground loop and keeping the aircraft from standing on its nose is beyond me to this day. This was another instance of the teamwork of our crew and the confidence we had in each other. Chambers and Karsten had instantly reacted to Scofield's voice without questioning or hesitation.

Chambers cut the engines quickly. We watched the other bomber land safely in the exact spot where we had been headed. They never saw us. All of us were weak and visibly shaking. And mad as hell!

We had narrowly escaped the worst kind of death. We were upset and determined to find out how something like that could happen. The tower could not see this second aircraft coming through the overcast. The pilot wasn't in the pattern and he was definitely not cleared to land. Later we learned it was a cripple coming in from another group to the south. In addition to radio problems, he was lost, and was within a few miles of home when he looked over and saw our airfield through a break in the clouds. To add to their problems, base scuttlebutt said both pilots were injured, as well.

Our airplane only suffered some minor damage, and was towed back to our hard stand and repaired during the night. The damage to our nerves was not as easily repaired.

The Bravest Thing
I think the bravest thing I ever saw in the war occurred one day, also late in my tour, while we were hitting Munich. As we

approached the target, we encountered especially heavy flak. Black smoke from the flak had turned the day into night. One pilot commented that it was so dark they had to start flying on instruments.

We had finished our turn and were departing from the target area when I looked out the waist at the formation following us into the target. There I saw a lone B-17. It had a couple of engines on fire, but was flying straight and level into the target, not wavering one bit as flak burst all around it. It continued into and over the target, all by itself. At times is was completely obscured by flak; it looked like every flak battery around Munich was firing at it.

Burning the last mile or two before reaching the target, we saw it drop its bombs. The pilot turned off target and started down in flames. We were quite a distance away by that time, and I was busy watching for fighters, but when I could I kept my eye on that plane going down in flames. No parachutes were visible coming from the stricken plane, which doesn't necessarily mean that none managed to get out. They could have bailed out at a lower altitude, or pulled their 'chute cords at a lower altitude, or they could have gone down with their plane.

I never saw this plane's number or squadron markings, never knew any of the names of the crew, but that B-17 epitomized what we were all about. While with the Second Bomb Group, I never once personally observed a single bomber in our squadron or group turning back from a target because of enemy opposition or pressure. Many times planes en route to the target turned back because of mechanical difficulties, weather, serious injuries or loss of oxygen, but not one turned back because the fighters were too many, or the flak too heavy. In all of my research on the Fifteenth Air Force in Italy and the Eighth Air Force in England did I ever read of an airplane turning away from the target because of enemy pressure. I always admired that plane and that crew. They were the essence of our fighting spirit and determination. They were heroes.

* * *

After my return to the States the remainder of my crew encountered a similar situation. We didn't consider ourselves heroes, we were just doing our job. Looking back, I shake my head at the fool hardiness of what we did, but at the time we saw nothing outstanding in our actions. A brief entry from Lesher's navigator's diary for 17 February 1945 speaks volumes.

> Feb. 17: *Bombed Lobau O/R [oil refinery] at Vienna.*
> *Feathered engine at IP & bombed about*
> *2 mi. behind sq'd on three engines. Flak HMA*
> *[Heavy (guns), Moderate (intensity), Accurate].*
> *95mph/headwind. -45 degrees c temp."*

Chapter 25

[1] Paul Wayne Chambers, born 2 December 1944, still lives in Winston-Salem, NC and has three children of his own.

16 December

Battle of the Bulge Intelligence

Our strategic planners made a serious mistake. They under-estimated the Germans' ability to carry the fight to us. Before our arrival in Italy, Allied planners had been overly optimistic in saying the Germans could never bring the fight back to us and could now only fight defensively. For about a year, our highest placed intelligence people had been saying that we had won the war. But they didn't tell the Germans that, and the Germans kept on fighting. During our stay in Italy, one day we would read that the Air Force claimed to have broken the back of the Luftwaffe. The next day we would read of some group being hit by a large pack of enemy fighters and many shot down. To us, the fighting seemed to be getting heavier and heavier.

Allied High Command intelligence ignored local intel-ligence observations before the Battle of the Bulge.[1] For three or four weeks, during our missions in early December, we saw columns of enemy armor streaming west from the Russian front. We duly reported this information. One observation was most curious to us. We had been using a particular ground reference as a navigational check for several months when we were in that area. In early December, as we passed over it, the navigator called out, "Wait a minute, there's something wrong here. There's a forest there today where there wasn't yesterday."

I looked out to see what he was talking about. Sure enough, it did look like a forest had sprung up overnight, but we decided it was more of their creative camouflage. Later we learned they had landed more than two hundred airplanes on the Autobahn and stood them on their noses. Covered with camouflage netting, they did look like trees in a forest. They were having a build-up and we observed it. All this unusual activity was reported to our intelligence.

My only objection to the way we were lead was that our leaders were abandoning the European war too quickly. They began to slacken their effort before we had actually won, thinking we had won. Our intelligence missed in this instance—badly.

Three Las Crucens

16 December we awoke to a very heavy fog. It was also raining. Visibility was very poor. The worst winter in fifty years had descended over the European continent. The Allied tactical air force was having problems getting missions off the ground. The weather also affected operations of the strategic Eighth Air Force in England.

In Italy, the weather was slightly better. The Fifteenth Air Force prepared for another mission, as usual planning strikes by both B-17s and B-24s. About the same time we were boarding trucks to drive to the flight line in Amendola, the German battle group launched an attack on our unsuspecting divisions in the Ardennes.

It was sweat time for us in the Second Bomb Group as we took off with low visibility and high ice levels. Climbing blind with other aircraft around us always presented the distinct possibility of collision. Our target that day was Brux, Czechoslovakia.

Forty-five miles south of Amendola, the B-24 field at Pantanella was also a beehive of activity. It was the home field of the 465th Bomb Group. Unknown to me, Donald Stern, from Las Cruces, New Mexico (where I had attended college), was preparing for his first mission with the 781st Squadron. At that time I didn't know Donald, but his parents and mine were good friends. Mr. Stern owned the dry goods store were my parents had purchased those expensive shoes so admired by the Italian musician. This was Don's first mission.

He and his crew had arrived in Italy by ship and were then trucked to Pantanella. Before their first mission they had been extensively briefed, as we all had, with the information they needed to survive if shot down. Don was a tail gunner.

Don had a problem most other airmen didn't. Don was Jewish. The Fifteenth Air Force made arrangements to provide false identity for Jewish airmen, because the rumor was circulating that the Germans hunted especially hard for Jewish airmen and gave them special treatment if captured. Everyone wore dog tags, and on the dog tags was stamped a "P" for Protestant, "C" for Catholic, "H" for Hebrew, or you could leave it blank. Don opted to leave his blank.

His mother had also worried about the possibility of his capture. Before he left the States, she taught him the Lord's Prayer, and insisted he memorize it verbatim, just in case he was captured.

For this first mission, Don and his crew were assigned *Flamin' Mamie*, a well-known Liberator. It was the pride and joy of one of the lead crews in the 781st Squadron, a crew that was not flying that day. Their AC was an old-timer, Lieutenant Tom Yancy, who had lost most of his crew and was giving Don's regular pilot, Marion A. Pitts, a Georgia boy, his check ride. Yancy gathered the crew together. "We won't have a milk run today. Today's mission is Brux. The B-17s of the Group have already lifted off and will cross the target ahead of us, getting the Germans all stirred up and madder than hell by the time we reach the target."

Their take-off and climb-out was scary, but uneventful. As their Group flew over the Alps between Salsburg and Innsbruck, they made a wide detour around Linz, the home of the heavily defended Hermann Goering Industrial Complex. They threaded their way around the defended towns in the area to a point northwest of Linz.

About that time, the Second Bomb Group had dropped its bombs and was turning off target. We sustained the usual damage. The B-24s, including *Flamin' Mamie*, were due at the IP ten to fifteen minutes after the 17s had cleared the target area.

Don, alert for fighter attacks, had been observing the sights. In the distance he could see Switzerland, the upper Alps, and Bavaria. They had experienced no problems up to that time. Suddenly, without warning, the #3 engine turned loose. Oil poured back over the wing and the pilots had problems feathering the propeller of the bad engine. They started dropping behind the formation. The Group leader told them to make their way home. To their great disappointment, they were having to turn back on their first mission.

Immediately after they had made their turn, the #4 engine began smoking and then quit. While the pilots frantically worked to feather that engine, they were smothered by flak. The pilot told them to dump everything overboard to lighten the aircraft, as he didn't think he could maintain altitude or a heading. Don came out of the tail. He and the other crewmen worked to drop the ball turret, followed by their bombs, ammunition and all the guns. All loose equipment was tossed overboard. Only parachutes, escape kits, and shoes were saved.

Yancy announced they still couldn't maintain altitude. The pilots were using all their leg strength on the rudders to keep the aircraft on a heading, but with two engines out on the same wing, it was a losing proposition. The pilot alerted the crew that they were going to have to bail out. When he rang the bell, they were to leave the airplane quickly. The crewmen hurriedly snapped parachutes onto their harnesses. A few seconds later the bell rang and he ordered them to bail out.

As tail gunner, Don's responsibility was to make sure everybody in his area, waist, tail, and ball had jumped. The crew split into two groups. Some left by the bomb bay, others jumped out the escape hatch in the rear of the airplane. When they had all jumped, Don called the pilots on the intercom and told them the others were gone. The pilot then ordered Don to jump. He hesitated at the escape hatch for a moment, looking back at *Flamin' Mamie.* By then her wing had started to burn. As Don bailed out, he saw Yancy leave.

His parachute opened with a vicious crack. World War II airmen used small 'chutes designed to get you to the ground in a hurry. You wanted to be a target for as short a time as possible, and also, we sometimes bailed out at high altitudes where there was little oxygen. Small 'chutes were hard on the body, especially of a large person, when you landed.

After his 'chute opened, Don could not see the rest of his crew. Below he could see fields. He quickly checked his escape kit, his shoes, and his dog tags. When he looked up to check his parachute, he saw, to his horror, a huge, ten-inch oil spot on one of the panels. An oil-soaked silk or nylon panel, under pressure, could disintegrate at any second. This upset him, and he made a mental note that if he ever returned to base, he was going to give the man who packed his 'chute a piece of his mind. That morning, his parachute had sported a brand-new inspection tag on it. Fortunately, the panel held until he landed.

Don hit hard. He immediately looked around for his pilot and saw him coming down about a mile away. Don hastily gathered his parachute, removed his Mae West and the rest of his gear and tried to hide it. Just as he turned in the pilot's direction, three German soldiers drove up and stopped immediately in front of him, covering him with their rifles. Out in the open there was no cover, no place to run or fight. Don held up his hands and surrendered.

(left) General Nathan Twining, commander of the Fifteenth Army Air Force at a debriefing session with 781st Squadron, 465th Bomb Group personnel. This was Donald Stern's unit. *(Courtesy Fifteenth Air Force Association) (right)* Donald Stern in the fall of 1945 after his release from POW camp. *(Courtesy: E.J. Stern, Jr.)*

As the Germans left the car, he thought they were talking about the pistol he wore in his shoulder holster and interpreted their conversation to mean they wanted him to give it to them. As he gingerly reached for it, one of the soldiers smashed him in the head with his rifle butt and removed the weapon himself. They threw Don into the back of the vehicle and drove off.

At their destination, he joined several other members of his crew and Pitts was brought in later. A majority of the crew had been quickly collected and brought to this location. Puzzled as to why they were in that particular spot, they soon had their answer. A Luftwaffe flak-battery commander, apparently the same battery which had fired at them, wanted to question them. They could tell from his questions, in English, that he wanted credit for the downing of *Flamin' Mamie*. He needed details of the encounter which he could submit to his superiors.

The first one he queried was Pitts. Pitts, as contrary as he could be, decided he wouldn't give them the time of day. When the flak officer asked him which shell had hit him, Pitts responded, "What flak are you talking about? We had mechanical troubles earlier and were returning home when we lost the other engine. Both engines went out on their own. We didn't take any hits from flak. The fact is, I didn't even see any flak."

When Don's turn came he took his cue from Pitts. "I'm sorry, I don't know what you're talking about. We didn't see or hear any flak. As far as I know, there wasn't any. We had mechanical problems and were going home."

The flak officer first tried cajoling them and when that failed even issued threats to make them admit that his battery had shot them down. He was obviously in desperate need of credit, but the American airmen calmly denied even seeing flak. they left him gnashing his teeth in rage.

Next, they were transported to a detention center in Linz. There the interrogation took a strange turn. Here they were questioned by professional interrogators. It soon was Don's turn to be questioned. The interrogators immediately noticed that his dog tags were unmarked for religious denomination. Don, knowing he was going to be singled out for special treatment, denied being Jewish. They tried everything they could think of to make him admit he was Jewish.

Another interrogation officer walked into the room and over to Don. After he checked Don's dog tags, he very smugly said, "If you aren't a Jew, you're either a Catholic or a Protestant. If you're a Catholic, say the Catechism. If you're a Protestant, tell us the Lord's Prayer."

Without a change of expression, Don recited the Lord's Prayer for the crestfallen officer. At that point they decided Don wasn't Jewish and he was returned to his crew. Don thanked his lucky stars for his mother's prescience. He would probably have been placed in a special camp where prisoners were starved, beaten, or put in the ovens. Many Jewish airmen disappeared and were never accounted for. The Germans never quit trying to find Jewish members among the prisoners of war. At that stage in the war the Germans were paying less and less attention to the Geneva Convention. The Malmedy Massacre was grim testimony to their lack of regard for the Convention.[2] Don was captured at noon. The next day, also at noon, 130 American infantrymen prisoners of war were slaughtered by the First SS Panzer Division.

From Linz, they were taken to a Stalag Luft in northern Germany. Don remained a POW until he was liberated at the end of the war. By liberation, his weight had dropped to 110 pounds. Since then he has tried never to miss a meal, and is still grateful that they never discovered he was Jewish.

16 December was a landmark day for nearly every Allied soldier fighting in Europe. It affected my life. It greatly affected Don Stern's life, and unknown at that time to either of us, it also affected the life of another Las Crucen, Arthur L. Valdez.

Valdez was a platoon leader in the First Battalion of the famed Forty-second Rainbow Division. On this same morning he was in a bunker when a field telephone rang. It was the CP (Command Post). They wanted to know what was causing all the noise. Arthur didn't know but would send out scouts. Very shortly the scouts returned, out of breath, and reported, "Our forward positions have been overrun. They're all around us, they're all over us. You can hardly see them it's so foggy, but we're sitting right in the middle of them!" As 88 shells rained about them, Arthur moved his men into their bunker. There they dug in and prepared to fight. And fight they did. They hung on by their teeth until 6 January 1945. Out of food and ammunition, with many injured and sick, and with German forces hitting them from both front and back, Arthur and his unit surrendered and spent the remainder of the war as prisoners. Ironically, on 6 January, the battle had turned in favor of the Allies and they began driving the Germans back.

Aftermath

Arthur now has a CPA firm not far from my office in Las Cruces and has been my accountant for many, many years. He talks little about the Bulge.

Don Stern operated The State Finance Company in Las Cruces. Several years ago he decided to attend his Bomb Group's reunion. At that gathering he received much kidding about his short combat experience. The regular *Flamin' Mamie* crew was still mad because Don's crew had lost it. He was also the butt of many jokes about not being a true veteran because of being shot down half-way through his first mission. Since then, he immensely enjoyed those reunions. Just prior to the publication of this book, Donald Stern died.

Among Don's most treasured possessions is that old pair of well-worn dog tags which he wore on the morning of 16 December 1944. They are on his key ring and every time he looks at them, he is reminded of that particular day and how the Lord brought him back.

About three or four months after my return to the States, I was notified by the War Department that the Fifteenth Air Force, because of its efforts to cut off the Germans' fuel supply during this battle, had been awarded a Bronze Campaign Star. All airmen who participated in missions during this period also received it.

Chapter 26

[1] The Battle of the Bulge, so named for the large bulge created in Allied lines by German forces, began 16 December 1944. It was the largest land battle fought by the U.S. Army in World War II. The German Army, supposed by the Allies to be on its last legs, achieved complete surprise against the Allies by marshalling and committing valuable armored, infantry, and air reserves in an attempt to drive a wedge between British and American armies and capture the port of Antwerp, Belgium. Twenty-five German divisions attacked along a sixty-mile front, but the offensive sputtered to an unsuccessful halt by early January 1945. Wheal, et al., 75-76.

[2] On 17 December 1944, near Malmedy, Belgium, approximately 130 American infantrymen, most of whom were from Battery B, 285th Forward Artillery Observation Battalion, surrendered after being overrun by elements of the First SS Panzer Division on the second day of the Battle of the Bulge. After they surrendered the Americans were marched into an open field and executed. The "Malmedy Massacre" was the most publicized, but not the only, indiscriminate slaughter of American POWs by SS troops during the opening phase of the battle. Charles B. McDonald, *A Time for Trumpets* (New York: Bantam Books, 1985), 201-221.

Christmas Day, 1944

It was Christmas Eve. My crew and I had spent all after-noon in a ground crewman's tent huddled around a big, jerry-rigged radio, apprehensively listening to music and news. We had searched the dial, desperately trying to get news about the Battle of the Bulge. Christmas carols serenaded us between newscasts. I had heard "The Twelve Days of Christmas" about fifty times already that day, and was getting sick and tired of it. Ever since I've hated 'Partridges in pear trees.' We'd listened to BBC, Voice of America, and Axis Sally.[1] I preferred Axis Sally because she played better music. Axis Sally was a fan of Bing Crosby, so she played a lot of Der Bingle's songs that day. For several days Sally had been urging all of the surrounded and fighting American soldiers to surrender, pledging offers of a warm bed, medical attention, and hot food. She made it sound like an ocean cruise. Nobody paid any attention to her offers, but her music was always good.

As was every other American in Europe, we in the Fifteenth Air Force were very concerned. Our ground forces were in a very serious situation. They were fighting a savage, highly motivated German Army in the fog, snow, and rain. It was bitterly cold. Many units, such as those soldiers in Bastogne,[2] were surrounded, out-numbered, out-gunned, cut off, and running low on food, medicine, and ammunition. We were painfully aware of what would happen if the Germans captured our supply center at the port of Antwerp.[3] Hitler was being particularly vindictive toward Liège and Antwerp in retaliation for the way they had welcomed the Allies. Thousands of civilians died as a result of a rain of V-1 and V-2 rockets upon those cities. Some were convinced that if Hitler recaptured these cities, he would slaughter the entire population. It was definitely a bad time.

Allied Intelligence finally admitted the Germans weren't in as bad a condition as they had supposed. They still had the capability of taking the fight to us. It was only after the first week of that battle that we began to understand the scope of the attack, and the danger facing the Allies.[4] The Germans, plundering their reserve, placed twenty-two divisions against a lightly held American sector. Some of these were Panzer divisions, equipped with plenty of Panther and Tiger tanks.[5]

Officers of the Fifteenth Air Force pored over maps and constantly listened to meteorological reports, trying to determine if it was possible for us to fly over the battlefield in aid of our beleaguered forces. The weather had been so bad in England that all our strategical and tactical forces had been grounded. Our tactical fighter and medium bomber forces in France had also been neutralized by the weather.

In Italy, we had flown missions up through 21 December, but then the weather turned bad for us as well, making it impossible for our forces to fly over the battlefields in Belgium, the Lowlands, and Germany. Since the 21st, the weather had become so bad it was impossible to lift off from the field, much less to cross the Alps.

It was a frustrating, sobering time for us. Many members of the Fifteenth had relatives fighting in the Bulge. We were proud of the way the Americans were fighting. We'd heard clerks, cooks and various other non-combatant personnel had been given rifles and helped plug the line. We also heard Congress was questioning the military, trying to determine how our Intelligence had allowed a German army of that size, attacking on a seventy-mile wide front, to move into an area almost in our front lines without being detected.

The ground personnel took good advantage of the down time between the 21st and the 24th and were busy patching up our planes and tending to the mechanical repairs. They had been working around the clock since the German drive began. I watched them at mess, their heads wrapped in scarves to cover their ears, their noses fiery red, and their hands cracked and bleeding. Our Group received three new crews from the States. They were given their indoctrination. We were all anxious for a break in the weather so we could help those American soldiers who were cut off in the Bulge. From 16 December, when the German offense began, until the 22nd when our planes were grounded due to the weather, we'd been doing our best, flying through nearly impossible weather conditions in order to knock out oil refineries and oil storage facilities in the marshalling yards. The Fifteenth was trying to stop the flow of fuel needed by the German army in this offensive.[6] Anyplace we struck was a top-priority target.

We were all dog-tired from the effort, and took advantage of the break for badly needed rest. Sickness was beginning to affect our air crews. I had a cold so deep that when I coughed it seemed to be coming from my toes. Influenza was spreading throughout the crews. Many were running high fevers. There was not a festive air on this Christmas Eve.

That day I had received my Christmas presents from my folks. They sent a fruit cake—which I dearly loved—a wool scarf, some dress gloves, along with another light bulb, and two cans of hot, green chile from the fields of New Mexico. I had been working on the fruit cake since early that morning. I had tried to eat my chopped chile on some cold, greasy Vienna sausages and it had upset my stomach. When I offered the rest of the crew some spoonfuls of the chile, they looked at me as if I had offered them rattlesnake meat. While I was eating and listening to the radio, somebody came by and said there were rumors we were going up on Christmas Day. No one believed Christmas Day would be a holiday. The Germans weren't going to take the day off, and we wouldn't either.

Late that afternoon, I walked to the squadron headquarters to look at the bulletin board to verify the rumor. As it was bitterly cold I bundled up for the walk in sheepskin clothing—gunner's leather cap with sheepskin lining hanging over my ears, a muffler, two pairs of pants, and fur flying boots. I must have looked like a combination of a grizzly bear and Big Foot. The only good thing about that cold weather was the ground was frozen so hard you didn't bog down into mud up to your ankles.

I arrived at headquarters, and as I walked up to the bulletin board where a loading list for the next day had been posted, someone told me that we were indeed flying. Evidently, there had been a small enough break in the weather to allow for a mission. The first thing I noticed on the loading list was that this was Ralph Chambers' first mission as a Captain. We'd known since the first of December that he was being promoted, but the promotion hadn't yet come through. Christmas Day would be his first flight as a Captain.

An anomaly was apparent with the lead aircraft, #461. The pilots listed to fly the squadron lead were Chambers, and Ralph Bischoff, two of the squadron's lead pilots. Why would they risk two squadron lead pilots in the same airplane, on the same mission? The explanation was that Bischoff had been scheduled to give Chambers his routine check ride on that day; later Chambers would, in turn, give Bischoff his check ride, as was customary in the Twentieth. Chambers, the pilot for the mission, had been assigned #461 which had a radome installed in the belly in place of the ball turret. Radome-carrying planes were called Mickey Ships, and no one wanted to fly them because of the lack of a gun in the belly. The Mickey operator was trained in radar bombing. The Twentieth was preparing to bomb by radar if necessary. Every crewman on #461 was an old timer.

I read through the remainder of the loading list, looking for my assignment. Upsher was listed as the pilot for #200. That crew was also a veteran; no rookies listed there. The last crewman named on #200 was George Teat Jr., a friend of ours. He lived in the tent next to ours, and he, like myself, was getting close to finishing his tour. Lieutenant E.C. Bender was to fly #650, and it was manned by another veteran crew. Both #200 and #650 carried the big target strike cameras in the camera well. Sergeant Jack Norwine was scheduled to fly right waist that day on #650. Jack was the oldest gunner, in seniority, in the Twentieth. During July 1944 he flew four missions in a row over Ploesti.[7] Later that month, he'd survived a terrible wound in his arm which placed him in the hospital through October. His original crew had been one of those lost on Mission 263 on 29 August. Jack had, after his return to the squadron, been friendly enough if engaged in conversation, but, although he smiled politely and returned conversation automatically, he made very few close friends after the loss of his original crew. Everyone liked him. He was an excellent crew member, but he didn't want to make any new friends and risk losing them as well. Jack was hit again after I completed my missions. He finally completed his fifty missions by the Spring of 1945, and returned to the States with a sackful of Purple Hearts.

What I saw on the briefing board made me feel good. Karsten was piloting #438, and leading the second element of our squadron. We would be flying off his wing. Leading the second element indicated that he was being groomed for squadron leader. More and more frequently, our own crew members were being given positions of responsibility. He, also, had nine brand-spanking new rookies assigned to him that day. Karsten was the only veteran in the crew. Jack would have his hands full.

LOADING LIST FOR THE 25 December 1944

Plane # 461
?	1st Lt.	R. F. Bischoff
CP	1st Lt.	R. E. Chambers
VN	1st Lt.	R. L. Sherwood
N	1st Lt.	A. A. Worth
B	1st Lt.	J. B. Atkins
UTG	T/Sgt.	H. L. Heck ✓
RWG	S/Sgt.	R. W. Finch
LWG	Sgt.	E. E. Williamson
TG	S/Sgt.	J. T. Griffin
ROG	T/Sgt.	R. L. Burns

Plane # 200 · *Camera*
P	1st Lt.	S. P. Upsher
CP	1st Lt.	C. W. Anderson
N	1st Lt.	H. Gluck
B	1st Lt.	J. A. Pasco
UTG	T/Sgt.	W. V. Burch Jr.
LTG	S/Sgt.	A. Barbarika
RWG	S/Sgt.	S. H. Krajozynski
LWG	S/Sgt.	M. K. Bjorn (c)
TG	S/Sgt.	E. J. Black
ROG	T/Sgt.	G. Teat Jr.

Plane # 650 *Camera*
P	1st Lt.	E. C. Bender
CP	1st Lt.	E. O. Ruhlin
N	1st Lt.	A. K. Benner
B	S/Sgt.	R. W. Phillippe
UTG	T/Sgt.	E. C. Camp
LTG	S/Sgt.	T. R. Lively
RWG	S/Sgt.	J. W. Korwine
LWG	S/Sgt.	B. D. Chesshir (c)
TG	S/Sgt.	C. A. Summerfield
ROG	T/Sgt.	O. J. Beardsley

Plane # 439 *Nickels*
P	1st Lt.	J. W. Karsten Jr.
CP	2nd Lt.	C. R. O'Donnell
N	2nd Lt.	F. D. Senior Jr.
B	2nd Lt.	W. E. Krehow
TG	Cpl.	T. B. King
TG	Cpl.	E. F. De Blascio
TG	Sgt.	W. Reinfold
LWG	Cpl.	W. T. Dood Jr.
TG	Cpl.	C. F. Pray Jr.
ROG	Cpl.	J. A. Gearhart

Plane # 428 *Nickels*
P	1st Lt.	J. W. Gallagher
CP	2nd Lt.	E. L. Mirowski
N	2nd Lt.	W. J. Hughes
B	S/Sgt.	M. W. McGuire
UTG	T/Sgt.	W. R. McKane
LTG	S/Sgt.	A. Novak
RWG	S/Sgt.	D. W. Jensen
LWG	S/Sgt.	M. E. Hollinger
TG	Cpl.	N. A. Tilbey
ROG	Cpl.	R. G. Cheney

Plane # 554
P	1st Lt.	R. D. McClure
CP	1st Lt.	W. J. Horton
N	1st Lt.	D. E. Durner
B	2nd Lt.	R. W. Kolodgy
UTG	S/Sgt.	J. F. Goodrich
LWG	S/Sgt.	I. D. Buckman
RWG	T/Sgt.	L. D. Pardee
LWG	S/Sgt.	T. D. Fletcher
TG	S/Sgt.	A. S. Czulada Jr.
ROG	T/Sgt.	C. S. Koco

Plane # 378 *Nickels*
P	1st Lt.	J. G. Tulley
CP	2nd Lt.	J. S. Clayton
N	2nd Lt.	C. E. Hannerty
B	1st Lt.	E. W. Henderson
UTG	T/Sgt.	S. C. Lewis
LTG	S/Sgt.	K. L. Fletcher
RWG	S/Sgt.	D. S. Tomaro
LWG	Cpl.	E. K. Freykes
TG	S/Sgt.	D. W. Back
ROG	T/Sgt.	R. L. Mosberg

CLIVE A. WALKER
Captain, Air Corps,
Operations Officer.

NOTE: 'Camera' identifies the aircraft carrying reconnaissance cameras. 'Nickels' were small bits of foil dropped from airplanes to confuse German radar. The airplane originally assigned to McGuire's crew was #411. Because of mechanical problems they were switched to #428.

His navigator's name gave me a laugh: F.E. Senior, Jr. Some clerk-typist would have fits with that name. Second Lieutenant C. R. O'Donnell was co-pilot with Karsten. This crew, in time, became one of best crews in the Second Bomb Group, but tomorrow they would fly their virgin mission with Karsten. Unless they were well-trained and disciplined, they would hear about it from Karsten in no uncertain terms. Karsten was a no-nonsense kind of pilot, and would not allow any horseplay or lack of radio discipline, if they were so inclined. This acclaimed crew lost only one member in action and the surviving nine are still a tightly knit group.

Other than Chambers and Karsten, I still had not located on the loading list the names of any other members of our crew, until I saw my assignment. I was to fly as bombardier with Lieutenant J. W. Gallagher. He was an excellent pilot and I liked to fly with Gallagher. E. L. Mirowski was listed as co-pilot; W. J. Hughes was the navigator, upper turret McKain, my friend Novak in the ball turret, Jensen, another friend, and Hollinger at the waist guns, and two rookies, Chenney and Tilbey on radio and back at the tail. Flying with Novak and Jensen would make up somewhat for not being with my old crew. I knew them, and could depend on them to do the right thing.

We were assigned #428, which brought a smile to my face, as this was that gleaming B-17G we'd flown from Lincoln to Italy, only to have it taken away from us upon arrival at Amendola. The prospects of flying with this mostly experienced crew, and in my old plane, made me feel a little better. From looking at the loading list, it was obvious the Twentieth was flying with its first team. Chambers, Karsten, and I were the only members of our crew scheduled to fly the next day. The target would not be revealed until briefing the next morning, but I knew wherever we were going it would be a top priority target, and undoubtedly well-defended. I returned to the tent to prepare for the mission.

I couldn't sleep at all that night and spent much of the time praying. I only needed two or three more missions to complete my tour, and was completely worn out. I tried to think of home, wondering what my family would be doing at that moment, allowing for the time differential. In no time at all, it seemed, the Charge of Quarters was waking up crews in the area. I got up and dressed carefully, putting on my best, cleanest woolen shirt and a heavy wool sweater. I laid out my personal effects—my class ring, billfold, and a letter I had written to my folks earlier that evening—on the old sweater, stuffed with towels, which I used for a pillow. I walked to the mess tent.

I didn't eat much; I wasn't hungry. The coffee, however, was great. From the mess tent I could see the vague outlines of the Amendola Ritz, covered with patches of snow and frost. After breakfast I returned to the tent and brushed my teeth, trying to be as quiet as possible so as not to wake the others. Fenstermaker was awake and whispered, "Good luck today, Mack, see you tonight."

With that I left the tent. As it was still dark, I was lucky to find another crewman with a real flashlight, not the generator-type that you had to keep squeezing to get light, and together we proceeded to the briefing tent. I laughed when we passed our famous Snow Woman. Created of snow, the sculpture fashioned by an unknown Michelangelo to Dolly Parton's specifications had turned to ice. She had melted somewhat and lost her left breast. As we walked to the briefing tent, we were greeted with some half-hearted "Merry Christmases" by unknown passers-by. One of our ground crewman who had been laboring all night walked up to me, patted me on the shoulder and wished me good luck. Everyone knew I was approaching the end of my tour.

The briefing room was warm and well-lit with the huge briefing map in front of the room. As I took my seat I anxiously stared at it: a long finger of red yarn, the route we were to fly, stretched from Amendola . . . to Brux. It was going to be Brux again! The briefing was short. We were given some news from the ongoing Battle of the Bulge. The Americans were still hanging on. Our Allies were frantically trying to get help for them and the battle had begun to stabilize. The Meteorological

363

Wayne Lesher and the 'Snow Woman.' *(Courtesy W. Lesher)*

Officer told us the weather was not going to be too bad; we would face heavy icing on our climb out, and could expect frost inside the airplanes. They couldn't guarantee us fighter escort on the mission, as it was still undetermined whether single-engine planes could take off in that weather. We could expect temperatures down to sixty or seventy degrees below zero. We were flying at high altitudes that day, and could expect to bomb visually but be prepared for PFF bombing if necessary. When the briefing was finished, I left as quickly as possible, waving to Karsten as I passed.

I managed a ride to the flight line with a man from the camera department. He carried some equipment in the back of his weapons carrier and delivered me to the equipment room. I drew my gear—parachute bag, escape kit, oxygen mask—and walked over to #428. I noticed its crew was already standing around it. Before I reached the plane, I stopped for a minute and looked it over from a distance. I always had a soft spot for that airplane, and always will. She was no longer the gleaming pet we'd flown from Lincoln. She was scorched, oil-streaked, burned and patched. The closer I came to her, the more damage I could see. She had patches in the fuselage, nicks in the plexiglass. The leading edges of the wings were dented and gashed from flak. Her props were nicked. I noticed the squadron markings on the tail had begun to fade, but she still looked like a smooth-running, business-like battle queen.

I walked up to the crew and introduced myself to those I did not know. "Good morning, my name is McGuire, and you are honored today with the presence of an esteemed bomb-dropper and noted ally of the Americans. Although I am from New Mexico and talk funny, I have been known to get hits as close as fifty miles from the target area." Some good-humored banter greeted my introduction. I walked around and chinned myself through the bombardier's escape hatch. With every mission it was getting more difficult to lift myself into the bombers, and that morning was no exception. Once inside I placed my parachute in a convenient location. I checked the oxygen equipment, made sure the intervelometer was set to the mission requirements, completed my pre-flight check very carefully but quickly. All of that completed, I walked back to the bomb-bay. Chills went through me when I saw those squat, ugly, rusty bombs snuggled neatly in their shackles. Earlier that morning, someone on the ground crew had chalked on one of the bombs, "Merry Christmas, Adolf." I checked the arming wires and the cotter keys stuck in the nose and tail fuses. Everything seemed to be in order.

I dropped out of the plane and waited with the rest of the crew for the arrival of the officers. I asked the radio operator if he would look at the bomb-bay after I released the bombs to make sure they had all dropped. Gallagher and the others arrived. We gathered around for our last briefing. He told us our target for Christmas Day was the Bergius Synthetic Oil Refinery in Brux, Czechoslovakia. It would be a long haul. We would have to be very careful not to touch any metal with bare flesh as we would be flying at twenty-nine thousand feet, and could expect very cold temperatures. He told us what he expected of us, and we had a short break before taking stations and start engine time. Each of us took a few minutes to pray, and then we entered the airplane and took our stations.

They fired the green flare and we started taxiing, as usual, nose-to-tail with the other aircraft and we took off when it was our turn. It seemed to take forever for #428 to come unstuck, but we finally lifted off the ground and climbed into the overcast. Around four thousand feet we broke into sunlight. All the aircraft in the Twentieth looked good. A short while later I told Gallagher that I was going to arm the bombs and then climbed into the tunnel behind the pilot, between the legs of the top turret gunner and opened the door to the bomb bays. I crawled onto the catwalk above the bomb-bay. There I took out a pair of pliers and started removing the cotter keys and tags from the nose and tail fuses of each of the twelve bombs. The bombs were then fully armed. I carefully recounted the cotter keys, making sure there were twenty-four, dropped them into a small bag and left the bag in the radio room. I made my way back to the bombardier's chair in the nose where I quickly climbed into my gear and put on my oxygen mask. I flexed the chin turret and dropped its gunsight in front of me.

As we climbed over the Italian coast, the weather was surprisingly good. We crossed the Alps without problems and were soon approaching central Europe abeam of Salzburg-Innsbruck. It was a smooth mission so far. We made our usual detour around Linz, that deadly area, home of the Hermann Goering Industrial Complex. Over the radio I heard reports of scattered flak. We knew the Germans weren't taking the day off because they were lighting smoke pots around some of the towns we were skirting.

When we were about five minutes away from the IP, Chambers' lead ship was slightly above and ahead of us in the formation. The weather around us was clear, good enough for enemy single-engine fighters to meet us. We were in a high state of alert watching for them. I had been exercising the chin turret to make sure the oil didn't get sluggish: I had been caught once trying to turn and fire a turret that didn't want to turn, and didn't want to go through that again. We reached our IP without incident, however, and turned onto the run to the target.

I quickly put on my flak vest and steel helmet, installed my stove lids, and moved the gun control pedestal to my right. Familiar landmarks on the ground that were marked on my map rolled past underneath the ship. It was unusually quiet as we started lining up. Our formation looked good as we loosened up somewhat for the bomb run. I turned and threw the lever to open the bomb-bay doors, and then called the pilot and told him they were coming open. Prepared for the worst, I began concentrating on my job.

As we approached the target, I knew down below there was a bustle of activity going on. German flak officers bent over radar screens were twisting dials and knobs, directing guns at us: They knew we would now fly straight and level with no evasive action for the next thirty miles as the lead bombardier flew the lead plane and, therefore, the formation into the target. Below us firemen were putting on asbestos suits and repositioning fire equipment around oil storage units built between earthen berms. Valves to these units were being closed, and alternate pipelines readied to shunt oil from damaged units to non-damaged ones. Non-essential personnel were racing into bomb shelters, while fire-fighters, including hundreds of slave laborers, were positioned to stop as much damage as possible. They knew how to fight fires and run refineries under war-time conditions. They had learned their lessons well at Ploesti.

There was no smoke over the target; this had to make them unhappy. Evidently the wind this Christmas morning was blowing hard, negating the efficiency of their smoke pots. We would not need to use the radar for the bomb dropping, as target visibility was excellent. We hunkered down for the bomb run. By then their flak batteries had fired some ranging shots. I groaned inwardly as the first four rounds fired from a small battery exploded exactly at our altitude, and just a little ahead of us. They would quickly adjust. Brux, one of the most heavily fortified industrial complexes left to the Germans, always took the prize for tracking fire.

Just then it seemed like all the imps of hell were turned loose on us. The sky just turned black and red with bursting shells. There was the usual mixture of black smoke from 88s, gray from the 105s, and white from the 128s. The sky began to shake. Planes began pitching from the turbulence and vacuum created by the exploding shells. The familiar sound, like hail hitting a tin roof, caused by spent, falling flak hammering on our plane indicated their shots were accurate. I ignored the tumult, my eyes riveted to the bomb-bay of Chambers' lead aircraft. The flak was so heavy it sometimes partially obscured his plane from my vision.

We neared the target, and the concentration of flak became more noticeable as we entered barrage-type flak. I was soaked in perspiration, even though it was sixty or seventy degrees below zero. Sweat ran down my forehead and into my eyes. My eyes started burning. With about two or three minutes to target, I reached down and flipped the covers off the bomb release and salvo switches. A quick look down to the green lights indicated everything was ready. I was hoping for a good bomb run.

Several lifetimes seemed to have passed before the first bomb finally dropped out of the lead Fortress. I quickly flipped my bomb release switch and turned to watch the intervelometer. Our bombs were dropping in good order. When the intervelometer showed zero, I hit the salvo switch just to make sure all of them were gone, and a second later called, "Bombs Away!" I reached to close the bomb-bay doors. The radio operator signaled that all the bombs had dropped. I called Gallagher and told him the doors were coming closed.

Right then, someone yelled, "Red Flak! Red Flak! Look out for fighters!" German flak batteries often fired colored bursts to signal to lurking fighter squadrons that the flak barrage was over, and they could jump on us without fear of getting hit by their own flak. I instantly grabbed the chin turret control and locked it into position.

Just at that moment, flak burst in front of Chambers' aircraft. It started jinking and skewing around, flying very erratically. I overheard someone say, "I think a pilot must have been hit." My heart leapt into my throat. Please not Chambers. God help them all if both pilots were hit. There was no time to watch after Chambers' plane, my job was looking for fighters. No fighters ever showed. To this day we don't know why they shot red flak at us. Maybe they were having fun and wishing us a Merry Christmas.

Gallagher told the navigator we were turning toward the rally point. The lead aircraft, flying erratically, had drifted a little out of formation. Another squadron plane took the lead. Someone in a squadron behind us reported an airplane going down. I pressed my face as close to the plexiglass as I dared to look behind us. The flak barrages lightened. We were through most of it. A short time later one of our gunners reported a plane out of the Ninety-sixth Squadron going down behind us. Novak, at the ball turret, reported some fires on the target. We had struck a nerve; we had hit something sacred that day.

Now I could turn my attention back to the lead plane. Although it had smoothed itself out, it would straggle in and out of formation. I was so worried about Chambers and Bischoff. All the way back to the base I was convinced one or both of them had been hit. Years later, I finally heard from Bischoff himself what had happened on that day.

As they released their bombs and right-turned off the target to the rally point, Chambers said, "Merry Christmas ya'll," in his soft southern accent. As he spoke, *bang*, that near flak burst sent a jagged, splintery piece of steel the size of a candy bar under the windscreen and into Ralph Chambers. Chambers immediately doubled up and slumped over the controls. Bischoff heard the steel slam into Chambers. Slumped over the controls, Chambers moved a hand inside his flak jacket, into the area of his heart and ribs while Bischoff fought to regain control of the aircraft, calling for help from his crew to get Chambers out of his seat. Chambers managed to lift himself off the pilots' column, and, straightening himself up as best he could, weakly smiled at Bischoff as he handed over the red-hot piece of flak. The flak was burning his gloves. "Here," he weakly told Bischoff, "Save this for me." Bischoff took the flak out of his glove, then flung it onto the instrument panel, it was so hot. In the confusion following landing, Bischoff forgot the flak, but returned later to retrieve it. Fortunately, it was still in the plane.

With help from the engineer and bombardier, he laid Chambers in the tunnel of the airplane. The flat side of the piece of flak had struck him in the left upper arm, shattering it in two places, and continued its trajectory under his flak vest, where it burned him until he fumbled for it and lifted it out. The flak probably would have cut him in two if it had hit him edgewise. Chambers was still talking when they stretched him out in the tunnel. They made sure he had oxygen and covered him as best they could. Throughout the four-hour flight back to Italy Chambers lay in the tunnel, extremely conscious of the pain in his shattered arm.

The bombardier climbed into Chambers' seat and helped Bischoff fly back to the field. They stayed in formation until we reached the Adriatic Coast, near Venice. At that point they pulled out of formation and began a rapid descent. With that maneuver, I knew something was seriously wrong. It is hard to describe my feelings when they left us. I can't explain why, but I knew it was Chambers who had been hit. Bischoff wanted to get Chambers to a hospital as quickly as possible. He, and some other aircraft which also had wounded aboard, flew into Foggia Main, where we had a good hospital. Bischoff had called ahead to alert the medical personnel and described Chambers' injury. When they landed Ralph was quickly unloaded and driven twelve miles to a large hospital with orthopedic surgeons standing by, ready to operate.

Our formation returned to Amendola through heavy clouds. Upon landing, I finished my business in the nose of the aircraft, told Gallagher I was going looking for Chambers, but would be back for debriefing, and left the plane as quickly as possible. I asked one of the ground crew if the lead aircraft had returned. He pointed to the empty hard stand where it was supposed to be.

Karsten's plane taxied up. When he disembarked, Karsten told me Chambers had been hit, but nobody knew how badly he'd been hurt. No one could tell me what happened. Nobody

Christmas Day, 1944

(above) Lieutenant Ralph Chambers after flight training graduation and being commissioned a pilot.
(below) Captain Ralph Chambers on his check ride after his release from the hospital. *(Courtesy R. Chambers)*

knew, just that Bischoff landed at Foggia Main and placed Chambers in the hospital. That was it.

The ground crewmen around me busied themselves with the damaged aircraft. There were many holes in the planes, but all of our airplanes in the squadron were accounted for. We didn't know the status of the other squadrons. I decided it was time to get back to debriefing. As I jumped on the truck taking us back to Group Headquarters, the Ninety-sixth started landing. Flares were fired indicating wounded. I noticed the usual feathered props, and smoking engines common to landings after a mission.

The truck, as always, delivered us into the big Italian-type courtyard in front of the Headquarters. Before the debriefing, we first were given a close inspection by medical aides. There were several industrial-type accident victims on this mission: a sprained knee, sprained ankle, broken wrist. An airman in front of me had severe lacerations on his forehead, and another man had had two fingernails completely ripped off one of his hands. These men were triaged. Those with the most severe injuries were sent to the hospital. Then we proceeded past four large wooden tables, each with markings appropriate to our squadrons, the Twentieth, the Forty-ninth, the 429th, and the Ninety-sixth. The traditional dose of medicinal whiskey was handed to each man. That was always welcomed, especially after long missions with exposure to seventy degree below temperatures. Everybody drank two carefully measured jiggers of whiskey. It didn't pay to try and sneak an additional dose off another squadron's table.

Once that ritual was finished, we walked over to the Red Cross wagon,[8] called "Betty's Choke Point for Chowhounds." A very nice Red Cross lady handed me a scalding cup of delicious coffee and one of her famous doughnuts. After each mission she had more than two hundred men converge upon her, each anxiously awaiting her goodies.

Then it was time to be interviewed by debriefing officers. In a very unusual move, Gallagher told the debriefing officers to take me first and get it over with in a hurry as my regular pilot had been hit. All this time I had been asking everyone if they knew anything about Chambers. Nobody knew anything. Evidently, we had had a successful strike that day. It had looked good to me when I peered behind us after the bomb drop. They finished my interview and I waited around until Karsten was also finished, and we could talk for a little while.

Karsten had learned that Chambers' arm was in pretty bad shape, but that the wound was not fatal. Because the piece of flak had hit him with its flat side, Chambers had lost very little blood. It was as if he had been hit by a truck. Karsten promised to keep me informed when he heard any more information. As we walked back to our area, Karsten reminded me that we were being served turkey since it was Christmas, and he was hungry. I suddenly remembered he'd flown with a green crew, and asked him how it went. He assured me they would make a fine crew. We approached squadron operations where Karsten waved goodbye and headed for the mess hall to take care of some turkey.

I waited for what seemed hours in the operations room. Finally someone called from the hospital; Chambers was doing well. His arm had been placed in a cast and he was hurting, but he would be all right. With that news, I returned to the world and became aware that I was starving. Even though it was getting late, I walked to the mess and had my Christmas dinner. All day I had been thinking about those canned turkeys the cooks had been saving for our Christmas dinner, and now all that was left were the necks and wings, everything else was gone. I was the only one in there. Everybody else had eaten and returned to their tents or back to their jobs.

I returned to our empty tent, where I sat on the edge of the cot and reflected on what had happened that day. Christmas Day. Suddenly, I desperately wanted to go home. I became tremendously homesick. I wanted to see my father, mother, brother. I wanted to see my old horse, older than I was then, the one that so much enjoyed hunting and camping with me in the hills of New Mexico. I remembered how all I had to do to call her was lift an ear of corn and she'd come up and search my pockets for the corn. I began thinking about Chambers and suddenly started shaking. I shook violently, teeth chattering, cold sweat pouring off me. It took several minutes before I was able to stop shaking and get myself back together. I was close to the end of my string. This couldn't go on much longer. Falling back onto the cot I immediately dropped off to sleep.

The crew came in and found me asleep on the bed still wearing my flight clothing. They removed my boots and jackets without disturbing my sleep. One more day, one more mission behind me.

At 0215 the next morning I heard the CQ coming by to wake the men for another mission. I had come to hate his voice.

I climbed wearily out of bed to face another damn day. . . .

Chapter 27

[1] Mildred Gillars was an American citizen in Berlin when the war started. An aspiring actress who taught English, she was sympathetic to the Nazi cause. Gillars was hired to broadcast propaganda to American troops after the Allied invasion of North Africa in an attempt to undermine morale. She never succeeded in that goal, but 'Sally,' with her sultry voice and salty stories about what was happening to the wives and girlfriends back home, was the source of endless speculation among GIs about her sexual prowess and appetites. GIs paid little attention to her propaganda, but they loved her music. She had good taste in swing music, and also popularized among American forces the famous "Lili Marlene," a popular German song of the period. She was captured after the war, tried and convicted of treason. She claimed she was motivated to serve as a Nazi mouthpiece because of her love for a German Foreign Minister. She was imprisoned until 1961, when she was pardoned. Parrish, 233.

[2] This critical road junction was held by the 101st Airborne Division, along with elements of a combat command of the Tenth Armored Division and soldiers from other divisions, from the beginning of the battle until 26 December, when they were relieved by Patton's Fourth Armored Division. For over a week they held out against the Fourth Panzer Corps and two German reserve divisions. When told to surrender by German officers, acting CO General Anthony McAuliffe replied, "Nuts!" Wheal, et al., 50-51; Parrish, 51.

[3] The port of Antwerp was the terminal objective for the Germans. The port had been liberated on 4 September 1944, but only came into use as the

Allies' main supply port on 28 November because Montgomery failed to clear the sixty-mile Scheldt estuary of German troops in his bid to pounce into Germany on the carpet of airborne armies in Operation Market-Garden. Hitler, in planning to capture Antwerp, attempted to drive a wedge between British and American forces and seize the initiative on the Western Front. Wheal, et al., 21; Mayer, 14; Parrish, 23.

[4] Before the offensive was finally repulsed in January 1945, 600,000 American soldiers were involved in the fighting. Parrish, 42-43.

[5] The Panther PzKpfw V was considered Germany's best tank design of the war. It was specifically designed to counter the excellent Soviet T-34 tank. Production started on the model in 1943. The tank was noted for its balance of speed, armor, weight, and firepower. The 47-ton tank, crewed by five men, driven by a 700 hp gasoline engine, fired a 75mm gun which was capable, with special ammunition, of penetrating 122mm of armor at 2,000 meters. It also was armed with two 7.92 machine guns. It had a range of 110 miles, top speed of 28-30 mph, and carried 100mm-120mm of well-sloped armor. 4,818 Panthers were built by the end of the war. Mayer, 194-195; Parrish, 619; Wheal, et al., 356.

The Tiger tank, PzKpfw VI, first went into production in 1937, but successes of lighter German tanks against England and France lulled the High Command into a false sense of security and production of this much heavier tank was discontinued. Production was quickly instigated beginning mid-1942, however, when Russians countered with their T-34 and KV tanks. 1,335 Tiger tanks had been produced by August 1944, when the line was discontinued for even heavier models. The Tiger was originally designed to serve as spearhead armor for Panzer Divisions, but problem areas in the engine, gearbox, and suspension made it more suitable for a defensive role. Armed with an 88mm cannon which could pierce 112mm of armament at 1,400 yards, and protected frontally with 110mm of steel, it was one of the most formidable tanks of the war. Manned by a five-man crew, it was powered by a 692 hp gasoline engine, enabling it to reach speeds of 24 mph. It had a range of 62 miles, and was additionally armed with two 7.92 machine guns. Wheal, et al., 47.

[6] Fuel shortages, indeed, eventually checked the advances of the German armored columns, although stubborn and heroic U.S. reinforcements and tactical air strikes brought the offensive to bay. Wheal, et al., 75-76.

American armored divisions, in the dash across France in Fall 1944, required eight times the tonnage in gasoline that they needed in food. Bradley, 245.

[7] Ploesti was the center of the Rumanian oil fields, conquered in 1941 by the Germans. The field yearly produced seven million tons of oil for the German war machine, and so was extremely valuable to that effort. It was the target of U.S. air raids from June 1942 until August 1944. It never stopped producing oil for the Germans until it was overrun by Soviet ground forces in September 1944. It was a tough target for American

bombers. Three hundred fifty aircraft were shot down while trying to knock it out. Parrish, 499-400; Wheal, et al., 371.

[8] The Red Cross, an international humanitarian organization, was established in the 1860s for the purpose of aiding military and civilian casualties of war. During World War II, the Red Cross provided such aide for all combatants, Axis and Allied. It supplied canteens such as the one McGuire mentioned, collected blood, provided ambulances and medical personnel, located families and friends of combatants and refugees, staffed major relief programs for refugees, and also aided prisoners of war.

– 28 –

The Last Mission

It was late afternoon, 26 December. We had been awakened, as usual, for that day's mission, but after dressing and breakfast were told the mission had been canceled due to heavy weather. The day before I was supposed to have gone to the clinic for a penicillin shot for the deep-seated cold that had been plaguing me for a long time. Flying on Christmas Day, and with Chambers being wounded, I had postponed it. I was feeling pretty good and planned to see Chambers at the Foggia hospital.

When I checked the ops (operations) board for the 27th, sure enough, I was scheduled to fly. It wasn't my own crew but they had been there a while and were a good crew. What was so unusual about the mission was the number of crews listed on the board. It was about everything the Twentieth could put into the air. An airman standing near me said, "Looks like we've got a maximum effort coming up tomorrow. We must be going to throw the kitchen sink at 'em. By the way, did you see your name?"

"Yeh, I'm scheduled to fly."

"No, look down at the bottom."

My eyes went to the bottom of the loading list: 'Fiftieth Mission - M.W. McGuire.' That was the first time I had ever seen that in writing for anyone. That notation by my name created a strange, indescribable feeling within me. Now, instead of seeing Chambers, it looked like I would be finishing tomorrow. Walking to the infirmary, I tried to fathom my own mixed feelings.

The medic asked for my name and problem. "I need a shot of penicillin and was supposed to have come yesterday but I flew, my pilot got hit and I forgot it," I replied. He pulled my file and about that time Doc Ihle walked in.

Doc asked the medic what I had and he said, "McGuire needs a shot of penicillin, doctor. He was supposed to have been in yesterday but he said his pilot got hit and he forgot about it. He's due for a shot."

Doc Ihle asked to look at the file. After a long look he said, "McGuire you've been here some time. You have a bunch of them don't you?"

"Yes, sir. I'm scheduled to fly tomorrow and that'll be my fiftieth."

"That's good news. I like to see some of you finish. Before you take that shot, take your clothes off and get on the scales." That could be a problem, I thought. I was even beginning to believe that maybe I would make it home. The last thing I wanted was to be grounded for a few days just before my last mission. Stripping down to my underwear, I got on the scales. Ihle said, "You've lost an awful lot of weight, McGuire, too much. How are you sleeping?"

Trying to underplay it, I replied, "I sleep pretty good, doctor. I pull a mission once in a while. If I was going to stay I would ask you for some R&R, but I'm alright. This cold is bothering me some, but it's no worse than it's been for a long time."

"McGuire, shut your eyes and touch your nose." Which I did. "Alright, now take your forefinger and touch mine." He held his finger up and I reached to put my finger on his and he moved it down and I almost fell on my face. "Alright, now let's put heel to toe and see if you can walk this line." I didn't do very well. "You're having balance, middle ear problems?"

"Yes, sir, a little bit. Not much."

"Tomorrow is your last one?"

"Yes, sir."

"Alright, McGuire, you can bend over and I'll give you a shot with my famous square needle in celebration of finishing your fiftieth tomorrow."

After I had re-dressed and started to leave he said, "McGuire, good luck. I really feel good when some of my boys get to go home. Good luck tomorrow." With that I walked back to the tent thinking how lucky I'd been. Doc Ihle had a way of looking deep into your soul and knew my condition was much worse than I admitted. I hadn't fooled him any at all, but he was going to leave me operational so I could finish and go home.

That night I didn't sleep well and was up when the CQ came to awaken us. It was very cold that morning and the briefing room was packed. I don't know how many crews were there, but every squadron was putting up every crew they had. That day, the Fifth Wing was divided into a Blue Force and a Red Force. My group, the Blue Force, would be hitting targets at Korneuburg, which was at the city limits of Vienna. The Red Force was assigned targets in the Linz area. If our target was more than two-tenths covered and not plainly visible for visual bombing, our orders were to proceed to Linz, our secondary target and hit the Hermann Goering Tank Works.

Korneuburg had a small, but very productive, high-test gasoline refinery set amongst many, many historic buildings and churches and was very difficult to see. Our bombing would have to be extremely accurate and we could not afford to take any chances if visibility was impaired. I groaned inwardly. This was a hell of a way to end it all by going to the two hottest targets going, if we had to also go to Linz.

The B-24s would precede us and bomb airfields along our route, particularly in the Klagenfurt area. They would also be hitting marshalling yards, viaduct bridges, transportation centers, and in general, disrupting German defense activities. We would have heavy escorts that day. This was to be a maximum effort by the Fifteenth Air Force.

My wish for something better than Vienna or Linz for my last mission was not to be. The takeoff was the usual white-knuckle job, but we were soon lined out on our mission. We crossed Croatia, bypassed Zagreb, and went over Slovenia. Below us was some fighter activity, but nothing had molested us so far. We entered the Vienna/Wiener Neustadt area, always a hotbed, and bypassed that cesspool of Vienna. We would make our bomb run on the way back and avoid Vienna proper, bypassing most of the defenses at Vienna. The few guns that morning were extremely accurate. We were taking a few hits when the lead airplane called to abort the bomb run; the target was obscured. We were to proceed to the secondary target. There was no way to avoid the defenses at Linz. The Hermann Goering Tank Works were part of the industrial complex there and their defenses would tear us apart. It was only ninety plus miles to Linz so it was a short trip, but a very long bomb run from Korneuburg to the Hermann Goering Tank Works that day. The Red force, which had preceded us over the target, encountered some problems. In one of the lead aircraft, the bombs came out simultaneously when the bomb bay doors were opened. Must have been a gremlin aboard. The remainder of the Twentieth hastily regrouped and the #2 ship took over the bomb run so the following aircraft could drop on him.

Between Vienna and Linz, I became aware of conversations between the engineer and pilots. The engineer said, "Lieutenant, I would suggest we feather that one the minute we can. It's really slopping up the fuel. I think there's a big leak in the main fuel lines of that engine."

"Here it comes," I thought. "My last mission and I'm going to be a straggler *again*, if I didn't become a piece of toast from an exploding shell setting off our leaking gas. I hope he doesn't try to cross that target with three engines." He didn't. The engine was smoking and the fuel gages were dropping drastically. At bombs away, when we turned off the target to head for the rally point, the pilot announced he was feathering the #3 engine to save fuel.

The rest of the formation left us and we spotted some EA. Even though they hadn't demonstrated any hostile intent toward us, we watched them intently. I was feeling very sorry for myself. A P-51 appeared, looked us over, slid in sideways, and radioed he could stick with us for a little while. A few minutes later we picked up a second P-51, the first pilot's wing man. They had been separated during a dog fight someplace else and were now headed for home. They escorted us for as long as their fuel supply permitted them to stay with us. Finally, we passed 'Old Snaggle Tooth,' my private name for Gross Glockner, and hit the Adriatic. Our pilot stuck the nose down and we headed for Amendola on three engines. Falling into the normal landing pattern, we arrived only about five minutes after the remainder of the squadron.

By then I was a basket case. Having made it that far, I could think of all the things that could happen to me on this final leg of my last mission: someone was going to ram us; some guy clearing his gun was going to kill me; *something* was going to happen. I was desperately trying to accept the idea that I was through, but kept looking for loopholes.

When we touched down someone in the tower called, "Congratulations on your fiftieth, McGuire." After the airplane had taxied up to the hard stand, I sat in the nose for a few minutes before tossing out my two parachute bags. Finally, I wearily crawled over to the escape hatch and dropped to the ground.

An official Air Force photographer demanded I kiss the ground as the ground crew and other locals crowded around with their Brownie cameras. "I don't want to kiss that stuff." For centuries that mud had been fertilized with human feces and it stunk. Besides, I didn't feel like kissing it.

They chided me, "It's protocol. You don't have to kiss the mud, kiss the Marston mat." So I dutifully bent down and kissed the mat. By then the crew was out of the airplane and joined the others in shaking my hand. All day they had kidded me about my fiftieth mission and I would bring them good luck. They crowded around congratulating me and patting me on the back. I was shaking so badly, all I wanted to do was go behind the tail and vomit.

Someone volunteered to carry the parachute bag I was turning in for the last time. The second bag I was planning to keep as I didn't want anyone to know about those stove lids. Two ground crewmen friends, Irv and Wolf, jumped out of a truck and came over to shake my hand before returning to their work. By then I was looking forward to those two fingers of medical whiskey, and going back to lie down on my cot. By myself. . . .

Upon arriving at the Group headquarters, someone announced it was customary for those who didn't want their medical whiskey to give it to the guy finishing. After three or four extra double shots, and by the time I had my coffee and donut and finished debriefing, I could have flown without an airplane. I staggered back to the tent, sat down, and cried. I was finished. . . . I was actually going home. . . .

The next day some of my crew flew. I didn't know when they left as I slept until shortly before noon. By that time, water was more plentiful and we were allowed to shower every other day, so I showered, shaved, and ate something before checking the squadron bulletin board. A note instructed me to contact the first sergeant.

Entering Tiny Atkerson's office he said, "Sit down Mack, and congratulations. How do you want to go home? By air on a war-weary (airplanes being retired from combat duty) or on a ship?"

"I've had my belly full of flying, Sarg, I need to go home on a boat."

"Alright, but we'll have to process you pretty quickly. We'll start tomorrow, so get your stuff all ready to go. There's a ship due in Naples that will only be there two or three days and we want to get you aboard it. I'll start processing your paperwork now. We'll probably fly you to Naples. If the weather is too bad, I'll send you down in a jeep, but get ready to go home. I heard today about Chambers. They tell me he's going to be there for another ten days and then they will let him come back to the squadron and rehabilitate. He has a bad arm and it's in a cast."

I thanked him. Then he added, "If you have any questions give me a call."

Out of force of habit I went by the ops room bulletin board and my crew was scheduled to fly the next day. Karsten was the pilot and all those left in our crew would be together again. With that I returned to the tent.

They left early the next morning, as usual, and I didn't hear them. It was one of the few times I didn't hear the CQ awaken them. I spent all day processing out, signing pay vouchers and mail transfers, and turning in any remaining equipment. The horsehair pad I put in the tent for one of my crew, but placed the four stove lids on the wall behind the tent for the navigator from another crew. They had been promised to him when he found out about them some time before. I was cutting my ties. . . .

About three o'clock the squadron began returning, so I went to headquarters and waited. I was becoming alarmed as my crew still had not returned. Tulley walked by and I asked him if he knew anything about Karsten. He responded, "Yeh, Karsten had some injuries aboard and took them in to Ancona. How bad they are or how many, I don't know. The airplane looked alright. Karsten dived out of the formation as soon as we reached the Adriatic and was headed toward Ancona. We heard that was where he landed safely, but we don't know anything more about it."

"Where were you today?"

"We went to Castel Franco, to hit the locomotive and boiler works there. We came off the target at Castel Franco and ran

(above) John Warren 'Jack'
Karsten after he became a
First Lieutenant.
(Courtesy W. Karsten)

(right) Warren Karsten at
Amendola Field.
(Courtesy W. Lesher)

across flak batteries between there and Udine. There was little flak, although it was accurate. He must have had somebody hit about that time, because it didn't take him long to head down." (Forty-eight years later I learned from Ralph Bischoff, squadron leader for that mission, that the Germans had moved mobile flak batteries, unknown to our Intelligence, into that area. The mission's return route was between Castel Franco and Udine, to get them back over the Adriatic. The first they knew of these unknown batteries was when Karsten's airplane was hit. There wasn't any other appreciable damage.)

That news was like being kicked in the face by a mule. Not knowing what else to do, I returned to the tent and waited. And waited. It seemed forever. . . .

About two or three hours after the other crews had returned, mine walked into the tent. I stood up, white-faced and shaken. Graham entered first, with tears running down his face. Sutton walked over to his bed, sobbing, Fenstermaker sat down with his head in his hands and I knew he was crying. Scofield came in shortly, very subdued and moist-eyed.

I asked, "What happened?"

Graham looked at me for a moment and said, "Mack, Thompson got hit and he's dead. He was killed." With that, I broke down. . . .

We sat around with tears running down our faces. It was a very quiet group. Thompson had been the crew favorite. The baby whom everybody had looked after, but the only one who really didn't need any looking after. He was simply the favorite. If there was ever a model son, brother or friend, it was Jim Thompson. The perfect crew mate, he was like a brother to me. Jim didn't say much, but when he did, it was something worthwhile. Tough, capable of handling anything, he always did more than his share and was the first to volunteer and help others. He was quietly religious. I recalled the Bible lessons we had from that little blue Bible he always carried. Jim was truly an All-American Boy with no bad habits. He didn't smoke, he didn't do anything that he shouldn't have, he didn't even cuss. That Hoosier from Columbus, Indiana was only about a half or quarter inch shorter and only a few months younger than I.

It was extremely rare for us to expose the chinks in our armor, but that day we all cried openly. That evening I became angry and bitter, and blamed myself for Jim's death. If I had been there, maybe I could have done something. Actually, there wasn't anything anyone could have done. When he was hit, he reported in a very matter-of-fact voice over the intercom, "This is the tail, I've been hit real bad."

Scofield and Graham scrambled back to him. Thompson was wearing a backpack parachute that day, the type they had recently begun issuing to tailgunners, along with the pilots. He was so big they couldn't get him out of the tail, so they had to cut off his backpack, Mae West and other equipment and then cut through his clothing. The wound was a very large hole in his chest. They bandaged him as best they could, but it was probably already too late.

After a sleepless night I finished processing, and picked up my orders. Upon my return, I was shocked to see in front of our tent, one of those eerie white bundles that contained the personal effects of my friend. The two efficient men with the neckties came out and nodded as they passed me. . . .

29

A Yard Full of Germans

The day after Thompson's death, I was shipped out of Amendola. My world had just been ripped apart. The crew was scattered. Chambers and Lesher were in hospitals somewhere. I wanted to see them, but didn't know where they were, or even if they were still alive. Fenstermaker had been assigned to fly with a general. Scofield was assigned to re-training returning gunners. Sutton, Graham, and McDonnell were scattered, flying in other crews. My life had become a mess, and rather than feeling elated at leaving alive, I felt sick and guilty.

I packed that morning and kept out my one good uniform and what I could carry in my B-4 bag. The rest of my belongings, valuables, souvenirs, and address book I hastily threw into that old parachute bag. It would travel in the ship's cargo hold. Many of those items I now wish I had been able to carry with me. Then I was driven out to the flight line. The airplane taking

McGuire, carrying his B-4 bag, says his farewells to the Amendola Ritz and his crew. Louis Scofield wrote on the back of the original photograph, "50 missions, the first to make it home." *(Courtesy L. Scofield)*

me to Naples taxied up to the runway. One look and a lump formed in my throat. It was *Flak Holes*. That afternoon *Flak Holes* flew me to Naples. Our old gremlin friend delayed our departure by invoking that characteristic mag drop in the #4 engine. Finally the ground crew had it running well, buttoned up the cowling and we took off and I flew away from Amendola.

We arrived in Naples late that evening. They pulled over to let me out, and then took off again, back to the field. I stood there in the gathering dark of the evening and watched *Flak Holes* disappear into the night. That plane had always returned us to safety. And once again, malfunctions and all, it had returned me to safety for the last time. Never again in my life would I love anything so ugly. . . .

They assigned me to some kind of a schoolhouse, a depot for those of us waiting for a ship home. I remember my first night there very vividly. My first thought when getting into the cot was, "Hey, I won't have to wake up at 0215. I won't have to fly over a target tomorrow, get shot at by flak, dodge and shoot at enemy fighters, or endure that bone-aching cold." There would be no more of that. No more. That tour had seemed like a lifetime. Instead it would be hamburgers, T-bone steaks, milk, my family, clean clothes, clean linens, a life.

I should have been happy, but I wasn't. My thoughts went back to the day the ten of us met for the first time as a crew in Lincoln. Young men, not that far removed from being boys. And I was the only one coming home. I thought, "Why me, Lord? Why me and not Thompson? What did I do to deserve this?" I should have been feeling some form of exultation, but I wasn't.

The rush to reach Naples to catch that ship proved unnecessary. The ship, coming from Norfolk, Virginia was forced to return to Norfolk for repairs, so I spent almost a month in Naples. They took very good care of us—hot chow and showers every day. Each day our numbers were swelled by new arrivals also going home, but for the first week or so there I recognized nobody. They left us alone, but the MPs were bad about staying on top of us if we transgressed. These rules and regulations-filled MPs who hadn't had seen any combat time, freely used their night sticks on combat men, particularly those from the Fifth Army.

One evening a truck pulled into the area and two or three men from the Group joined us. They looked like I must have when I got back from Amendola. The driver I recognized as a ground crewman from the Second. It was impossible to contact my crew, so I knew nothing about what had happened in Amendola since my departure. I asked the driver what he knew about my crew. He hesitated for a few minutes, reluctant to tell me anything, then finally said, "Mack, I think your crew went down yesterday in that old airplane you bitched so about. All of them. The ship took a direct hit in the bomb bay over target and just blew to pieces." I couldn't believe it and didn't. With our seniority, there was no way they would be flying *Flak Holes*. After the driver left one of the new men approached me. I recognized him as Sutton's friend and fellow radio operator.

He told me, "Mack, *Flak Holes* did go down, but I'm pretty sure your crew wasn't on board. I think jets got them somewhere around Breslau.

This news completely crushed me. I started blaming myself, but as I learned later, this was perfectly normal behavior. You rationalized; if I had been there, this wouldn't have happened. These guys, my crew, my family, all gone in a flash, all of them good men.

We embarked shortly afterwards, but instead of feeling elated about going home, I felt empty and drained. There were about three thousand of us shipping home on the *Richardson*, a brand-new transport ship embarking, unescorted, on the return leg of its maiden voyage with a mostly green crew. The Navy figured the ship was so fast it didn't need destroyer escorts.

We had food, lots of it. The food was outstanding. But then, any food was outstanding to us. The first night on board they served us pork chops, all the milk we could drink, ham sandwiches, and all of the fresh coffee we could hold. You could even ask for seconds after everybody had been fed. Among the returnees were infantry veterans of the Forty-fifth Division. While we sailed in the Mediterranean, they did well. As soon as we hit the rough Atlantic, they began getting seasick, and quit eating. We airmen, quite used to three dimensional motions didn't have problems with squeamish stomachs, found there was plenty of food at every meal. For a while I was eating six or seven times a day and gained a pound a day during the voyage.

The Atlantic was quite rough at that time of year. Because the ship's crew was new and green, many of the sailors were as seasick as the soldiers. We airmen liked to railbird, stand on the rails and give wise and unsolicited advice. It was great fun to catch seasick sailors and give them a hard time. One day while railbirding, we heard peculiar but distinctive sounds coming from the line of fellow railbirders. Airmen lined up along the railway down at the end of ship were throwing up, one after the other, as if it was contagious, and it was heading our way. I noticed a sailor walking slowly behind the men who were throwing up. He wasn't saying a word, just walking slowly past them. Whenever he walked past, they vomited. Finally, he walked past us. Behind him he dragged a raw pork chop on a string. The sight of a raw pork chop in a rough sea is generally guaranteed to make anyone sick to his stomach. We threatened to kill him, and took away his pork chop.

On the way home my mouth, once again, got me into trouble. I became claustrophobic down in the hold where I was supposed to be. It was most uncomfortable down there. There were no escape hatches to jump out, no parachutes, no Mae Wests. Therefore, I went up on deck as much as possible. While up there I was not content to leave well enough alone, spending much time on deck leaning against the rails and giving unsolicited and unwelcomed advice. During gun drills, I let it be known what I, as a crack Air Force waist gunner, felt about the Navy's inabilities to hit even the ocean. I talked so much I offended one of the executive officers, because he quickly assigned me to man a 20mm Oerlikon anti-aircraft gun for part of the journey home. That wasn't very good duty in the Atlantic in the middle of storms, but almost anything beat the chaos below.

We were caught in the middle of a wild storm while crossing. One night, in response to a report that a submarine had surfaced ahead of us, the skipper threw our ship in reverse. The ship shuddered so violently I thought we'd been torpedoed. We evaded the U-boat and finally arrived in Norfolk, Virginia.

There the ship took on a pilot, who steered us toward shore. From the ship we could see big crowds of people standing on the dock, waving and cheering. A band was playing, but they were too far away for us to hear. Just then, about a mile or two from the dock, the pilot grounded us on a sandbar. The word was that he was drunk, but you never knew about rumors. Regardless of the reason, this was too much for some who had waited so long to get home. Guys started jumping off the ship and swimming to shore, and it was a long, long swim. They put out little launches to scoop up those idiots who were in such a hurry to get home. The tide and some tugboats finally helped us off the sandbar. After waiting for four hours, we finally docked.

The crowd was still there, as was the military band. We all lined up waiting our turn to go down the gangplank. I noticed one of the musicians, a T5, who every now and then hit his drum. I thought to myself, what kind of a job is that? I turned to a soldier at my elbow, a major who had been crippled, and pointed out the drummer. I said, "Major, look. Now there's a guy that's got it made. His daddy must be a senator or something." The major yelled something at him, and the rest of the soldiers waiting at the rails picked it up. The drummer didn't seem to mind. Every now and then he hit his drum.

We all marched down the gangplank, and everybody was milling around, laughing, kissing, when somebody marched a company of German POWs, former SS troops, past us. These men had been captured a long time ago, and were working as roustabouts on the dock. Marching past, the Germans broke out in song. This was after the Malmedy Massacre. Because of it, and other atrocities, the SS had not made themselves popular. A fight broke out. It looked like the whole Forty-fifth Division and half of the Fifteenth Air Force jumped those men. They finally pried us off the Germans.

Right after they broke up the fight, they herded us into a huge auditorium for a welcome-home briefing. They were nice at first, telling us where we could get uniforms, or extra money for emergencies. But we were getting restless and a speech was the last thing we wanted to hear. All we wanted to know was the location of good clubs where we could get good bourbon and meet women. Then some nitwit from the welcoming committee gets up and starts passing around brochures on how to use flush toilets, evidently for those of us who had been gone so long we had forgotten how. It was disgusting. That really did it. They also passed out condoms and started a lecture on VD. That was the last straw. The men began throwing everything handed to them on the floor. It was getting ugly. Eventually, the officer in charge decided he'd better end the briefing, so they took us to a huge mess hall.

We immediately noticed that German POWs were standing behind the food tables ready to serve it. Another welcoming officer jumped on top of a table and said, "We've got some real fine food for you. We're all ready for you. We would appreciate it if there are no further incidents with the German prisoners. They're here against their will."

From our crowd came a voice, "Yea, tell them about Malmedy!" The officer ignored him, and we all lined up for food.

A little infantry major stood immediately ahead of me in line. He put his plate out for some potatoes, and the German prisoner gave him some. The major asked for some more. The German scooped up a big spoonful, looked the major in the eye, and slapped a mound of potatoes onto the tray so hard he knocked the tray out of the major's hands. The major quickly picked up the tray, looked at it, then stepped up and wrapped it around the German's face. And just for good measure, I hit him too. Another fight then erupted all down the line. The MPs had the honor of breaking up another fight.

We stayed in Norfolk for only a short time awaiting orders home. While there we had our pictures taken. Those of us in the Fifteenth Air Force were not very photogenic. Our skin was still a spotted orange from the Atabrine. When it came my turn, the photographer tried to mask the color by putting powder on my face. That really didn't seem necessary because it was a black and white picture. I look like death warmed over in that picture.

They finally loaded those of us who lived in the Southwest on a nice, well-appointed troop train, and shipped us home. The Army was doing its best to be nice to its returnees. Unfortunately, they made the mistake of stopping in New Orleans. We left the train when it stopped, but when the train started again there were fewer than twenty-six of us on it. There were, however, exactly ninety-six bottles of whiskey. Someone had counted the bottles, and I remember the final tally. At departure time, men ran from everywhere to catch the train. Some didn't make it. The MPs gathered up the stragglers and somehow had them waiting for us at the next train stop.

I spent two or three days in Fort Bliss , getting new uniforms and catching up on my back pay. I hitched a ride to Las Cruces, and then hitched another out to my father's farm in Hatch.

This was the moment I had waited for for so long; the object of all my true desires during my last months in Italy. Home. I drove up to my yard.

It was full of Germans!

POWs.

SS and Africa Corps. Die-hard Nazis.

I scrambled out of the car, blistering mad and screaming, "I traveled five thousand miles to fight these sons of bitches, and I come home and find the yard full of them. What are these guys doing here?" Oh, I was having a fine fit.

My father ran over and hastily explained they were in the yard to pour a sidewalk.

I said, "What?"

He explained, "Yea, they're working. We're paying them a salary." You could hire them as day labor from their POW camps. They kept some of the money and the government kept the rest for their subsistence. The Germans warily eyed me, and I heard mutterings about "*der combatant flieger*" as I stood there ranting, with Dad at my side sputtering explanations. They looked very nervous. Finally, my father's foreman told them to get away from the house and join the others in the fields because there were plenty of rifles in the house and I might start my hunting early. They didn't waste any time leaving.

Being reunited with family and friends was wonderful. There were times of sadness when I met the family of friends who had not returned. But, there were also times of joy in being with old friends who had returned. Tom Case had served in the Navy on escort duty. Frank Simpson had not gone down with the *U.S.S. California*. His family received the welcome news on Christmas Eve after Pearl Harbor. That was one Christmas the Simpson family will never forget. Both Frank and Tom happened to be in Hatch while I was there and we had a great reunion.

During that leave, I visited my aunt and uncle who operated a combination clothing-tailor-dry cleaning business in Hatch. The local Rexall Drug Store was famous for its root beer floats. Walking to the drug store, I saw Frank Simpson. He, too, had about ten days left on his leave before reporting to Bremmerton, Washington, where his ship, the USS *California*, was in dry dock undergoing major repairs after an engagement in the Pacific. At the end of this leave, I would report to Santa Ana, California for reassignment and rehabilitation.

Frank was dressed much as I was, nothing to indicate we were military. I yelled at him, "Let's go down and get a root beer float. I haven't had one in years." He agreed. When we entered the store we were greeted very warmly by the two ladies behind the soda fountain. The older one was married and had been Frank's classmate. The other was Danny's age and I had attended school with some of her family. The four of us had just begun a lively conversation when three soldiers walked into the drug store.

A casual glance at their sunburned faces told us they were fresh out of basic training. They had been drinking and were feeling their oats, and were obviously looking for girls. Their attempts to attract the notice of the two behind the soda fountains met with a remarkable lack of success. We four continued our animated conversation.

Finally, one said, "Guess they prefer 4-F, draft-dodging, unpatriotic guys who wouldn't fight for their country, over real Americans. He looks healthy enough to me," as he pointed in my direction.

Frank stopped drinking his root beer float and asked me, "Is that ignoramus talking about us?"

"I think so," I replied.

"I'm not going to put up with this."

"Hold the phone, Frank, we best finish our floats first. We can always hit them later. Besides we don't want to start a fight in this place." The drug store was crammed with glass counters and breakables, definitely not a place for a knock-down, drag-out fight. The newcomer kept mouthing off, obviously still trying to impress the two ladies. The other two nodded their heads in agreement. "Frank," I continued, "keep your shirt on and finish your drink. After we pay, we can get them outside. Let's don't start any problems in here and tear up the drug store."

"I'll try," responded Frank. We were both grinning from ear-to-ear. Frank loved to fight. One of the women ran, panic-stricken to the back and told the druggist, "Those soldiers up there just called Frank Simpson and Melvin McGuire 'a couple of 4-F, draft-dodging, unpatriotic, cowardly Americans,' and there is going to be a terrible fight in here. Do something!" Without even checking the situation, Mr. Busby raced out of the drug store in search of the deputy sheriff.

After Frank and I had finished our floats and paid for them, I said, "I'll take the loud-mouthed one and you can have the other two, but let's get outside." He agreed. Just as we were about to leave the drug store, we saw Mr. Busby running back with a deputy sheriff in tow. As they entered the store, you could see the relief on the druggist's face when he saw that his store was still intact.

The deputy sheriff addressed the three, "You guys come with me."

"What did we do?"

"For several reasons you need to get out of here immediately and come with me. We like to have service men up here. We appreciate what you're doing, but you're here and starting some trouble that you can't handle. I've known these two guys since they were babies, and either one could eat you alive. First, I'd have to lock you up after you got out of the hospital. You were about to get hurt real bad. Second, one has just returned from fighting in the Pacific and the other from Europe. They're war heroes. You couldn't carry around the fruit salad (medals) they wear on their uniforms. Right now I'm going to do you a big favor." The drug store was the the bus stop, and the driver, a local man, was unloading papers from the bus. The deputy marched the three over to the bus.

"Jim," he said, "take these fellows to Las Cruces and don't stop or even slow down for the railroad tracks. They were in the drug store calling Frank Simpson and Melvin McGuire 4-F, draft-dodging, unpatriotic Americans. If you can't take them, I'm going to lock them up so they don't get hurt." The three, badly shaken soldiers climbed meekly onto the bus. The driver was grinning broadly and there's no telling what he said to them on the way to Las Cruces. That was the last Hatch ever saw of them.

Mr. Busby was eternally grateful that his business escaped total destruction.

On V-J Day I was senior enlisted gunnery instructor at a Florida base training B-29 air crews for the war in the Pacific. Uncle Johnny and I also worked on that bottle of Scotch. We had a fine time until Rosita bit me, again.

I recall celebrating the end of the war with a terrible hangover.

30

Epilogue

Postwar

After the war I returned to New Mexico A & M and eventually achieved my dream to became a pilot. I started a charter service in New Mexico and flew there for awhile, as well as in California, before returning to New Mexico where I graduated from the State Police Academy, Class of 1949. I served as chief pilot for the State Police and later served as chief pilot for the State Highway Commission for many years before retiring in 1964. After retiring, I went into real estate work and also served as Commissioner for Real Estate in New Mexico where I was on the lecture circuit on defensive practices in the real estate industry. During this period I also attended the National Judicial College at the University of Nevada-Reno. After retiring for the second time, I decided to write about my crew and our war-time experiences.

Epilogue

That extra parachute bag I had packed in Amendola had been misdirected and, in 1947, the Hatch postmistress called me to pick up my bag. The smell from it was driving them out of the post office. Evidently, it had been all over the Pacific because it was filled with fungus and rot. In addition to my dirty clothes, that parachute bag contained all of my souvenirs, personal papers, and most important, my address book. I hastily dug into the bottom of the bag to retrieve the address book. Finding nothing but a green, smelly, slimy goo, I took the bag and burned it. All information about my crew and friends, and personal papers were irretrievably lost. I had no way of contacting their families, so for almost fifty years I believed that my crew had not survived. I had left Italy with the horrible thought that my entire crew had gone down. Either with *Flak Holes*, as I had been told in Naples, or by the other airman who said they had been shot down by jets over Breslau.

During those years I couldn't help wondering what had actually happened to them. I wanted to know how they died, but couldn't bring myself to believe they were all dead. Perhaps that was why, in my many travels across the United States as a pilot, every time I dropped into a city, I always looked in the local telephone book for the names of my crew—Chambers, Karsten, McDonnell, Graham, Sutton, Fenstermaker, Lesher, Scofield. I theorized that many veterans gravitated back to their hometowns when they returned from the war, the way I had returned to Las Cruces. My problem was I couldn't remember their hometowns, except Scofield's and Sutton's. I remembered Scofield was from Lincoln because that was where our crew had met, and of course I recalled that last meal with his family. Scofield's family had left Lincoln, and nobody seemed to know anything about him. Sutton, I remembered was from St. Louis, Missouri. There was no system to my search, and I never had any success except what I learned about Sutton.

In the 1950s, I was first pilot on a late-night route from Santa Fe to St. Louis to Oklahoma City and back to Santa Fe. On one trip, the weather was marginal before receiving clearance for landing in St. Louis. The co-pilot noticed the #2 engine was throwing oil in rather large quantities. The St. Louis center quickly gave us clearance for a direct approach to the ILS (instrument landing system) and we landed there. After the passengers had deplaned, I took the aircraft to the maintenance hanger and was told it would take an hour or more to make repairs.

Armed with a handful of coins and a phone book, I settled down in the pilot's lounge to look for Suttons. I had great expectations of talking to Jimmy. My last contact with him had been on 29 December 1944. Jimmy could tell me about the rest of the crew. When I dialed the number for James Sutton a woman answered.

In the excitement of wanting to surprise Jimmy, I neglected to tell her who I was and just asked, "Is Jimmy Sutton there?"

Instantly, a hysterical tirade flooded through my end of the phone. Ghoul and weird creature were two of the names I could recognize from her hysterical explosion. I was really taken back. When she finally stopped for a breath I managed to interject, "Lorraine, Lorraine. This is Melvin McGuire, Mack McGuire. I was with Jimmy in Italy. We were crew mates. Jimmy and I were together on most of our missions. I would like to talk to him if possible. I haven't called you before."

The phone line was quiet for a moment. Then she cautiously said, "Is this Mack?"

"Yes. Is this Lorraine Koelka (her maiden name)?"

She said, "Yes."

I continued, "I'm now a pilot and my aircraft is laid up for repairs here in St. Louis and I thought I would try to find Jimmy. Is something wrong?"

"Jimmy was buried about a week ago. He was killed while walking on a sidewalk in a busy area of St. Louis. Several stories above him where they were repairing a window some equipment fell from the scaffolding and struck him on the head. He was killed instantly!"

The news floored me.

She continued, "Since his obituary came out in the papers, I have received dozens of obscene calls, and calls from people claiming they were the Devil and he had arrived all right. Some of the callers claimed that he ordered equipment and there have been some fake bills come in the mail." At that moment she was expecting the police to tap her line. She mentioned that this was not an uncommon occurrence in St. Louis and the police were anxious to catch them.

This was no time to bother her. I mumbled my apologies and said I would call back in a few weeks. After reminding her that Jimmy was my friend, I told her I lived in Santa Fe and was in the phone book if she needed me. The news of Jimmy's death dashed my hopes of learning about the rest of my crew.

Several months later, when I again called Lorraine, that number had been disconnected and there was no way to trace her. She had been so faithful about writing to Jimmy. Each day he wrote her a V-mail letter, no matter how tired he was, that he had spent much time composing. I have never seen a man who loved a woman so much. They were married shortly after his return. He was only a few missions behind me, and left Italy shortly after I did.

It took several days to get over that blow. James Sutton was a pleasant, efficient radio operator and an asset to any crew. He was always so jolly and joined us in pranks when he wasn't writing to Lorraine. It was such a tragic way to die after surviving fifty missions over Central Europe.

Meanwhile, I had joined the Second Bomb Association. It wasn't until 1989 that I could attend any meetings. I had medical problems with a bad leg at the time, and still do, but bad leg and all I was going to attend that year's reunion in Tucson, Arizona.

I took that group picture we had had taken in Lincoln, which I had sent my parents and was still in its original frame, to the reunion. There I displayed it with labels to identify the people. "Did anybody there have any knowledge of these guys?" I had been talking to several ex-POWs from the Second. Good records were kept of POWs, and the POWs themselves had a system while they were prisoners to remember other POW's names so they could pass this information along in case the Germans killed them.

I wasn't having any luck until later that evening a man came over and introduced himself as Ralph Bischoff, a former B-17 pilot with the Twentieth Squadron. Bischoff said, "McGuire, you're looking for your crew? Well, I was with Ralph Chambers the day he was hit." This excited me, and I then recognized him from the time I had flown with him. Not flying with Chambers that day, I never knew the details and result of his injuries. All I could remember was that he was hit on Christmas Day. Before learning anything else about his injuries, I was rotated home. Now I would finally learn what had happened! The story Bischoff told me has been included in Chapter 27, Christmas Day, 1944. Bischoff never saw Chambers again, but he believed Chambers had survived his wound and the war.

After hearing Bischoff's story, I remembered Chambers telling us he was from North Carolina. Back home after the reunion, I decided to try and find Chambers as quickly as possible. Contacting a North Carolina telephone operator, I told her I was a World War II veteran, and it was a long shot, but she might be able to help me with my problem. There was a possibility that my aircraft commander, whom I had given up for dead all these years, might still be alive. I told her his name, and asked if she could locate anybody named Ralph Chambers in North Carolina. She was most sympathetic and the quest intrigued her. "Hon," she said, "I'm from South Carolina and if that rascal is anywhere in the Carolinas and has a telephone, I'll find him." She was about to take her lunch break, and she would call me back in a few minutes. I will be eternally grateful to that AT&T operator who spent her lunch hour searching for any Ralph Chambers in either North or South Carolina.

About thirty minutes later she called—there were eight Chambers in North Carolina, and two or three were listed as either Ralph or R. something or other. She read the list to me. When I called the first name on the list, a woman answered. I asked if this was the Chambers' residence. She replied that it was. I then said, "This sounds silly, but was your husband a B-17 pilot in the Second Bomb Group of the Fifteenth Air Force in Italy?", and then I heard her turn from the phone and yell, "Honey, it's Mack! It's Mack!"

It was Rachel Chambers. She still remembered my New Mexico voice. I heard him yelling from across the room. By coincidence, the very evening I called they had been watching the "Wings" program on the Discovery Channel. It was a segment on the B-17 in which I had been one of those interviewed.

Chambers quickly got on the phone, and we both started crying. He told me Karsten, Fenstermaker, and Scofield had made it through the war, but Fenstermaker was the only one with whom he had kept in contact. We talked for a long, long time. I couldn't believe, after all those years of thinking he and the others had been killed, that I was actually talking to him. Ralph went into the banking business, working his way up to Vice-President and being put in charge of a large branch bank. Problems with arthritis—having a knee replaced with metal—forced him to take an early retirement. We finally ended our conversation, but not before promising to keep in touch with him, and also not before he gave me Fenstermaker's number.

I called Fenstermaker and talked to him, but Chambers had beat me to the punch by calling him first. John finished his tour as flight engineer for a general, and waited until Chambers completed his tour so they could be rotated back to the States together in the spring of 1945. Lesher had left Italy a month before they did. This was near the end of the war. Chambers finished the war as a Deputy Wing Leader. The two had stayed close over the years.

Fenstermaker wanted a college education, so after the war he went to Penn State. He needed a few extra credits, so as a lark, took some ceramics courses. Making little birds, ashtrays and knickknacks didn't appeal to him, but when they brought in a glass-blower he immediately took to it and became quite good at it. He had a talent for glass blowing, and when he finished the class, employers were lined up waiting to hire him. He could blow scientific and experimental glass to precise specifications. The salary they paid him, he said, was obscene. This son of a Pennsylvania coal miner has done well for himself.

It was Fenstermaker who found Karsten. Fenstermaker had attended a Second Bomb Association reunion in Dayton, Ohio, when they dedicated a group memorial at Wright-Patterson Field, and there was Karsten. Karsten had returned to his home state Missouri, and had become involved in cotton ginning and politics. He is still heavily involved in big ginning operations in cotton country.

Scofield found me by watching one of the "Wings" programs. His wife has an uncle in the Confederate Air Force and through the CAF Locator, they found me. After the war Scofield enrolled in the University of Nebraska, but couldn't stand the thought of another cold winter after the Amendola Ritz, so he ended up at the University of Texas, eventually earning a Ph.D. in geophysics. I now tease him that he really wanted to be a

McGuire, in Confederate Air Force flight uniform, discussing the merits of a restored airplane. *(Courtesy Robert Hadley)*

gynecologist but couldn't spell it so became a geophysicist instead. He was very successful in the oil business before he, too, took an early retirement. Early retirement actually did not end his working days as he continued to do special consulting work for oil companies all over the world, spending a lot of time in Turkey and, at one time, Iran.

I told them about Sutton. Of course, we knew that Jimmy Thompson had been killed.

That accounted for seven out of our crew of ten. Nobody knew anything about Lesher, McDonnell, or Graham. The five of us remembered their home towns, but thorough inquiries as to their possible location, if they indeed were alive, came to nothing.

The Reunion

That was three years ago. We had decided to get together, and that decision was hastened by a happy event. In early 1992, while at a local business, I noticed a couple my age sitting next to me. They had driven up in a car with Michigan plates. Starting a conversation with them, I discovered they were from East Lansing. Mentioning that my navigator, Lesher, had lived there before the war, I asked if they, by some wild chance, knew him. They didn't, but the woman thought she knew the family. We thought he had been killed during the war, but his old crew wanted to find out about him. Since he was a Michigan State alumni, I had twice written the alumni organization to inquire, but never received an answer. The woman had relatives working at the alumni office, and she would find out what they knew about him.

Ten days later she called. Lesher was alive and currently vacationing in Florida. She provided his telephone number, and I called him. It was now Dr. Lesher. Lesher had received his Ph.D. in education. After the war he had buried himself in school. He was very candid and open. Life had been good to him, except for the long period when he couldn't get his war experiences out of his mind. Finally, he blanked out all of those memories.

I told the others about finding Lesher, and they were as happy as I was. We finalized plans for the reunion, our first meeting in forty-eight years. Dallas, being mid-continent and a major airline hub, was chosen as the meeting place because it would not involve so much traveling for old flyers with war wounds. March 1992, was the date and they asked me to organize the reunion.

So many, many people helped us coordinate this reunion. I had mentioned our plans to my colleagues in the Confederate Air Force, Wallace and Martha Dillard. If we had special needs, they offered to consult with the CAF. I was hesitant about asking for help with the meeting, but Wallace insisted that I needn't spend my time with arrangements. The CAF was well-qualified to locate and make arrangements with a hotel which could provide us with a meeting room, lounge, and restaurant. We also wanted to visit the modern Twentieth Bomb Squadron, now a B-52 outfit, at Carswell Air Force Base.

Before I knew it, everything was arranged. Local and national newspapers reported that the crew of *Flak Holes* was getting together after forty-eight years. Colonel Jerry Bishop of Graham, Texas, a retired Air Force pilot, and member of the Confederate Air Force, called me for a crew roster and inquired about any physical conditions or special problems which needed consideration. Bishop drove from Graham to Carswell to obtain a copy of the unit's modern history so we could be brought up-to-date on its activities.

The next call was from Duane Neifert. He had negotiated with the Wyndham Gardens Hotel in Irving, Texas, and they were providing a complimentary conference room and reserved tables at the restaurant. Neifert reported that Colonel Tom Hill, another retired Air Force officer and Confederate Air force member, had arranged for all our transportation, including baggage pickup at the airport and cutting through any red tape.

The Eighth Air Force Association relayed word that they stood ready to help if needed. They also volunteered to host a meeting to argue the relative merits of the B-24 versus the B-17, or the Eighth versus the Fifteenth. They also offered their assistance if anyone became ill. Considering the age of the group, this was a comforting offer.

The most exciting news was a call from the Executive Officer of the Twentieth Bomb Squadron, Captain Mark Clardy. They asked us to be special guests of the Twentieth on one day during our visit. I immediately accepted. An opportunity to visit the modern-day version of the Twentieth would, indeed, be a thrill. Lieutenant Jason Xieques would meet us and be our escort. That didn't leave much for me to do except to call the crew. They were as excited and as curious as I was to see if the contemporary squadron was carrying on the traditions that we had left.

Except for Lesher, we were all feeling great about this reunion. He had never talked to anybody about the war, even his late wife, and expressed serious reservations about even meeting with the crew. He would come, but we should not expect much from him at the meeting. He didn't remember anything about the war, didn't feel comfortable talking about it, and didn't want to talk about it, but he would still show up. Unfortunately, Fenstermaker had health problems and couldn't attend.

Scofield rode the Amtrak to El Paso to help me with the plans. We all arranged to arrive at the Dallas-Fort Worth International Air Port. The hotel had reserved a conference room for us, and we went into a marathon session that lasted into the early morning hours. I shouldn't have worried about Lesher. Once he started talking, he had no more problems. In the early morning hours we were all ready for bed.

The next day we visited the Twentieth Squadron and received the red-carpet treatment. We were shown one of the Twentieth's B-52s which had participated in Desert Storm, and given an inspection of modern aircraft and weapons simulators. Afterwards we were taken to the ready room where they had spent many, many years on alert for Strategic Air Command. In their ready room we had a question and answer session with the entire Twentieth Squadron personnel, both ground and air.

Most of them were history buffs so many of their questions were about our time in Italy. We shared the photographs we'd brought. The room was packed to capacity and the overflow crowd stood out in the hallway. The pictures disappeared into the hallway, made the rounds there, and then came back to us. Pilots from other squadrons were very interested in what we had to say, so they, too, had come to listen.

During lunch at the officer's club, I was asked to give a presentation on the traditions we upheld when we flew with the Twentieth. To us, the most important was that no plane had ever turned back from a target because of enemy opposition. They were unaware of Mission 263; it wasn't in their squadron history. My emotions threatened to choke me as I explained how the Twentieth was lost to the last man the day we arrived in Amendola, and the debt of gratitude the Twentieth owed the people of Czechoslovakia. At one point in my speech I looked up and noticed there wasn't a dry eye among my crew mates, and quite a few moist eyes, as well, in the audience.

Then they brought in the Twentieth battle standard. It was huge, because its history goes back a long way. The Twentieth was one of the four original squadrons created in World War I. When they showed us the ribbons we had put on it, there wasn't a dry eye in the entire meeting room. The Wing Commander addressed us, and said he liked what he was seeing and hearing. This had been educational for his men, and he thought they may have started a tradition of keeping in touch with former airmen of the squadron. They presented each of us the modern Twentieth's patch. There were a few laughs as we razzed them about having 'Pineapple Pete,' the Twentieth's mascot, running in the wrong direction. As we bid farewell to the officers and men of the Twentieth, we were convinced our old squadron was in good hands, and the taxpayers were more than getting their money's worth. It is still an elite outfit. On the drive back to the hotel, one of us commented that he didn't see a man there with whom he wouldn't have been proud to serve. They were a little older group than we were when we served in Italy.

Another marathon session began that also lasted until the early hours of the morning.

The next day, the end of our reunion, we were staggering from lack of sleep as we left the hotel for the airport. We walked together down the concourse and stayed together as each man boarded his flight. Scofield, the first to leave, had been the best shot of us all. I remembered him blowing up the stove and the subsequent wiener roast. And, the time he was sick for two days from swallowing that plug of chewing tobacco.

Then it was time for Jack Karsten and his wife Mary to go. I remembered my vivid impression of him when we first met in Lincoln and how impressed I was with him. I liked him, and the feeling grew as we came to understand and trust each other under combat conditions. I recalled the day we landed on the British base and they had confronted us. Karsten had scrambled back into the plane, turned on the master switches to power up our guns and turrets, and then manned the top turret himself.

Next to leave were Ralph Chambers and his dear wife Rachel. It hurt to see Chambers walk so painfully on that artificial knee. My thoughts went back to the time he was a trim, handsome, cool officer who had lead us on so many successful missions without making any errors. He understood us, and got the most out of us. He made us feel like brothers more than soldiers, but he never let us forget we were soldiers. I can't remember him ever giving us an order. He always asked us to do things. As he limped down the ramp I couldn't help but recall how, hands on hips in front of that plane at the British base, he faced that British officer who far outranked him, and told him that he had flown a crippled plane all the way from the Polish border trying to stay alive and nobody, but nobody, was going to arrest any of his men. One of the reasons he was so successful as a leader was that he was an honestly, genuinely, quietly religious man. Before the war he had sung in his church choir. When he arrived in Amendola, he sang in the group choir. He set the moral tenor for the rest of us. This was the guy who finished the war flying as Deputy Group Leader, tough as a boot to the last.

The Ralph Chambers crew at a Second Bomb Association reunion, September 1993. *(l to r.)* Chambers, Scofield, McGuire, Lesher, and Karsten. Surrounding the group are the other crew members: *(l to r.)* Sutton and Thompson, deceased; McDonnell and Graham, unknown; and Fenstermaker, who was unable to attend the reunion. *(Courtesy Rachel Chambers)*

Epilogue

I still remember Ralph's face and the tears in his eyes when he told about returning to the Squadron and Group in mid-January 1945. His crew had dissolved: Thompson killed, Sutton and I had finished and gone home, and McDonnell and Graham had been assigned as navigator and flight engineer to other crews. Karsten was flying as A/C with new crews and trying to put together a crew of his own from orphans from other crews. Scofield was giving additional gunnery training to navigators and bombardiers as well as gunners who hadn't flown for some time. He also gave survival lessons to ball turret gunners. Fenstermaker was still assigned to a general's plane. The only bright spot was Lesher's return from sick leave and he had flown as squadron lead navigator on several missions. The crew he had loved so well, and trained with for so long, was dissolved and gone. When he told about the awful loneliness and voids in his life during that period, I couldn't help listening, with tears also running down my face. I, too, shared his grief.

During our visit to Carswell, I had several conversations with the commanding officer of the Twentieth Squadron. What had impressed him about us was that we obviously cared so much for one another; there was a genuine friendship among us; we were solicitous and considerate of one another. We obviously had forged bonds in the roughness and danger of combat that had lasted for almost half a century. When I told him that neither Chambers nor Karsten had ever issued us a direct order, the commander found it difficult to believe. Chambers and Karsten both chimed in, saying there was never any reason to give a direct order because the crew always did the right thing. Everybody performed well under fire. Everybody was cool. Orders were superfluous. We had genuinely liked one another, and as a result, we were a family as well as a crew. Chambers and Karsten set the example in their conscientious way, and we tried to follow. No one ever raised a voice to another. No one was ever disciplined or punished, or even came close to it.

This wasn't lost on the men of Twentieth. They wanted to know the secrets of how a crew could be made that close. How did we bond? When we left, we believed we had given them the answer: We were never short for good leaders.

Then it was Lesher's time to leave. Lesher was one of the bravest men in our crew. How he kept his mind working on all of those numbers during some of those messes we were in I will never know, but his skill as a navigator saved our lives on numerous occasions. Wayne Lesher, a pleasant man and true gentleman. I remembered the first time we heard him cuss. He was working diligently on his numbers at his navigator's table when a heavy flak burst directly over us and flung hot metal all over him. His charts had burning holes in them, and his E6B computer was shot out of his hands. With his charts ruined and his numbers all scrambled, he really let loose, but I think under the circumstances he was entitled to it. I also remembered that bad day over Brux, the day when we had so many decisions to make. A flak burst came so close to him that it tore off his oxygen mask and numbed his lips so badly that he had a hard time talking. In spite of these obstacles he charted us a course back home, weaving through German air bases, flak concentrations, over the Alps, and back to Italy.

When we recalled Wayne's audience with the Pope, he laughed and said he has a friend who is a Catholic priest. That friend turns green with envy when he sees that rosary blessed by Pius XII.

Finally they had all left but me, but even then I wasn't alone. While waiting for my plane, I thought about the ones who had not made it to the reunion: Fenstermaker, Thompson, Sutton, McDonnell, Graham. The reunion would have been perfect if Fenstermaker had made it. He was the best flight engineer in the Fifteenth Air Force, or so we thought. He had come a long way from being one of eleven children of a coal miner. Regular Army. Hot-headed on occasion. Tough as a boot anytime, though usually quiet and gentle, but competent in everything he did. I remembered always seeing him reading technical manuals. There wasn't a rivet or bolt on the B-17 that he didn't know about. His knowledge always paid off. His fuel transfer innovations saved our lives after the Brux mission. He was always thorough in preparing before every raid, and a good shot on top of everything else. I recalled, while we were in Italy, watching him wander off to talk to a group of crew chiefs, listen to their discussions, and join in about the plane. Always cool under fire, he never panicked. He seemed to perform better under pressure. We couldn't have asked for a better crew member.

Thompson was killed, of course, before I left Italy, but we have never found out where, when, or how the others died. I recalled Thompson, the All-American kid, everybody's favorite, giving me Bible lessons before takeoff, always doing the right thing, always there to help.

Sutton, reading the latest letter from his fiance before every mission, to bring himself luck. I thought about how much he missed her. At the reunion, Karsten said that he, too, had tried to contact Jimmy in St. Louis, but the man who answered the door said the Sutton's didn't live there any more. He had bought it from the James Sutton estate.

Graham, or 'Snaf,' was always right at my back at the right waist gun. The always dependable Graham with that mischievous grin. McDonnell, the teacher from Wyoming. I wondered what happened to them.

Finally, my plane arrived, and it was my turn to go.

Selected References

Bailey, Ronald H. *The Air War in Europe.* Chicago: Time-Life
 Books, Inc., 1981

Bradley, Omar. *A Soldier's Story.* New York: Henry Holt &
 Company, 1951.

Bruce, Anthony. *An Illustrated Companion to the First World
 War.* London: Michael Joseph Ltd., 1989.

Caiden, Martin. *Black Thursday.* New York: Ballantine Books,
 1960.

Galland, Adolf. *The First and the Last.* New York: Ballantine
 Books, 1954.

Gray, Randal. *Chronicle of the First World War*, Vol. II, 1917-
 1921. New York: Facts on File, 1991.

Jablonski, Edward. *Flying Fortress.* Garden City, NY: Doubleday & Company, Inc., 1965.

Keegan, John. *The Second World War.* New York: Penguin
 Books, 1989.

Luck, Hans von. *Panzer Commander.* New York: Dell Publishing Company, 1989.

Marshall, Richard, ed. *Great Events of the 20th Century.* New
 York: The Reader's Digest Association, Inc., 1977.

Mayer, S. L., ed. *The Rand McNally Encyclopedia of World War
 II.* Chicago: Rand McNally & Company, 1977.

McDonald, Charles B. *A Time for Trumpets.* New York:
 Bantam Books, 1985.

Parrish, Thomas, ed. *The Simon and Schuster Encyclopedia of
 World War II.* New York: Cord Communications Corpo-
 ration, 1978.

Regan, David. *Who's Who in Hollywood, 1900-1976.* New
 Rochelle, NY: Arlington House Publishers, 1976.

Rust, Kenn C. *Fifteenth Air Force Story in World War II.* Terre
 Haute, IN: Sun Shine House, Inc., 1976.

Wheal, Elizabeth-Ann, Stephen Pope, and James Taylor. *A
 Dictionary of the Second World War.* New York: Peter
 Bedrick Books, 1990.

INDEX

419

About the Authors:

Melvin McGuire finally achieved his dream of becoming a pilot. After a career with the New Mexico State Police in the Criminal Division and on the Governor's Staff in charge of Investigations & Security, he was Chief Pilot for the State Police and then Chief Pilot for the New Mexico State Highway Commission, flying VIPs around the country. He also served seven years as a New Mexico Real Estate Commissioner.

Robert Hadley is a freelance writer and photographer. Since 1975 his work has been published in numberous local, regional, and national publications. He graduated from the University of Texas and completed his Masters Degree at San Angelo State University.